Presupposition and Assertion
in Dynamic Semantics

Studies in Logic, Language and Information

The *Studies in Logic, Language and Information* is the official book series of the European Association for Logic, Language and Information (FoLLI).

The scope of the series is the logical and computational foundations of natural, formal, and programming languages, as well as the different forms of human and mechanized inference and information processing. It covers the logical, linguistic, psychological and information-theoretic parts of the cognitive sciences as well as mathematical tools for them. The emphasis is on the theoretical and interdisciplinary aspects of these areas.

The series aims at the rapid dissemination of research monographs, lecture notes and edited volumes at an affordable price.

Managing editor: Robin Cooper, University of Gothenburgh

Executive editor: Maarten de Rijke, University of Amsterdam

Presupposition and Assertion in Dynamic Semantics

David I. Beaver

CSLI Publications
Center for the Study of Language and Information
Stanford, California
&
FoLLI
The European Association for
Logic, Language and Information

Copyright © 2001
CSLI Publications
Center for the Study of Language and Information
Leland Stanford Junior University
Printed in the United States
05 04 03 02 01   5 4 3 2 1

Library of Congress Cataloging-in-Publication Data

Beaver, David I., 1966–
Presupposition and assertion in dynamic semantics / David I. Beaver.
p.   cm.
(Studies in logic, language, and information, no. 16)
Includes bibliographical references (p.) and index.

ISBN 1-57586-121-6 (cloth : alk. paper)
ISBN 1-57586-120-8 (paper : alk. paper)

1. Presupposition (Logic). 2. Semantics.
I. Title. II. Series.
P39.B43   2001
401'.43–dc21   2001037374
CIP

∞ The acid-free paper used in this book meets the minimum requirements of the American National Standard for Information Sciences—Permanence of Paper for Printed Library Materials, ANSI Z39.48-1984.

CSLI was founded early in 1983 by researchers from Stanford University, SRI International, and Xerox PARC to further research and development of integrated theories of language, information, and computation. CSLI headquarters and CSLI Publications are located on the campus of Stanford University.

CSLI Publications reports new developments in the study of language, information, and computation. In addition to lecture notes, our publications include monographs, working papers, revised dissertations, and conference proceedings. Our aim is to make new results, ideas, and approaches available as quickly as possible. Please visit our web site at
http://cslipublications.stanford.edu/
for comments on this and other titles, as well as for changes and corrections by the author and publisher.

Contents

Preface

In ordinary talk, we presuppose a great deal. That is, we take things for granted, assuming that the other conversational participants share our knowledge of them. This book is about linguistic presupposition, how what we take for granted is reflected in what we say.

In the book I first explore what around a hundred previous researchers have had to say about presupposition, and then make my own contribution. That contribution is set within the framework of *dynamic semantics*, an approach to meaning that has been developed especially (but not exclusively) in the work of Karttunen, Stalnaker, Heim and Groenendijk and Stokhof. Classical semantics, in the style of e.g. Frege, Russell, Tarski or Montague, involves a static relationship between linguistic form and reality, not changing between different parts of the same utterance. In dynamic semantics, the form/reality relationship is fluid, mediated by an evolving context of interpretation. Although the use of such a semantics for presupposition is not original to my work, I innovate by providing solutions to problems in three main classes: compositionality, quantification and *accommodation* (the adaption a hearer makes when a speaker presupposes too much).

This book has its own presuppositions, things I took for granted that readers would be familiar with. But I have tried to make sure that those presuppositions will present no problem to anyone who has taken the equivalent of a graduate level course, or possibly two, in semantics and pragmatics. I assume the reader is familiar with the basics of classical propositional, first-order and modal logic and lambda calculus, with standard accounts of the semantics of predication, quantification, anaphora and modality, with Montague Grammar and with Gricean pragmatics. The reader need have no prior knowledge of presupposition or dynamic semantics. Apart from whatever worth the book has as a presentation of original research results, is my hope that it may be useful both as a reference work and as a pedagogical tool, perhaps the basis of a graduate level course on presupposition. It is to be hoped that the index and bibliographic references will help serve these goals.

This book is a reworked version of my thesis (Beaver 1995). I have added to, subtracted from and corrected what was in the original, but the structure of the work and the fundamental ideas are essentially unchanged. Much of the overview of previous work on presupposition, Part I of the book, appeared in a heavily adapted form in Beaver (1997). Some of the ideas of Part II have appeared in Beaver (1994b;a; 1999a;b), Beaver and Krahmer (2001). These presentations follow the same line of thinking as you will find in the current work, but are distinct in both detailed content and textual form.

Since the completion of my thesis, six years ago, both presupposition theory and dynamic semantics have moved on, as has my own thinking. Intervening developments mean that the coverage I gave of prior accounts is incomplete, and, although I have updated various aspects of the text, I have not added detailed discussion of recent work. But work in the area has tended to proceed step-wise, and there have been no dramatic shifts in semantics and pragmatics or in presupposition theory specifically. I must let the reader judge the significance of the ideas I present here, but I would comment that their significance has not changed greatly in the time since they were first presented.[1]

There are many people in who's intellectual debt I stand. Creditors no longer able to collect what is due include Jon Barwise, Gottlob Frege, Richard Montague, Bertrand Russell, Peter Strawson and Alfred Tarski. The remaining creditors, whom I hope to pay off in installments, include Paul Dekker, Jeroen Groenendijk, Irene Heim, Hans Kamp, Lauri Karttunen, Reinhard Muskens, Rob van der Sandt, Robert Stalnaker, Martin Stokhof, Frank Veltman and Henk Zeevat. As you see, my debts are onerous, and yet I must also give credit to two other researchers who, independently of me and each other, described closely related dynamic treatments of presupposition: Gennaro Chierchia and Jan van Eijck. Given the great extent to which my thinking overlaps with theirs, I am happy to recommend that the reader studies their work first-hand: see Chierchia (1995), van Eijck (1993; 1994; 1995).

Those who's direct help I must gratefully acknowledge include two anonymous referees for the SiLLI series who provided extensive commentary on an earlier version of this manuscript. Along with detailed guidance from the series' executive editor, Maarten de Rijke, this has greatly affected the final form of the book. The manuscript may have never seen the light of day without the unique qualities of Dikran Karagueuzian at CSLI Publications: he and his staff, particularly Christine Sosa, have been very

---

[1]The liveliest criticism of ideas presented here is found in work by Bart Geurts and Rob van der Sandt: see Geurts (1996; 1999), Geurts and van der Sandt (1999). Two papers that have appeared posing problems for dynamic semantics in general are Geurts (1997), Stalnaker (1998).

helpful. Ela Widdows did a wonderful job of proof-reading and editing. Ewan Klein at the University of Edinburgh was my main thesis advisor. He and my second advisor, Robin Cooper, helped shape both me and my thesis. My Ph.D. examiners, Gerald Gazdar and Paul Schweizer provided extensive comments on the thesis, which have also greatly affected the form and content of the book you now read. There are many others who in a less official capacity have been of enormous help to me, sometimes providing detailed comments on a version of this manuscript or a related work, and sometimes altering or helping refine my views, whether during presentations, in preciously human minutes snatched in a conference break, or in drawn out conversations over a beer. These include: Dorit Abusch, Nic Asher, Johan van Benthem, Martin van den Berg, Patrick Blackburn, Steve Berman, Johan Bos, Gennaro Chierchia, Francis Corblin, Paul Dekker, Jan van Eijck, Tim Fernando, Kai von Fintel, Claire Gardent, Mark Gawron, Jelle Gerbrandy, Bart Geurts, Jeroen Groenendijk, Willem Groeneveld, Irene Heim, Herman Hendriks, Lex Holt, Larry Horn, Hans Kamp, László Kálmán, Marcus Kracht, Emiel Krahmer, Peter Krause, Manfred Krifka, Alex Lascarides, Alice ter Meulen, Frederike Moltmann, Michael Morreau, Reinhard Muskens, Kimba Newton, Breanndán Ó Nualláin, Barbara Partee, Jeff Pelletier, László Pólos, Stanley Peters, Craige Roberts, Mats Rooth, Robert van Rooy, Antje Rossdeutscher, Kjell Johan Sæbø, Rob van der Sandt, Remko Scha, Jerry Seligman, Martin Stokhof, Anatoly Strigin, Zoltán Szabó, Ken Turner, Enric Valduvi, Frank Veltman, Henk Zeevat, Ede Zimmerman, and Ryszard Zuber.

I must also thank my colleagues, students and friends at the Center for Cognitive Science in the University of Edinburgh, at the Department of Philosophy at the University of Amsterdam, and elsewhere at the Institute for Logic, Language and Computation in the University of Amsterdam, in the Computational Linguistics group at the University of Tilburg, and at the Department of Linguistics at Stanford University. I have been very fortunate to work in a sequence of environments combining great friendliness with an extraordinarily high degree of intellectual stimulation.

The people who have sustained me most over the decade since I embarked on the project that has culminated in this book, are my family. My love and gratitude go to Allan and Muriel Beaver, to Alexis, Simon, Lauren and Max Blum, to Michelle and Damien Taylor, to Eszter Csanyi, and, especially, to, Moni, Anna and Noah. I most especially thank Moni, without whom neither I nor the index (which she worked Perl magic on) would be in one piece.

Stanford, July 2001
David I. Beaver

Part I

The Presupposition:
A Critical Survey of
Presupposition Theory

Overview of Part I

Russell once commented (Russell 1946, p.212) that all the significant advances in philosophy have been made in the teeth of opposition from the disciples of Aristotle. The introduction of the notion of *presupposition* is no exception:

> "For manifestly, if Socrates exists, one of the two propositions 'Socrates is ill', 'Socrates is not ill' is true, and the other false. This is likewise the case if he does not exist; for if he does not exist, to say that he is ill is false, and to say that he is not ill is true." (From the *Categories*, Aristotle 1950/350 BC, Ch.10:13b pp. 27-35)

> "That the name 'Kepler' denotes something is just as much a presupposition for the assertion 'Kepler died in misery' as for the contrary assertion." (From Frege's *On Sense and Meaning*, McGuinness 1984, p.168.)[1]

Russell, who clearly enjoyed being in the right, in one respect had helped engineer the truth of his own observation. After his criticism in Russell (1905) of Frege's radical departure from Aristotelian dogma, presupposition seems to have been largely forgotten, and when, half a century later, Strawson rediscovered the notion, Russell was once more on hand to fight a rear-guard action.[2] That this action, although fairly successful, did not completely halt the further development of the theory of presupposition is

---

[1]The term *presupposition* in quotations of Frege is translated from *voraussetzung* in the original. Note that in most cases Frege talks of people presupposing, not sentences. The above quote is one of few which suggests that it might be an expression, or an assertion of an expression that has a presupposition, not a person.

[2]It has been suggested by Larry Horn that the mediaeval philosopher Petrus Hispanus, possibly the only logician ever to have become pope, should be credited with the first introduction of a notion of presupposition. Horn (noting that the reference differs from that of Horn 1985) has pointed out to me a striking passage from the final tract of Petrus Hispanus' *Summulae Logicales*, in translation and original in Mullally (1945).

attested by Sag and Prince's collected bibliography of works dealing with presupposition in Oh and Dineen (1979), which contains more than three hundred items.

In the years since the Sag and Prince bibliography was collated, work on presupposition has continued apace, so that the discussion in this book does not and could not provide a comprehensive survey of the voluminous existing literature. But the five chapters in Part 1 of this book are devoted to a critical examination of at least a significant part of that literature. It is to be hoped that this part of the book will at least provide the mathematically inclined reader with a grasp of empirical and linguistic issues, and the linguistically inclined reader with a grasp of relevant formal methods and logical issues: the aim is thus not to summarise the existing literature, but to make it more accessible to logicians and linguists alike.[3]

The first chapter in Part I is largely introductory, tackling the basic concepts and setting the methodological scenes. In the four chapters thereafter some of the more influential formal attempts to explain presupposition related inferences are outlined and discussed. The grouping of proposals cannot in any sense be standard, because it is not obvious whether there is any standard taxonomy of different theories. The division of theories across chapters 2–5 does not reflect the philosophical interpretation which the original progenitors advocated, but is fixed by my own perspective

---

This is the first surviving reference to presupposition, and probably the first ever reference to the presuppositions of discourse connectives: "We now discuss reduplicative signs. Reduplicative signs are those which imply the reason according to which something is attributed to another, as 'insofar as', 'according as', 'by reason of the fact that' and so on.[...] [A] reduplicative word presupposes [*praesupponit*] a certain predicate to be in a certain subject and denotes [*denotat*] that that to which it is immediately attached is the cause of that inherence." The *praesupponit/denotat* distinction made here does not play a central role in Petrus' philosophy, and in the paraphrases he gives during the following analysis he simply conjoins presuppositions and assertions.

A big topic of research three quarters of a millennium ago concerned what was called *suppositio*, but despite the superficial morphological similarity, this field has no obvious connection with the study of presupposition. *Suppositio* is related to *supponere*, meaning to substitute, and this mediaeval field is more closely connected with paradoxes and problems of substitutivity and intensionality. Moving back to the twentieth century, and Russell's part in maintaining Aristotelian dogma, it is only fair to point out that although Russell defended bivalence in cases of reference failure, he was at the time advocating a move away from another aspect of Aristotle's doctrine, namely the assumption that sentences can be analysed into subject-predicate form.

[3] The reader is also pointed to a number of excellent previous surveys: Levinson (1983) provides a gentle introduction to the important issues . Soames (1989) has provided an excellent overview article, whilst van der Sandt (1988, pp. 1–154) is not only insightful but also unsurpassed for breadth of coverage. More recently a couple of shorter overview articles have appeared, Horn (1994) and Seuren (1991). Contemporary PhD theses are of course a mine of information: see for instance the literature overviews by Bridge (1991) and Marcu (1994), both of which are strong concerning the more computationally oriented accounts of presupposition, and especially Geurts (1994; 1999), Krahmer (1995; 1998), Schöter (1995).

on the technical apparatus underlying the proposals. The division loosely represents four different ways in which the dynamics of the interpretation process is used to explain inferences arising from presuppositions. Here is a summary (some of the technical terms mentioned in the summary have not yet been introduced):

Chapter 1: "Presuppositions and How to Spot Them" Basic concepts and methods are introduced, and some of the underlying assumptions of presupposition theories are discussed.

Chapter 2: "Multivalence and Partiality" In this chapter models are presented in which the dynamics of the interpretation process plays no role at all. In these purely static theories the possibility of presupposition failure is tied to the presence of extra truth values in a multivalent (or partial) semantics.

Chapter 3: "Cancellation and Filtering" Here we discuss models in which the context of evaluation affects which presuppositions are projected. Such models can involve an *inter-sentential dynamics* or *dynamic pragmatics* since the context of evaluation is modified with each successive utterance, although this intersentential dynamics is generally relatively simple and involves only incrementation with new propositions.

Chapter 4.1: "Dynamic Semantics" In these models presuppositions constrain the local contexts in which a presupposition trigger is admissible. These theories involve not only incrementation of context with successive sentences, but also *sentence internal* dynamics. For a given context of evaluation for a complex sentence the dynamics of the interpretation process determines what the local contexts of evaluation will be for the parts of the sentence, and given that the parts are only admissible in certain contexts, this in turn determines whether the sentence as a whole is admissible.

Chapter 5: "Accommodation" Accommodation based theories of presupposition allow for a much more sophisticated dynamic pragmatics than in the earlier chapters. This dynamics manifests itself in a process of accommodation. This allows repair or modification of contexts of evaluation so that presuppositions are justified, but the thus modified contexts may be local contexts of evaluation rather than the global context in which the sentence as a whole is interpreted.

1

Presuppositions and How to Spot Them

1.1 Introduction

The non-technical sense of the word *presupposition* serves as a good basis for understanding many of the various technical definitions which have been given. Certainly this is true of the notion of presupposition introduced by Frege, according to whom presuppositions are special conditions that must be met in order for a linguistic expression to have a denotation. He maintained that presuppositions constitute an unfortunate imperfection of natural language, since in an ideal language every well-formed string would denote something. The possibility of what we would now call *presupposition failure*, which in a Fregean picture would mean cases when a well-formed expression failed to denote, was repugnant to him. He cites, as well as the 'Kepler' sentence quoted earlier, the following examples (both from Frege 1892) :

E1   Whoever discovered the elliptic form of the planetary orbits died in misery.

E2   After the separation of Schleswig-Holstein from Denmark, Prussia and Austria quarrelled.

For Frege, the propositions, respectively, that the name 'Kepler' designates something, that somebody discovered the elliptic forms of the planetary orbits, and that Schleswig-Holstein was once separated from Denmark, are not part of the "thoughts expressed" by the above examples, but are presupposed by them. An important aspect of Frege's separation of *sense* and *reference* is his contention that linguistic expressions may have a sense, yet lack a reference. This aspect of the Fregean scheme is often ignored, and, for instance, is absent from Richard Montague's otherwise essentially Fregean PTQ (Montague 1974).[1] Thus for Frege noun-phrases like those

---

[1] It is not obvious why Montague chose against fully implementing this part of Frege's theory. The possibility of propositional formulae having sense but no reference would

underlined in E1–E2 could have failed to have any reference, at least if the world had been different and there had not been any relevant entities to which they could refer. In this case the sentences containing the noun phrases would themselves have had a sense but no reference, which, given that the Fregean reference of a sentence is the True or the False, would have meant that the sentences did not have a truth value.

Most authors follow the Fregean line of relating presuppositions to assumptions that have been made. That is, presuppositions concern either the way in which utterances signal assumptions, or, conversely, the way in which utterances depend upon assumptions in order to be meaningful. However, some words of caution are in order. It is not the case that all technical uses of the term presupposition involve reference to assumptions. Indeed, if by *assumptions* we mean the assumptions of some agent, then the notion of an assumption is essentially a pragmatic one, whereas for some theorists presupposition is a purely semantic relation. Phenomena that one theorist explains in terms of what is assumed, another may explain without essential reference to assumptions, and yet both theorists may use the term *presupposition*. It is not even the case that all proponents of pragmatic accounts of presupposition take assumption as a central notion. For instance, Gazdar's influential theory of presupposition (Gazdar 1979a;b) does not involve a commitment to presuppositions being in any sense *assumed*. And although Frege's choice of terminology clearly reflects the idea that presupposition to be related to assumptions, Frege's proposal to model presupposition as definedness of reference provides the standard way of defining a semantic presupposition relation which is independent of the speaker.

Having mentioned the terms *semantic* and *pragmatic*, I must warn the reader that they are bandied about rather freely, and indeed confusingly, in the presupposition literature: I will attempt to clarify.

In a semantic theory, presupposition is usually defined as a binary relation between pairs of sentences of a language. What makes this relation semantical is that it is defined or explicated solely in terms of the semantic valuation of the sentences, or in terms of semantical entailment. Thus a definition in terms of semantic valuation might, following one interpretation of Strawson's work, say that one sentence (semantically) presupposes

---

have complicated the (already messy) logic of IL: a natural method of implementation might involve making Montague's *cup* operator (which maps senses onto references) into a partial function. Yet partialising PTQ requires care: see Muskens (1989; 1995). Less formally detailed proposals for partialising PTQ, intended specifically for the inclusion of presupposition data, were made some years earlier by Hausser (1976) and von Kutschera (1975). A system presented by Karttunen and Peters (1979), discussed in the next chapter, can be construed as providing yet another means of encoding a Fregean theory of presupposition into Montague Grammar, although the authors do not intend the systems they present to be thought of in this way.

another if the truth of the second is a condition for the semantic value of the first to be *true* or *false*. Other such notions will be explored in Chapter 2 below.

In pragmatic theories the analysis of presupposition involves the attitudes and knowledge of language users. In extreme cases such as Stalnaker (1974), presupposition is defined without any reference to linguistic form: Stalnaker talks not of the presuppositions of a sentence, but of the *speaker's presuppositions*, these being just those propositions which are taken for granted by a speaker on a given occasion. Other pragmatic theories are less radical, in that linguistic form still plays an essential role in the theory. The majority of well-developed pragmatic theories concern the presuppositions not of a sentence (as in semantic theories) or of a speaker (as in Stalnaker's theory) but of an utterance. In some theories, utterances are explicated as pairs consisting of a sentence and a linguistic context, and as a result presupposition becomes a ternary relation, holding between two sentences and a context.[2] In other theories, the presuppositions of a sentence are seen as conditions that contexts must obey in order for an utterance of the sentence to be felicitous in that context.[3]

The post-Fregean philosophical study of presupposition has been dominated by an assumption-based conception, but, given the range of linguistic and philosophical theories which have been formulated during the last twenty years, such a characterisation is no longer apt.

Furthermore, saying that presuppositions are not part of what is asserted but of what is assumed does not in itself provide any practical method of identifying presuppositional constructions in language, or even of showing that there are any such constructions. If one theorist argues that a definite description asserts the existence of a (unique) object satisfying the description, and another theorist maintains that the existence of a relevant object is not asserted but presupposed, how are we to tell who is right? This issue was at the heart of the famous Russell-Strawson debate. Neither party could offer a solid empirical justification of his position, since the debate appeared to hinge on whether a simple sentence containing an

---

[2]Strawson's account can be seen as the first such theory, although Frege's sparse remarks on presupposition are already suggestive. See Strawson (1950) and the reconstruction by Soames (1989). Chapter 3 introduces a number of such theories, and it is there suggested that (the second version of) the theory due to Karttunen (1973) is the first in which a definition of utterance presupposition is formally realised.

[3] Keenan (1971, p. 49) defines pragmatic presupposition as follows: "A sentence pragmatically presupposes that its context is appropriate." On the other hand Karttunen writes: "Strictly speaking, it would be meaningless to talk about the pragmatic presuppositions of a sentence. Such locutions are, however, justified in a secondary sense. A phrase like "the sentence A pragmatically presupposes B" can be understood as an abbreviation for "whenever A is uttered sincerely, the speaker of A presupposes B" (i.e. assumes B and believes that his audience assumes B as well.)"(Karttunen 1973, pp. 169–170)

unsatisfied description was false, as Russell claimed, or meaningless, as Strawson, taking his lead from Frege, maintained. Judgements on whether sentences are meaningless or false are typically hazy — indeed, it is hard even to know how to pose to a naive informant the question of whether a given sentence is meaningless or false — and the debate arguably never reached a satisfactory conclusion.[4]

So what is the defining characteristic of the recent linguistic study of presupposition? We will see that a large class of lexical items and grammatical constructions, including those identified as presuppositional by philosophers such as Frege and Strawson, produce distinctive patterns of inference. It is difficult to find any common strand to current analyses of presupposition, save that they all concern (various parts of) this class.

Although many categories of expression have been identified as presuppositional, the bulk of discussion in this book concerns definite noun phrases and factive verbs. The fact that I concentrate on certain constructions to the exclusion of others reflects a general bias in the presupposition literature, one which is presumably of historical origin – in modern times presuppositions were first discussed in the context of definite NPs and (later) factive verbs. The huge majority of work on presupposition assumes that relevant phenomena are constant across presupposition types, and there is relatively little convincing evidence to the contrary. Zeevat (1994) does offer evidence suggesting a split between presuppositional inference behaviour for different types of trigger, and this is discussed below in §5.9.3. Nonetheless, in the absence of a thorough empirical comparison of the full range of presuppositional constructions, the current work is incomplete as an account of presupposition. The following list, which contains many of the constructions that are commonly identified as presuppositional, together with some references to literature on them, provides a partial remedy for this lacuna:

Definite NPs The Russell-Strawson debate centred on whether definites should be seen as presuppositional Strawson (1950; 1964), Russell (1905; 1957). The literature is enormous, but see e.g. the following selection: (Hawkins 1978, Clark and Marshall 1981, van Eijck 1993, Heim 1982, Kadmon 1990, Lasersohn 1993, Neale 1990). The class of definites may be taken to include proper names, possessives, 'this'- and 'that'-clauses, and some wh-phrases.

Quantificational NPs presupposing existence of a non-trivial domain of quantification. See e.g. de Jong and Verkuyl (1985), Lappin

---

[4]The main references for this debate are Strawson (1950; 1964), and Russell (1905; 1957). Note that the 1964 Strawson paper is quite conciliatory. Recently proposals have been made which go some way towards predicting judgements of truth and falsity of sentences with non-referring definite descriptions (Lasersohn 1993, von Fintel 2001).

and Reinhart (1988), von Fintel (1995), Abusch and Rooth (2000), Bergmann (1981) for an example of a formal system where such presuppositions are built in, or Heim and Kratzer (1998) for an extensive recent discussion starting at an introductory level.

Factive verbs and NPs presupposing truth of the propositional complement. E.g. 'regret', 'know', 'the fact that X' and 'the knowledge that X'. There is a large literature on factives, starting with the landmark Kiparsky and Kiparsky (1970). There has been much discussion as to whether *cognitive factives* (which concern knowledge of facts) and *emotive factives* (which concern emotional attitudes towards facts) manifest different presuppositional behaviour, as first suggested by Karttunen (1971c). See e.g. Klein (1975), Gazdar (1979a), Stalnaker (1974). Other work on factives includes e.g. Postal (1972), Zuber (1977), Peterson (1979).

Clefts An it-cleft 'it was x that y-ed' is argued to presuppose that something 'y-ed', or perhaps that there is a unique such entity. Similar presuppositions are produced by wh- and pseudo-clefts. See e.g. Prince (1986), Delin (1989; 1992), Ramsey (1992).

Wh-questions presuppose existence of an entity answering the question, or speakers' expectation of such an entity. See e.g. Belnap (1969), Prince (1986), Rullmann and Beck (1998). Note also that answers may be said to presuppose openness of questions — see e.g. the account of accommodation of questions of Larsson *et al.* (2000).

Counterfactual conditionals have been claimed to presuppose falsity of the antecedent. See Karttunen (1971a), Kasper (1992), von Fintel (1998), and the arguments against there being a presupposition from Karttunen and Peters (1979) and Böer and Lycan (1976).

Intonation Destressed or unstressed material is sometimes thought to induce a presupposition, so that e.g. 'X y-ed' with stressed 'X' might presuppose that somebody 'y-ed'). See e.g. Halliday (1967), Chomsky (1971), Prince (1986), Reinhart (1982), Sgall *et al.* (1973), Sgall (1995), Horn (1986), Blok (1993), Gawron (1995), Rooth (1987).

Sortally restricted predicates presuppose rather than assert that their arguments are of the appropriate sort. E.g. 'dream' presupposes animacy of its subject, and predicative use of 'a bachelor' presupposes that the predicated individual is adult and male. Also sometimes referred to as *categorical* restrictions. See e.g. Fillmore (1971a), Seuren (1988a), Thomason (1972).

Signifiers of actions and temporal/aspectual modifiers Most verbs
signifying actions (to use standard aspectual terminology, *accomplish-
ments* and *achievements*) carry presuppositions that the preconditions for the action are met. For instance both 'climbing' a mountain
and 'reaching' its summit involve preconditions that one is not already
there at the time, and that one is not a banana. Such preconditions
could be conceived of as a special case of sortal restriction. Modifiers
such as the verbs 'stop' and 'continue', and the adverbs such as 'still'
are discussed more often in the literature: all of them can be seen as
placing presuppositional requirements on the initial state. The modifiers may be clausal, as in 'before' and 'after' clauses. See van der
Auwera (1993), Lorenz (1992), Heinämäki (1972), ter Meulen (1995).

Iterative Adverbs such as 'too' and 'again' are said to presuppose something that is being repeated, often an event, but possibly a state.
These are discussed e.g. in Kripke (ms), Zeevat (1994), Kamp and
Rossdeutscher (1994), Rossdeutscher (1994). Iteratives occur in other
syntactic classes (e.g. the determiner 'another', and, relatedly, the
noun modifier 'other'), and may even be seen as extending below the
lexical level to the morpheme 're-'.

Various other presupposition triggers have been identified, for instance
Karttunen's (1971b) *implicatives* (e.g. 'manage','succeed'), Fillmore's *verbs
of judging* (e.g. 'criticise') (Fillmore 1971b), the *focus-sensitive* particles
'even' and 'only' (Horn 1969, Krifka 1992), and discourse connectives such
as 'although' and 'because' (Lagerwerf 1998). Keenan also suggests that
presuppositions may arise from attributive (i.e. *non-restrictive*) relative
clauses (which pass the negation test, yet are invariably used to convey
new information) and what he terms *pragmatic felicity conditions* (e.g. use
of polite forms).

1.2 Projection/Heritability

Taking $\models$ for the moment to be classical semantic entailment (also termed
necessitation or *consequence*), it does not follow from $\phi \models \psi$ that $\neg\phi \models \psi$,
and, for an arbitrary choice of χ, it does not follow that $\phi \rightarrow \chi \models \psi$.
Neither does it follow that $\Diamond\phi \models \psi$, where $\Diamond$ is a classical modal possibility
operator. These properties of classical entailment mirror the standardly
recognised properties of inference between sentences of natural language.
For example, Frege's E1, repeated below,[5] has E3 as one of its implications,
and it is no surprise that E3 does not follow from any of E4–E6.

---

[5]When repeating examples I follow a convention of adding an apostrophe to the
original numbering, so that e.g. E1 becomes E1'.

E1′   Whoever discovered the elliptic form of the planetary orbits died in misery.

E3   Somebody died in misery.

E4   Whoever discovered the elliptic form of the planetary orbits did not die in misery.

E5   If whoever discovered the elliptic form of the planetary orbits died in misery, he should have kept his mouth shut.

E6   Perhaps whoever discovered the elliptic form of the planetary orbits died in misery.

However, consider E7, which Frege claims to be presupposed by E1. Strikingly, E7 seems to be implied by E1, but also by all of E4–E6. We may say that one implication of E1 is *inherited* or *projected* such that it also becomes an implication carried by the complex sentences in E4–E6, whereas another implication of E1 is not inherited in this way.

E7   Somebody discovered the elliptic form of the planetary orbits.

This takes us to the curse and the blessing of modern presupposition theory. Certain implications of sentences are inherited more freely to become implications of complex sentences containing the simple sentences than are other implications, and such implications are called presuppositions. In its guise as curse this observation is called (following Langendoen and Savin 1971) *the presupposition projection problem*. The problem is twofold. First, we must say exactly when presuppositions are inherited, and, second, we must say why. But the observation is also a blessing, because it provides an objective basis for the claim that there is a distinct presuppositional component to meaning, and a way of identifying presuppositional constructions: a linguistic test for presupposition on a methodological par with, for instance, standard linguistic constituency tests.

To find the presuppositions of a given grammatical construction or lexical item, one must observe which implications of simple sentences are also implications of sentences in which the simple sentence is embedded under negation, under an operator of modal possibility or in the antecedent of a conditional. To be sure, there is nothing sacred about this list of embeddings from which presuppositions tend to be projected, and the list is certainly not exhaustive. The linguist might equally well choose to consider different connectives, such as in E8, or non-assertive speech acts, as with the yes-no question in E9 — questions having been considered as test-embeddings for presuppositions by Karttunen — or the imperative in

E10.[6] E9 is not a question about whether anybody discovered elliptic form of the planetary orbits, and E10 does not act as a request to guarantee that somebody has discovered the elliptic form of the planetary orbits. Rather, we would take it that an utterer of either of these sentences already held the existence of a discoverer of the elliptic form of the planetary orbits to be beyond doubt. Thus the sentences could be used as evidence that E7 is presupposed by the simple assertive sentences from which E9 and E10 are derived.[7]

E8   Unless whoever discovered the elliptic form of the planetary orbits died in misery, he was punished in the afterlife.

E9   Did whoever discovered the elliptic form of the planetary orbits die in misery?

E10   Ensure that whoever discovered the elliptic form of the planetary orbits dies in misery!

Returning to projection *qua* problem rather than *qua* test, it is often forgotten that, from a semantic perspective, the projection problem for presuppositions fits quite naturally into a larger Fregean picture of how language should be analysed. The projection problem for presuppositions is the task of stating and explaining the presuppositions of complex sentences in terms of the presuppositions of their parts. The larger problem, which strictly contains the presupposition projection problem, could naturally be called "the projection problem for meanings", i.e. the problem of finding the meanings of complex sentences in terms of the meanings of their parts. Of course, this larger problem is conventionally referred to as the problem of *compositionality*.

1.3   Cancellation/Defeasibility

The projection test is dependent upon a source of data which has been central to semantical inquiry since Aristotle, namely our intuitions concerning

---

[6]The behaviour of presuppositions in imperatives is discussed by Searle (1969, p. 162).

[7]Burton-Roberts suggests the following generalisation of the standard negation test for presuppositions: "Any formula equivalent to a formula that entails either p or its negation, and the negation of any such formula, will inherit the presuppositions of p."(Burton-Roberts 1989b, p.102) Such a generalisation seems problematic. For if we allow that a contradiction entails any sentence, then it follows that a contradiction presupposes everything. But any tautology is standardly equivalent to the negation of a contradiction, so all tautologies must presuppose everything. Further, if a tautology is entailed by any other sentence, it immediately follows that every pair of sentences stands in the relation of presupposition. I fear Burton-Roberts presupposes too much.

which pairs of sentences stand in the relation of implication. But the notion of implication is not always one we can take for granted, especially when presuppositions are involved.

In the first place, and specifically with regard to examples E9 and E10, we must be careful when talking about the *implications* of a non-assertoric speech act. But if we say that 'A implies B' means that any utterance of A indicates that the speaker believes B, then it is safe to say that both E9 and E10 imply E7, but do not imply E3.

A more serious problem is that many of the inferences on which we base the identification of a presupposition have an worryingly *will-o-the-wisp* character: if you look hard at them, they sometimes disappear. Suppose that we wished to back up Strawson's position in his debate with Russell by showing that there was an identifiable presuppositional component to the meaning of a sentence containing a definite description, and that this component behaved quite differently from ordinary assertions. We might begin by considering embedding under negation of a simple sentence, e.g. the *locus classicus* of presupposition theory E11:

E11   The King of France is bald.

E12   The King of France is not bald.

E13   Somebody is bald.

E14   There is a king of France.

Asking naive informants whether E14 follows from E12 produces a mixture of bemused looks, positive and negative replies. Such a result is hard to interpret: it seems plausible that the world knowledge of the informants, the fact that they know there is no King of France, is affecting the way they answer. To factor out the effect of world knowledge, one may follow Gazdar (1979a) and replace 'France' with the name of a less familiar place name, such as 'Buganda', before re-asking the question. This has a quantitative rather than qualitative effect, increasing the proportion of respondents who will attest that (the *Bugandalised* version of) E14 follows from (the Bugandalised version of) E12. It would be a brave scientist who, on the strength of such results, would assert that the negative sentence entails the existence of an object satisfying the definite description. Even more problematically for one who wished to assert the presence of such an entailment, it is easy to invent contexts where a Bugandalised version of E12 might be uttered without any commitment to the existence of a Bugandan king:

E15
    A: The King of Buganda is bald.
    B: Come now A, Buganda is not even a monarchy.
    A: OK, I was wrong then. The King of Buganda is not bald.
    Perhaps it was the president I was thinking of?

Many presupposition theorists argue that cases like E15 are somehow deviant or exceptional. For instance, it has often been claimed that there are not one, but two negations in English (and presumably other languages), and thus that the occurrence of E12 in the discourse E15 involves a different negation to the more *everyday* truth conditional negation. Others argue for E15 being exceptional on the basis of its highly marked intonation contours. If E15 is highly marked, then even without explaining why speaker A need not be committed to E14 after E15, it might still be possible to maintain that utterances of E12 with neutral stress (e.g. no deaccenting, no mid-sentence focal stress) imply the existence of an appropriate king.[8]

Others, especially since Kempson (1975; 1979) and Wilson (1975), have taken the *defeasibility* or *cancellability* of presuppositions to be one of their defining characteristics. But rather than being disturbed by the tendency of presuppositional implications to disappear in certain contexts, some theorists would regard such behaviour as grist to the mill of one trying to defend the existence of a distinct presuppositional realm of meaning. Presuppositional implications are defeasible, they argue, whereas ordinary entailments are not. This is certainly a justifiable position when one considers in detail the data on which the identification of presuppositions is based, for occasional disappearance of claimed presuppositional implications is not restricted to sentences involving negation. Given any characteristically presuppositional implication, that is, an implication of a sentence which appears to remain as an implication in various embeddings, it is usually possible to find contexts in which utterance of the complex embedding does not yield the purported presupposition as an implication. For example, the first of the two following monologues contains an embedding of 'the King of Buganda' in the antecedent of a conditional, and the second contains the same definite noun phrase in a yes-no question, and yet in neither case would we think that an utterer of the monologue was committed to the existence of a king:

---

[8] As it happens, speaker B is wrong: Buganda has been a monarchy for approximately 600 years, at time of writing the King being His Majesty Ronald Muwenda Mutebi II. Confusingly, there is a President as well, although the President is head of the larger state Uganda which incorporates the Kingdom of Buganda, so B may be pardoned for his ignorance. In fact A is wrong too, since, so far as I can tell, His Majesty is not bald. Note that when Gazdar discussed the example there was no Bugandan King: the King in exile died in 1969, and the monarchy was not restored until 1993. I trust that readers will be able to ignore their knowledge of Bugandan politics when evaluating examples.

E16   I don't know for sure whether the King of Buganda is alive, although I've heard it rumoured that he is 90 and completely bald. I have only one comment on the issue. If the King of Buganda is bald, then that must be somebody else inspecting the troops.

E17   You maintain that Buganda has a king, and that he's a recent ex of yours. Well, as it happens I saw the Bugandan head of state opening parliament. I'll ask you just one question about him, and if you can answer correctly and without hesitation, I'll grant that you're right. Is the King of Buganda bald?

All of the following examples may be viewed as cases where a presupposition is cancelled:

E18   If Mary's married then her husband must be very tolerant.

E19   If Jack has children, then all of Jack's children are bald.
       (Karttunen 1973)

E20   You say that somebody in this room loves Mary. Well, it isn't John who loves Mary, and it certainly isn't Sandy who loves her, (and so on, everybody in the room being enumerated). So, nobody in the room loves Mary!
       Example adapted from Keenan (1971).

E21   If I realise that I was wrong I'll tell everybody.
       Example adapted from Karttunen (1971c).

E22   (Teacher to Pupil) I wasn't aware that you were allowed to smoke behind the bicycle sheds!

E23   If the King of France is bald, then I'm a Dutchman: there is no King of France.

E24   If Kennedy knows the war is over, the war is over!
       (Gazdar 1979a)

E25   Nobody has yet discovered that protons are influenced by the CIA!
       (Gazdar 1979a)

E26   (A man is seen in the park crawling around the bushes and whistling.) If he's lost his dog, that would explain his strange behaviour.
       Example adapted from Kay (1992).

E27   (Same situation.) He's either lost his dog or he's lost his mind!

E28   (Same situation.) Perhaps he's lost his dog?

Even if the occasional disappearance of claimed presuppositional implications does not force us to give up analysing various implicational properties of language in terms of presuppositions, it at least forces us to be
careful when defining tests for presuppositional constructions. It will not
do simply to say "a sentence S has a presuppositional implication P if any
utterance of S or of various (listable) complex sentences containing S shows
that the speaker believes P". It is not easy to give a simple restatement
of the identification conditions for presuppositions, one which allows for
defeasibility. A rough and ready reformulation might run along the lines
of "... utterances of S or of various (listable) complex sentences containing
S where the linguistic context provides no relevant information about the
speaker's attitude towards P, provide evidence that the speaker believes
P".

1.4 Applying Presupposition Tests

There are many grammatical constructions which cannot easily be embedded as the tests demand. For example, texts consisting of several sentences
cannot be embedded under negation, in the antecedent of a conditional or
under a modality. Do we want to conclude from this that texts do not
have presuppositions? It seems more natural to remain agnostic, accepting
that we cannot directly obtain data about the presuppositions of texts and
thus that the consequences of any particular theory regarding the presuppositions of texts are untestable. Similar remarks apply to non-assertoric
speech acts. It is sometimes suggested that a wh-question presupposes
the existence of an object satisfying the properties predicated of the wh-
element, yet such a claim is difficult to test: what is the negation of a
question? ('What is not the negation of a question?' ?)

For another example, consider presupposing polarity items (discussed
by van der Sandt in his thesis): sentences containing the positive polarity
item (PPI) 'still' are hard to negate (at least without the feeling of *denial,*
which is just what we want to avoid), and on the other hand a sentence
containing the negative polarity item (NPI) *any more* normally is negative,
so that further negation is highly marked.[9]

The following are all cases where a naive application of presupposition
tests yields bogus presuppositions. The (a) sentence of E29, for example
implicates the (c) sentence, that Mary did not eat one of the two bananas,

---

[9]In broad terms, an NPI is a word or phrase that tends to occur only in non-positive
contexts (e.g. embedded in the antecedent of a conditional), or, in some cases, only
in a clearly negative context (e.g. within the scope of the quantifier 'nobody'). Correspondingly, a PPI tends to occur felicitously only in positive contexts (such as simple
un-negated sentences).

which is also entailed by the negation of (a), in (b). The remaining triples are all based on scalar implicatures.

E29 a. Mary ate one of the two bananas

    b. Mary didn't eat one of the two bananas

    c. (Mary didn't eat one of the two bananas)

E30 a. Mary's total assets are worth $10.

    b. Mary's total assets are not worth $10.

    c. Mary's total assets are not worth $11.

E31 a. Jane submitted one abstract in her entire academic life.

    b. Jane did not submit one abstract in her entire academic life.

    c. Jane did not submit two abstracts in her entire academic life.

E32 a. It is possible that Bill is happy.

    b. It is not possible that Bill is happy.

    c. Bill is not necessarily happy.

E33 a. I think Bill is happy.

    b. I don't think Bill is happy.

    c. I don't know Bill is happy.

So called *scalar implicatures* are thought of as being generated in the presence of a *linguistic scale*. Such a scale is found whenever two expressions have similar distributional properties, but a simple sentence involving the first is logically stronger than the sentence with the second expression substituted for the first. For instance, 'know' might be analysed as higher on a scale than 'believe' (which may be notated 'know'>'believe') since E33a is strictly entailed by 'I know Bill is happy'. Generally, given a scale such that A< B then if S contains A, S implicates the negation of S with A replaced by B, which we may write 'Not S[A\B]',[10] and 'Not S' also carries this entailment. Therefore, one standard presupposition test indicates that for any such B > A and S containing A, S presupposes 'Not S[A\B]'.[11]

As a final type of case where tests indicate what might be seen as a bogus presupposition, consider parentheticals, as in the following example drawn from the Guardian newspaper:

---

[10] Here, and in future, expressions of the form 'Not A' are used to denote the negation of A, it being assumed irrelevant how that negation is realised unless specifically indicated to the contrary.

[11] Gazdar (1979a, p.108) attributes this type of example to Andrea Howard.

E34   Sweden may export synthetic wolf urine — sprayed along roads to keep elk away — to Kuwait for use against camels. — **Associated Press**, January 19, 1995

Syntactically, the parenthetical 'sprayed along roads to keep elk away' appears within the scope of the modal operator 'may': presumably it could be analysed as an attributive relative clause acting as adjunct to the NP 'synthetic wolf urine'. One would infer both from a non-modal version of the example (e.g. with 'may export' replaced by 'is exporting'), and from the example as it stands that synthetic wolf urine is sprayed along roads to keep elk away. Thus, according to the embedding-under-modals test (and others can be applied with the same result) this inference should be designated as presuppositional. But many theories associate presuppositions with information which is in the common ground between interlocutors, or assumed by the speaker to be in this common ground. On such an account the anti-elk application of synthetic wolf urine would not appropriately be termed presuppositional, since the writer of the text very likely does not expect readers to have any previous knowledge of the subject.[12][13] This is not to say that in this case presupposition tests are definitely wrong. Rather, there is no pre-theoretical right and wrong in the matter, and a theoretician has to choose which subsets of phenomena that tests indicate are presuppositional are given a unitary explanation in terms of a theoretical notion of presupposition. Karttunen and Peters have argued that the set of phenomena which tests identify as presuppositional is in fact highly heterogeneous, and indeed that no single sub-group of these phenomena even merits the name *presupposition* (Karttunen and Peters 1977; 1979).[14]

----

[12]The strong definition of *common ground* offered by Clark and Marshall (1981) would suggest that for presuppositional status relevant anti-elk technology should be mutual knowledge, i.e. both hearer and speaker know, and know that each other know, and know that each other know that each other know, and so on. This is obviously a stronger assumption for the speaker to make than merely assuming hearer knowledge. However, this strength is mitigated by the possibility that the speaker merely acts as if the knowledge is mutual, so that use of a presuppositional expression may help speaker and hearer *construct* mutual knowledge. To demonstrate that an expression type is non-presuppositional against a view that allows for a speaker merely to act as if there was mutual knowledge would require evidence that could not be gleaned by looking at one or two tokens. Rather, we would presumably have to show that this expression type was *typically* used when there was no presumption of common knowledge. I hypothesise that utterers of parentheticals do not typically assume mutual knowledge, but have not catalogued sufficient examples to decide the issue.

[13]Tests for presupposition might be understood to indicate that footnotes, which can be seen as a notation for parantheticals, are presupposed. For the negation of a sentence containing a footnote reference would usually suggest the author's belief in the footnote just as much as the corresponding positive sentence would. But I would hesitate to say that this footnote (or any other) is presupposed.

[14]Note that Böer and Lycan (1976) also argue against the presuppositionality of attributive relative clauses.

1.5 Formal Models of Projection

> "... this will suggest ... the appearance of wonderful new 'logical' connectives, and of rules of 'deduction' resembling the prescriptions to be read in *The Key of Solomon.* Since no one expects that standard logic texts shall ever read like witches' grimoires, this inclines one to dismiss the technical study of presuppositions as a mathematical parlor game." (van Fraassen 1969)

For a first glimpse of what is to be expected of a formal presupposition theory, it should be observed that there are some *prima facie* difficulties involved in attempting to explain presupposition related inferences in terms of classical logic. For instance, a purely semantic characterisation of presupposition may begin with the idea that presuppositions can follow both from a formula and its negation. Indeed, this is often taken as the basis of a formal definition of a presupposition relation between sets of formulae: ϕ presupposes ψ iff $\phi \models \psi$ and $\neg \phi \models \psi$. But classically we have that if $\phi \models \psi$ and $\neg \phi \models \psi$, then $\models \psi$. In other words, the above definition together with classically valid patterns of argumentation would yield the unwelcome consequence that only tautologies could be presupposed.

To give another example, since presuppositions are commonly taken to project from the antecedents of conditionals, it might be suggested that if ϕ presupposes ψ, then $\phi \rightarrow \chi \models \psi$ (for arbitrary χ). If this were allowed, then, on natural assumptions about the presuppositions of definite descriptions, we would have 'If the King of France has a bald head then the King of France has a head' entailing that 'There is a King of France.' Now, it seems reasonable to insist that whatever logic is employed should support an inference from 'The King of France has a bald head' to 'The King of France has a head'. However, a consequence of the logician's beloved *deduction theorem* is that from $\phi \vdash \psi$ we can conclude $\vdash \phi \rightarrow \psi$. But then 'If the King of France has a bald head then the King of France has a head' is a tautology, and from this *a fortiori* 'There is a King of France' must also become a tautology. This is an unpalatable consequence. Should we be prepared to accept, for example, the loss of the deduction theorem as one way of breaking down this argument?

Apparent defeasibility of presuppositions suggests abandonment of other classically valid inference patterns. Right monotonicity allows derivation from $\phi \vdash \psi$ that $\phi, \chi \vdash \psi$ (for arbitrary χ). Projection of presuppositions from negated contexts means that 'The King of Buganda is not bald' should normally licence an inference to 'There is a King of Buganda'. However, 'The King of Buganda is not bald. There is no King of Buganda.' apparently does not licence this inference, so maybe right monotonicity should not be valid in a logic for presuppositions.[15]

The philosopher's traditional, intentionally oversimplified picture of interpretation involves mapping sentences of natural language into *similar* sentences of classical logic. The above observations suggest that a formal model of the presupposition projection problem requires a significant departure from such a picture. There are several different strategies for effecting this departure:

1. Changing the interpretation of Logical form (see e.g. the theories in Chapter 2);

2. Complicating the relation between surface structure and logical form (this is the basis of the neo-Russellian account discussed immediately below);

3. Adding pragmatic mechanisms to act in parallel with semantic interpretation (e.g. the theories in Chapter 3).

Many of the theories that are be described in the coming pages could not be said to adopt just one of these, but are hybrids combining several. In particular, the approach which is introduced in the second part of this work is a hybrid of strategies 1 and 3.

1.6   Are Presuppositions Conventional?

We have seen that theories differ as to whether presuppositions are viewed semantically or pragmatically. Another dimension of variation along which theories can in principle differ concerns whether presuppositions are understood to be conventional or not. By a theory of conventional presupposition I mean one in which the grammar explicitly encodes that a certain subset of constructions are presuppositional, and determines for each such construction with what presuppositions it is associated. These constructions are

---

[15]Note that Gazdar's solution to the projection problem, the best known theory which takes defeasibility as its basis, preserves right monotonicity, but effectively removes left monotonicity: if previous sentences contradict the presuppositions of a sentence, the presuppositions are not added to the context. Note also that all the above examples concern meta-logical rules of inference, inferences from the validity of one argument pattern to the validity of another, such as are found in Gentzen Sequent systems. There has been little systematic study of how presupposition in particular bears on general properties of proof systems. The only discussion I am aware of is due to van Fraassen (1975). But van Fraassen makes no attempt to connect the systems he presents with natural language. On the other hand Thomason (1972; 1979) does apply a variant on van Fraassen's supervaluation approach to natural language, although there the discussion does not have the (perhaps excessively rarefied) generality of van Fraassen's work.

known as *presupposition triggers*. Many accounts involve a difference between the presuppositions attached to utterances and those attached conventionally (and independently of utterance context) to the trigger, and this may be reflected terminologically, typically by referring to the presuppositions associated with triggers as *elementary, primitive* or *potential* presuppositions. When referring to theories of conventional presupposition, I include such accounts: although in some cases it might be argued that it is inappropriate to call the utterance presupposition itself *conventional*, the utterance presupposition still originates from a conventional stipulation in the grammar.

A conventional specification of elementary presuppositions is fundamental to all of the formal theories of projection to be discussed in detail in the coming chapters of this monograph. Before ploughing into description and inter-comparison of these theories it is as well to put them into some perspective by asking just how solid their basic foundation is. Must presuppositions be conventionally marked in the grammar? I now present some accounts which appear to provide, and in some cases perhaps really do provide, the basis of a negative answer to this question.

Scope Ambiguity

Although Russell did not find the concept of presupposition to be useful, his theory of definite descriptions (as well as the updated and extended version of that theory of Neale 1990) provides a serious candidate for a treatment of some phenomena taken by others to be presuppositional in nature. It would be a mistake to overlook Russell's simple and elegant account for the sake of philosophical dogma. Furthermore, in §5.9.2 it is be shown that the Russellian analysis of definites is not so distant from current presupposition theory as some might imagine, so that it is well worth taking the trouble to see how Russell's ideas extend to other phenomena usually taken to be presuppositional. Others have proposed how Russell's program might be extended to account for the problems of modern presupposition theory, including Delacruz (1976), Cresswell (1973, pp. 168-169) and Grice (1981), and the extension I propose is perhaps most like the first of these.[16]

A radically Russellian theory of presupposition might be based around the following tenets:

1. The logical form (LF) of language is homogeneous, in the sense that there are no semantically distinct presuppositional and assertional components.

---

[16]Recently, Heim (1992) has also suggested that scope ambiguity might have a role to play in explaining projection facts, postulating that this might provide the explanation of projection from attitude contexts.

2. The LF of a sentence may differ markedly from its surface form, since certain expressions can take semantic scope which is very unconstrained with respect to the syntactic domain in which they are realised at surface structure. Call these expressions the *free scopers*.

3. Call whatever is entailed by all formulae having such an operator at wide scope, the *basic assertions* of the operator (e.g. the existence of a king should be a basic assertion of the operator corresponding to the noun-phrase 'the king'.) To say that a presupposition is cancelled is to say that the embedding at LF of the operator introduced by the presupposition is such that the basic assertion of that operator is not entailed by the LF, and to say that a presupposition is projected is just to say that the basic assertion is entailed.

4. In general a complex sentence will have a large number of LFs. The claim that "presuppositions tend to project" must be explained as a pragmatic preference across alternative LFs, such that one LF will be preferred over another if *ceteris paribus* a free scoping operator has wide scope over a non-free scoping operator in the first LF, but not in the second.

Given that ι is a Russellian description operator *there is one and only one*, the reader will probably recall that according to Russell E12 is subject to a scope ambiguity.[17] Its meaning can correspond to either of two logical forms:

E35 $\quad \iota x[\text{king-of-france}(x)] : \neg(\text{bald}(x))$

E36 $\quad \neg(\iota x[\text{king-of-france}(x)] : \text{bald}(x))$

The first of these readings entails the existence of a unique French King, and is thus comparable to the reading derived in a presuppositional theory where the definite description remains embedded under the negation at LF but where some semantic or pragmatic mechanism allows the presupposed existence of a unique French king to be inherited as a presupposition of the whole sentence. The second reading, in which the definite remains embedded under the negation, of course corresponds to what in a presuppositional theory would be a case of presupposition cancellation.

---

[17]The Russellian need not be committed to analysing definites as introducing a scope bearing sentential operator. Instead, a term forming version of the ι may be defined. Whitehead and Russell (1910) adopted a syntactically awkward hybrid approach when they took over and modified the iota notation from Peano. Grice (1981) is an example of someone who prefers to take the iota as a term operator. However, I follow Neale (1990) in assuming an operator treatment.

Given that these two readings are approximately those commonly discussed in the presupposition literature, what is wrong with Russell's theory? One point of weakness is Russell's uniqueness restriction. At the very least, it is clear that there are some uses of definites which do not entail that there is a unique satisfier of the description:

E37 At the Françaises-celebres masquerade Napoleon gets a cheap laugh by offering his hat to one of the Kings of France, of whom several are present. The King of France is bald, and soon loses his head.

Russell's account fails to allow for anaphoricity of presuppositional expressions such as definites. Whether Russell's uniqueness constraint could be defended against such examples, perhaps by separating anaphoric and non-anaphoric uses of definites, uniqueness effects are far from straightforward, and there is no competing theory which fully accounts for them.[18] More to the point, we are interested in whether Russell's account of definites can serve as the basis of a more general theory of phenomena treated elsewhere as presuppositional. Uniqueness effects are peculiar to a limited set of constructions (definites and clefts), and would presumably not figure as part of the more general theory. On the other hand, there is another idea in Russell's analysis, that of justifying the presence both of projection and cancellation readings in terms of an underlying scope ambiguity, which could conceivably be of general applicability.

For instance, suppose that we worked in a semantic universe sufficiently rich to allow variables to range over propositions (or over individual correlates of propositions). We might then define a language with expressions $[x - \phi](\psi)$, where this has meaning ϕ *holds, and under the assignment of x to the individual correlate of ϕ, ψ holds.* Then we might analyse sentences containing a factive verb along the lines of the following examples:[19]

E38 a. Pooh realises that Eeyore is sad.

b. $[x - \mathsf{sad}(e)](\mathsf{realises}(p, x))$

---

[18]See e.g. Kadmon (1990) and McCawley (1979) for discussion of uniqueness. Anaphoricity of presuppositional expressions other than definites is discussed in §4.6, below. Note that Russell was aware that definites are used when they do not uniquely refer, but appears to have taken a prescriptivist line that such uses are merely sloppy: "we do, it is true, speak of 'the son of So-and-so' even when So-and-so has several sons, but it would be more correct to say 'a son of So-and-so'."(Russell 1905) Such an invocation of human frailty would fail in the case of non-unique anaphoric definites, and in other cases where paraphrase of a definite using an indefinite produces a change in truth conditions.

[19]The structure in E38b is somewhat reminiscent of the type of syntactic analysis suggested by Kiparsky and Kiparsky (1970). Kempson (1975, pp. 130–135) provides a similar semantic analysis of factives to that here, tracing her equivalent to the $[x - \phi](\psi)$ construction back to Reichenbach's *fact functions* (Reichenbach 1947).

E39   a.   Pooh doesn't realise that Eeyore is sad.

        b. $[x - \mathsf{sad}(e)](\neg\mathsf{realises}(p, x))$

        c. $\neg(\ [\mathsf{sad}(e)](\mathsf{realises}(p, x))\ )$

Once again, both cancellation and projection readings are found for the negative case. Where then, might the weaknesses of such an analysis lie? Most importantly, our neo-Russellian theory cannot be easily stated without introducing a class of presuppositional constructions, even if by another name.[20] For given that presuppositions can project from much more deeply embedded constructions than are found in the above examples, and given that projection is to be explained as wide scope, presuppositional constructions will have to be interpreted as a class of operators which can take extra-clausal (and perhaps completely unbounded) scope. Thus in the following example, the factive complement of 'realise' (and also the definite description 'the forest') must be allowed to take extra-clausal scope, which appears to be forbidden for the scope bearing quantificational NP 'every animal':

E40   If every animal in the forest realises that Eeyore is sad, they will organise a party.

Of course, there are other operators which are less constrained as to their possible scope than the bulk of quantificational NPs. For instance, neither indefinite NPs nor sentential connectives are subject to a constraint on extra-clausal scope. What would make the analysis of presuppositional constructions unusual is that they would have to be given wide scope *as a default*, for it is well known that the cancellation (i.e. narrow scope) readings only occur in very specialised circumstances, such as when consequences of the wide scope reading are explicitly contradicted. It is not obvious how the preference for wide scope could be explained, but it is at least clear that the explanation would have to make clear why this preference applied to presuppositional constructions and not other scope bearing elements, and thus that some class of presuppositional constructions would have to be distinguishable in the theory.

One final observation on the neo-Russellian theory. If presupposition triggers were a special sort of scope bearing element, then there would

---

[20] Grice (1981, p.280) also comes to the conclusion that, at least for some constructions, it will be difficult to explain the data without postulating conventional marking of presuppositions: "I do not see that it is going to be particularly easy to represent the implication in the case of *regret* as being one of a conversational kind. It does not look as attractive as the Russellian case." Here by the "Russellian case" he refers to the Russellian treatment of definite descriptions. Grice then proceeds to suggest marking certain presuppositional expressions using special brackets, and suggests a rewriting operation on logical forms which effectively gives the presuppositions wide scope. He later describes this as "a minimal strengthening of a Russellian pattern of analysis by the addition of a purely syntactical scope device. . . ."

presumably often be other readings than just wide and narrow scope with respect to all other operators. For example, E40 should be expected to have a reading where the sadness of Eeyore outscopes 'every animal' but remains within the conditional (i.e. 'If Eeyore is sad and every animal realises it, then they will have a party'). Readings of this sort occur in the context of a quite different style of presupposition theory, where they are produced by a mechanism called *intermediate accommodation*. The relationship between the mechanisms of accommodation and scope variability is discussed in §5.9.2.

Underspecification

Atlas (1976; 1977), Kempson (1975) and Wilson (1975) have all presented theories of presuppositional phenomena which, like the neo-Russellian account above, do not involve the postulation of a semantic division between presuppositions and assertions. Further, these authors were amongst the first to show that sentences involving a factive verb (or definite description) under a negation do not always implicate the truth of the factive complement (or existence of an object satisfying the description), demonstrating that in some contexts of utterance the implication is lacking. Yet all three authors objected to the postulation of Russellian scope ambiguities as an explanation for this instability. Indeed, all three argue that negation in standard (for English) VP-modifier position bears fixed, wide scope semantically. Thus for them 'Jane realises that Bill is happy' simply entails that Bill is happy, and the negation of this sentence 'Jane does not realise that Bill is happy' entails that it is not the case both that Bill is happy and that Jane realises it: the negative sentence does not entail that Bill is happy. The occasional surfacing of *presuppositional* inferences, in this case the inference that Bill is happy, is to be explained not in terms of semantic entailment, but in terms of Gricean argumentation, utilising general principles such as informativeness and relevance.

The three authors differ considerably in the details of their pragmatic analyses. Kempson seems to suggest that definite descriptions are in some sense (syntactically) more complex than indefinites, this complexity consisting in an extra "[+ def]" feature. She constructs an argument to the effect that when a speaker chooses to use a definite over an indefinite a generalised conversational implicature is generated, the hearer having to explain what extra information is signaled by the choice of a definite. But since "the definite article can only be construed as offering extra information if it is used to convey the same information as its obligatory (anaphoric) use" (Kempson 1975, p. 178), the hearer concludes that the speaker is using the definite *as if* it were anaphoric on some previously introduced entity, and the existence of an appropriate entity is inferred.[21] Although Kempson does not invoke any principles of analysis specific to presupposition, and terms the inference to the truth of a presupposition a *conversational impli-cature*, her theory nonetheless counts as a theory of conventional presupposition on the rather broad definition which I have provided, for what is the [+ def] feature if not a means of conventionally marking presuppositions? In the case of definite descriptions the presence of the special feature can be independently justified as signaling a preference for an anaphoric use, but this explanation does not seem appropriate in the case of other presuppositional classes, such as aspectual verbs and factives. Furthermore, it is not obvious that there would be any descriptive difference between Kempson's theory and a version of that theory where the [+ def] marked constructions directly triggered a conventional implicature. This is essentially the idea of the cancellation theories of presupposition to be considered in Chapter 3, of which Kempson's account can be seen as a forerunner.

Wilson (1975), by contrast seems not to be a theory of conventional presupposition.[22] I will exemplify the account with her treatment of negative sentences involving factive verbs (pp. 99-100). This analysis depends on listing a certain set of cases in which the sentence would be semantically correct, and then providing arguments why in various of these cases the sentence would be pragmatically inappropriate. For instance, if 'Jane does not realise that Bill is happy' is uttered and the field of alternatives has been narrowed down to the case where Bill is not happy (which she argues entails that Jane is not in the state of realising that Bill is happy), and the case where Bill is happy but Jane does not realise it, then the first case can be ruled out. If the speaker knew that Bill was not happy, then simply uttering 'Bill is not happy' would be more perspicuous. The analysis depends heavily on selecting the right cases: the hidden premise seems to be that the speaker has complete knowledge of the situation being described, and is not, for instance, in a state of knowing that either the first or second of the above cases holds, but not knowing which.

For Atlas, presuppositional inferences arise in order that negative sentences may be informative, and in order that they may tie in with entities and topics already under discussion in a discourse. Witness the

---

[21]Kempson applies the same analysis to factive verbs, assuming, as mentioned, that at deep structure the propositional complement of a factive verb also involves a [+ def] feature. However, the argument seems to me rather weaker than in the case of definite descriptions, for there the analysis apparently rests on the speaker having the choice of either using a definite or an indefinite. So to construct the same argument for factive verbs one would need choices of semantically similar predicates which lacked the [+ def] feature. In general, such choices appear to be lacking.

[22]On the other hand, Wilson's joint account with Sperber (Wilson and Sperber 1979) does involve conventional stipulation, but this stipulation is (a) much finer grained than the standard presupposing/non-presupposing contrast, and (b) not in general attached to specific lexical items but to different grammatical constructions and stress patterings.

following from Atlas (1976): "The presuppositional understanding of a negative sentence will be logically stronger and more informative than the non-presuppositional one." [p.150]; "The presuppositional understandings of sentences are logically stronger than the non-presuppositional understandings. Claims about the world are more informative when singular terms designate, predicates have non-null extensions, modifiers are modifiers of something..." [p.152]. I wish to draw out one theme from this analysis which seems relevant to any theory of presupposition: the fact that presuppositions tend to project might be explained in terms of a general preference for logically stronger interpretations over weaker ones.[23] This approach to ordering interpretations I will term "the Atlas method", it being appropriate that a thus-named scholar should have formulated a preference for brute strength over semantic weakness. Whereas for Atlas this strengthening is a matter of further specifying a single weak logical form, for the neo-Russellian scholar the strengthening would be a matter of picking the logically stronger of the available readings. The fact that $\iota x[\text{king-of-france}(x)] : \neg(\text{bald}(x))$ entails $\neg(\iota x[\text{king-of-france}(x)] : \text{bald}(x))$, but not *vice versa*, would justify choosing the first reading over the second. The first, the wide scope definite reading, of course corresponds to what others would term projection of the definite's presupposition. I leave it to the reader to consider examples where the alternative scope readings are not ordered by logical entailment, and to establish whether there is indeed any preference for the projection readings in these cases.

The program of showing that there is no need for presuppositions to be conventionally marked in the grammar is perhaps carried to its furthest extent in Atlas and Levinson's joint work (Atlas and Levinson 1981). But even here, where the range of presuppositional constructions dealt with is not large, and where there is attention to formal precision, the difficulty of executing the general program satisfactorily is manifest. The main difficulty is that whilst the cornerstone of the program must be essentially Gricean, formalisation of Gricean argumentation is notoriously problematic. Not only are we lacking any generally accepted statement of the Gricean maxims, we are also lacking any generally accepted logic which is able not just to encode those maxims, but also to support the sort of reasoning that would be required. If an anti-presuppositionalist claims to have completely eliminated the need for presupposition, but that claim rests on

---

[23]This is not to say that any evidence has been presented here, or by Atlas for that matter, that there is such a general preference. But it is at least an interesting and not implausible hypothesis that such a preference exists. The possible relevance of logical strength to the ordering of interpretations in a theory of presupposition was pointed out to me by Henk Zeevat, who suggested that it would be an alternative basis for ordering the readings available in van der Sandt's theory. The approach has been under discussion recently: see Geurts (2000) and references therein.

a Gricean account of pragmatics which is still not adequately formalised, then the claim must remain, in part, mere whistling in the wind.

There is no *a priori* reason to introduce a notion of presupposition into grammar. If a grammar can be developed in which the class of constructions which have been called presuppositional are not distinguished in any special way, but the combination of this grammar and a general theory of utterance interpretation can predict the type of inferences which are commonly thought of as presuppositional, then the notion of presupposition, conceived of as something to be encoded explicitly in grammar, will have been rendered superfluous. However, seen in this way, at least two of the theories considered in this section, Kempson's theory and the neo-Russellian theory, do not take us any nearer this goal. For these two can be seen as presuppositional theories, in that the class of constructions commonly identified as presuppositional must be distinguished in the grammar.[24] But if Gricean theory could be adequately formalised, and it could be demonstrated that presuppositional inferences arose as mere side effects, that would surely count as a tremendous success. Furthermore, such an explanatory success might not necessarily conflict with the presuppositionalist's program. For even if conversational principles can explain presuppositional inferences, the possibility remains that what were once conversational inferences have become conventionalised. Thus Geurts (1994; 1999) discusses the possibility that "what started off as a pragmatic regularity has been encoded in the grammar", and Grice himself (Grice 1981, p. 282) says of his own account that it could be "regarded as a conventional regimentation of a particular kind of non-conventional implicature." So it is at least possible that the type of argumentation developed by Wilson, Atlas and Levinson could be interpreted not as replacing presuppositional theories, but as supplementing them, as providing an account of how linguistic presuppositions came into being in the first place and providing an interpretation for whatever formal apparatus the presuppositionalist proposes.

As I have indicated, all the remaining theories to be discussed involve presuppositions (occasionally under another name) being conventionally marked in the grammar, some function being utilised which maps simple positive sentences onto a set of propositions called the presuppositions (or *elementary/primitive/potential* presuppositions) of the sentence.[25] This is not to say that conventional stipulation of presuppositions has been validated, but it has not been invalidated either.

---

[24] As I have indicated, Kempson distinguishes presuppositional constructions with a [+ def] feature, and the neo-Russellian seems forced to distinguish a class of *free-scopers*.

[25] One might think that the definition of this function would be the central part of presupposition theory. But in fact most authors either assume such a function, or only define it for a small subset of constructions. Geurts (1994; 1999) contains an illuminating discussion concerning the difficulty of defining a function from simple sentences to their elementary presuppositions.

2

Multivalence and Partiality

2.1 Introduction

This chapter concerns a subset of approaches to presupposition which follow the first of the options mentioned in §1.5, namely modifying not the logical form itself, but the interpretation of that logical form. In general this refinement may concern the interpretation of objects of any syntactic category, but I concentrate on the meaning of sentence level units, or, when looking at artificial languages, on the interpretation of formulae rather than of terms. The subset of approaches now to be discussed are those in which the interpretation of a formula defines not only a set of worlds such that when interpreted relative to one of these worlds the formula is true (call this set T), and a set where it is false (F), but also a set where its presuppositions are satisfied (P) and a set where they are not (N).[1]

There are three standard ways in which this redefinition is achieved. First, there is trivalent semantics in which the Boolean domain of truth values $\{t, f\}$ may be extended to include a third value $\star$, such that the T, F and N worlds are those where the formula has the value t, f and $\star$ respectively, and $P = T \cup F$. Second, there is partial semantics. Here the domain of truth values is allowed to remain Boolean, but the interpretation function is partialised, such that for a given formula T is the set relative to which the valuation produces t, F is that against which the valuation produces f, P is still the union of T and F, but now the set N is not a set relative to which the formula is given some particular valuation or valuations, but rather it is the set of worlds against which the valuation function is not defined for the formula. Third, there are two dimensional systems, where the valuation is split into two parts, or dimensions, each of the two sub-valuations being boolean. There is some variation in how the split is made, but the approaches I describe make a split between a presuppositional and an assertional sub-valuation. For the assertional

---

[1] Some might prefer to read *models* where I write *worlds*.

sub-valuation T is the set of worlds where the formula has value t, and F is the remaining set where the formula has the value f, and for the presuppositional sub-valuation, P is the set of worlds where the formula has value t, and N is the remaining set where the formula has the value f.

If the trivalent, partial and two-dimensional accounts differ as to the precise refinement from classical interpretation which they utilise, they nonetheless share a basic approach to presupposition projection:

1. Presuppositions are constraints on the range of worlds/models against which we are able to evaluate the truth or falsity of predications and other semantic operations, or against which this evaluation is legitimate.

2. If these constraints are not met, semantic undefinedness, or illegitimacy of the truth-value, results.

3. Presupposition projection facts associated with a given operator are explained compositionally, in terms of the relation between the definedness/legitimacy of that operator and the definedness/legitimacy of its arguments in some model, and this relation is recoverable from the semantics of the operator alone.

For the purposes of the following discussion, partial and trivalent semantics are collapsed. This is possible because the discussion is restricted to systems where the connectives are defined *truth functionally*. Truth functionality is taken to mean that, for any compound formula the only information needed for evaluation relative to some world is (1) the semantics of the head connective, and (2) for each argument whether there is a valuation in the given world, and, if so, what that valuation is. Given such a restriction, from a technical point of view all systems which are presented as trivalent could be presented as partial, and *vice versa*, whilst maintaining extensionally identical relations of consequence and presupposition.[2] I

---

[2]This restriction to truth functional systems does exclude one important method of supplying partial interpretations, namely the *supervaluation* semantics developed by van Fraassen. See van Fraassen (1969; 1975), Thomason (1972; 1979), and the discussion of Martin (1979). One advantage of the supervaluation approach is that it allows a logic, say classical first order logic, to be partialised such that logical validities remain intact. (Note that classical validities are also maintained in the two dimensional approaches which are discussed below.) Van Fraassen's account is discussed at greater length in Beaver (1997).

The choice between using a partial or a trivalent logic has few if any empirical consequences for the treatment of presupposition data. (Supervaluation account may provide an exception, but see Karttunen's (1973) discussion of van Fraassen.) However, in saying this I am taking for granted a conventional use of the term *partial logic* by logicians (see e.g. Blamey 1989), whereby, for instance, versions of both Kleene's strong and weak systems are sometimes referred to as partial logics. Seuren (1985; 1990a) offers

first consider trivalent systems, then two dimensional systems, and then discuss some of the general advantages and disadvantages, showing why most contemporary proponents of such approaches accept that presuppositional data cannot be explained in purely semantic terms, but require some additional pragmatic component.

2.2 Trivalent Accounts

In a trivalent logic,[3] where the semantic valuation of a formula ϕ with respect to a model M (here written $[\![\phi]\!]_M$) may take any of the three semantic values, typically thought of as true, false and undefined $(t, f, \star)$, presupposition may be defined as follows:

Definition D1 (Strawsonian Presupposition) ϕ presupposes ψ (also written $\phi \gg \psi$) iff for all models M, if $[\![\phi]\!]_M \in \{t, f\}$ then $[\![\psi]\!]_M = t$.

Let us assume, for the moment, a Tarskian notion of logical consequence as preservation of truth ($\phi \models \psi$ iff for all models M, if $[\![\phi]\!]_M = t$ then $[\![\psi]\!]_M = t$). Let us further assume that a negation $\neg$ is available in the formal language which is interpreted classically with respect to classically valued argument formulae, mapping true to false and *vice versa*, but which preserves undefinedness. This defines a so-called *choice* negation having the following truth table:

ϕ	$\neg\phi$
t	f
f	t
$\star$	$\star$

Given these notions of consequence and negation, it is easily shown that the above definition of presupposition is equivalent to one mentioned earlier:

Definition D2 (Presupposition Via Negation) ϕ presupposes ψ iff $\phi \models \psi$ and $\neg\phi \models \psi$

---

an alternative characterisation whereby only Kleene's weak system (the internal system of Bochvar 1939) would count as a gapped/partial logic. This is because he implicitly limits consideration to systems which are truth functional in a stronger sense than is given above, such that a compound formula can only have a value defined if the valuation of all the arguments is defined. On the other hand, Burton-Roberts (1989a) offers a system which he claims to have the only *true* gapped bivalent semantics, and which just happens to contain exactly the connectives in Kleene's strong system.

[3]Standard references for trivalent logics such as presented below are Strawson (1952), Kleene (1952). For further discussion, see Beaver (1997), Beaver and Krahmer (2001), the introductory material in Gamut (1991), McCawley (1981), or the overview and critical discussion of Soames (1989).

These, then, are the standard approaches to defining presupposition in three-valued logics. One author who offers a significant deviation from these definitions is Burton-Roberts (1989a). He defines two separate notions of logical consequence, *weak* consequence, which is just the notion $\models$ above, and *strong* consequence, which is here denoted $\models_s$, and is defined by: $\phi \models_s \psi$ iff (1) $\phi \models \psi$, and (2) for all models M, if $[\![\psi]\!]_M = f$ then $[\![\phi]\!]_M = f$. Thus for one proposition to strongly entail another, the truth of the first must guarantee the truth of the second, and the falsity of the second must guarantee the falsity of the first.[4] Burton-Roberts then suggests that presuppositions are weak consequences which are not strong consequences:

Definition D3 (Burton-Roberts Presupposition) ϕ presupposes ψ iff $\phi \models \psi$ and $\phi \not\models_s \psi$

This seems an attractive definition, and is certainly not equivalent to the standard definitions above. However, it has some rather odd properties. For example, assuming this definition of presupposition and Burton-Roberts' quite standard notion of conjunction, it turns out that if ϕ presupposes ψ, then ϕ presupposes $\psi \wedge \phi$. Let us assume that 'The King of France is bald' presupposes 'There is a King of France'. According to Burton-Roberts' definition it must also presuppose 'There is a King of France and he is bald', which seems completely unintuitive. More generally, if ϕ presupposes ψ then according to this definition it must also presuppose the conjunction of ψ with *any* strong consequence of ϕ.[5] I see no reason why we should

---

[4]Wilson (1975) took a definition of consequence like $\models_s$ as fundamental, and used it as part of her argument against semantic theories of presupposition. In a more technically rigorous discussion, Blamey (1989) also suggests that the strong notion should be the basic one.

[5]Burton-Robert's system uses Kleene's strong *falsity preserving* conjunction, whereby a conjunction is true if and only if both conjuncts are true, and false if and only if at least one conjunct is false. The following argument then shows that a proposition must presuppose any conjunction of a presupposition and a strong entailment:

1. Suppose ϕ presupposes ψ in Burton-Roberts system
2. Then (a) $\phi \models \psi$, and (b) $\phi \not\models_s \psi$
3. From 2, $[\![\psi]\!]_M = f$ and $[\![\phi]\!]_M \neq f$ for some model M
4. Suppose $\phi \models_s \chi$
5. By definition of $\models_s$, we have that $\phi \models \chi$
6. By 2(b), 5 and definitions of $\wedge, \models$, it follows that $\phi \models \psi \wedge \chi$
7. Relative to the same model M, where ψ is false, falsity preservation of $\wedge$ tells us that $\psi \wedge \chi$ is false
8. Since there is a model (M) where ϕ is not false and its weak entailment $\psi \wedge \chi$ is false, it follows that $\phi \not\models_s \psi \wedge \chi$
9. Hence ϕ must presuppose $\psi \wedge \chi$ in Burton-Roberts system. Q.E.D.

accept a definition of presupposition with this property.

Moving back to the standard definitions, we can examine the presupposition projection behaviour of various three-valued logics. A simple picture of presupposition projection is what is known as the *cumulative hypothesis* according to which the set of presuppositions of a complex sentence consists of every single elementary presupposition belonging to any subsentence.[6] As far as the projection behaviour of the logical connectives is concerned, such a theory of projection would be modelled by a trivalent logic in which if any of the arguments of a connective has the value $\star$, then the value of the whole is also $\star$. Assuming that combinations of classical values are still to yield their classical result, this yields the so-called *internal Bochvar* or *weak Kleene* connectives:

Definition D4 (Weak Kleene or Internal Bochvar Connectives)

$\phi \wedge \psi$	t	f	$\star$
t	t	f	$\star$
f	f	f	$\star$
$\star$	$\star$	$\star$	$\star$

$\phi \rightarrow \psi$	t	f	$\star$
t	t	f	$\star$
f	t	t	$\star$
$\star$	$\star$	$\star$	$\star$

$\phi \vee \psi$	t	f	$\star$
t	t	t	$\star$
f	t	f	$\star$
$\star$	$\star$	$\star$	$\star$

ϕ	$\neg \phi$
t	f
f	t
$\star$	$\star$

It should be mentioned that the above is not the only definition of presupposition that Burton-Roberts offers: it seems to be intended as a definition of the elementary presuppositions of a simple positive sentence. Presuppositions of compound sentences are given by a relation of *Generalised Presupposition*, which I do not discuss here.

[6]The cumulative hypothesis is commonly attributed to Langendoen and Savin. However, this may be wrong on two counts. First, the term is explicitly introduced by Morgan (1969), and Morgan offers the cumulative hypothesis as a straw-man. He dispenses with this straw-man by showing cases of non-projection. Second, Langendoen and Savin's view appears to have been more sophisticated than some have suggested. Regarding examples where a presupposition of the consequent of a conditional does not become an implication of the conditional as a whole, they comment (Langendoen and Savin 1971, pp. 58): "A conditional sentence has the property that its presupposition is presupposed in a (possibly imaginary) world in which its antecedent is true...and no mechanism for suspending presuppositions is required." Although the informality of their proposal makes it difficult to evaluate, it is clear that Langendoen and Savin were aware of cases where presuppositions of an embedded sentence are not implications of the whole and did not see them as counterexamples to their theory. Indeed, on a charitable reading (where it is read as a generic about a property holding of worlds which satisfy the antecedent of a conditional) the above quote seems to prefigure the inheritance properties that Karttunen later attributed to conditionals.

A naive version of the cumulative hypothesis, such as is embodied in the definition of Bochvar's internal connectives, is not tenable, in that there are many examples of presuppositions not being projected. Let us consider first how this is dealt with in the case that has generated the most controversy over the years, that of negation.[7] In a trivalent semantics, the existence of cases where presuppositions of sentences embedded under a negation are not projected, is normally explained in terms of the existence of a *denial* operator (here $\natural$) such that when $[\![\phi]\!]_M = \star$, $[\![\natural\phi]\!]_M = t$. Typically the following *exclusion* (sometimes called *weak*) negation operator results:

ϕ	$\natural\phi$
t	f
f	t
$\star$	t

Since there apparently exist both cases where a negation acts, in Karttunen's terminology, as a *hole* to presuppositions (allowing projection) and cases where it acts as what Karttunen called a *plug* (preventing projection), the defender of a trivalent account of presupposition appears not to have the luxury of choosing between the two negations given above, but seems forced to postulate that negation in natural language is ambiguous between them. Unfortunately, as is argued at great length by Horn (1989), and by Atlas (1989), convincing independent evidence for such an ambiguity is lacking. There may at least be intonational features which mark occurrences of denial negation from other uses, and thus potentially allow the development of a theory as to which of the two meanings a given occurrence of negation corresponds.[8]

---

[7]Horn (1985) provides an excellent overview of treatments of negation and considers cases of presupposition denial at length. For a longer read, Horn (1989) is recommended. Extensive discussion of negation within the context of contemporary trivalent accounts of presupposition is found in Seuren (1985; 1988b) and Burton-Roberts (1989c;a). These latter publications produced considerable debate, to a degree surprising given that Burton-Roberts, though innovative, presents what is essentially a reworking of a quite well worn approach to presupposition. This refreshingly vehement debate provides the definitive modern statements of the alternative positions on negation within trivalent systems: see Horn (1990) and Burton-Roberts' (1989b) reply, Seuren (1990a) and Burton-Roberts' (1990) reply, and also the reviews by Seuren (1990b) and Turner (1992).

[8]If the *raison d'etre* of a trivalent denial operator is to yield truth when predicated of a non-true and non-false proposition, then in principle some choice remains as to how it should behave when predicated of a simply false proposition. Thus the denial operator need not necessarily have the semantics of the exclusion negation, although, to my knowledge, only Seuren has been brave enough to suggest an alternative. Seuren's preferred vehicle for denial is an operator which maps only $\star$ onto t, and maps both t and f onto f. *Contra* Horn, Seuren has also marshalled empirical evidence that negation is in fact ambiguous, although the main justification for his particular choice of denial operator is, I think, philosophical.

There is a frequently overlooked alternative to postulating a lexical ambiguity, dating back as far as Bochvar's original papers (Bochvar 1939). Bochvar suggested that apart from the normal mode of assertion there was a second mode which we might term *meta-assertion*. The meta-assertion of ϕ, $A\phi$, is the proposition that ϕ is true: $[\![A\phi]\!]_{\mathrm{M}} = t$ if $[\![\phi]\!]_{\mathrm{M}} = t$ and $[\![A\phi]\!]_{\mathrm{M}} = f$ otherwise. Bochvar showed how within the combined system consisting of the internal connectives and this assertion operator a second set of *external* connectives could be defined: for instance the external conjunction of two formulae is just the internal conjunction of the meta-assertion of the two formulae (i.e. $\phi \wedge_{\mathrm{ext}} \psi =_{\mathrm{def}} A(\phi) \wedge_{\mathrm{int}} A(\psi)$), and the external negation of a formula is just the exclusion negation given above, and defined in the extended Bochvar system by $\sharp\phi =_{\mathrm{def}} \neg A(\phi)$.[9] Thus whilst the possibility of declaring natural language negation to be ambiguous between $\neg$ and $\sharp$ exists within Bochvar's extended system, another possibility would be to translate natural language negation uniformly using $\neg$, but then allow that sometimes the proposition under the negation is itself clad in the meta-assertoric armour of the A-operator.

There is no technical reason why the Bochvarian meta-assertion operator should be restricted in its occurrence to propositions directly under a negation. Link (1986) has proposed a model in which in principle any presupposition can be *co-asserted*, where co-assertion, if I understand correctly, essentially amounts to embedding under the A-operator. Let us term a theory where all occurrences of cancellation are explained away in these terms a *floating-A theory*. Such a theory is flexible, since it leaves the same logical possibilities open as in a system with an enormous multiplicity of connectives: for instance if the A operator can freely occur in any position around a disjunction, then the effects of having the following four disjunctions are available: $\phi \vee \psi$, $A(\phi \vee \psi)$, $A(\phi) \vee \psi$ and $\phi \vee A(\psi)$. It is then necessary to explain why presuppositions only fail to project in certain special cases. Link indicates that pragmatic factors will induce an ordering over the various readings, although he does not formalise this part of the theory. Presumably a default must be invoked that the A operator only occurs when incoherence would result otherwise, and then with narrowest possible scope. The term *incoherence* must then be ex-

---

[9]External negation, given that it can be defined as $\neg A(\phi)$ where A is a sort of truth-operator, has often been taken to model the English paraphrases 'it is not true that' and 'it is not the case that'. Although it may be that occurrence of these extraposed negations is high in cases of presupposition denial — I am not aware of any serious research on the empirical side of this matter — it is certainly neither the case that the construction is used in all instances of presupposition denial, nor that all uses of the construction prevent projection of embedded presuppositions. Thus the use of the term *external* for the weak negation operator, and the corresponding use of the term *internal* for the strong, is misleading, and does not reflect a well established link with different linguistic expressions of negation.

plicated: perhaps it can be understood as semantic undefinedness in the set of models corresponding to our assumptions about the world. At base then, a floating-A theory consists of a semantic component generating multiple meanings encoding varying degrees of presupposition projection, and a pragmatic component selecting between these meanings. This selection could, for instance, be based on the Atlas method, the principle of preference for logically stronger readings — see §1.6. In §2.4 we will see that, given an argument in essence due to Soames, the defender of a trivalent account of presupposition might be forced into some version of a floating-A theory. For the moment let us merely observe that in a floating-A theory the lexical ambiguity of negation which is common in trivalent theories is replaced by an essentially structural ambiguity, and in this respect is comparable with the Russellian scope-based explanation of projection facts.[10]

So far we have only considered cases where presuppositions of each argument are either definitely projected to become presuppositions of the whole, or definitely not projected. Fittingly, in the land of the *included middle*, there is a third possibility. The presupposition may, in effect, be modified as it is projected. Such modification occurs with all the binary connectives in Kleene's *strong* logic:

Definition D5 (Strong Kleene Connectives)

$\phi \wedge \psi$	t	f	$\star$
t	t	f	$\star$
f	f	f	f
$\star$	$\star$	f	$\star$

$\phi \rightarrow \psi$	t	f	$\star$
t	t	f	$\star$
f	t	t	t
$\star$	t	$\star$	$\star$

$\phi \vee \psi$	t	f	$\star$
t	t	t	t
f	t	f	$\star$
$\star$	t	$\star$	$\star$

ϕ	$\neg\phi$
t	f
f	t
$\star$	$\star$

To see that under this definition it is not in general the case that if ϕ presupposes π then $\psi \rightarrow \phi$ presupposes π, we need only observe that if $[\![\psi]\!]_{\mathrm{M}} = f$ then $[\![\psi \rightarrow \phi]\!]_{\mathrm{M}} = t$ regardless of the valuation of ϕ. Presuppositions of the consequent are weakened, in the sense that in a subset of models, those where the antecedent is false, undefinedness — read *presupposition failure* — of the consequent is irrelevant to the definedness of the whole. However, in those models where the antecedent is not false, the

---

[10]Horn (1985, p.125) provides a similar explication to that above of the relation between theories postulating alternative 3-valued negations and theories involving a Russellian scope ambiguity. A joint article by Emiel Krahmer and myself contains further discussion of a floating-A theory (Beaver and Krahmer 2001).

presuppositions of the consequent are significant, so that presupposition failure of the consequent is sufficient to produce presupposition failure of the whole. The presuppositional properties of the strong Kleene logic may be determined by inspection of the truth tables, and may be summed up as follows (where $\gg$ is defined as in D1):

Fact 2.1 Under the strong Kleene interpretation, if $\phi \gg \pi$ then:

$$\neg\phi \;\gg\; \pi$$
$$\phi \wedge \psi \;\gg\; \psi \to \pi$$
$$\psi \wedge \phi \;\gg\; \psi \to \pi$$
$$\phi \to \psi \;\gg\; (\neg\psi) \to \pi$$
$$\psi \to \phi \;\gg\; \psi \to \pi$$
$$\phi \vee \psi \;\gg\; (\neg\psi) \to \pi$$
$$\psi \vee \phi \;\gg\; (\neg\psi) \to \pi$$

If models are restricted to those where ψ is bivalent, these are maximal presuppositions, in the sense that the right hand side represents the logically strongest presupposition, all other presuppositions being entailed by it.

The occurrence of conditionalised presuppositions can be argued for on the basis of examples like the following:

E41   If Jane is married, then her husband is not here.

Given that the consequent of E41 carries the presupposition that Jane has a husband, the implication as a whole is predicted to carry the presupposition that if Jane is married then she has a husband. If we restrict our attention to models in which this natural — one is tempted to say *analytic* — condition is satisfied, the (logical rendering of the) sentence will always have a classical truth valuation. Thus, appropriately in this case, the presupposition of the consequent is weakened to the point of triviality, and the sentence does not presuppose (nor entail) that Jane is married. We return to conditionalised presuppositions, which occur in some two dimensional accounts as well as in Strong Kleene, below.

2.3   Two Dimensions

There are no obvious empirical reasons for using more than three truth values in the treatment of presupposition, and thus Occam's razor commonly makes trivalent semantics the preferred basis for a multivalent treatment of presupposition.[11] However, quite apart from the fact that four valued logics are sometimes thought to be technically more elegant than their three valued cousins, the use of four truth values affords theorists the space to pursue a *divide and conquer* strategy, separating issues of presupposition from those of classical truth and entailment. The idea was developed independently, but in rather different forms, in Herzberger (1973) and Karttunen and Peters (1979), Herzberger's formulation having been further developed by Martin (1977) and Bergmann (1981). The semantic domain is considered as consisting of two two-valued coordinates (*dimensions*), which I will call *assertion* and *presupposition*.[12] Thus, if the four values are represented using a pair of binary digits, with the first representing the assertion, and the second the presupposition, then, for instance, $\langle 0, 1 \rangle$ will mean that the assertion is not satisfied, although the presupposition is.

Treating a four valued semantics as consisting of two boolean coordinates allows for a straightforward introduction of the tools of classical logic to study an essentially non-classical system, and this enabled Karttunen and Peters to provide compositionally derived two-dimensional interpretations for a fragment of English using the classical IL of Montague (familiarity with which I assume). To illustrate the approach, let us suppose that expressions of English are associated with two translation functions, $\mathcal{A}$ and $\mathcal{P}$. $\mathcal{A}$ maps expressions to IL formulae representing its assertion, and $\mathcal{P}$ likewise maps to an IL representation of the presupposition. Given that the assertion and presupposition of an expression are assumed by Karttunen and Peters to have identical IL types, and that for English sentences this type is that of truth values, the two dimensional interpretation of a sentence S relative to an IL model M and assignment g will be $\langle [\![\mathcal{A}(S)]\!]_{\mathrm{M,g}}, [\![\mathcal{P}(S)]\!]_{\mathrm{M,g}} \rangle$. Now we might associate with conditionals, for instance, the following translation rule pair:

$$\mathcal{A}(\text{If S1 then S2}) = \mathcal{A}(\text{S1}) \rightarrow \mathcal{A}(\text{S2})$$
$$\mathcal{P}(\text{If S1 then S2}) = \mathcal{P}(\text{S1}) \wedge \mathcal{P}(\text{S2})$$

This particular rule pair defines a notion of implication comparable with

---

[11]Cooper (1983) presents an interesting empirical justification for the use of a fourth value, suggesting that whilst the third value is used to represent presupposition failure, a fourth value is required to signal acts of presupposition denial. This idea, which enables Cooper to give some explanation of cancellation effects without postulating an ambiguity of negation (or other operators) has not, to my knowledge, been taken up elsewhere.

[12]What are here called *assertion* and *presupposition* are for Herzberger *correspondence* and *bivalence*, and for Karttunen and Peters *entailment* and *conventional implicature*. The theories differ considerably in philosophical motivation, in that whilst Herzberger's could be reasonably termed a semantic account, Karttunen and Peters' is not presented as such. However, the fact that Karttunen and Peters give a pragmatic explication of their second dimension of evaluation is irrelevant to most of the technicalities.

the Bochvar internal implication. If we associate the value $\langle 1,1 \rangle$ with t, $\langle 0,1 \rangle$ with f, and the remaining two values both with $\star$, then a sentence 'If S1 then S2' will take the value $\star$ just in case either S1 or S2 takes this value, and otherwise will take the standard classical value.[13]

The same approach can be extended to other types. Let us suppose that a sentence of the form 'The guest Xs' involves the assertion of the existence of a guest with property X and presupposition of the uniqueness of the guest, and that a sentence of the form 'y curtsied' carries the assertion that y performed the appropriate physical movement, and the presupposition that y is female. Then assuming appropriate basic translations, constants *guest, curtsied* and *female*, and meaning postulates guaranteeing that, for instance, the constant *curtsied* stands in the correct relation to other constants relevant to the physical act of curtseying, part of the derivation of the meaning of the sentence 'The guest curtsied' ('S') might run — departing somewhat from Karttunen and Peters' original system — as follows:

$$
\begin{aligned}
\mathcal{A}(\text{the guest}) &= \lambda X[\exists y\, guest(y) \wedge X(y)] \\
\mathcal{P}(\text{the guest}) &= \lambda X[\exists y\, guest(y) \wedge \forall z[guest(z) \to x = z] \wedge X(y)] \\
\mathcal{A}(\text{curtsied}) &= curtsied \\
\mathcal{P}(\text{curtsied}) &= female \\
\mathcal{A}(\text{S}) &= \mathcal{A}(\text{the guest}).\mathcal{A}(\text{curtsied}) \\
&= \lambda X[\exists y[guest(y) \wedge X(y)]](curtsied) \\
&= \exists y[guest(y) \wedge curtsied(y)] \\
\mathcal{P}(\text{S}) &= \mathcal{P}(\text{the guest}).\mathcal{P}(\text{curtsied}) \\
&= \lambda X[\exists y[guest(y) \wedge \forall z[\text{guest}(z) \to x = z] \\
&\quad \wedge X(y)]](female) \\
&= \exists y[guest(y) \wedge \forall z[guest(z) \to x = z] \wedge female(y)]
\end{aligned}
$$

Thus we derive the assertion that a guest curtsied, and the presupposition

---

[13]This two dimensional version of Bochvar's internal implication is found in the first systems proposed in Herzberger (1973). Note that the other Bochvar internal connectives can be defined similarly, such that in each case the assertion is defined entirely in terms of the assertion of the arguments, and the presupposition is defined entirely in terms of the presuppositions of the arguments. This yields what is termed (following Jankowski) a cross-product logic. However, both Herzberger and Karttunen and Peters also define operators for which this property does not hold. For instance, the two dimensional version of Bochvar's assertion operator considered by Herzberger, thought of as a semantics for the English 'it is the case that' locution, could be defined:

$$
\begin{aligned}
\mathcal{A}(\text{it is the case that } S) &= \mathcal{A}(S) \wedge \mathcal{P}(S) \\
\mathcal{P}(\text{it is the case that } S) &= T
\end{aligned}
$$

Here the assertion is defined in terms of both the assertion and presupposition of its argument.

that there is exactly one guest and that guest is female. The approach
seems quite general, but Karttunen and Peters observe, in a by now infamous footnote, that there is a problem associated with their interpretation
of existentially quantified sentences. According to their theory, a sentence
of the form 'An X Ys' carries the assertion that an individual in the assertional extension of X has the property given by the assertional component of
Y. Further, the sentence carries the presuppositions (1) that some individual is in the presuppositional extension of X, and (2) that some individual
in the assertional extension of X is in the presuppositional extension of Y.
What might be referred to as *the binding problem* is that there is no link
between the variables bound in the assertion and in the presupposition.
In particular, there is no guarantee that any entity satisfies both the assertional and the presuppositional requirements. Let us see why this is
problematic for the sentence 'Somebody curtsied':

$$
\begin{aligned}
\mathcal{A}(\text{somebody}) &= \lambda X[\exists y\, person(y) \wedge X(y)] \\
\mathcal{P}(\text{somebody}) &= \lambda X[\exists y\, person(y) \wedge X(y)] \\
\mathcal{A}(\text{curtsied}) &= curtsied \\
\mathcal{P}(\text{curtsied}) &= female \\
\mathcal{A}(\text{somebody curtsied}) &= \mathcal{A}(\text{somebody}).\mathcal{A}(\text{curtsied}) \\
&= \lambda X[\exists y\, person(y) \wedge X(y)](curtsied) \\
&= \exists y\, person(y) \wedge curtsied(y) \\
\mathcal{P}(\text{somebody curtsied}) &= \mathcal{P}(\text{somebody}).\mathcal{P}(\text{curtsied}) \\
&= \lambda X[\exists y\, person(y) \wedge X(y)](female) \\
&= \exists y\, person(y) \wedge female(y)
\end{aligned}
$$

Thus the sentence is given the assertion that somebody performed the
physical act of curtseying, and the presupposition that somebody is female.
Crucially, this interpretation fails to enforce the common-sensical constraint
that the person who curtseyed is female. One possible fix would amount
to making all presuppositions also assertions, which is standard in some
of the accounts to be considered in the next chapter. In fact, as will be
discussed there, there is a separate reason to make presuppositions also
part of the asserted content, for without this one cannot easily explain
why although presuppositions are commonly defeasible, presuppositions of
simple positive sentences are not. If the presupposition is also part of the
assertion, then the reason for this indefeasibility has nothing to do with
the presuppositional dimension itself, but derives from the fact that one
cannot ordinarily deny one's own assertions, or make assertions which one
knows to be false.

2.4 Limitations of Semantic Accounts

More effort has gone into the development of partial and multivalent solutions to the problems of presupposition theory than into any other general
approach. It is thus striking that even the treatment of basic logical connectives in this paradigm remains troublesome. The following discussion
presents a number of challenges for a purely semantic multivalent/partial
account of presupposition, and thus provides motivation for either considering pragmatic additions to the semantic theories, or for considering
alternative accounts of presupposition.

2.4.1 Negation

In many multivalent and partial treatments multiple homophonous negations are posited, even though postulation of a lexical ambiguity of negation
is, if defensible (see Seuren 1985), nevertheless controversial. Further, the
problems associated with cancellation in sentences involving negation are
parallelled by cancellation cases involving other connectives. Witness the
following example (related to one discussed by Kempson 1975, p.93) which,
although it involves no explicit negation, manifests cancellation behaviour
which would be typical of a simple negative sentence:

E23'   If the King of France is bald, then I'm a Dutchman: there is no King
       of France!

The theorist who explains cancellation in negative sentences by postulating multiple negations would seem to be led by such examples in the
unattractive direction of postulating multiple homophonous conditionals.
A further difficulty with the multiple negations story is that if a cancellation negation is posited in some sentence, then all presuppositions will be
blocked, and not only those which the discourse explicitly determines to be
problematic. But it seems to me that in the following example, whilst the
presupposition that there is a King of France is blocked, the presupposition
that the addressee has a son is not:

E42   The King of France didn't give your son the *Royaume Medaille d'Honeur*.
      France is not a monarchy, and there is no such award.

Thus either of the following continuations seem natural, and in both
cases the main NP ('he' or 'Johnny') can be understood as coreferential
with the just mentioned son.

E43   Besides, he's only three years old!

E44   Besides, Johnny is only three years old!

2.4.2 Disjunction

Apart from negation, disjunction turns out to be particularly resistant to analysis in terms of multivalent semantics. Although disjunction is also problematic in other approaches, the difficulties are particularly clear cut for multivalent logics based on a standard semantic definition of presupposition. The trouble (c.f. Soames 1979, on which the current discussion leans heavily) is that we can quite easily provide an exhaustive listing of all the connectives that manifest the basic logic of disjunction in a given system, and we can quite easily show that no single definition of the connective would predict all the cases of projection and cancellation which are found. I will consider the following examples from the point of view of a trivalent system:[14]

E45   Either the King of Buganda is now opening parliament, or the Mayor of Nozdrovia hasn't arrived yet.

E46   Either the King of Buganda is now opening parliament, or else the person who told me Buganda is a monarchy was wrong.

E47   Either the person who told me Buganda is a monarchy was wrong, or else the King of Buganda is now opening parliament.

E48   Either the King of Buganda is now opening parliament, or the President of Buganda is conducting the ceremony.

In E45 presuppositions of both disjuncts appear to project, and in a trivalent system with standard semantic definition of presupposition, this would naturally be explained by assuming that whenever either disjunct has the value $\star$, the whole disjunction also has this value. However, it seems that in a case where the left disjunct of E46 has the value $\star$, the whole disjunction will in fact be true, the truth of the right disjunct in such a case apparently being sufficient to guarantee this. A mirror argument can be applied in the case of E47, suggesting that whenever the left disjunct of a disjunction is true, the whole disjunction should be true. We are left

---

[14]One aspect of these examples which I will not consider in detail is the presence of the word 'either'. As Prince (1978, p.372) pointed out, the presence of this word is essential to the felicity of many examples where a presupposition triggered in a disjunction is cancelled. Prince conjectures that the 'either' acts as a signal to the hearer to "delay attribution" of information in the disjuncts, which she suggests may lead to the presuppositions not being regarded as beliefs of the speaker.

with the following truth table, which is Kleene's strong disjunction:

$\phi \vee \psi$		ψ	
ϕ	t	f	$\star$
t	t	t	t
f	t	f	$\star$
$\star$	t	$\star$	$\star$

Although under this semantics it is not the case that presuppositions uniformly project, we are at least left with weakened presuppositions from both disjuncts. As mentioned above, if ϕ presupposes ψ, then $\phi \vee \chi$ presupposes $\neg\chi \rightarrow \psi$, where "$\rightarrow$" is the strong Kleene implication, and similarly for the other disjunct.

But now consider sentence E48, which is of a type first considered by Hausser (1976).[15] Here the disjuncts carry conflicting presuppositions: if there is a King of Buganda, then there is no president, and *vice versa*. Let us suppose that the Bugandan head of state is either a president or a King, and assume that 'opening parliament' is synonymous with 'conducting the ceremonies'. We can concentrate on two exclusive and exhaustive possibilities: (1) the head of state opened parliament, or (2) the head of state did not open parliament. In case (1), at least one of the disjuncts must be true, and since (under the above strong Kleene interpretation) truth of a disjunct guarantees truth of the disjunction, it must be that the disjunction as a whole is true. In case (2), it can be seen that one of the disjuncts must be false, and the other undefined. In this case the above table tells us that the disjunction as a whole must be undefined. We thus see that E48 can be either true (if the head of state opened parliament) or undefined (if the head of state did not open parliament), but not false. This seems rather odd. For we are then forced to say that the (standard, internal) negation of E48, perhaps E49 or E50, could never be true. This seems blatantly inappropriate.[16]

---

[15] See also the discussions of Gazdar (1979a, pp. 95, 117). Gazdar terms such examples "Hausser-Wilson sentences, and makes the memorable comment "These sentences are to presupposition theories what Bach-Peters sentences are to pronominalization theories." Landman (1986) has proposed analyzing such examples in terms of Robert's (1987) *modal subordination*. The proposal relies on a special form of *accommodation*.

[16] Burton-Roberts (1989a, pp. 169–170) seems to regard cases of conflicting presuppositions as being unproblematic in his system, which does assume a strong Kleene disjunction. He argues that a case like E48 is always given the values true or false, and is never undefined. But it seems to me that his argument is flawed. He assumes that the disjuncts have a common *strong entailment*, which is taken to be bivalent, and in this case might be a proposition something like X = 'There is exactly one head of state and that head of state opened parliament'. Burton-Roberts begins, as above, by dividing into two cases (1) X is false, and (2) X is true. But with regard to case (1), Burton-Roberts

E49   It is not the case that either the King of Buganda is now opening parliament or the President of Buganda is conducting the ceremony.

E50   Neither is the King of Buganda now opening parliament, nor is the President of Buganda conducting the ceremony.

2.4.3   Conditionals and Conditionalised Presuppositions

Presuppositions of conditionals provide yet another battleground. In the strong Kleene system both the antecedent and consequent presuppositions can be said to be weakened in the course of projection. In Karttunen and Peters' system, with respect to which I have not yet discussed the treatment of conditionals, the antecedent presupposition projects unmodified, but the consequent presupposition is weakened just as in the Strong Kleene system.

In the Strong Kleene system with a Strawsonian notion of presupposition, if ϕ presupposes π, then $\phi \to \psi$ does not automatically presuppose π, but does presuppose $(\neg\psi) \to \pi$. I know of no empirical evidence in favour of this weakening of the antecedent presupposition in the Strong Kleene system, and am unable to construct any. It does seem odd that if the consequent is true in a model, then the implication as a whole is defined (and true) independently of the definedness of the antecedent. This might be felt to be a weak point of the Strong Kleene system *qua* logic for presupposition,[17] since truth of the consequent of a conditional is manifestly not

---

diverges from the argument above. Since, by assumption, X is a strong entailment of both disjuncts, and since (by definition of strong entailment) if A strongly entails B and B is false then A is false, it follows that both disjuncts are false. From this it follows that if X is false, the disjunction as a whole is false, and not undefined as argued above.

In this way Burton-Roberts avoids the disjunction as a whole ever being undefined. But crucial to his argument is the premise that both disjuncts strongly entail X. By fiat he is thus declaring first that whenever the head of state did not open parliament, the proposition 'The king opened parliament' is false, irrespective of whether there is a king, and second that 'The president opened parliament' is false irrespective of whether there is in fact a president. This seems completely unjustified to me. It could well be that the type of argumentation Burton-Roberts develops later in his book, concerning the question of when presupposition bearing elements are truth valueless, could be applied successfully to such cases, but the discussion on pp. 169–170 does not settle the point.

[17]Kleene, like Lukasiewicz, did not motivate his semantics in terms of linguistic presupposition but in terms of certain issues in the foundations of mathematics. Bochvar's motivation at least concerned the philosophy of language. For him the third value signaled *nonsense*, but he used this notion to refer to the denotation of a *paradoxical* sentence, rather than one in which the presuppositions fail. The Strong Kleene connectives are the ones most commonly utilised by presuppositionalists. For instance, they are found in work of Hausser (1976), Seuren (1985), who adds an extra negation, Burton-Roberts (1989a) and Link (1986), the latter using Blau's (1978) system which contains the Kleene connectives as a subsystem. None of these authors, however, simply combine Strong Kleene with a Strawsonian definition of presupposition and no other pragmatic component.

sufficient for a conditional to be interpreted as felicitous:

E51   If the Pope's current obsession with water skiing is anything to judge by, then he hasn't much of a future in professional ice hockey.

Here the consequent is true, but I would hesitate to judge the conditional as a whole as true. I certainly would not infer that if the pope has a future in professional ice hockey then he is obsessed with water skiing. However, I don't know that this is a knock down argument against the Strong Kleene treatment of presupposition *per se*. The difficulties of understanding material implication as representing natural language conditionals are well known, and conditionals with known-to-be-true consequents are generally odd. Strong Kleene extends material implication to a third value so as to maintain what Kleene took to be the basic intuitions of the material implication itself. As Andreas Schöter (p.c.) has pointed out to me, that Strong Kleene predicts E51 to be true independently of whether the pope is currently obsessed with water skiing might best be seen as a reflex of the non-presuppositional problems facing the material implication.

Regarding the weakening of the consequent presupposition, there has been considerably more controversy. Both the Strong Kleene system and Karttunen and Peters' system make the prediction that if ϕ presupposes π, then $\psi \rightarrow \phi$ does not automatically presuppose π, but does presuppose $\psi \rightarrow \pi$. The examples which have caused controversy are of two basic types, those where the antecedent seems unrelated to the presupposition of the consequent, and those where, under certain assumptions which may be taken to restrict the relevant models of evaluation, the antecedent entails the presupposition of the consequent. An example of the first type is the following:

E52   If I go to London, my sister will pick me up at the airport.

A hearer would be expected to infer from an utterance of this sentence that the speaker has a sister, but the Strong Kleene and Karttunen and Peters systems predict only a weaker conditionalised presupposition, namely that if the speaker goes to London then the speaker has a sister. Karttunen and Peters recognised this problem, and informally suggested a pragmatic line of solution. Although Gazdar (1979a, p.115) suggests a number of examples where a superficial examination seems to indicate that Karttunen and Peters' solution does not work, and where, in Gazdar's words "remarkably zany predictions" result, all of these examples are dealt with in Soames (1982, pp. 542–543). I will not detail Karttunen and Peters' informal solution here, but point the reader to Soames (1982) and to the even more critical evaluation in Geurts (1999). However, later in this monograph, a formal solution will be given to the problem of conditional presuppositions in examples like E52.

Regarding the second type of example, those where the antecedent entails the presupposition of the consequent, I am afraid the standard of argumentation in the literature has sometimes been disappointing. Otherwise excellent critiques of Karttunen and Peters' system by Gazdar (1979a) and van der Sandt (1988) are marred by the presentation of supposed counterexamples to conditionalised presuppositions, but examples in which the conditionalised presupposition is blatantly irrelevant. Consider Gazdar's E53 (which is not discussed by Soames) and van der Sandt's similar E54 :

E53   If John murdered his father, then he probably regrets killing him, but if he killed him accidentally, then he probably doesn't regret having killed him.

E54   If John murdered his wife, he will be glad that she is dead, but if she took those pills herself . . .

A hearer of examples E53 and E54 would typically infer that a close relative of John (father or wife, respectively) is dead. Such a presupposition (or, in the first case, a slightly stronger presupposition) is triggered in the consequent of the first conditional in each example, but this presupposition is weakened in the Strong Kleene and Karttunen and Peters' systems to a trivial proposition that can be glossed 'If John murdered relative X then relative X is dead', and there is no prediction of any non-trivial presupposition. Are these counterexamples? Not at all. The inference to relative X being dead has absolutely nothing to do with the factive in the consequent of the respective conditionals. In the following examples the consequents have been replaced with non-presupposing clauses, but in each case the inference to relative X being dead seems just as clear as with the original cases:

E55   If John murdered his father, then he'll go to prison, but if he killed him accidentally, then he could inherit a fortune.

E56   If John murdered his wife, he will go to prison, but if she took those pills herself . . .

It is clear that the presupposition, if that is what it is, arises not in the consequent of the conditional, but in the antecedent. It is presumably linked with the contrastive stress that one would expect to find in an utterance of these examples. Further, I have nothing to say about the inference to X's death, except that it manifestly has nothing to do with the issue of conditionalised presuppositions, and that the reader who wishes to know where the inference does come from should look to an account of the interaction between presupposition and stress/topicality. The relevant literature stretches back to Strawson (1964), who suggested that reference failure only produced truth-valuelessness in case the presupposition was topical, and includes accounts (like Strawson's) of how topicality affects presupposition projection, accounts of the presuppositions generated by sentence stress, and accounts which conflate presupposition and topicality. See, for instance, Wilson and Sperber (1979), Reinhart (1982), Sgall *et al.* (1973), Hajičová *et al.* (1998), Horn (1986).[18]

Stress is quite obviously central to the analysis of another purported counterexample. Soames (1982, p.497) gives E57 as an example which backs up Karttunen and Peters' predictions. In this example, the cleft in the consequent carries a presupposition that the problem has been solved, but the weakened presupposition, that if someone at the conference solved the problem then the problem has been solved, is trivial.

E57   If someone at the conference solved the problem, it was Julius who solved it.

Van der Sandt (1988, p.159) has a different opinion. He maintains that E57 has an interpretation where the presupposition of the consequent is preserved unmodified, observing that "one way to achieve this [interpretation] is to read *at the conference* with contrastive stress", which he notates as in E58. Van der Sandt backs up his claim that the presupposition is preserved by noting that that the continuation in E59 "is completely natural, and clearly presupposition preserving":

E58   If someone AT THE CONFERENCE solved the problem, it was Julius who solved it.

E59   If someone AT THE CONFERENCE solved the problem, it was Julius who solved it, but if it was solved at the Nijmegen Institute of Technology, it certainly wasn't Julius.

But why should we accept the legitimacy of adding stress? It seems to me that the stressed antecedent itself tends to produce an inference to the problem having been solved, whether one wants to call this presuppositional or not. As far as I can tell, E60 and E61 below, in which the cleft has been removed, are most plausibly uttered in situations where it has been established that the problem has been solved, and the only remaining questions are where it was solved and by who. These examples suggest

---

[18]What I have to say about the interaction between topicality and presupposition, which is more the statement of a problem than the suggestion of any formal solution, can be found in Beaver (1994a).

that the problem has been solved to just the extent that E58 and E59 do, which shows that the conditionalisation of the consequent presupposition is, once again, completely irrelevant.

E60   If someone AT THE CONFERENCE solved the problem, then JULIUS solved it.

E61   If someone AT THE CONFERENCE solved the problem, then JULIUS solved it, but if it was solved at the Nijmegen Institute of Technology, it certainly wasn't Julius.

Van der Sandt seems to assume that stress does not determine which interpretations are available, but merely helps us find readings which are there anyway. But why is it that in the following example, E62, I cannot find any 'interpretation' at all whereby it is established that the problem is solved? The simplest answer would be that in this example, unlike in E58, the antecedent does not itself carry a presupposition that the problem is solved, and the presupposition of the consequent is, as predicted in the Strong Kleene and Karttunen and Peters' models, weakened to the point of triviality.

E62   If someone at the conference SOLVED/(FINALLY solved) the problem, it was Julius who solved it.

Conditionalised presuppositions are problematic, but I know of no convincing general arguments against them. The discussion above, combined with that of Soames (1982), dispenses with all purported counterexamples with which I am familiar. In the Strong Kleene and Karttunen and Peters' systems, such presuppositions arise not only from conditionals themselves, but also from disjunction and conjunction. Disjunction is discussed above. Regarding weakening of presuppositions in conjunctions, I think that the weakening of presuppositions on the right hand side is appropriate, but I am sceptical about weakening of presuppositions on the left, this latter weakening being found in Strong Kleene, but not in Karttunen and Peters' system. In the following two examples another member of the family falls foul of John. The question is whether in each case it is presupposed that John's mother is dead, this being, let us assume, triggered by the factive *regrets*:

E63   John killed his mother but regrets that she's dead.

E64   John regrets that his mother is dead, but he killed her.

We can answer this question by embedding the sentences in the antecedent of a conditional, which produces the following pair:

E65   If John killed his mother but regrets that she's dead, he'll give himself up.

E66   If John regrets that his mother is dead, but he killed her, he'll give himself up.

I believe that that E65 does not suggest (without stress on *killed*, c.f. the discussion above) that John's mother is dead, but that E66 does indicate this. If this is right, then the weakening of the left conjunct in Strong Kleene is incorrect, but the weakening of the right is justifiable.[19] I will return to the issue of conditionalised presuppositions repeatedly throughout this monograph.

2.4.4 Pragmatic Extensions

Given such difficulties facing multivalent and partial accounts, it is not surprising that little if any recent work has advocated a pure multivalent / partial account of presupposition. Rather, even where multivalence / partiality is taken as the core of a treatment of presupposition, it is usually assumed that some pragmatic component will be required in addition:

- Karttunen and Peters (1979) assume that conversational implicatures will strengthen some of the weak presuppositions generated.

- Link (1986) assumes a cancellation-like mechanism whereby a presuppositional expression can sometimes be *co-asserted*. Whether an expression is indeed co-asserted must be controlled by pragmatic factors (c.f. discussion of the floating-A theory, above).

- Seuren (1985) embeds a trivalent system within a general theory of discourse interpretation. Further, he supposes that a mechanism of *backward suppletion* (similar to that which is below called *accommodation*) will repair the discourse context in cases of presupposition failure.

- Burton-Roberts (1989a) discusses a *meta-linguistic* use of negation which he argues enables treatment of cancellation cases without postulation of a lexical ambiguity of negation. He also provides essentially pragmatic argumentation to establish whether the falsity of a sentence's presupposition leads to the undefinedness of the sentence.

- Kracht (1994) argues that processing considerations can influence the way in which a connective is interpreted, and in this way reasons to each connective having multiple (trivalent) realisations.

---

[19] We will see some more examples later where weakening of a presupposition on the right hand side of a conjunction seems appropriate, e.g. E108 in Chapter 3.

Rather than exploring pragmatic extensions to multivalent/partial accounts of presupposition, in the bulk of this book I examine treatments of presupposition which blend semantics and pragmatics quite differently, but I do return to the topic in chapter 10. Readers interested in the further development of a multivalent account of presupposition, and in discussion of how pragmatic mechanisms could be formalised, might consult Beaver and Krahmer (2001).

3

Cancellation and Filtering

3.1 Introduction

The theories to be discussed in this chapter have two things in common. First, they are, in a sense, the only true projection theories: the set of presuppositions associated with the utterance of a complex sentence is a subset of the set of elementary presuppositions of that sentence. We can thus say that these theories define (relative to a context) a projection function which determines for each elementary presupposition whether it is projected or not. Second, this projection function is context sensitive. Thus, whereas in the theories discussed in the previous chapter presupposition was understood as a binary relation between sentences (or formulae), the theories to be discussed now involve definitions of presupposition as a three place relation between a pair of sentences and a context of evaluation. Alternatively, if an utterance is defined as a pair of a sentence (or set of sentences) and a linguistic context, then presupposition becomes a two place relation between an utterance and a sentence.

What are termed here cancellation and filtering are usually regarded as opposing approaches to the treatment of presupposition. However, the two are closely related variations on a single theme:

1. The grammar and lexicon together encode a way of calculating for each simple sentence a set of *potential presuppositions*, each of which is a proposition.

2. The set of presuppositions of a complex sentence is a subset of the union of the potential presupposition sets of the simple subsentences. Call this subset the *projection set*.

3. The calculation of the projection set is sensitive to linguistic context (conceived of as a set of sentences), and relies on one or both of the following two strategies:

Local filtering For each subsentence S consisting of an operator embedding further subsentences as arguments, S not only carries its own potential presuppositions, but also inherits a subset of the potential presuppositions of the arguments.

Global cancellation Pragmatic principles determine a function from tuples consisting of the context, the set of potential presuppositions, the assertive content of the sentence, and (except in the version in van der Sandt 1988) a set of Gricean implicatures of the sentence, to that subset of the potential presuppositions which is projected.

I will review the filtering theory of Karttunen, and then discuss the cancellation accounts of Gazdar, Mercer and van der Sandt. Finally it will be shown that although filtering and cancellation accounts can be combined into a theory which is descriptively superior to any of the individual filtering or cancellation accounts, there remain serious problems.

3.2 Plugs, Holes and Filters

Karttunen (1973, p. 178) introduced the following taxonomy:

Plugs: predicates which block off all the presuppositions of the complement sentence [examples include 'say', 'mention', 'tell, ask'];

Holes: predicates which let all the presuppositions of the complement sentence become presuppositions of the matrix sentence [examples include 'know', 'regret', 'understand', 'be possible', 'not']; ;

Filters: predicates which, under certain conditions, cancel some of the presuppositions of the arguments [examples include if-then, 'either-or', 'and'].

3.2.1 The First Version of Local Filtering

Assume we are given a function π mapping simple sentences or complex constructions onto sets of potential presuppositions, and some taxonomic division of sentential predicates (apart from conditionals, disjunctions and conjunctions) into the classes of plugs and holes. Representing the set of presuppositions associated with a sentence 'A' as $P(A)$, the first version of Karttunen's filtering conditions in his 1973 paper may be stated recursively as follows:

Definition D6 **(Karttunen '73, Sentence Presuppositions)**

1. $P(\mathsf{S}) = \pi(\mathsf{S})$ for simple sentences S.

2. $P(\mathsf{S}') = P(\mathsf{S}) \cup \pi(\mathsf{S}')$ where S' consists of a hole-predicate embedding a sentence S.

3. $P(\mathsf{S}') = \pi(\mathsf{S}')$ where S' consists of a plug-predicate embedding embedding any further sentence.

4. If S is 'If A then B' or 'A and B' then $P(\mathsf{S}) = P(\mathsf{A}) \cup \{p \in P(\mathsf{B}) \mid \mathsf{A} \not\models p\}$.

5. If S is 'Either A or B' then $P(\mathsf{S}) = P(\mathsf{A}) \cup \{p \in P(\mathsf{B}) \mid \neg\mathsf{A} \not\models p\}$.

Let us see how these definitions apply to an example. In E67, A, B and C are the substrings marked by the relevant brackets:

E67   If [$_A$ Jane and her husband are going on holiday], then [$_B$ it's possible that [$_C$ their neighbours don't realise that Jane and her husband are going on holiday]]

1. Set D = 'their neighbours realise that Jane and her husband are going on holiday'. Now $P(\mathsf{A}) = \pi(\mathsf{A}) = \{$ 'Jane has a husband'$\}$, and $P(\mathsf{D}) = \pi(\mathsf{D}) = \{$ 'Jane and her husband have neighbours', 'Jane and her husband are going on holiday'$\}$.

2. Since 'not' and 'it's possible that' are both holes and introduce no further potential presuppositions, $P(\mathsf{B}) = P(\mathsf{C}) = P(\mathsf{D})$.

3. So P('if A then B') = $\{$ 'Jane has a husband'$\} \cup \{p \in P(\mathsf{B}) \mid$ 'Jane and her husband are going on holiday' $\not\models p\} = \{$ 'Jane has a husband', 'Jane and her husband have neighbours'$\}$.

Thus E67 is predicted to presuppose that Jane is married and that she and her husband have neighbours. The potential presupposition that Jane and her husband are going on holiday (triggered in the consequent) is filtered out.

3.2.2 The Revised Version of Local Filtering

Karttunen notes the following counterexample to the first version of his filtering conditions. Suppose that Fred thinks Mormons wear special 'holy underwear', and he suspects that Geraldine is a Mormon. One voyeuristic night Fred catches sight of Geraldine wearing an ordinary bra and panties, and exclaims:

E68 Either [$_A$ Geraldine is not a Mormon] or [$_B$ she has given up wearing holy underwear].

Karttunen maintains that the presupposition from the second disjunct (that Geraldine used to wear holy underwear) ought to be filtered out, but it is not filtered because it is not entailed by the negation of 'Geraldine is not a Mormon.' He suggests that the problem should be repaired by relaxing the filtering conditions to take into account the propositions holding in the context previous to the utterance. Thus rather than cancelling presuppositions which are entailed by the negation of the first disjunct alone, he suggests cancelling of presuppositions which are entailed by a combination of some set of propositions holding in the context of utterance and the negation of the first disjunct. Similar modifications for the other connectives result in the following revised filtering rule, where F is some possibly null set of "assumed facts" (a notion he never makes fully explicit):

Definition D7 (Karttunen '73, Utterance Presuppositions)

1. $P(S) = \pi(S)$ for simple sentences S.

2. $P(S') = P(S) \cup \pi(S')$ where S' is a syntactic construction containing a hole-predicate embedding a sentence S.

3. $P(S') = \pi(S')$ where S' is a syntactic construction containing a plug-predicate embedding any further sentence.

4. If S is 'If A then B' or 'A and B' then $P(S) = P(A) \cup \{p \in P(B) \mid (F \cup \{A\}) \not\models p\}$.

5. If S is 'Either A or B' then $P(A) = P(A) \cup \{p \in P(B) \mid (F \cup \{\neg A\}) \not\models p\}$.

Here is how the new definition applies to E68:

1. $P(A) = \emptyset$, and $P(B) = \{$ 'Geraldine has worn holy underwear'$\}$,

2. Set the context $\sigma = \{$ 'All Mormons have for some time worn holy underwear'$\}$.

3. Assuming that the negation of 'Geraldine is not a Mormon' is just 'Geraldine is a Mormon':
   P('either A or B') = $\emptyset \cup \{p \in$P(B)$\mid\{$ 'All Mormons have for some time worn holy underwear', 'Geraldine is a Mormon'$\} \not\models p\} = \emptyset$. Thus no presupposition is predicted.

Karttunen's revised filtering conditions probably constitute the first formal definition of presupposition which concerns the presuppositions of utterances rather than sentences, although the philosophical remarks of Strawson (and arguably of Frege) had also pointed to the relevance of context. However in Karttunen's original formulation it is unclear whether the "(possibly null) set of assumed facts", is relative to some particular occasion of utterance or existentially quantified over all occasions. It seems natural to assume the former, especially in the light of Karttunen (1974), which will be discussed in the next chapter.

3.3 Global Cancellation

The model presented by Gazdar (1979a), like Karttunen's revised filtering model, is context sensitive, provides an account of the presuppositions of utterances rather than sentences, and predicts the presuppositions of an utterance to be a subset of the potential presuppositions of the component sentences. Unlike Karttunen's model, the presuppositions are not calculated by bottom-up filtering but by a global cancellation mechanism. All the potential presuppositions of component sentences are collected together into one set, and from that set are removed any members which conflict with (1) propositions in the previous context, (2) the entailments of the utterance, (3) various implicatures associated with the utterance, or (4) each other. Those potential presuppositions surviving this tough selection process go on to become full presuppositions of the utterance.

The basic idea that something cannot be presupposed if that would conflict with implicatures of the utterance is already found in Stalnaker (1974, pp. 207–210), a discussion of Karttunen's full-factive/semi-factive distinction. Further, Soames proposed independently of Gazdar that defeat by implicature should be the central notion of a theory of presupposition projection: "A speaker who utters a truth-functional compound, question or epistemic modal indicates that he is presupposing all of the presuppositions of its constituents unless he conversationally implicates (or explicitly states) otherwise." (Soames 1979, p.653). Kempson (1975) and Wilson (1975), as discussed earlier, both recognise that conversational factors determine whether or not a presupposition is projected, although their general strategy is of trying to find implicature-based explanations of all cases where presuppositions do project, rather than assuming by default that they project and only seeking implicature-based explanations of cases where presuppositions are cancelled.

Gazdar's theory of presupposition, however, provides the first formalisation of this type of account. It is set within a dynamic model of meaning, in which discourse contexts — sets of propositions — are progressively updated with the information in succeeding utterances. Note that the dynamism is found only at the level of texts, and does not extend downwards to the interpretation of the constituents of sentences. In this respect Gazdar's model contrasts with the accounts of presupposition proposed in Karttunen (1974) and Heim (1983b), as well as with the accounts of anaphora proposed by Kamp (1981), Heim (1982; 1983a) and Groenendijk and Stokhof (1991b), all of which employ dynamic interpretation at the subsentence level.

Central to Gazdar's model is his notion of *satisfiable incrementation*. The satisfiable incrementation of a context X with a set Y of propositions (denoted $X \cup !Y$) is just the original context plus all those propositions in Y which cannot introduce inconsistency. Here a proposition y *cannot introduce inconsistency* just in case all consistent subsets of $X \cup Y$ are still consistent after addition of y. The following definition (almost identical to Gazdar's) results:

Definition D8 (Consistency, Satisfiable Incrementation)

$$\text{cons}(X) \quad \textit{iff} \quad X \not\models \bot$$
$$X \cup !Y \quad = \quad X \cup \{y \in Y \mid$$
$$\forall Z \subseteq (X \cup Y) \ (\text{cons}(Z) \to \text{cons}(Z \cup \{y\}))\}$$

For example, if $X = \{p, q\}$ and $Y = \{\neg p, r, s, \neg s\}$, with all atomic formulae assumed logically independent, then $X \cup !Y = \{p, q, r\}$. The proposition $\neg p$ cannot be added because it is inconsistent with X, s cannot be added because there are consistent subsets of $X \cup Y$ (e.g. $\{p, q, \neg s\}$) which become inconsistent when s is added to them, and similarly for $\neg s$.

3.3.1 Cancellation without Implicatures

Gazdar is concerned with reasoning about the hearer's knowledge of the speaker, and for that reason the propositions in a Gazdarian context are formulae of an epistemic logic, in fact Hintikka's logic of knowledge and belief (Hintikka 1962). For the moment, let us simplify by ignoring implicatures. In that case updating a context σ with the information conveyed by some utterance of a sentence S proceeds as follows: first the proposition that the speaker knows what is asserted by S to be true is added to the context, and the resulting context is satisfiably incremented with the potential presuppositions. Thus if the assertion is α, and the set of potential presuppositions of the sentence is π (obtained by taking the union of the potential presuppositions of all the constituents), then the final context is simply given by $\sigma' = (\sigma \cup \{K(\alpha)\}) \cup !\pi$.[1]

---

[1]Note that because $K\phi \models \phi$ is valid in Hintikka's logic, the context σ' will entail the assertion α, although this is not added explicitly.

All the potential presuppositions are also assumed to be prefaced with a K operator: we will have more to say about this assumption later. The actual presuppositions of the utterance are just those members of π which survive in σ'. Consider E69:

E69   Mary doesn't KNOW that Bill is happy: he isn't.

1. Suppose the initial context $\sigma = \emptyset$. Take the assertion $\alpha = \neg K_m(happy(b)) \wedge \neg happy(b)$, and the set of potential presuppositions $\pi = \{K(happy(b))\}$.

2. The update of σ with E69 is given by: $(\sigma \cup \{K(\alpha)\}) \cup !\pi = \{K(\neg K_m(happy(b)) \wedge \neg happy(b))\} \cup !\{K(happy(b))\}$.

3. Since the assertion α entails $K(\neg happy(b))$, and this is inconsistent with the only potential presupposition, the potential presupposition is not added, and is not a presupposition of E69 in this context (or, for that matter, in any other context).

3.3.2   Adding Implicatures

A striking aspect of Gazdar's theory is that the same mechanism is used for implicature as for presupposition, in both cases the notion of satisfiable incrementation being central. A sentence is associated with *potential implicatures* of various sorts, as well as potential presuppositions, and the actual implicatures of an utterance are just those potential implicatures which survive satisfiable incrementation. Crucially, the context is updated with the implicatures before the presuppositions, and this has the effect that implicatures can cancel presuppositions. I will not discuss implicature in general, and I will not distinguish between different types of implicature as Gazdar (following Grice) does. Rather I will focus on one type of *conversational implicature*, that arising from hypothetical statements to the effect that the speaker does not know the hypothesis to be true and does not know it to be false. This type of implicature, arising from the presence of an embedded clause which is not entailed by the whole sentence, is known as a *clausal* implicature. For example, the sentence 'If Mary is sleeping then Fred is boring' carries potential (conversational) implicatures $\{\neg K\,sleeping(m), \neg K \neg sleeping(m), \neg K\,boring(f), \neg K \neg boring(f)\}$.

Definition D9 (Gazdarian Update) If sentence S has semantic content α, potential implicatures ι, and potential presuppositions π, then the update of a context σ with S is:
$\sigma' = ((\sigma \cup \{K(\alpha)\}) \cup !\iota) \cup !\pi.$

Let us consider the treatment of an example:

E70   If Mary is sleeping then Fred is annoyed that she is sleeping.

1. Set the context $\sigma = \emptyset$,
   set the asserted content $\alpha = sleeping(m) \rightarrow annoyed(f, sleeping(m))$,
   set the potential implicatures $\iota = \{\neg K sleeping(m),$
   $\neg K \neg sleeping(m), \neg K annoyed(f, sleeping(m)),$
   $\neg K \neg annoyed(f, sleeping(m))\}$,
   and set the potential presuppositions $\pi = \{K sleeping(m)\}$.

2. All the potential implicatures survive satisfiable incrementation, so:
   $(\sigma \cup \{K(\alpha)\}) \cup! \iota = \{K(\alpha)\} \cup \iota$.

3. Since the only potential presupposition is inconsistent with the implicature $\neg K sleeping(m)$, which has now been added to the context, the
   potential presupposition does not survive satisfiable incrementation,
   and is predicted not to be a presupposition of E70 in this context.

3.4 Projecting By Default

One might say that in Gazdar's model whilst Hintikka's logic of Knowledge
and Belief plays centre stage, the performance is kept running smoothly
only by considerable off-stage direction. This is not to say that Gazdar's
model is not thoroughly formalised: it is, but that formalisation is defined
at a meta-level. For instance, the notions of incrementation and satisfiable
incrementation, although well defined and linguistically motivated, are not
expressed using the same logic as is used to encode presuppositions. This
is not in itself problematic for the linguist, but a logician or computational linguist might find such devices technically *ad hoc*, and wonder if
the notions which Gazdar utilises could be located in a more general (computational) framework, a general logic of information interchange. Part of
the motivation for the theory of presupposition due to Mercer (1987; 1992)
seems to be to express within a logic some of the machinery that in Gazdar's theory is extra-logical. In particular, Mercer takes Gazdar's insight
that presuppositions *normally* project, and are only cancelled as a result of
conflict with context or implicatures, and formalises that by explicitly encoding Gazdar's potential presuppositions as default inference rules within
Reiter's default logic. Mercer assumes that such a rule is associated with
each presupposition trigger, so for instance the rule associated with the
lexical item 'regret' runs:[2]

---

[2]Reiter's default rules have the form $\dfrac{A:B}{C}$, meaning that if given information establishes A and is consistent with B, then C should be inferred.

$$\frac{\neg(regret(x, \phi)) \land LF(regret(x, \phi)) : \phi}{\phi}$$

This can be glossed as: if a theory (a set of propositions closed under ordinary first order logical consequence) includes the proposition that x does not regret ϕ, and it includes the proposition that the Logical Form of an utterance contains (arbitrarily deeply embedded) the formula $regret(x, \phi)$, and ϕ is consistent with the theory, then, by default, the theory should be extended by addition of ϕ (and further classical logical closure).

By and large, Mercer's theory makes much the same predictions as Gazdar's. As in Gazdar's system, presuppositions triggered in the lexicon become integrated in a hearer's information state (i.e. *projected*) only by default, and, as in Gazdar's system, the main factors controlling that integration are consistency with asserted facts and consistency with implicatures. One difference is that Mercer does not attempt to prioritise implicatures over presuppositions, presumably because Reiter's default logic does not allow for prioritisation of different defaults (although related non-monotonic logics do allow such prioritisation). As a result Mercer cannot treat conversational implicatures as defaults, since that would result in conversational implicatures and presuppositions mutually cancelling each other, contrary to Gazdar's evidence that implicatures cancel presuppositions. Instead, Mercer treats implicatures not as being defaults, but as being indefeasible. This has the effect that they are able to cancel presuppositions, but given that such implicatures clearly are defeasible[3] this is not a desirable move. However, I take this as a purely technical problem, and not in itself reflective of any new philosophical considerations. A more serious objection to Mercer's theory is simply that the improvements over Gazdar's theory are quite marginal, and one certainly could not claim mathematical beauty as a justification for the introduction of default logic, given that its model theory can best be described as "work in progress", and its proof theory involves a computationally awkward fixed-point construction.

In one respect Mercer's theory deviates significantly from Gazdar's. Karttunen (1974) describes one of the goals of his work as that of avoiding a theory of *part-time presupposition*. Yet Gazdar provided just that, in the sense that in his account unwanted presuppositions simply vanish. In a Mercer type account, on the other hand, presuppositions, which are default rules, could be allowed to remain in the context whatever other pragmatic or semantic information is available. Projection or cancellation do not correlate with maintenance or removal of the presuppositional rule, but with the logical validity or invalidity of certain inferences associated with the application of the rule. Mercer identifies a philosophical difference

---

[3] For instance, in a *modus ponens* argument 'ϕ and if ϕ then ψ, so ψ', a clausal implicature $\neg K\phi$ is cancelled.

between his theory and Gazdar's, in that Mercer does not even see his account of the projection data as a theory of projection, but as a theory of certain types of inference. In essence this is an inference which allows a hearer to select, from amongst the set of models which satisfy an uttered sentence, a subset of models which are pragmatically preferred. In this respect Mercer's theory may be thought of as a proof-theoretic version of the less formalised theories of Kempson (1975), Wilson (1975), except that Mercer does assume that presuppositional constructions are conventionally marked as presuppositional in the lexicon, whereas it is not clear that Wilson would wish to accept this.[4]

A consequence of the fact that in Mercer's theory presuppositional rules remain in the context is that presuppositional inferences which would be licensed by a one sentence text could be induced to disappear when additional text is added afterwards. For instance the first sentence of E71 in isolation would be predicted to licence an inference to the existence of a son, but the complete text does not licence this inference.

E71   Jane definitely doesn't beat her son: she's not the violent type. Besides, I'm not even sure that she has a son.

On the other hand in Gazdar's theory, where sentences are processed one at a time, a decision has to be reached at the end of processing the first sentence as to whether the proposition that Jane has a son should vanish into thin air, or be added irretrievably to the context. The theory predicts that the proposition will be added, so that the text is incorrectly predicted to be contradictory. This is not to say that this is a fatal flaw with Gazdar's theory. One could imagine modifying the theory such that speech acts rather than sentences were processed as units, and claiming that E71, although it consists of more than one sentence, comprises only a single speech act. On the other hand, one could also see the stability of presuppositional rules, and the instability of presuppositional inferences, in Mercer's theory as a disadvantage. For if a presuppositional inference follows from a sentence, it is very strange for the utterer to deny the conclusion of that inference a dozen sentences (or several speech turns) later. It seems that if you are going to deny the presuppositions of part of your utterance, you must do it

---

[4]Recent cancellation accounts include Marcu (1994), Morreau (1995), Gervas (1995), and Schöter (1994; 1995). These accounts specifically target the defeasibility of presuppositions but have, to my taste, a clearer model theoretic interpretation than Mercer's, and as such perhaps capture the Kempson/Wilson intuitions even better. Other cancellation accounts which I should have liked to discuss in detail are by Bridge (1991), Gunji (1981) and Horton (1987), Horton and Hirst. (1988). All of the above cancellation theories, like Gazdar's, differ from Kempson's and Wilson's accounts significantly: Kempson and Wilson wish to find conversational principles which explain cases of projection, whereas recent cancellationist theories take projection as the norm, and only try to explain away cases of cancellation.

as soon as reasonably possible. Clearly Mercer's theory would need some modification to account for this.

3.5 The Pre- in Presupposition

In what sense is Gazdar's theory an account of 'presupposition'? I do not mean to suggest that it does not provide an account of presuppositional data. I merely mean that the account does not bear any relation to the fairly intuitive notion of presuppositions as previous assumptions. Indeed, since presuppositions are the last things to be added in Gazdar's definition of update, perhaps it would be more natural to call them *post-suppositions*.[5]

My own predilection, as will hopefully become clear in the course of this monograph, is for a theory that takes the *pre* in *presupposition* seriously, and which in some way associates presuppositions specifically with the initial context in which a sentence is semantically interpreted, or with the initialisation of that context. To me, at least, the major achievement of the theory first presented in van der Sandt (1982), which only appeared in English somewhat later (van der Sandt 1988), is that it does succeed in reconciling ideas from Gazdar's cancellation account with what I take to be the intuitive notion of presupposition. I will term van der Sandt's 1982/88 account his *cancellation* theory, to distinguish it from his later DRT-based theory, to which we will turn shortly.

One crucial but disarmingly simple insight could be said to drive van der Sandt's cancellation theory. Suppose a sentence S can be coherently uttered in a context σ, and that one of the constituents of S carries a potential presupposition expressible using the sentence P. If in σ the text made up of P followed by S is coherent, then utterances of S in σ will carry the presupposition P, i.e. P is projected, and otherwise P is cancelled (see van der Sandt 1988, pp. 185–189). For example, given a context of utterance which is neutral regarding Bugandan and Adnagubian politics, E72 presupposes that there is a King of Adnagub (since E73 is coherent), but not that there is a King of Buganda (since E74 is incoherent).

E72 The King of Buganda is not balder than the King of Adnagub since Buganda has no King.

E73 There is a King of Adnagub. The King of Buganda is not balder than the King of Adnagub since Buganda has no King.

---

[5] Given the almost identical way in which presuppositions and implicatures are treated in Gazdar's model, one might think presuppositions could better be labelled as a subtype of implicature. This would be in tune with Karttunen and Peters' (1977, 1979) suggestion that presuppositions in fact comprise an assortment of different implicatures, largely *conventional* implicatures. Karttunen and Peters' arguments have not produced a generally accepted change in use of terminology, if such was their aim.

E74 ⋆ There is a King of Buganda. The King of Buganda is not balder than the King of Adnagub since Buganda has no King.

Coherence of a sentence, what van der Sandt expresses as "acceptability in a context", here comes down to the requirement that every clause is both consistent and informative. Van der Sandt's precise definition of acceptability, which is based upon a dynamic view of the interpretation of the logical connectives like that to be discussed in the following section, need not concern us here. So far as sentences containing logical connectives are concerned, a good approximation, which appears adequate for the examples van der Sandt discusses, is to define acceptability of a sentence S in a context σ as the requirement that for each clause S' appearing in S (other than within a presuppositional expression) σ neither entails S' nor entails the contrary of S'. If this requirement is not met, then S will not be a maximally *efficient* (i.e. compact) way of communicating whatever information it conveys in that context. I simplify by taking a context to be a set of sentences, although van der Sandt allows for contexts to contain certain additional information.

Definition D10 **(Presuppositions in van der Sandt '82/'88)**
Given that all the potential presuppositions (or *elementary presuppositions* in van der Sandt's terminology) of S are collected in the set π, the presuppositions of S in context σ are those propositions φ such that:

1. $\phi \in \pi$

2. For any $\psi \in \pi$, $\sigma \cup \{\phi, \psi\} \not\models \bot$

3. S is acceptable in the context $\sigma \cup \{\phi\}$

Although there are problems associated with this definition,[6] the intuition is clear, as the treatment of E70 (repeated below) should illustrate:

---

[6]The definition is essentially that given by van der Sandt (1988, p.203) as "D-7". There appear to be two major errors. A first problem is that the second clause only checks for consistency of pairs of potential presuppositions. It is easy to manufacture an example where all pairs are consistent but the triples are not. Suppose the context σ contains the proposition that exactly two people whistled, and that S= 'Sherlock has discovered that Watson whistled, or he's discovered that Mycroft whistled, or he's discovered that Moriarty whistled'. Now we might take π to be the set { 'Watson whistled', 'Mycroft whistled', 'Moriarty whistled'}. Any pair of elements of this set is consistent with σ although, assuming non-identity of Watson, Mycroft and Moriarty, the three elements together are inconsistent with σ. The above definition would incorrectly predict that all elements of π become full presuppositions even in a context where their joint addition produces inconsistency.

A similar problem ensues from the third clause, which checks that addition of each presupposition to σ would not make S unacceptable, but does not ensure that if all the presuppositions are added to σ the resulting context accepts S. Again we can manufacture a rather artificial example to illustrate the point. Suppose σ is empty, and S

E70'   If Mary is sleeping then Fred is annoyed that she is sleeping.

Suppose that the context is empty. For E70, π is just the singleton set {*Mary is sleeping*}, the one potential presupposition being triggered by the factive 'annoyed'. We can test whether the potential presupposition is actually presupposed by adding it to the context and checking that all the subsentences in E70 not appearing in presuppositional expressions are neither entailed nor contradicted in the resulting context. Since the resulting context {*Mary is sleeping*} entails one of the subsentences, i.e. the antecedent of the conditional, we can conclude that the proposition that Mary is sleeping is not being presupposed, for if it were then E70 would be inefficient, and hence unacceptable.

3.6   Presupposition and Entailment

Uncertainty is sometimes expressed about whether potential presuppositions of a simple sentence should also be considered as part of the asserted content (i.e. amongst the entailments) of the sentence. Since in a traditional trivalent account of presupposition it is not even possible to define unentailed presuppositions, one naturally wonders whether the possibility of defining presuppositions which are not also assertions gives the cancellation account significant extra empirical coverage, or whether this possibility is just an artefact. The same issue arises with respect to two dimensional accounts such as Herzberger's, or that of Karttunen and Peters, which also allow presuppositions not to be part of the asserted content.

Let me digress to point out that although the question has been posed both with respect to different presuppositional constructions, and with respect to various different models of presupposition, it is not always the same question. In particular, whereas Gazdar's model involves presuppositions being epistemic statements, with content like 'The speaker knows that there is a French King', this is not the case in most other models of

---

= 'If John is an only child then he doesn't regret that he has no brothers and he doesn't regret that he has no sisters.' It seems plausible that π should be the set {John has no brothers, John has no sisters}. Since these are consistent with each other, and since S is acceptable in either of the contexts produced by adding an element of π to σ, van der Sandt predicts that both members of π become full presuppositions. This is inappropriate, since both elements of π taken together entail that John is an only child, so that if both are being assumed then the antecedent of the conditional is uninformative. In a context to which those presuppositions have been added, S will convey only the same information as the sentence 'John doesn't regret that he has no brothers and he doesn't regret that he has no sisters.'

Clearly the technical apparatus proposed by van der Sandt does not quite square up with what I take to be the intuition behind that apparatus, namely that in a context containing the presuppositions, S should be maximally efficient. See also Burton-Roberts' (1989c) review article, for some quite different criticisms of van der Sandt's D-7.

presupposition, and the question of whether such an epistemic statement is entailed by 'The King of France is bald' is obviously different from the question of whether 'There is a King of France' is entailed. However, the epistemic aspect of Gazdar's potential presuppositions could fairly easily be removed.[7] Suppose that the potential presuppositions π were just taken to be the standard expressions triggered by various lexical items etc., and not statements of the form $K(\phi)$, and that the asserted content of an utterance was added to the previous context *simpliciter*, also without embedding under a K operator. Thus the update of a context σ would be given by $((\sigma \cup \{\alpha\}) \cup! \iota) \cup! \pi$. As things stand this would prevent conversational implicatures, which are inherently epistemic statements, from interacting properly with presupposition, but this is easily rectified. We simply replace the definition of consistency with: $\mathrm{cons}(X)$ iff $\{K(x) \mid x \in X\} \not\models \perp$. So this is just Gazdar's theory but with the Ks added at a later stage. It is not significant that the implicature expressions end up doubly embedded under K operators in the consistency test, because of the validity of $K \neg K \phi \models \neg K \phi$ and $K K \phi \models K \phi$ in the modal logic which Gazdar uses (Hintikka's epistemic logic).

To return from the digression, regarding Gazdar's account it is very easy to answer the question of whether presuppositions should be part of the asserted content, at least for the majority of presuppositional expressions. Although presuppositions arising from triggers in embedded contexts produce defeasible presuppositional inferences, the corresponding inference connected with a trigger in a simple affirmative sentence is typically indefeasible. Gazdar (1979a, pp. 119–123) describes the inferences associated with factive verbs, definite descriptions, aspectual verbs, and clefts as being indefeasible in simple affirmative sentences. Since potential presuppositions are always defeasible in Gazdar's model, and since the only inferences which are indefeasible in his model are those associated with the asserted

---

[7]Both Blok (1993) and Horton (1987), in developing theories of presupposition along Gazdarian lines, have suggested refinements of the underlying epistemic logic. Presumably, then, they would disagree with the impression I have given that the epistemic nature of Gazdar's presuppositions is inessential. But here I should qualify my intentions. I do think that most (or all) of the data dealt with by Gazdar (1979a) could be handled without making presuppositions into intrinsically epistemic statements, but I accept first that there may be philosophical motivation for presuppositions being epistemic, and second that there may be further applications of the theory for which the epistemic operators are essential. With regard to the first point, it should be noted that in this book presuppositions will be given an epistemic interpretation (roughly as what the speaker believes, or acts as if he believes, is mutually known), although this *epistemicity* will not be explicit in the formal system. With regard to the second, both Blok and Horton model the beliefs of multiple agents in a dialogue setting, whereas Gazdar concentrates on just the beliefs of just one agent (the speaker). When providing a full account of the evolution of multiple sets of beliefs, it is natural to utilise explicit belief operators.

content, Gazdar is forced to claim that the potential presuppositions of these constructions are also entailments.

Although Gazdar hedges with regard to the question of whether presuppositions should be part of the asserted content for other classes of presupposition trigger, he discusses at least one example where it is crucial to his analysis that the trigger does not entail the presupposition. The following, from Gazdar (1979a, p.150), is of a type discussed by Heinämäki (1972):

E75   Max died before he finished his autobiography.

Standard projection tests indicate that the complement of a before clause is presupposed. But in E75 the presupposition (that Max finished his autobiography) is apparently cancelled, in spite of the fact that the 'before' clause occurs in a simple positive context. Gazdar's successful treatment of this example implicitly assumes that the presupposition is not entailed. Van der Sandt (1988, pp. 196–198) makes it clear that he regards the flexibility of a theory in which presuppositions do not have to be entailed as a major boon. Apart from 'before' clauses, van der Sandt also suggests that three other types might be non-entailed.

First, there are *verbs of judging* (Fillmore 1971b), verbs like like 'accuse' and 'criticise': E76 is claimed to presuppose but not entail E77. Second, van der Sandt mentions emotive factives, like 'is glad', 'regrets', a class of verbs which Gazdar (1979a, pp. 122–123) argues to entail their presuppositions. Gazdar's claim runs *contra* to earlier observations of Klein (1975), discussed by Gazdar, that utterances of sentences like E78 do not indicate the complement of 'regret' to be true. Third is the particle 'even': E79 has been claimed (and this dates back as far as Horn 1969) to be truth conditionally synonymous with E80.

E76   John criticised Harry for writing the letter.

E77   Harry wrote the letter.

E78   Falsely believing that he had inflicted a fatal wound, Oedipus regretted killing the stranger on the road to Thebes.

E79   Even John left.

E80   John left.

There is good reason to remain suspicious of non-entailed presuppositions, for making this move creates as many problems as it solves. Consider 'before'. According to cancellation accounts, presuppositions can be suspended if they contradict entailments or implicatures. Thus E81, where the presupposition that Max won is explicitly denied, and E82, where the first sentence carries an implicature that the speaker does not know whether Max won, should both be cases where the presupposition associated with the **before** clause is unproblematically cancelled. Yet both examples are very odd.

E81 ? Max trained assiduously before he won the race, and/but never did win it.

E82 ? Perhaps Max won the race. He trained assiduously before he won the race.

In cases where the presupposition of a 'before' clause is cancelled, there is always some causal connection between the sentence which the 'before' clause modifies and the main clause. Thus in understanding E75 we are able to make a causal connection between the sentence 'Max died' and the 'before' complement 'Max finished his autobiography'. Perhaps we could say that there is a hypothetical causal chain which runs from a time just in advance of Max's death to a time when Max's autobiography is complete, but that this chain is interrupted by Max's death.[8] Regarding instances of **before** in positive contexts, it appears crucial to the cancellation that the interruption to the relevant causal chain is announced by the main clause. This is not reflected in current cancellation accounts, all of which allow a wide range of extraneous conflicting information to cancel the presupposition.

An additional problem with postulating an unentailed presupposition occurs with embedding of the presuppositional construction in an intensional context: Sentence E83 suggests E84. If the 'before' complement is not entailed, none of the cancellation accounts predict this inference.[9]

E83   John thinks Max trained assiduously before he won the race.

---

[8] This suggestion that the presence of a causal chain is crucial is reminiscent of Moens and Steedman's analysis of the oddity of examples like 'When my car broke down, the sun set' (Moens and Steedman 1988, p.23).

[9] On the other hand, assuming an entailed presupposition, whilst it would produce an inference from E83 to E84, would not predict defeasibility of such inferences. Thus 'Jane thinks Max died before he finished his autobiography.' does not suggest that Jane thinks Max finished his autobiography. So I am not saying we should conclude outright that the complement of 'before' is part of the asserted content, but that no current theory gets the data right whether or not this conclusion is accepted. Another open problem is the licensing of negative polarity items in 'before' (but not 'after') clauses, as in 'Max died before finishing anything'. Explanations have been offered for this (see e.g. Sanchez Valencia *et al.* 1994), no unitary explanation has been offered both for the negative polarity item and for the cancellation data. I am (unjustifiably) optimistic that one day, when we really find out what 'before' means, a clear link between the two phenomena will emerge.

E84   John thinks Max won the race.

An argument from embedding in an intensional context can be applied in the case of emotive factives. If the emotive 'regret' presupposes its complement but does not entail it, then cancellation accounts will fail to predict that E86 follows from E85, although they will typically predict that E87 follows:

E85   John thinks Mary regretted leaving.

E86   John thinks Mary left.

E87   Mary left.

Moving to the case of 'even', here, I think, the argument that there is a non-entailed presupposition simply falls flat on its face. It may be attractive to analyse E79 as being truth-conditionally equivalent to E80, but I know of no good reason to doubt that the presupposition is entailed. Horn's original suggestion of truth conditional synonymy was not couched within a formal theory where it was possible to make a distinction between entailed and non-entailed presuppositions, and the evidence he presented in Horn (1969) does not bear on the issue. It is natural to take the presupposition of E79 to be E88. But the negation of E88 is inconsistent with a simple positive assertion of E79, as witnessed by the oddity of E89. To account for this in a cancellation theory, the natural move, maybe the only move, would be simply to assume that the presupposition was also an entailment.[10]

E88   People other than John left.

E89   ? Even John left, but nobody else did.

I am left with the conclusion that the strongest case for non-entailed presuppositions rests with Fillmore's verbs of judging. If this class of verbs provide the only data standing in front of the very general principle that elementary presuppositions are entailed in unembedded contexts, then we might wonder whether the inferences that Fillmore and others have classed as presuppositions in these cases could be implicatures. For instance, we might reason that it is typically only when someone has done something that they are criticised for it, or that the question of whether they were criticised for it arises. It would then be this typical association of sentences of the form 'A criticised B for C-ing' with situations in which B has C-ed that lead to a default inference that B has C-ed.[11] I will not attempt to develop such an account of verbs of judging here.

---

[10]Embedding 'even' in an intensional context does not appear to produce clear results. This may be because even is an *anaphoric* trigger, of the type discussed later in §5.9.3.

[11]Levinson (2000) uses such argumentation in his neo-Gricean theory of pragmatics. Inferences to prototypical situations of occurrence are analysed as *I-implicatures*.

3.7 Combining Cancellation and Filtration

The cancellation and filtering theories are largely complementary in terms of which data they get right. For instance, Karttunen's theory fails (without the introduction of a second *plug* negation, as well as other plug connectives) on presupposition denial cases, whilst Gazdar's theory fails on a class of examples like the following (as discussed by Heim 1983b and Soames 1982):

E90   If none of Mary's friends come to the party, she'll be surprised that her best friends aren't there.

E91   If John is munching his way through a packet of biscuits, then Bill will be glad that John is eating something.

These are cases where the antecedent of a conditional strictly entails a presupposition of the consequent, so that Karttunen, correctly I think, predicts cancellation. Thus I take it that a hearer would not infer from E90 that Mary's best friends will not be at the party, and would not infer from E91 that John is eating, although these presuppositions are triggered in the respective consequents of the conditionals.[12] In each case, all of the cancellation accounts discussed predict projection of the presupposition. Earlier I discussed a case E70 where a presupposition triggered in the consequent of a conditional was cancelled by a clausal implicature generated in the antecedent. But in E90 and E91 the relevant implicature is not strong enough. For instance, in E91 a clausal implicature is generated that the speaker does not know whether John is munching his way through a packet of biscuits, but this implicature does not imply that the speaker does not know whether John is eating at all, and the presupposition remains unchecked. To put this in terms of van der Sandt's cancellation model, addition to the context of the elementary presupposition that John is eating something does not make the conditional inefficient (for believing that John is eating something does not determine whether or not he is munching his way through a packet of biscuits, and does not determine Bill's mental state), and so this presupposition is added.[13]

---

[12]In E90, focal stress on 'surprised', especially combined with destressing of 'that her friends aren't there', does seem to encourage the presuppositional inference. Similar comments apply in the case of E91. A possible line of explanation for this type of phenomenon is developed in Beaver (1994a).

[13]Landman (1981) suggests a solution to this problem, which essentially consisted of strengthening conversational implicatures so as to force cancellation of the problematic presuppositions. This may solve the immediate problem with presuppositional predictions, but in the process creates quite undesirable effects from the implicatures themselves. See Soames (1982). It should be noted that the problems faced by cancellation models with this type of example do not result from the 'if-then' construction

To move to a different type of example which is discussed by van der Sandt (1988), consider the following:

E92   John claimed that the President of France is coming to dinner: the idiot doesn't realise that France is a monarchy!

Karttunen identifies 'claim' as a plug, so that on his account the presupposition that France has a President vanishes, whilst the presupposition that France is a monarchy is projected. However, on Gazdar's or Mercer's cancellation accounts, the potential presuppositions that there is a President of France and that France is a monarchy conflict, so these accounts incorrectly predict that a hearer of this example would not infer that the speaker takes France to be a monarchy.

There are, then, many cases where Karttunen correctly predicts that some presupposition is filtered, but where various of the cancellation accounts incorrectly predict projection. On the other hand, there are numerous examples where the cancellation accounts correctly predict that some presupposition is cancelled, but where Karttunen's filtering model incorrectly predicts projection. Witness, for instance, the following two examples repeated from above. In the first, the elementary presupposition that there is a King of France is cancelled, and in the second the elementary presupposition that there is a King of Buganda is cancelled. In both cases this is predicted by the cancellation models, but not by Karttunen's filtering model.

E23'   If the King of France is bald, then I'm a Dutchman: there is no King of France!

E46'   Either the King of Buganda is now opening parliament, or else the person who told me Buganda is a monarchy was wrong.

Having observed the complementarity in coverage between Gazdar's theory and a later version of Karttunen's theory, Soames (1982) proposed a synthesis of the two accounts. However, the later version of Karttunen's theory (to which we will turn shortly) is not a filtering theory in the sense

---

specifically, since variants on the examples which do not use this construction are still problematic. In the following triple, the cancellation models predict a contrast between the (a) and (b) sentences. Specifically, they predict that the presupposition glossed in (c) is cancelled in the (a) case by a clausal implicature, but projected in the (b) case. I am unable to detect any such contrast.
(a) Either Mary's best friends will come to the party, or she'll be surprised that her best friends aren't there.
(b) Either some of Mary's friends will come to the party, or she'll be surprised that her best friends aren't there.
(c) Mary's best friends won't be at the party

defined above. The presuppositions that a complex sentence is predicted to have are not a subset of the potential presuppositions of its parts. This complicated Soames' attempt to unify the insights of the two account in a single theory. To give an idea of the difficulties faced, ask yourself this question: when looking for a synthesis between two accounts, where the first account makes all presuppositions members of the set of potential presuppositions, and the second account does not, should the resulting theory be expected to make all presuppositions members of the set of potential presuppositions? (Soames answers in the negative.) A much simpler integrated theory, but one which still preserved Soames' insight of complementarity, could be formed by combining the Karttunen 1973 theory, as discussed above, with Gazdar's. The most obvious way to join the two theories so as to address both defeat of presuppositions by inconsistency and filtering of presuppositions which are locally entailed, would simply be to take the intersection of the set of presuppositions predicted by each of the two models. Such a joint Gazdar-Karttunen model would provide a formidable account of presupposition, combining relative simplicity with a clear improvement over any of the other models discussed in this section. But it would still face a number of problems common to all cancellation and filtration theories, and most of these problems remain unsolved in the combined account that Soames did in fact propose.

3.8 Quantification in Cancellation and Filtering Models

The cancellation and filtering models can be likened to the two dimensional theories discussed in the previous chapter in that meaning is divided into separate presuppositional and assertional components, although the method the models discussed in the current chapter use to calculate the presuppositional component is quite different from that in the two dimensional accounts. It was shown in the previous chapter that in a two dimensional theory such as that of Karttunen and Peters difficulties arise regarding the treatment of quantified presuppositions, i.e. cases where an elementary presupposition appears free in some variable, and that variable is bound by a quantifier. Those problems arise precisely because presuppositional and assertional components are separated, so that no variable binding can occur between them. Thus one should expect that similar problems will occur with cancellation and filtering theories. To my knowledge, none of the cancellation and filtering models discussed in this chapter have been applied to the problem of quantified presuppositions.

One thing that marks the cancellation theories apart from Karttunen and Peters' model is that for most triggers, cancellationists assume that the presupposition is also part of the asserted content. This assumption alleviates somewhat the problem of quantified presuppositions. For instance, if 'curtsied' not only carried a presupposition that its argument is female, but also entailed it, then 'Somebody curtsied' would presumably entail that some female curtsied. But if examples like 'Somebody curtsied, and I was surprised to see that it was a man' lead us to postulate that the presupposition, by virtue of its cancellability in positive sentences, was not part of the asserted content, problems would ensue. For without the assumption of an asserted presupposition, 'Somebody curtsied' would, just as in the Karttunen and Peters model, presuppose that somebody was female, and assert that somebody performed the act of curtseying, and not provide any implication that the performer of the curtseying act was female.[14]

Even if presuppositions are assumed to be asserted, problems arise. For instance, it seems reasonable to maintain that the following sentence cannot be true unless there is some watch-owning woman who realised that if her watch was slightly wrong she'd be in danger of shooting the wrong man:

E93   Exactly one woman realised that if her watch was slightly wrong, she'd be in danger of shooting the wrong man.

If 'her watch' is taken to have a presupposition of the form $has\text{-}a\text{-}watch(x)$, an open proposition, then it is completely unclear what should be done with this proposition in a cancellation theory. Saying that the open proposition is presupposed (with the effect of universal quantification) is inadequate, because the presupposition is clearly only relevant to some salient set of women. On the other hand, the mere fact that $has\text{-}a\text{-}watch(x)$ is asserted in its local context does not help, for the phrase 'her watch' occurs within a conditional. The assertion would be predicted to be something along the lines of 'exactly one woman came to believe that if she owned a watch and that watch was slightly wrong then she would be in danger of shooting some wrong man', but this would not enforce that it was a watch owning woman who had the relevant realisation.

---

[14]This could be construed as yet another argument (c.f. §3.6) for not allowing non-asserted presuppositions in the cancellation models, for allowing any non-asserted presupposition would present major problems as soon as quantification into presuppositions was allowed. Take the case of 'before'. If the presupposition (that what is described in the complement of 'before' actually took place) were not entailed, then it is hard to see how any sensible interpretation could be given for a sentence like 'Everybody knocked before entering'. An assertion that everybody knocked and presupposition that everybody entered, even if such a presupposition could be derived, would still fail to enforce the proper temporal relationship between each knocking event and the following entering event.

3.9 Conditional Presuppositions

Consider the following stock examples (as in Karttunen (1973, p.184), the general type and the second example being attributed by him to McCawley):

E94   If LBJ appoints J. Edgar Hoover to the cabinet, he will regret having appointed a homosexual.

E95   If Nixon Invites Angela Davis to the Whitehouse, then Nixon will regret having invited a black militant to his residence.

In the consequent of E94 the elementary presupposition that LBJ will have appointed a homosexual is triggered, and in the consequent of E95 the elementary presupposition that Nixon will have invited a black militant to his residence is triggered. In neither case would one expect a hearer to conclude that the elementary presupposition holds, so it is reasonable to claim, as Gazdar does with respect to a slight variant, that the presupposition is simply cancelled. Gazdar (1979a, pp. 151–152) suggests that his treatment of this type of example represents one of the strengths of his theory. I suggest the contrary, first because I believe examples like these do carry non-trivial presuppositions (albeit not the elementary presuppositions triggered in the consequents), and second because I do not accept the assumptions Gazdar makes in order to demonstrate that his system yields cancellation. Gazdar's argument as he applies it to a slight variant on E95 appears to run as follows:

1. A clausal implicature is triggered of the form 'The speaker does not believe that Nixon invites Angela Davis.'

2. The context contains the fact that Angela Davis is a black militant.

3. The phrase 'a black militant' can be anaphoric on the NP 'Angela Davis', so that the potential presupposition can be given as 'The speaker believes Nixon invites Angela Davis.'

4. The clausal implicature conflicts with the potential presupposition, and correctly prevents projection.

My first objection stems from the fact that when somebody who (like me) has no knowledge of Angela Davis' skin colour or political tendencies is confronted with E95, they will tend to infer that she is a black militant. Thus the assumption that the context contains the fact that Davis is a black militant seems unjustified, and irrelevant to peoples' understanding of the example. Likewise, if somebody who has no presumptions about

Hoover's sexual preferences is confronted with E94, I would suggest that they would tend to infer that Hoover is a homosexual. That such inferences occur can be seen as offering support for the claim that there are non trivial presuppositions. In the Strong Kleene and Karttunen and Peters accounts discussed earlier, in the hybrid model which Soames actually did propose in Soames (1982), and in some of the dynamic semantic accounts to which I will shortly turn, conditionalised presuppositions are predicted for such examples. These presuppositions can be glossed as follows:

E96   If LBJ appoints Hoover he will have appointed a homosexual.

E97   If Nixon invites Davis, he will have invited a black militant.

As stated, these glosses do not strictly entail that Hoover is a homosexual or that Davis is a black militant, although the glosses are highly suggestive of these conclusions. Some strengthening is needed, and an appropriate mechanism will be introduced later, in Chapter 9. With or without explicit formalisation of a strengthening mechanism, prediction of a conditionalised presupposition needs to be justified. An argument for the view that there is such a presupposition can be developed, as usual, by considering behaviour under embedding. Since we are considering the (conditional) presupposition of an entire conditional, embedding can be awkward. Nonetheless, utterance of any of the following five examples clearly implies that if Nixon invites Davis, he will have invited a black militant, just as for the initial unembedded example E95. A theory in which this implication was an unpresupposed entailment of E95 would leave such projection behaviour unexplained.

E98   Perhaps if Nixon invites Davis he will regret having invited a black militant.

E99   It is likely that if Nixon invites Davis he will regret having invited a black militant.

E100   Is it likely that if Nixon invites Davis he will regret having invited a black militant?

E101   If Nixon invites Davis he will probably not regret having invited a black militant.

E102   It is sometimes claimed that if Nixon had invited Davis he would have come to regret having invited a black militant.

My second objection to Gazdar's analysis concerns his assumption that the indefinite NP in the consequent is anaphoric, which I will argue against.

Before that, I wish to point out that even if anaphoricity were present in the original examples, it could not be used to explain away very similar variants. Consider the following:

E103 If LBJ appoints J. Edgar Hoover to the cabinet, he will regret that his cabinet is no longer entirely made up of heterosexuals.

E104 If Nixon invites Angela Davis to the Whitehouse, then Nixon will regret that his house is no longer devoid of black militants.

I take it that hearers of E103 would not uniformly infer that LBJ's cabinet is no longer entirely made up of heterosexuals, so that Gazdar might wish to say that the potential presupposition is (or at least can be) cancelled. Similarly, he would presumably want to say that in E104 the potential presupposition that Nixon's house is no longer devoid of black militants is cancelled. But in this variant there is no expression which can act anaphorically on the NP 'Angela Davis', and the argumentation offered for the original examples would fail.

Now we briefly consider whether there was any anaphoric link in the original examples. Consider the following:

E105 If LBJ appoints J. Edgar Hoover to the cabinet, he will realise that he has appointed a homosexual.

E106 If Nixon invites Angela Davis to the Whitehouse, then Nixon will realise that he has invited a black militant to his residence.

E107 If Nixon invites Angela Davis to the Whitehouse, then Nixon will realise that he has invited the black militant to his residence.

Examples E105 and E106 are both examples where assuming the indefinite NP in the consequent was coreferential with the proper name in the antecedent might be problematic. We would not want to say that E106 says only that if Nixon invites Davis then he will realise that he has done so. This is exactly the (peculiar) reading we would get in a truly anaphoric case such as E107, which has an interpretation such that even if Nixon invites Davis, he does not necessarily realise that she is a black militant, although the speaker does realise this. Conclusion: the indefinite 'a black militant' in E106 is not anaphoric, at least not in the sense that in the LF of E106 'a black militant' acts as if it were merely a repeat of the NP 'Angela Davis', which is the type of assumption that would enable Gazdar's argument to go through. A similar conclusion can be drawn regarding E95.[15]

---

[15] Another possibility to be considered is that 'a black militant' does not act merely as a repeat of 'Angela Davis', but rather as a definite description, akin to 'the black

So, if we take it that 'a black militant' in E95 is non-anaphoric, or we consider examples like E104 or E106, what results does the cancellation model predict? This can be answered very easily. Whether or not the fact that Davis is a black militant is taken to be in the context, the clausal implicature that 'The speaker does not believe that Nixon invites Angela Davis' will not conflict with the potential presupposition 'The speaker believes that Nixon invites a black militant'. In fact, on any of the cancellation accounts, E95 should be expected to presuppose, incorrectly, that Nixon has invited a black militant (except in very special contexts, such as those already containing the negation of this proposition, or containing the assumption that Nixon invited at most one person).

Both Karttunen's revised 1973 account and the joint Gazdar-Karttunen model proposed above correctly predict filtering provided the proposition that Davis is a black militant is assumed to be in the initial context. But these models still fail to account for the fact that even hearers who are not aware of Davis' skin colour and militancy will tend to infer it. A better model would be one which predicted a conditionalised presupposition as discussed above.

If a sentence has the form 'If A then B$_C$' (meaning that B carries presupposition C), then the relevant conditionalised presupposition is 'If A then C'. As it happens, the relevant 'If A then C' conditional is part of the *asserted* content for the cancellationist. This is because factives are assumed to carry their potential presuppositions as entailments. For example, the assertion of the McCawley sentence E95 may be paraphrased 'If Nixon invites Davis, he'll have invited a black activist and regret it', which classically entails 'If Nixon invites Davis, he'll have invited a black activist.' Thus if one sets up the initial context so as to force cancellation, then although cancellation models do not yield conditionalised presuppositions for the McCawley sentences, they do still predict that the speaker is committed to the relevant 'If A then C' proposition. An example of such a context is that set up by the modal statement 'Perhaps Nixon will invite a black militant to the Whitehouse', where an implicature is triggered that the speaker does not know whether Nixon will invite a black militant.

It might then seem that there is hope for the cancellationist, if only the conditions for cancellation could be strengthened in these cases so that

---

militant'. But it is essential to Gazdar's position that the elementary presupposition associated with 'realise' in E106 does contain information that is not present in the antecedent. In particular, this elementary presupposition should not mention ethnicity or militancy, since that would prevent the presupposition being cancelled. However, by the arguments above, the proposition towards which Nixon would (hypothetically) stand in the realisation relation should mention Davis' ethnicity and militancy. So Gazdar would seem to be forced to a position where the elementary presupposition associated with 'realise' is distinct from the proposition expressed by its complement. This position, while consistent, is unattractive.

the elementary presupposition itself is cancelled as Gazdar claimed. Then what others might claim to be the conditional presupposition of a McCawley sentence would be identified as part of the asserted content by the cancellationist. But this appearance of hope is illusory, for it is easy to find cases for which other theories would still predict a rather plausible conditional presupposition, but where the cancellation model will not predict this conditional to be either a presupposition or an assertion:

E108　If LBJ appoints J. Edgar Hoover to the cabinet and regrets having appointed a homosexual, he will try to fire him.

E109　If Nixon invites Angela Davis to the Whitehouse and regrets having invited a black militant to his residence, then he will organise a cover-up.

　　Strong Kleene, the theory of Karttunen and Peters, that of Soames, and the dynamic theories in the next chapter all predict the same conditional presuppositions for E108 and E109 as for E94 and E95 respectively, and I argued above that this prediction is appropriate. But for the latter pair of examples there is no prospect of a cancellation theory reproducing the relevant conditional presupposition as an assertion. The cancellationist's assertion for E109 could be glossed as 'If Nixon invites Davis and has invited a black militant and regrets it, he will organise a cover-up.' Clearly this does not entail 'If Nixon invites Davis then he will have invited a black militant', which the other models mentioned would, correctly I think, predict as a presupposition. To summarise, not only is it the case that, as was shown in the previous chapter, there are no solid arguments against conditionalised presuppositions, it is also the case that cancellation and filtering theories are demonstrably inadequate in their coverage of a range of cases where other models do predict a conditionalised presupposition, and where this presupposition seems appropriate.

4

Dynamic Semantics

4.1   Introduction

All of the major contemporary theories of presupposition projection are in one way or another dynamic theories, making crucial use of the way in which the epistemic state of an agent changes as the interpretation process proceeds. We have already seen that the cancellation theories of Gazdar, van der Sandt and Mercer, although based on a classical static semantics, involve pragmatic mechanisms controlling the evolution of a set of accepted propositions. Another theory which combines a static (although non-classical) semantics with a dynamic pragmatics is that of Seuren (1985). In all these theories we may say that the static interpretation of a sentence acts as a middleman between the syntax of language and pragmatic processes controlling the changing state of the language user. In this chapter we will be concerned with theories which try to cut out this middleman, so that language is interpreted directly into a domain of state-changing operations. The term *dynamic semantics* will be used to describe systems in which strings of sentential category are mapped onto a certain class of operations, and these operations act on the state of information of some agent to produce a new state.

In general, the successful performance of an operation may require that certain preconditions are met. Open heart surgery requires a steady hand and a fair amount of equipment, and the operation of buttering toast also requires both a steady hand and a certain minimal set of ingredients. The central idea of the dynamic semantic approach to presupposition is that the operation of modifying an information state may require certain of the *ingredients* to be already present. For instance 'Oh no! I've dropped the knife.' may be understood as an operation to update a state which in some way determines a salient knife (the crucial ingredient) with the information that the object in question has been dropped. This will lead to a formal model of *presupposition* which is intuitive in the sense that it accords closely

79

with the everyday usage of the term as *a proposition taken to be accepted in advance*. The outline of the model runs as follows:

- An information state is comparable to a partial model, with respect to which some propositions are satisfied, some are falsified, and others are neither satisfied nor falsified.

- Sentences are interpreted as update operations mapping states to states. However, it may be that for some state the update operation cannot succeed, in which case the sentence is said to be inadmissible in that state. One sentence presupposes another if all states admitting the first satisfy the second.

- When evaluating a complex syntactic expression in a certain input context, the semantics of the functor should determine what input states are used locally in the evaluation of the argument expressions. Basic projection facts are explained by assuming that a complex expression is only admissible in a state if the argument expressions are all admitted in their local input states.

To reiterate, the use of the term *dynamic semantics* is not meant to imply that the theories to be discussed will be semantic theories in the classical sense of concerning a static relation between *the word* and *the world*. The chief philosophical advance of the models to be discussed is the combination of what had been thought of as distinct pragmatic and semantic aspects of meaning and interpretation into unitary theories, and there is now little consensus as to what should be termed *semantic* and what *pragmatic*. In this monograph, the term *semantic* is used when talking of rules of interpretation which are associated with particular syntactic features or are intended to be folded into the compositional description of a grammar. Rules of interpretation are termed *pragmatic* if they do not include reference to syntactic features, or act over and above the compositionally defined part of the grammar. On this basis Gazdar's model of the interpretation process, for instance, could be separated into (1) a semantic part which generates the assertion, the sets of potential implicatures and the set of potential presuppositions, and (2) a pragmatic part which updates an agent's state on the basis of these components without direct reference to the grammatical features which produced them. In this system, calculation of the potential presuppositions is, in my terms, semantic (since it is assumed to depend on the details of specific lexical items and syntactic structures), but calculation of the actual presuppositions is pragmatic. On the other hand, with regard to Karttunen and Peters' system, I would use the term *semantic* for the generation of both the assertion and the presupposition (what they term the *conventional implicature*), since they are calculated in strict rule-by-rule correspondence with the syntactic derivation, although Karttunen and Peters do suppose that there are further pragmatic mechanisms determining some presupposition related inferences.

I will begin the discussion of dynamic semantic accounts with Karttunen's 1974 dynamic reformulation of his earlier filtering theory (as discussed in the last chapter), and will then show how this reformulated model was further adapted by Heim to produce a first integrated dynamic model of presupposition and anaphora. In Heim's model of presupposition information states are given an abstract formulation in terms of possible worlds. Information states can be thought of as mental representations, and much recent work on the dynamics of the interpretation process has concentrated on providing accounts of structured representations and how they are manipulated. Heim's model of interpretation was originally stated in this way, and DRT (Kamp 1981, Kamp and Reyle 1993), is another good example of this type of approach. Prior to the work of Heim and Kamp, linguistic context had typically been modelled as a set of parameters such as a speaker parameter, a hearer parameter, and/or a single *world of evaluation*. In a few accounts, principally those discussed in the last chapter, linguistic context had been given more structure, being defined as a set of propositions, and had been allowed to evolve in an interesting way in the course of a conversation. Both Heim's account and DRT provide sophisticated notions of linguistic context as information states of agents, and such notions of context facilitate a type of treatment of presuppositions that might be termed *anaphoric*. In such a treatment, presupposition triggers may stand in a relation to previous linguistic material which is analogous to (or, according to van der Sandt, *identical with*) the relationship between an anaphoric pronoun and its antecedent. The last part of this chapter will be taken up with describing phenomena which motivate such an anaphoric account of presupposition, and showing how it may be realised in the frameworks set up by Heim and Kamp.

4.2 From Projection to Satisfaction

The second of Karttunen's two 1973 definitions of presupposition, as discussed in the previous chapter, involved a special contextual parameter for "a set of assumed facts", utterance presuppositions being calculated relative to such a set. However, it is not clear in this theory how the set of assumed facts and the set of (utterance) presuppositions are to be understood, and what, from a philosophical perspective, is meant to be the relation between them. Karttunen (1974) brilliantly resolved these difficulties, essentially by turning the projection problem, as then conceived, on its head. Instead of considering directly how the presuppositions of the parts of a sentence determine the presuppositions of the whole, he suggests we should first consider how the global context of utterance of a complex sentence determines the local linguistic context in which the parts of the sentence are interpreted, and derive from this a way of calculating which global contexts of utterance lead to local satisfaction of the presuppositions. He gives a formal definition of when a context satisfies-the-presuppositions-of — or *admits* — a formula. A simple sentence S will be admitted in a context σ (here written $\sigma \triangleright S$) if and only if the primitive presuppositions of S are satisfied in σ. Here the logical form of a sentence S is written in italics, S, a context is understood as a set of such logical forms, and the natural notion of contextual satisfaction is just classical entailment. When a complex sentence is evaluated in some context, however, presuppositions belonging to the parts of the sentence need not necessarily be satisfied in that context. For example, if a sentence S of the form 'S$_1$ and S$_2$' occurs in a context σ, the conditions for S to be admitted in σ are that S$_1$ is admitted in σ and S$_2$ is admitted in a new context produced by adding the logical form of S$_1$ to σ. Note that essentially the same idea was independently developed by Stalnaker, who comments in the case of conjunction: "If one asserts a proposition using a conjunctive sentence ... the presuppositions will change in the middle of the assertion. The first conjunct will be added to the initial presuppositions before the second conjunct is asserted." (Stalnaker 1973, p.455) In reading this quote it is perhaps illuminating to substitute *information state* for *presuppositions*, since Stalnaker's notion of presupposition is intended to capture something like the set of propositions assumed by the speaker to be in the common ground, and not any specific set of propositions attached to a sentence. Definition D11, where the π-function is, as above, assumed to map a simple sentence to its presuppositions, collects Karttunen's admittance conditions for simple sentences and for the logical connectives:

Definition D11 (Admittance in Karttunen '74)

$$
\begin{array}{rcll}
\sigma \triangleright S & \textit{iff} & \sigma \models \pi(S) & \text{for any simple sentence S} \\
\sigma \triangleright \text{not } S & \textit{iff} & \sigma \triangleright S \\
\sigma \triangleright S_1 \text{ and } S_2 & \textit{iff} & \sigma \triangleright S_1 \textit{ and } \sigma \cup \{S_1\} \triangleright S_2 \\
\sigma \triangleright \text{if } S_1 \text{ then } S_2 & \textit{iff} & \sigma \triangleright S_1 \textit{ and } \sigma \cup \{S_1\} \triangleright S_2 \\
\sigma \triangleright S_1 \text{ or } S_2 & \textit{iff} & \sigma \triangleright S \textit{ and } \sigma \cup \{\text{not } S_1\} \triangleright S_2
\end{array}
$$

Presupposition may be defined as follows:

Definition D12 (Dynamic Presupposition)

$$
\phi \gg \psi \quad \textit{iff} \quad \forall \sigma \ \sigma \triangleright \phi \rightarrow \sigma \models \psi
$$

The empirical motivation Karttunen presents for this theory is much the same as for his earlier theory. Let us consider an example:

E110   If [$_A$ Jane noticed that [$_B$ Fido was hungry]], and [$_C$ she fed him], then [$_D$ he'll be glad that she fed him].

1. The elementary presuppositions are given by $\pi(B) = \pi(C) = \emptyset$, $\pi(A) = B$, and $\pi(D) = C$.

2. We want to know for which contexts σ it is the case that $\sigma \triangleright$ 'If A and C, then D'. From definition D11, this will hold just in case: (i) $\sigma \triangleright A$, (ii) $\sigma \cup \{A\} \triangleright C$, and (iii) $\sigma \cup \{A, C\} \triangleright D$.

3. From the first clause of D11, and given that $\pi(A) = B$, we see that (i) only holds if $\sigma \models B$ does. Since $\pi(C) = \emptyset$, (ii) imposes no further constraint. And since $\pi(D) = C$, (iii) will hold just in case $\sigma \cup \{A, C\} \models C$, which is trivial, so (iii) also imposes no constraint.

4. So the example is admitted in any context which entails B. In other words E110 presupposes that Fido was hungry (and all entailments of this sentence).

This is similar to the result that would have obtained in the Karttunen '73 theories discussed earlier: the elementary presupposition in the antecedent of the conditional is projected, but the elementary presupposition in the consequent is effectively cancelled. The difference is that Karttunen (1974) predicts not only that B is presupposed, but also that all its entailments are presupposed, while this is not the case with the models of Karttunen (1973). This difference is revealing, for it shows that Karttunen (1974) is not a filtering model at all: the presuppositions of a sentence are not in general a subset of the elementary presuppositions of its parts.[1] Furthermore, the difference is not just that entailments of presuppositions are predicted to be presupposed. More interestingly, we will see that there is a whole class of cases where D11 predicts a non-trivial presupposition which is not a

---

[1] Under the condition that π always mapped simple sentences onto logically closed sets of elementary presuppositions, the Karttunen '74 theory would of course also be a filtering theory. For that matter, so would the multivalent and partial accounts of Chapter 2. However, without this restriction, the Karttunen '74 model, and most of the accounts of Chapter 2 could not be described as filtering theories. One difference is that in filtering/cancellation accounts, tautologies will not normally be presupposed, whereas in all the accounts described formally in Chapter 2 and in Karttunen's '74 model, all tautologies are presupposed by every sentence. In Karttunen's '73 filtering account, a tautology will only be presupposed if it is an elementary presupposition of the leftmost subsentence.

member of the elementary presupposition set at all, when the earlier Karttunen model would predict no presupposition at all.[2] Here is a summary of the presupposition projection properties arising from definitions D11 and D12:

Fact 4.1

If A presupposes B then:

1. 'Not A', 'A and C', 'If A then C', 'A or C' all presuppose B.

2. 'C and A' and 'If C then A' both presuppose 'If C then A'.

3. 'C or A' presupposes 'Unless C then A' (i.e. 'If not C then A').

It can be seen that when a presupposition trigger is found on the right-hand side of a connective, a conditional presupposition results, although this conditional will not in general be one of the elementary presuppositions itself. Let us consider a concrete case where the predictions of the earlier and later Karttunen models vary (sticking to the earlier labellings for the subsentences) :

E111   If [$_B$ Fido was hungry], [$_D$ he'll be glad that [$_C$ Jane fed him]]

Given that B $\not\models$ C, the first version of the '73 theory (that specified in D6) will simply predict projection of C, so that the sentence presupposes that Jane fed Fido. On the other hand, it can be seen from 4.1 that the '74 theory will predict a presupposition 'If B then C', i.e. that if Fido was hungry then Jane fed him. The second version of the '73 theory D7 presents an interesting halfway house: if the set of assumed facts associated with an utterance of the sentence entails 'If B then C' then there will be no presupposition, but otherwise C will be presupposed.[3] I have already discussed, in §2.4.3 and §3.9, structurally similar examples to E111 (conditionals with presupposition triggers in the consequent), and have argued in favour of 'If B then C'-type conditionalised presuppositions, which also

---

[2] A similar point concerning the difference between Karttunen's '73 and '74 models is made by Geurts (1994).

[3] Having observed that there are differences between the '73 and '74 theories, one might wonder what the relation between the models is. It is straightforward to formally define the Karttunen '74 notions of admittance and presupposition in terms of the '73 definition of utterance presupposition. I will write 'X 73-presupposes$_F$ Y' if, on the Karttunen '73 model as defined in D7 in Chapter 3, Y is a presupposition of X relative to a set of assumed facts F. Then we have:

1. σ admits X iff for any proposition Y such that X 73-presupposes$_\sigma$ Y, σ entails Y.

2. X 74-presupposes Y iff for any σ, if there is no Z such that X 74-presupposes$_\sigma$ Z, then σ entails Y.

arise in the Strong Kleene and Karttunen and Peters' systems. Of course, it is scarcely surprising that the Karttunen '74 and Karttunen and Peters' systems manifest the same behaviour, since the latter was developed from the former. Despite the fact that that Karttunen and Peters system is historically the more recent of the two, it is less radical than the Karttunen '74 theory in that, from a technical perspective, the Karttunen and Peters' system is based on a multivalent but static semantics, whereas the Karttunen '74 system utilises a dynamic conception of the interpretation process. In Chapter 10 I will discuss the insights (originally due to Peters, Peters 1977) which allowed a connection to be drawn between dynamic and multivalent systems.

4.3 Context Change Potential

Although Karttunen's 1974 model resolved the tension created by the simultaneous presence in his earlier work of distinct notions of assumption and utterance presupposition, it left unresolved one crucial issue: what is supposed to be the relationship between the definition of admittance for an expression and the semantics of that expression? Judging from the developments in Karttunen and Peters' later joint work, one might conclude that admittance conditions and semantics are separate and unrelated parts of a grammar, but some authors see this as a weakness of the theory. Gazdar (1979b, pp.58–59), which does not distinguish between Karttunen's '73 and '74 accounts, caricatures Karttunen's justification for why presuppositions sometimes disappear as "Because those presuppositions have been filtered out by my filter conditions." Gazdar suggests that an explanatorily adequate model should not only stipulate filtering conditions, but provide independent motivation for why those conditions are as they are. Although it is difficult to give any definitive characterisation of exactly when a theory of presupposition is explanatorily adequate — and Gazdar provides no such characterisation — it is at least clear that it would be desirable to justify a particular choice of filtering or admittance conditions. Heim (1983b) attempts to provide such a justification, and at the same time to clarify the relationship between admittance conditions and semantics. In particular, Heim provides a method of stating semantics, based on the approach developed of Heim (1982), in such a way that admittance conditions can be read off from the semantic definitions without having to be stipulated separately. Crucially, Heim's semantics involves a significant deviation from the classical Tarskian approach, in that rather than viewing meaning as a static relation holding between language and truth in the world, she takes the meaning of an expression to be a method of updating the information state of communicating agents. As will be seen in Chapter 6, Heim's claim of providing independent motivation for the semantics she specifies has proved difficult to establish, and a goal of this book is to bolster her position.

Following Stalnaker (1979), Heim initially takes an information state, or *context*, to be a set of possible worlds, representing the set of alternative worlds compatible with an agent's knowledge. For a simple sentence, the admittance condition must be stipulated by the grammar, as in other approaches. Thus a simple sentence with a factive will be admitted in a context if and only if all the worlds in the context are worlds where the propositional complement of the factive is true. The Context Change Potential (CCP) of the sentence is a procedure for updating a context to provide a new context. In the case of a simple sentence S, standard semantics must be taken to provide a set of worlds where S is true, call these the S-worlds. The CCP is an operation of intersection between the set of worlds in the old context, call it σ, and the S-worlds, the result being denoted $\sigma+$S. But this CCP should only be applied to a context in case the sentence is admitted in that context, in which case the CCP will provide an update:

Definition D13 **(Heimian Update, Admittance)**

$$\sigma + S \quad = \quad S'(\sigma) \text{ where S' is the meaning of S}$$
$$\sigma + S \text{ is defined} \quad \textit{iff} \quad \sigma \vartriangleright S$$

In the case of simple sentences, the admittance conditions must be defined by fiat, such that the sentence is only admitted in its local context if its presuppositions are satisfied in that context. Here the notion of satisfaction is different from that of Karttunen, since the notion of context is different. A sentence S is satisfied in a Stalnakerian context just in case the context contains only S-worlds. The important innovation over Karttunen's approach is that for complex sentences the admittance conditions are not given directly, but are derived from the definitions of CCPs for complex sentences. She gives the following definitions of the CCPs for negative sentences and conditionals, where the slash denotes set subtraction:

Definition D14 **(Heimian Negation and Conditionals)**

$$\sigma + \text{Not S} \quad = \quad \sigma\backslash(\sigma + S)$$
$$\sigma + \text{If A} then \text{B} \quad = \quad \sigma\backslash((\sigma + A)\backslash(\sigma + A + B))$$

Thus to update a context with the negation of a sentence, find the result of updating with the sentence, and subtract the resulting set of worlds from the original context. To update with a conditional, find the set of worlds where the antecedent is true, take away those worlds where both the antecedent and consequent are true, and subtract the result from the original context. Admittance conditions are now definedness conditions on updating, so σ admits 'Not S' just in case $\sigma \backslash (\sigma + S)$ is defined, which will be the case whenever $\sigma + S$ is defined. Thus the admittance conditions for S are identical to those for 'Not S', just as in Karttunen's system above. Similarly, a context admits 'If A then B' just in case $\sigma + A$ and $\sigma + A + B$ are defined, so that σ must admit A, and σ incremented with A must admit B. Again, this yields the same admittance conditions as Karttunen gave.

These CCPs for complex sentences are supposed to serve two purposes. First, and as we just saw, they provide a means for predicting whether a complex sentence is admitted in a context in terms of admittance of the parts of the sentence in local contexts. Second, they provide an account of the new information conveyed by complex sentences, encoding the normal truth conditional meaning in such a way that truth conditions can always be read off from a CCP.[4] She says "I believe, without offering justification here, that ... a compositional assignment of CCPs to the sentences of a language can fully replace a compositional assignment of truth conditions of the sort normally envisaged by semanticists, without any loss of empirical coverage." As I indicated in the introductory chapter, a principal goal of this book is to show in detail how such a compositional assignment of CCPs to the sentences of a language can be achieved, and to demonstrate not only that it can replace the classical paradigm of compositional assignment of truth conditions, but also that it can improve on the empirical coverage available in that paradigm.

4.4 Quantification in the CCP Model

One of the main claims of Heim (1983b) is that the CCP model provides a way to deal with the presuppositions of open sentences — sentences which at LF might be expected to contain a free variable bound only externally to the sentence. Heim suggests that contexts should register not only factual information, information determining which world we are in, but also information about the values of variables. To achieve this she introduces the notion of a *sequence*, a mapping from indices (natural numbers) to the domain of individuals, and redefines contexts as sets of sequence-world pairs. Thus the CCP of a sentence 'She$_i$ is happy', if 'she$_i$' is treated as a variable free in the sentence, becomes an intersective operation on this new type of

---

[4] Heim (1983b, p.118) provides the following definition for truth of a sentence in terms of its CCP: "Suppose σ is true (in w) and σ admits S. Then S is true (in w) with respect to σ iff $\sigma + S$ is true (in w)." Adapting from her definition (18) which concerns contexts as sequence-world pairs rather than worlds, a context will be true in a world just in case the context contains that world.

context, mapping a set of world-sequence pairs onto that subset containing only pairs $\langle g, w \rangle$ where the index i is mapped by the sequence g onto an individual that is happy in w. Heim then gives (essentially) the following CCP for universal sentences:

Definition D15 (Heimian Universal) If g_a^i is an i-variant of g, differing only by mapping i to some a, an element of the domain of individuals $\mathcal{D}$ (it being assumed that $\mathcal{D}$ is constant across worlds), then:

$$\sigma + \text{Every}_i \text{A}, \text{B} \;=\; \{ \langle g, w \rangle \in \sigma \mid \forall a \in \mathcal{D}, (\langle g_a^i, w \rangle \in \sigma + \text{A} \;\rightarrow$$
$$\langle g_a^i, w \rangle \in \sigma + \text{A} + \text{B}) \}$$

Heim also places an additional requirement that i is a "new variable" in σ, which she takes to mean that for any sequence-world pair $\langle g, w \rangle$ in σ, and for any individual a, there is another sequence-world pair $\langle g_a^i, w \rangle$ in σ. In other words, as far as σ is concerned i could have any value at all in any world in the context.[5] So, the definition says that the update of a context σ with a sentence 'Every$_i$ A, B' is the set of sequence-world pairs $\langle g, w \rangle$ in σ such that all the i-variants of g that survive update with the restrictor also survive sequential update with the restrictor and then the scope. To what admittance conditions does this definition lead? The conditions are parallel with those for conditionals: the restrictor (A) must be admitted in the input context, and the scope (B) must be admitted in the context formed by updating the input context with the scope. Suppose A contains a presupposition that is itself free in the quantified variable, as in the following example from Heim (1983b):

E112 Everyone$_i$ who serves his king will be rewarded

On the relevant reading, the phrase 'his king' is understood to mean the king of the individual x_i's country, and the presupposition is thus that x_i has a king. The restrictor will be admitted in an input context σ only if the proposition that x_i has a king is satisfied in that context. But for that to be the case, it must be that every value onto which index i is mapped in σ, by assumption every individual in the domain, must be established to have a king in σ. Heim predicts (*contra*, for example, Karttunen and Peters 1979, and *contra* the empirical survey in Beaver 1994b) that in general bound presuppositions in a quantificational sentence become universal presuppositions of the whole sentence, and, in particular, that 4.4 presupposes that everybody has a king.[6]

---

[5]Note that this requirement of i being unconstrained corresponds to what is enforced in semantics for programming languages by the operation of *random assignment*. In the recent spate of work on dynamic semantics initiated by Groenendijk and Stokhof (1991b), the requirement is normally made explicit in the semantics of the quantifier.

[6]As Heim points out, a mechanism of local accommodation (to which we will turn shortly) could make these predictions no more than a default.

The problem seems more serious in connection with the treatment of indefinites. Witness the presuppositions assigned to the following example, again from Heim (1983b):

E113 A fat man was pushing his bicycle.

Heim, in common with Kamp (1981), assumes that indefinites carry no quantificational force of their own, but merely mark that their index represents a new variable. Taking i as the indefinite's index, updating a context σ with E113 consists in first adding that x_i is a horizontally challenged adult male to form an intermediary context σ', and then updating with 'x_i was pushing x_i's bike.' But this latter sentence is assumed only to be admitted in contexts which satisfy 'x_i has a bike', so that in order for update to continue, every sequence-world pair in σ' must map x_i onto a bike owner. Since in σ' there are valuations mapping x_i onto each individual in each world such that the individual is a fat man in that world, the whole sentence is predicted to presuppose that every fat man owns a bicycle. This, of course, conflicts with intuition.[7] In Chapter 8 a solution to the problem of universal presuppositions from existential sentences, and a more generally adequate treatment of presuppositions of open sentences, will be presented.[8]

4.5 Projection from Propositional Complements

D11 omits Karttunen's 1974 account of how presuppositions triggered within propositional complements are projected. Karttunen divides lexical items taking a propositional complement into three classes: verbs of saying (e.g. *say, announce*), verbs of propositional attitude (e.g. *believe, want*), and others. The 'others' class includes various presupposition triggers, such as factive verbs, as well as an assortment of predicates which Karttunen takes to be *holes*, such as modals and internal negation. On Karttunen's account, the simplest cases are the first and the third: presuppositions

---

[7]Heim does suggest a possible line of solution, utilising the mechanism of local accommodation to be discussed in the following chapter. To jump ahead, the solution involves locally accommodating the presupposition within the scope of the existential. I refer the reader to the discussion of Soames (1989, pp. 559–600) where it is shown that Heim's solution is not without problems of its own.

[8]The particular problem of universal presuppositions from existential sentences does not occur in some other recent dynamic systems, such as those of Chierchia (1995), van Eijck (1993; 1994; 1995), Krahmer (1993; 1994; 1998), and is also resolved in Beaver (1992). I regret that I have been unable to include a full discussion and comparison of these proposals, but should point out that the current work contains more discussion of the interaction between quantification and presupposition, particularly as regards presentation of relevant data, than any of these predecessors.

triggered within the complement of a verb of saying do not impose any constraint on the context of utterance, whilst for members of the third class all presuppositions triggered within the complement must be satisfied. Thus 'John says that the king of France is bald' should be acceptable in any context, and 'John knows that the king of France is bald' should only be acceptable in contexts where there is a (unique) king of France. For a sentence with propositional attitude verb as matrix, Karttunen argues that it is the beliefs of the subject of the sentence which are crucial: for a context σ to admit the sentence, the beliefs of the subject in that context must satisfy all the presuppositions of the propositional complement. So 'John hopes that the king of France is bald' should only be admitted in contexts where it is satisfied that John believes there to be a king of France. In favour of this analysis is the fact that for instance the discourse 'Although France is not a monarchy, John believes that there is a reigning French king. He hopes that the King of France is bald', although contrived, is felicitous.

Assuming that neither verbs of saying nor verbs of propositional attitude induce any new presuppositions, and omitting members of the *other* class apart from factives, the following are essentially Karttunen's acceptability conditions:

Definition D16 (Karttunen '74 Attitudes)

$$\sigma \triangleright \text{saying-verb}(x, S)$$
$$\sigma \triangleright \text{attitude-verb}(x, \mathsf{S}) \quad \textit{iff} \quad \{\phi \mid \sigma \models \textit{believes}(x, \phi)\} \triangleright \mathsf{S}$$
$$\sigma \triangleright \text{factive-verb}(x, \mathsf{S}) \quad \textit{iff} \quad \sigma \models \mathsf{S}$$

For dynamic semantics of attitude verbs embodying such admittance conditions, the reader might consult Heim (1992). Note, however, that the semantics presented there involves essentially a stipulation of Karttunesque admittance conditions within the definitions of the context change potentials associated with attitude verbs. It is not the case that Heim claims motivation of these admittance conditions independently of presuppositional phenomena, through any 'deep' understanding of the concepts associated with such verbs. Zeevat (1992), however, does give a dynamic semantics for 'believe' in which Karttunen type admittance conditions arise quite naturally.

4.6 Anaphoricity

In this section the parallel between anaphora and presupposition will be considered. The basis of that parallel is empirical, as will be shown, but there is also a theoretical side to it: anaphora and presupposition motivate similar models of the dynamics of interpretation. For this reason, I place the discussion in the context of the dynamic theories of presupposition discussed in this chapter. However, the best developed theory which takes the parallel between anaphora and presupposition seriously uses a component that is not discussed in the current chapter, namely the mechanism of *accommodation*. That mechanism will be discussed separately in the next chapter, and the following discussion should provide some preparatory background.

Over the last decade a number of authors, most notably van der Sandt (1989; 1992a) and Kripke (ms), have argued that there is a tight connection between presupposition and anaphora. Van der Sandt has pointed out that for every example of what might be called *discrepant* anaphora, by which I mean those cases where the anaphoric link is not naturally treated using standard binary quantifiers to interpret determiners and bound variables for pronouns, parallel cases of *discrepant* presupposition can be found. In the following four triples, the (a) examples exemplify discourse anaphora, donkey anaphora, bathroom sentences and what Roberts (1987) has termed *modal subordination*, respectively. In each case, a corresponding example is given, as (b), in which a presupposition is triggered (by the adverb 'still') in the same structural position as the anaphor occurred, but in which this presupposition is satisfied.[9] The third member, (c), completes the

---

[9]Although I have defined formal notions of presupposition satisfaction, I have not said what it means as a description of a text to say that in the text a certain (elementary) presupposition is satisfied. Indeed, such terminology is commonplace in recent presupposition literature, but I do not know of any pre-theoretic analysis of satisfaction. Perhaps a direct test for satisfaction could be developed. To start the ball rolling, I propose the following method of determining whether an elementary presupposition P in a text segment T uttered in a context C is satisfied (where the presence of an elementary presupposition must be determined by standard embedding tests applied to the clause containing the putative elementary presupposition).

Satisfaction Test. If the dialogue consisting of:

A: I don't know whether P.
B: I see. Well, T.

is felicitous in context C, then the elementary presupposition P is satisfied in the text T in this context.

For example, set T and P as follows:

T = 'If Mary is vigilant, then she knows that someone ate a biscuit', and

P = 'A biscuit was eaten'. I find it hard to imagine a context in which the following dialogue would be felicitous:

A: I don't know whether a biscuit was eaten.
B: I see. Well, if Mary is vigilant, then she knows that someone ate a biscuit.

On the other hand set T = 'If John ate a biscuit, then Mary knows that someone did', and P = 'A biscuit was eaten'. The dialogue

A: I don't know whether a biscuit was eaten.
B: I see. Well, if John ate a biscuit, then Mary knows that someone did.

is, if still rather strained, more acceptable than the previous one, especially if B's reply

circle, showing that the argument of the presupposition trigger can itself be pronominalised with no change of meaning.[10]

E114 a. A farmer owns a donkey. He beats it.

  b. Wanda used to beat Pedro. She still beats him.

  c. Wanda used to beat Pedro. She still does.

E115 a. If a farmer owns a donkey then he beats it. [*Geach*[11]]

  b. If Wanda used to beat Pedro then she still beats him.

  c. If Wanda used to beat Pedro then she still does.

E116 a. Either there is no bathroom in this house or it's in a funny place. [*Partee*]

  b. Either Wanda never beat Pedro, or she still beats him.

  c. Either Wanda never beat Pedro, or she still does.

E117 a. A wolf might come to the door. It might eat you.

  b. Perhaps Wanda used to beat Pedro, and perhaps she still beats him.

  c. Perhaps Wanda used to beat Pedro, and perhaps she still does.

The parallel is compelling, and furthermore similar examples are easily constructed involving all standard presupposition types. But evidence for the anaphoricity of presuppositions goes beyond cases, like those above, where the presupposition is satisfied because it is in some sense anaphoric

---

is followed by 'Perhaps she can help you.' Similarly, applying the test to the (c) example in E114 we obtain a felicitous text, and so conclude that the presupposition is satisfied:

A: I don't know whether Wanda beats Pedro.
B: I see. Well, Wanda used to beat Pedro. She still does.

I leave it to the reader to apply the test to the remaining (b) and (c) examples.

[10]Note that although examples E114–E117 demonstrate the parallel between anaphora and presupposition that motivates van der Sandt's work, not all of the examples are dealt with in the theory that he proposes. In particular, E116 and E117 are not dealt with in van der Sandt (1989; 1992a). Progress on these issues (via a presuppositional account of modal subordination) is however made by Geurts (1999).

[11]Although Geach (1962) originated examples of donkey sentences, it is generally overlooked that the problem of donkey anaphora was already discussed by Frege (1892). Frege, presenting what I take to be potential counterexamples to what we would now call compositionality, introduced the following "number" sentence: "If a number is less than 1 and greater than 0, its square is less than 1 and greater than 0." Frege's prescient observation is that a single clause need not correspond to a complete *thought*: in other words, we must consider linguistic context when seeking an interpretation. He also presents other comparable examples, including some involving temporal relationships between antecedent and consequent. Thus Frege not only anticipated Geach, but also much contemporary work in DRT.

on a textual antecedent. The reverse of the coin is that, for at least some types of presupposition trigger, if a textual antecedent is not present the presupposition *cannot* be satisfied. Kripke observes that a common analysis of 'too' would make the presupposition of sentence E118, below, the proposition that somebody other than Sam is having supper in New York tonight. However, this proposition seems uncontroversial, so the standard account provides no explanation of why the sentence, uttered in isolation, is infelicitous.

E118   Tonight <u>Sam</u> is having supper in New York, too.   (Kripke ms)

Notably, E118 is felicitous when it follows a sentence saying of somebody other than Sam that he is having dinner in New York tonight, e.g. 'Saul is having dinner in New York tonight...'. It might be argued that E118 places a requirement on its local context that there is a salient having-supper-in-NY-tonight event. Although one could imagine introducing event discourse markers, and some ontology of events, into the framework we have sketched so far, less effort will be required if we restrict ourselves to an alternative suggestion of Heim (1990). This is the hypothesis that E118 is felicitous in contexts where there is a discourse entity of which it is locally satisfied that the entity is having supper in New York tonight.[12] Adapting from Heim somewhat, we might give the following sketch of an admittance condition for a sentence of the form 'S too', where the word 'too' is assumed to be co-indexed with some focussed NP:[13]

Definition D17 (Heimian 'too') Let $S[i/j]$ represent the sentence S with all instances of NPs indexed i replaced by x_j. Then:

$$\sigma \rhd S \ too_i \quad \text{iff} \quad \sigma \text{ satisfies } S[i/j] \text{ for some index } j.$$

E118 would be indexed 'Tonight Sam$_i$ is having supper in New York, too$_i$', and would only be admitted in contexts where for some j, 'Tonight x_j is having supper in New York' was satisfied.[14] We would thus expect E118

---

[12]To back up the suggestion that the presence of a discourse marker is essential to the felicity of 'too', observe that of the following two discourses (adapted from a well known pronominalisation example due to Partee) A is odd, but B is felicitous.
A: I have ten marbles and you have one. Only nine of mine are transparent. Your marble is opaque too.
B: I have ten marbles and you have one. One of mine is not transparent. Your marble is opaque too.

[13]Kripke does not limit his consideration to cases where an NP is in focus, and, of course, a fuller analysis than that given here would allow non-NPs to be focussed constituents as well.

[14]In order for definition D17 fully to meet Kripke's objections, an additional constraint on Heimian contexts would be required, roughly that they contain only information introduced in the immediately previous discourse. Otherwise an instance of 'too' might be predicted to be satisfied by material that was not introduced in the preceding text.

only to be admitted in a restricted range of contexts, but 'If Saul is having supper in New York tonight, then <u>Sam</u> is having supper in New York, too.' to carry no presupposition at all.[15]

For which presupposition triggers is an anaphoric analysis appropriate? Van der Sandt gives a straightforward answer: all presupposition triggers are anaphors. Perhaps it can be imagined how analyses like that for 'too' above could be given for other presupposition types. For instance, to make factives anaphoric, one might introduce discourse markers for propositions and facts, a development which would anyway be essential to treat propositional anaphora within texts (c.f. Asher 1993). One could then make acceptability of a factive verb with propositional complement ϕ conditional on the presence of a factual discourse marker (perhaps a discourse marker identifying a proposition satisfied in the local context) with interpretation related to ϕ in some yet to be specified manner. The addition of discourse markers for uttered propositions would yield a fine grained notion of infor-

---

[15]Kripke makes the provocative claim that the presupposition of a discourse like 'If Herb comes to the party the boss will come too' is that Herb and the boss are distinct individuals. This is interesting, and perhaps it is right in the pragmatic sense of presupposition, in as much as it would be usual for the speaker to be assuming distinctness. But I do not think that this is a presupposition which is conventionally associated with 'too', and I am not sure it is helpful to call it a presupposition at all. Consider first the following dialogue segment:

A: If Clark is at the party then is Lois in Washington?
B: No. If Clark is at the party then Lois is in New York too.

In the B sentence, the antecedent of the conditional acts as an anaphoric antecedent for the presupposition in the consequent, and we arrive at a presupposition to the effect that if Clark is at the party then Clark is in New York. And indeed, there does seem to be an assumption associated with the sentence that Clark, and hence the party, is in New York. This presupposition can be removed by adding extra information to the antecedent, as in 'If the party is in New York and Clark is at the party, then Lois is in New York too.', but it cannot be cancelled simply by adding contradictory information. The following dialogue segment is infelicitous if it occurs discourse initially (when there is no other possible antecedent for the 'too'):

A: If Clark is at the party then is Lois in Washington?
B: ? No. If Clark is at the party then Lois is in New York too, although the party is in Seattle.

However, the claimed distinctness presupposition behaves differently, and can be cancelled simply by denying its truth later. The following discourse *is* felicitous:

A: I never see Clark Kent and Superman together, so if Clark Kent is at the party, then Superman isn't.
B: If Clark is at the party, then Superman is definitely there too, since Clark is Superman!

I would favour a Gricean explanation of the distinctness implication, whereby each clause of a sentence or discourse is normally required to be informative. A sentence 'X Ys too' will only be informative if in its local context X is not established to Y. But if the presupposition that some salient entity Ys is satisfied by X itself, then clearly 'X Ys too' does not add any new information to that context. Note that on this basis van der Sandt's DRT-based theory, which incorporates such an informativeness constraint as a condition on DRS well-formedness, could account for Kripke's distinctness effect without any need to specify distinctness in the lexical entry for 'too'.

mation. An information state would record in much greater detail exactly what statements had been used to update it than is found in the dynamic systems discussed above. For instance, Stalnaker's notion of an information state as a set of worlds can only distinguish between asserted statements up to classical equivalence, and Heimian contexts go only a little further. Van der Sandt's approach to providing an anaphoric account of presupposition does not, however, involve refining Stalnaker's sets of worlds or Heim's contexts. Instead van der Sandt utilises a rather different sort of dynamic system, Kamp's DRT (Kamp 1981, Kamp and Reyle 1993), with which I will assume the reader's familiarity.

Van der Sandt is not the only one to have provided an account of presupposition in DRT, but his is the most developed account, and others, such as Kamp and Rossdeutscher (1994), Rossdeutscher (1994) are closely related. Accordingly, when discussing the relevance of the dynamics of DRT interpretation to presupposition, I will concentrate on van der Sandt's account. Note that in this chapter I will only be discussing the part of van der Sandt's account which takes advantage of the inherent dynamism of standard DRT, and it is only in the next chapter that I will discuss the considerable further developments that van der Sandt has made in the form of a theory of accommodation.

Discourse Representation Structures provide a very fine grained notion of information state, one which is ideal for an anaphoric account of presupposition, since so much of the original surface structure of utterances is recorded. But crucially, although van der Sandt's model operates under the motto *presupposition is anaphora*, it does not treat presuppositions as anaphors in the strict sense of requiring a *textual* antecedent. Rather, van der Sandt claims that a presupposition trigger is anaphoric at the level of discourse representation. The heart of the theory involves a structural relation between the position at which a presupposition trigger is represented in a DRS, and the point at which its *antecedent* is represented. The antecedent must be represented somewhere along the *anaphoric accessibility path* from the representation of the trigger, this condition being exactly the same requirement as is placed on anaphoric pronouns and their antecedents in standard DRT. The treatment of E119a should illustrate.

E119 a. Fred is escaping, but Mary doesn't realise that somebody is escaping.

Initially a DRS like the following, in which the presence of a presupposition is indicated using a double thickness box, is constructed:

E119 b.

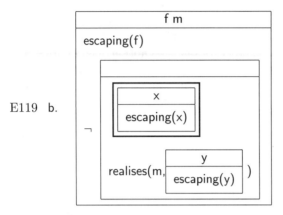

The global DRS is accessible from within the negation. The marker x can be resolved with the marker f, and in this case both the universe of the presupposition (now f) is accessible in the global universe, and the condition in the presupposition is accessible as a global condition. Thus the presupposition has an antecedent. The double-lined presupposition box, which plays no further role in DRS construction, and does not enter into the model theoretic interpretation of the completed DRS structure, is simply removed, to yield the final logical form:

E119 c.

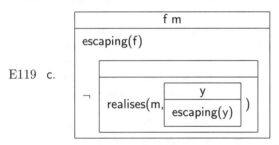

Note that it would make little difference to the treatment of E119 if the word 'somebody' had been replaced by 'he'. Van der Sandt thus provides an interesting twist to the DRT treatment of noun phrase semantics, since in his extended DRT an indefinite can (when embedded in a presuppositional environment) behave to some extent anaphorically.

This model of presupposition resolution, as will be seen shortly, is just one part of van der Sandt's theory of presupposition. Let us explore the relation between van der Sandt's resolution model and the other dynamic theories considered in this section, a job done much more thoroughly by Zeevat (1992). The dynamics of van der Sandt's model is not stated in terms of update functions as in Heim's work. Although some effort has been devoted to providing a more declarative statement of the model (see van der Sandt 1992a, van der Sandt and Geurts 1991), it remains explicitly procedural. For instance, it is important that the anaphors and presuppositions of a sentence are dealt with only after processing of previous discourse is complete. The dynamics can be said to reside in at least three aspects of the theory: the (extended) DRS construction algorithm, the standardly dynamic DRT semantics of implication and quantifiers, and the statement of anaphoric accessibility conditions.

The notion of accessibility is implicitly directional, in that it is invariably defined using an anti-symmetric relation, and reflects Karttunen's conditions on context incrementation. We might restate accessibility conditions in a way that brings this out. Say that a DRS α is a pair $\langle \alpha_0, \alpha_1 \rangle$, with α_0 a set of discourse markers and α_1 a set of conditions. Define $var(\alpha)$ as the set of markers mentioned in the conditions α_1, and take the context σ of any sub-DRS to be a set of discourse markers: this should be thought of as the set of markers external to a DRS which are accessible from within it. The markers of a DRS α in a context σ are completely accessible, written $\sigma \succ \alpha$, if $var(\alpha) \subseteq \alpha_0 \cup \sigma$. Then the following two rules state whether the variables in the sub-DRSs of negations and implications are accessible:

$$\sigma \succ \alpha \to \beta \quad \text{iff} \quad \sigma \succ \alpha \ \text{ and } \ \sigma \cup \alpha_0 \succ \beta$$
$$\sigma \succ \neg \alpha \quad \text{iff} \quad \sigma \succ \alpha$$

These rules, which must be extended to allow for van der Sandt's notion of accessibility of DRS conditions as well as DRS markers, are obviously close to Karttunen's admissibility conditions, as given above (definition D11). Differences arise with conjunction and disjunction, however. Regarding disjunction, it is fair to say that Karttunen's, Heim's and van der Sandt's theories all have problems. The problems with Karttunen's and Heim's accounts are analogous to those facing multivalent accounts of presupposition — see the discussion in Chapter 2. The difficulties with disjunction in van der Sandt's model will be discussed in the following chapter, after the main component of van der Sandt's theory, the accommodation mechanism, has been introduced. The absence of any conjunction operation between DRSs in standard DRT makes comparison on this count difficult, but at least in the case of sentence sequencing, the fact that sentences are processed in a definite order will have the effect that the context of one sentence includes information from previous sentences, which is just what is given in Karttunen's admittance rule for conjunction (again in D11). In other cases there will be a difference in predictions. Van der Sandt's model, unlike the Karttunen or Heim theories, does not seem to predict any difference in acceptability between the following two examples:

E120 If John has children and John's children are at home, he's elsewhere.

E121 ?If John's children are at home and John has children, he's elsewhere.

To deal with this in van der Sandt's theory, one would presumably have to replace the set of conditions in a DRS with a sequence of conditions, and make one condition accessible from another within the same DRS only if the first preceded the second in the sequence. To make such an adjustment, of course, would increase even further the similarity between van der Sandt's model and the other dynamic accounts which have been discussed.

Anaphoricity is generally understood as a structural relation, whether the structures involved are texts, syntactic trees, or DRSs. But it must be pointed out that whilst such structures place some constraints on which items can stand in the relation, it would be wrong to suppose that this was the end of the story. The following examples all concern counterfactual conditionals, although I think the points I will make could be addressed to any intensional predicate which creates a local context that might be inconsistent with the global context:

E122   Mary owns a donkey. If she had been a farmer, she would have beaten it.

E123 ? Mary owns a donkey. If she had not owned any animals, she would have beaten it.

E124 ? Mary owns a donkey. If she had owned a mule instead, John would have owned a donkey too.

The first of these, E122, shows that in principle a pronoun in the consequent of a counterfactual conditional can stand in an anaphoric relation to an object introduced outside of the conditional. In DRT terms, one would have to say that the global DRS is accessible from the consequent DRS of a counterfactual conditional just as it is from the consequent box of a non-counterfactual conditional. But E123, which I take to be infelicitous, shows that one cannot arbitrarily resolve pronouns in the consequent of a counterfactual to relevant objects in the global box. There seems to be some extra non-structural condition: perhaps, given an appropriate theory of the semantics of counterfactual conditionals, one could say that not only must the antecedent to a pronoun be on the accessibility path, it must also correspond to an object which *exists* (in an intuitive sense which I will not attempt to clarify) in the local DRS. But in stating such a constraint, we would be complicating our notion of anaphoricity, placing semantic preconditions on when an anaphoric link could hold. In other words, we would be providing pronouns, the paragons of anaphoricity, with something like semantic presuppositions.[16] Similarly, in E124 it seems that regarding the

---

[16] Gender and number requirements can also be seen as semantic presuppositions, but there is at least the possibility of defining these requirements as grammatical constraints which are determined syntactically.

structural relationship between 'Mary owns a donkey' and 'owned a donkey too', anaphora should be licensed. Van der Sandt's model, as it now stands, would certainly predict simple resolution of the presupposition. But this is clearly wrong. E124 is infelicitous, and this shows us that conceiving of the anaphoricity of 'too' purely structurally, whilst a good approximation in many cases, does not work in general.[17] It is at least arguable that the Heim-style 'too' given above, which involves semantic constraints on the local context, should fare better in such cases, but such a claim remains vacuous in the absence of a CCP semantics for counterfactual conditionals. Heim (1992) discusses such a semantics, but I will not attempt to combine it with the above analysis of 'too' here.

---

[17]One anonymous reviewer of this book correctly points out that the above arguments (and those elsewhere in this volume) fail to show that *no* structural theory of presupposition could account for examples like E122–E124. Ultimately, if we allow for arbitrarily many applications of arbitrary syntactic manipulations, we would presumably arrive at structural theories with the power of a Turing machine, and thus the ability to reproduce any conceivable human (or superhuman) reasoning. So the conclusion we reach on the basis of data such as I have considered is not that working structural theories are in principle impossible. Rather the conclusion must be that an attractive structural account is impractical, since it would have to be sufficiently sophisticated to mirror some quite involved semantic and pragmatic relationships. What I have shown is only that a simple structural account based on a very small number of applications of pattern matching and movement/copying operations, as in van der Sandt's analyses, is problematic.

5

Accommodation

5.1 Introduction

> "... ordinary conversation does not always proceed in the ideal orderly fashion described earlier. People do make leaps and short cuts by using sentences whose presuppositions are not satisfied in the conversational context.... But ... I think we can maintain that a sentence is always taken to be an increment to a context that satisfies its presuppositions. If the current conversational context does not suffice, the listener is entitled and expected to extend it as required. He must determine for himself what context he is supposed to be in on the basis of what is said and, if he is willing to go along with it, make the same tacit extension that his interlocutor appears to have made." (Karttunen 1974, p. 191)

The process Karttunen here describes, whereby a "tacit extension" is made to the discourse context to allow for update with otherwise unfulfilled presuppositions, is what Lewis later called *accommodation* (Lewis 1979).[1] Theories which utilise a mechanism of accommodation are not classical *static* theories of meaning, but rather theories about the dynamics of the interpretation process. Yet theories of accommodation could reasonably be said to involve a *dynamic pragmatics*, in that accommodation is not usually thought of in compositional terms, but as an extra process operating in addition to the normal composition of meanings.

---

[1]Stalnaker (1972, p. 398) expresses similar sentiments to those in the above Karttunen quotation, commenting that presuppositions "need not be true", and that in some cases "Minor revision might bring our debate in line with new presuppositions." Interestingly, in the same paragraph Stalnaker talks of certain things being "accommodated" in the light of new presuppositions, although what he is describing here is not how we change our assumptions (the Lewisian notion of "accommodation"), but how *after* we have changed our assumptions we may reinterpret earlier observations.

In this chapter I will describe the contributions of Heim and van der Sandt to the theory of accommodation, and will detail van der Sandt's recent theory of presupposition and accommodation in DRT, this being by far the most comprehensive and fully specified current theory of presuppositional accommodation. A large part of the chapter will be taken up with discussion of van der Sandt's model, with a number of sections devoted to its empirical inadequacies, but also some discussion of the strengths it has above competing theories of presupposition. In the penultimate section of this chapter I will attempt some synthesis of different approaches to presupposition, showing that a wide range of superficially quite different theories of presupposition can be recast in terms of accommodation. Finally, I will briefly comment on the relevance of Langendoen and Savin's notion of projection to an accommodational theory of presupposition.

5.2 Heim and van der Sandt

Two questions are central to understanding what characteristics a theory of presupposition based on accommodation might have:

1. Given that the interpretation of a discourse involves not one linguistic context, but a series of contexts corresponding to different parts of the interpretation process and different parts of the discourse's meaning, in which context should accommodation occur?

2. Given some decision as to the context in which accommodation occurs, exactly how should a hearer determine what the new context is supposed to be?

Heim (1983b) was the first author to recognise the significance of the first question, noting that quite different effects could result according to which point in the interpretation of a sentence accommodation occurs. In the Heim/Karttunen account one can distinguish two types of context. There is the *global* context which represents the information agents have after complete interpretation of some sequence of sentences of text, but there are also *local* contexts, the contexts against which sub-parts of a sentence are evaluated.

Under definition D14 above, updating a context σ with a conditional 'If A then B' will involve local contexts $\sigma+A$ and $\sigma+A+B$ (to be read left-associatively) which are involved during the calculation of the update. Suppose that B contains some presupposition which is unsatisfied in the context $\sigma+A$, so that σ does not admit the conditional. In that case accommodation must occur, adjusting one of the contexts involved in the calculation so that A is admitted in its local context of evaluation. This might take the form of adding some sentence P directly to the local context in which B is to be evaluated, so that the final result of updating with the context would not be $\sigma\backslash(\sigma+A \backslash (\sigma+A+B))$, but $\sigma\backslash(\sigma+A \backslash (\sigma+A+P+B))$: this would be called *local accommodation*. On the other hand, an agent might backtrack right back to the initial context, add a sentence Q to the global context, and then start the update again. This is termed *global accommodation*, and the result of updating would be $\sigma + Q \backslash ((\sigma + Q + A \backslash (\sigma + Q + A + B))$. There is at least one other possibility. The agent might just backtrack as far as the evaluation of the antecedent, and add some extra information, say a proposition R, into the context in which the antecedent is evaluated, producing a result like $\sigma\backslash(\sigma + R + A \backslash(\sigma + R + A + B))$. Since this last option involves accommodation into a context intermediate between the global context and the context in which the problematic presuppositional construction is actually evaluated, it can be termed *intermediate accommodation*. Clearly the Heimian view on accommodation is highly procedural, and the exact options which are available for accommodation will be dependent on the details of how updating actually occurs, such processing details not being fully specified by the CCP alone.

The Heimian answer to question (1), then, is that accommodation might take place at any time during the interpretation process so as to ensure later local satisfaction of presuppositions. Put another way, accommodation might potentially take place in any of the discourse contexts used in the calculation of a sentence's CCP. Unfortunately, Heim has given no indication of how question (2) should be answered.[2] The first theory of accommodation which provides a fully explicit answer to both questions is that of van der Sandt (1992a), and having described one part of that theory in the previous section, I will now present the theory in full. As mentioned, in van der Sandt's theory Heimian contexts are replaced by explicit discourse representations. Consequently, whereas for Heim accommodation must consist in augmenting a set of world-sequence pairs, van der Sandtian

---

[2]Witness the following quote from Heim (1983b): "Suppose [a sentence] S is uttered in a context σ which doesn't admit it.... simply amend the context σ to a richer context σ', one which admits S and is otherwise like σ, and then proceed to compute σ' [updated with] S instead of σ [updated with] S." Here she does not specify the relation between σ and σ', except to say that σ' is richer than σ, and strong enough to admit S. Her later comparison with Gazdar's theory, a comparison to which we will turn shortly, does seem to suggest that she considers accommodation to consist in adding exactly the proposition that Gazdar would have labelled the *potential presupposition*, but, as Heim (p.c.) has pointed out, she nowhere says this explicitly. It seems I was mistaken in assuming, in an earlier version of this work (Beaver 1993b), that Heim was committed to a *structural* account of accommodation, a term which will be explained shortly. Zeevat (1992) also assumes that Heimian accommodation consists in adding the proposition signaled as presupposed by the trigger. On the other hand, Geurts (1999) supposes that the most natural way of making Heim's theory explicit would involve accommodation of the logically weakest proposition needed to guarantee local satisfaction.

accommodation is simply addition of discourse referents and conditions to a DRS. This difference could be minimised if the CCP model were presented in terms of Heimian *filecards* (c.f. Heim 1982; 1983a), so that accommodation would consist of either creating new filecards, or adding conditions to existing ones. Regarding question (1), van der Sandt's theory shares the flexibility of Heim's. If a presupposition lacks an antecedent in a DRS, van der Sandt allows accommodation to take place in any discourse context that is accessible from the site of the trigger. Thus once again we can talk of *local accommodation*, meaning accommodation in the DRS where the trigger is represented, *global accommodation* meaning addition of material in the global DRS, and *intermediate accommodation* meaning addition of material in any DRS intermediate on the accessibility path between the global DRS and the site of the trigger.

Van der Sandt's answer to question (2), the question of what is accommodated, is as simple as it could be: if a trigger has an antecedentless presupposition, then accommodation essentially consists of transferring the discourse markers and conditions of the presupposition from the trigger site to the accommodation site. An example will demonstrate the power of the accommodation mechanism. At the same time, the example should illustrate an analogy that might be drawn between van der Sandt's theory and a transformational account of syntax, with van der Sandt's equivalent of *move-α* being an operation on DRSs.

E125 a.   If Mary chose the Chateau Neuf, then she realises it's a good wine.

Assuming, just so that we can concentrate on the treatment of the factive 'realises', that 'Mary' and 'the Chateau Neuf' and 'it' are simply represented as discourse markers, we derive the following DRS:

E125 b.

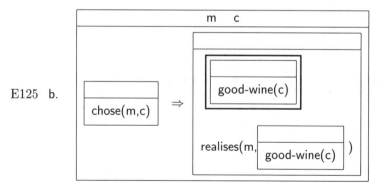

To produce a DRS in which there is no antecedentless presupposition, a transformation must take place whereby α, the presupposition [ ][goodwine(c)],[3] is moved to one of the three sites accessible from the site of the trigger.

Global accommodation produces E125c, which can be glossed as 'CN is good, and if Mary orders it then she realises it's good.'

E125 c.

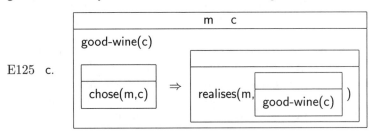

Intermediate accomodation produces E125d, which can be glossed as 'If CN is good and Mary orders it, then she realises it's good.'

E125 d.

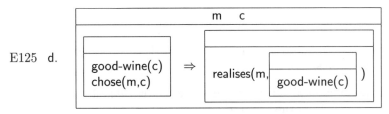

Finally, local accommodation produces E125e, which can be glossed as 'If Mary orders CN then it's good and she realises it's good.'

E125 e.

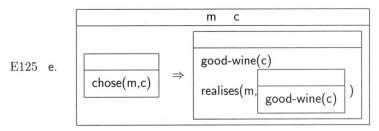

Given all these forms of accommodation, and, in van der Sandt's theory, additional options when resolution is possible, how are we to decide which treatment is preferred? Heim offered only one heuristic: "I suggest that the global option is strongly preferred, but the local option is also available in certain circumstances that make it unavoidable." (Heim 1983b, p.120) Van der Sandt provides much more detail. He offers a way of ranking alternative forms of binding and accommodation, including a preference for global over

---

[3]When giving DRSs in the running text, I use a linear notation, whereby [a,b][p(a,b),q(a)] represents a DRS which introduces markers a and b, and has conditions p(a,b) and q(a).

local accommodation, and describes a number of absolute constraints that any solution must obey.

Van der Sandt (1992a) does not state the ranking over alternative binding and accommodation options directly. It arises as a side effect of an algorithm for resolving presuppositions: on encountering a presupposition, first check each DRS on the accessibility path from the trigger, moving successively outwards, and attempting to bind the presupposition, and if after reaching the top box no resolution site has been found, check each box in the reverse direction (i.e. from the top box to the trigger site) attempting to accommodate.[4] Thus simple resolution by binding is attempted first, and only if that fails can accommodation occur. We may state the effects of this procedure declaratively as a preference ranking between possible outcomes:

Definition D18 (Preferences Between van der Sandtian Solutions)

1. Resolution is preferred to accommodation.

2. One resolution is preferred to another if the first is more local (i.e. closer to the site of the trigger).

3. One accommodation is preferred to another if the first is more global (i.e. further from the site of the trigger).

As specified by van der Sandt (1992a) the absolute constraints that must be obeyed by any binding or accommodation of a presupposition include the following five (partly renamed), in which K_0 is an incoming DRS for a new sentence to be merged with the earlier DRS, K_1 is the result of such a merge, and $K_{1'}$ is what might result from resolving all the presuppositions in the result:

Trapping "No condition ... contains a variable which is free" [p.365]

Global Informativity "$K_{1'}$ is informative with respect to K_0, that is K_0 does not entail $K_{1'}$" [p.367]

Global Consistency "Resolving K_0 to $K_{1'}$ maintains consistency"

---

[4]Van der Sandt states on p.362 of van der Sandt (1992a) that the bind-then-accommodate algorithm is to be implemented by generating all possible solutions and then ranking: "the resulting set [of alternative solutions] is ranked by a preference order, which is determined by full versus partial matching, relative distance along its projection line, discourse principles, and non-linguistic knowledge." (p. 363) Unfortunately, he does not give any further indication as to how this ranking is to be spelt out, although I believe he and Geurts have carried this part of the analysis further than can be seen in published work.

Local Informativity "Resolving K_0 to $K_{1'}$ does not give rise to a structure in which ... some subordinate DRS K_i is entailed by the DRSs which are superordinate to it." [p.367]

Local Consistency "Resolving K_0 to $K_{1'}$ does not give rise to a structure in which ... [the negation of some subordinate DRS K_i] is entailed by the DRSs which are superordinate to it." [p.367]

Before discussing the function of these constraints, I will offer a variant formulation. The most important change is to make precise what it means to describe a sub-DRS as *entailed* by superordinate DRS. Since I am not familiar with any standard notion of local entailment of a DRS, I have formulated a natural notion which is based on the idea that an entailed sub-DRS is one which could have been replaced by a tautology with no effect on the truth conditions of the global DRS containing it. The second modification I make is to fold the two consistency conditions into one, since Global Consistency can be seen as a special case of Local Consistency in the special case that the subordinate DRS K_i is the global DRS and is inconsistent. The following formulations of the preferences and constraints are mine rather than van der Sandt's, but they make the account more tractable, and will be used as the basis for the following discussion:

Definition D19 (Modified Consistency and Informativity Constraints)

Global Informativity If some DRS K is incremented with information from a new sentence, such that after solution of all presuppositions the new DRS is K', then $K \not\models K'$.

Local Informativity No sub-DRS is redundant. Formally, if K is the complete DRS structure and K' is an arbitrarily deeply embedded sub-DRS, K' is redundant if and only if $\forall M, f$ $(M, f \models K \leftrightarrow M, f \models K[K'_\top])$. Here $K[K'_\top]$ is a DRS like K except for having the instance of K' replaced by an instance of a DRS with the same universe as K' but no conditions, and $\models$ denotes the DRT notion of *embedding*.[5]

---

[5]The versions of the local informativity and consistency conditions presented here are different from that in Beaver (1995; 1997). Those earlier versions suffered from two problems. First, they failed to keep track of discourse markers introduced in redundant DRSs. I am grateful to Patrick Blackburn and Johan Bos for pointing out to me that this would lead to problems. Second, the earlier version inadvertently incorporated an implication where there should have been (and is now) a bi-implication: I am grateful to one of the anonymous referees of this book for pointing out that error. Implemented versions of van der Sandt's informativity and consistency constraints, and indeed the entire theory of van der Sandt, are discussed in Blackburn *et al.* (1999), Blackburn and Bos (ms). These authors succeed wonderfully in doing something that had seemed to

Consistency No sub-DRS is inconsistent. Formally, if K is the complete DRS structure and K' is an arbitrarily deeply embedded sub-DRS, K' is locally inconsistent if and only if $\forall M, f \; (M, f \models K \leftrightarrow M, f \models K[K'_\perp])$. Here $K[K'_\perp]$ is a DRS like K except for having the instance of K' replaced by an instance of a DRS with the same universe as K' but inconsistent conditions.

I will illustrate these constraints with some examples. First, trapping:

E126   a.   Nobody regrets leaving school.

Initially the following DRS might be constructed:

E126   b.

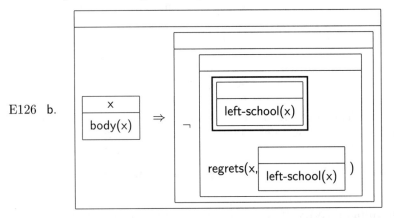

The presupposition cannot be accommodated globally because the discourse marker x would become unbound. The next most preferred accommodation site is in the antecedent box. This produces the final structure, the meaning of which can be glossed as 'Nobody who leaves school regrets having left school':

E126   b.

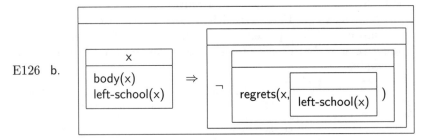

Next, let us consider application of the local informativity constraint. This is exemplified by E127:

---

me to be impractical, namely automating an inference based account of presupposition resolution and accommodation.

E127 a.   If Jane is married then her husband is on holiday.

Global accommodation of the presupposition that Jane has a husband (triggered by 'her husband') would produce the following DRS:

E127 b.

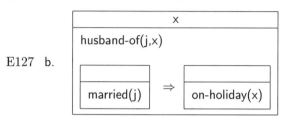

But, on the assumption that models are constrained by meaning postulates in such a way that if somebody has a husband then they are married, this DRS breaks the local informativity constraint: replacing the DRS in the antecedent of the conditional, [ ][married(j)], by the empty DRS [ ][ ] would not alter the range of models in which the global DRS could be embedded. Thus, once again, intermediate accommodation is preferred, producing a structure glossable as 'If Jane is married to x, then x is on holiday':

E127 c.

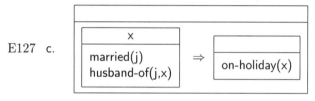

The next two examples, which I will not discuss in detail, illustrate the consistency and global informativity constraints, respectively:

E128 Either Jane is a spinster, or else her husband is on holiday.

E129 Jim is Fred's friend, and Fred is married. He is married too.

The reader should verify that for E128, the consistency constraint prevents global accommodation of the presupposition that Jane is married, forcing local accommodation, and that for E129 the global informativity constraint prevents resolution of the variable associated with 'he' to the discourse marker for Fred.[6]

---

[6]Note that in van der Sandt's system pronouns are treated in the same way as standard presupposition triggers, except that the presupposed DRS associated with a pronoun (something like [x][ ]) is assumed to contain insufficient conditions to support accommodation.

Note that in Geurts' (1999) detailed presentation and extension of van der Sandt's model there are no local informativity and consistency constraints. Most cases that van der Sandt would explain using these constraints, Geurts instead explains using Gricean implicatures. Since the implicatures and mechanism for generating them are not formalised, the predictions of his account are in some cases unclear, and I prefer to stick with (my formulation of) van der Sandt's earlier proposal.

Like the combined Gazdar-Karttunen theory described earlier, or Soames' similar synthesis of Gazdar's and Karttunen's work, van der Sandt's DRT-based model of presupposition gets right the cases which Gazdar's theory handles well (i.e. where presuppositions are either explicitly denied, or appear to be out-competed by implicatures) *and* the cases which Karttunen's theories handle well (typically where a presupposition is entailed in its local context). However, *none* of the cancellation accounts discussed, *none* of the various theories proposed singly or in joint work by Karttunen, and *neither* the above combined Gazdar-Karttunen theory *nor* Soames' own combined model provides an adequate account *either* of presupposed open propositions and their interaction with quantifiers, *or* of Kripkean cases of anaphoric presupposition. Van der Sandt's model treats both of these phenomena. It is on this basis that I would claim that the most successful fully formalised[7] model of presupposition to date is van der Sandt's, whose theory, with a judicious mixture of resolution and accommodation, successfully handles a wide range of problems from the literature and more besides.[8]

However, there remain considerable problems for van der Sandt's theory. Some of these difficulties are of such a general nature as to be relevant to any theory of accommodation, but first I will discuss problems which seem particular to van der Sandt's account.

---

[7]What it is for a model to be *fully formalised* is a matter of judgement. Nonetheless, it is clear that van der Sandt's model goes further than most of its competitors. For instance, perhaps Seuren's model will in principle yield comparable coverage, but at least one central component of the theory, i.e. *backward suppletion*, Seuren's equivalent of accommodation, remains unformalised to my knowledge (but see the developments in Chapter 10 of this book). Heim, though presenting an account with many superficial similarities to van der Sandt, has likewise not offered a detailed formal model of accommodation. One could transport a van der Sandtian view of accommodation into Heim's model (as indeed Zeevat has done Zeevat 1992) or into Seuren's, but then one produces, not surprisingly, a model with very similar descriptive coverage to van der Sandt's account. Or take the accounts of Burton-Roberts and Link. Both have offered promising starting points, but push much of the work over to an as yet unformalised pragmatic component. Another justification for calling van der Sandt's account "fully formalised" is that it has reached a stage where it can be implemented in an NLP system — see van der van der Sandt and Geurts (1991) and Bos (1994).

[8]For the "more besides" see §5.8 below on anaphora from accommodated presuppositions. Also see Sæbø (1996), and the most wide ranging application (and development) of van der Sandt's theory, Geurts (1999).

5.3 The Cancellationist Heritage

Many cases where the various Karttunen-derived models would predict no substantive presupposition, because the presuppositional requirements of the trigger are entailed in their local context, are, as has been discussed, problematic for cancellation theories. Van der Sandt's DRT based model does not filter out entailed presuppositions, but presuppositions which have an anaphoric antecedent. Van der Sandt is able to show that in the standard cases where local entailment plays a role in the theories of Karttunen, Karttunen and Peters, and Heim, his model predicts that there is a suitable anaphoric antecedent (or else one can be unproblematically constructed), and thus that no presuppositions are globally accommodated. However, the cancellationist history of van der Sandt's model shows itself in the treatment of the following examples:

E130 Either John didn't solve the problem or else Mary realises that the problem's been solved.

E131 Unless John didn't solve the problem, Mary realises that the problem's been solved.

E132 Either Mary's autobiography hasn't appeared yet, or else John must be very proud that Mary has had a book published.

E133 Unless Mary's autobiography hasn't appeared yet, John must be very proud that Mary has had a book published.

I do not think that E130 and E131 presuppose that the problem has been solved, or that E132 and E133 presuppose that Mary has had a book published.[9] In a Karttunen derived satisfaction model one might explain that the local context in which the second disjunct of, for instance, E132 is evaluated is one in which the negation of the first disjunct has been added. Since the negation of 'Mary's autobiography hasn't appeared yet' entails (given appropriate meaning postulates on autobiographies, books, etc.) that Mary has had a book published, no substantive presupposition is predicted. However, given the DRT notion of accessibility, the negation of the first disjunct is not anaphorically accessible from within the second disjunct, so anaphoric resolution is ruled out. Van der Sandt will then predict that the preferred reading is one involving global accommodation of

---

[9]However, E130 and E131 are certainly compatible with the problem having been solved, and with suitable stress perhaps this inference will be made. But I do not think the inference can arise from the presupposition of the factive *realises* alone. Similar comments apply to E132 and E133. See Beaver (1994a) for discussion of such issues. It is not essential to my arguments that there is no presuppositional reading, but only that the non-presuppositional reading is available, which I take to be uncontroversial.

the presupposition, yielding a DRS having interpretation corresponding to 'Mary has had a book published and either her autobiography hasn't appeared yet or else John must be very proud that Mary has had a book published.' The same comments apply *mutatis mutandis* to E130. Further, if *unless* is analysed in DRT simply as setting up a two box structure, with one box for the *unless* clause, and one for the matrix, then we will similarly not expect the negation of the *unless* clause to be anaphorically accessible from within the matrix, and van der Sandt's model will make the same erroneous prediction of preferred global accommodation.

5.4 Accommodation of Unbound Presuppositions

A relatively minor problem with van der Sandt's model, but still one that requires attention, involves the fact that unbound presuppositions can become accommodated into quantificational contexts. Consider the following two peculiar examples:

E134   a.   ? If the Pope fails to appear then he has measles. But every Catholic realises that the Pope has measles.

       b.   ? If the Pope fails to appear then he has measles. But every protestant who realises that the Pope has measles is converting.

After processing 'the Pope', the DRS for E134a might be:

E134   c.

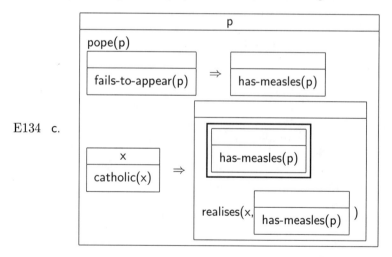

Global accommodation of the condition has-measles(p) would render the first conditional uninformative, and hence is blocked. The next option is accommodation in the restrictor of the universal quantification, to produce:

E134 d.
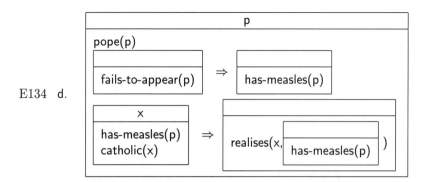

This DRS is then predicted to be the final meaning of the example. Its truth conditions may be glossed as follows: 'if the Pope fails to appear he has measles, but if he has measles then every Catholic realises it.' Now, while this is a perfectly good meaning for a discourse to have, it is not the meaning of the first example above, and there is no explanation of why the sentence is odd.[10] Clearly, the problem would recur in the analysis of E134b, which I will not describe in detail. The problem could perhaps be solved by adding an extra constraint on accommodation: call it *releasing*, since it is approximately the reverse of *trapping*. Whereas *trapping* prevents bound presuppositions leaving the quantificational context of the binder, *releasing* would prevent presuppositions not free in a certain variable from being accommodated in a quantification over that variable.

5.5 The Partial Match

Another problem with the theory of van der Sandt (1992a) is that anaphoric resolution is under-constrained. If what is known about a discourse referent does not conflict with known information about a presupposed referent, then resolution can occur, identifying the two referents, and adding information about the previously introduced referent. In (van der Sandt and Geurts 1991, van der Sandt 1992a, Geurts 1999), the formal statement of the theory does not separate cases where resolution consists only of the identification of referents, and cases where resolution adds information about a pre-existing referent. But in presentations and unpublished work (e.g. van der Sandt 1992b), van der Sandt has identified as a distinct process the latter from of resolution, where information about a referent is

---

[10]It might at first seem that the misanalysis is connected with the fact that I have represented the universal quantification using a conditional DRS, as in early DRT. But this is not relevant. Using a more recent version of DRT would still yield an interpretation glossed as above.

added, using the term *partial match*.[11] If we follow van der Sandt (1992a), then partial matches, as a form of binding, will be preferred to accommodation. On the other hand, in at least some of van der Sandt's unpublished work,[12] it is clear that partial matches are to be considered on a par with accommodation. Either way, I now show that the theory results in bizarre predictions.

In the following, van der Sandt's theory predicts that each of the (a) sentences can have the same meaning as the (b) sentences,[13] at least on the preferred interpretation:

E135 a. Every farmer who owns a donkey realises that a farmer has been injured.

    b. Every injured farmer who owns a donkey realises that a farmer has been injured.

E136 a. Every farmer who owns a donkey realises that a purple farmer-eating donkey is on the loose.

    b. Every farmer who owns a purple farmer-eating donkey which is on the loose realises that a purple farmer-eating donkey is on the loose.

---

[11]A thoughtful elaboration of van der Sandt's account of partial match has recently appeared in Krahmer and van Deemter (1998), to which the reader is recommended. Geurts' (1999) reformulation of van der Sandt's theory does not refer explicitly to partial matches, but his discussion of bridging does make reference to the phenomenon. Geurts makes an observation (p.77) showing that he recognises that the theory will have to be adapted to take such cases into account: "Is [a case where both partial match and accommodation readings are available] a counterexample against Principle B of the binding theory, which says that binding is preferred to accommodation? Not really. It is just that since this principle was introduced we have extended the concept of binding." Geurts does not give an explicit formal statement of his theory which incorporates the distinction he wants to make between basic cases of binding and the extended cases which we here term partial matches.

[12] van der Sandt (1992b, p. 12) states "In case of a partial match we have two possibilities. Either direct anaphoric linking or the creation of a discourse marker at some higher accessible level [...]. In case of a full match, anaphoric linking is obligatory [...]." The same statement is found in earlier versions of van der Sandt (1992a) distributed as talk handouts. The subtlety of separating partial match from full match, and stipulating that in partial match cases binding is optional improves the theory. However, without further constraints the more refined unpublished version still results in considerable over-generation. All the incorrect readings I discuss in the main text are produced by both van der Sandt's published and unpublished versions of the theory, although the readings are not automatically preferred in the unpublished versions.

[13]For example, in E136a, the presupposition that there is a purple farmer-eating donkey on the loose is triggered in the scope of a universal. In the restrictor DRS of the quantifier there is a marker for a donkey, and since being a donkey is compatible with being a purple farmer-eating donkey on the loose, anaphoric resolution can take place, adding to the restrictor the extra material necessary so that the presupposition has an adequate antecedent.

E137 a. If a farmer owns a donkey, he realises that a farmer has been injured.

b. If an injured farmer owns a donkey, he realises that a farmer has been injured.

E138 a. If a farmer owns a donkey, he realises that a purple farmer-eating donkey is on the loose.

b. If a farmer owns a purple farmer-eating donkey which is on the loose, he realises that a purple farmer-eating donkey is on the loose.

Let us reconsider the McCawley conditional E95, and its variant E109:

E95' If Nixon invites Angela Davis to the Whitehouse, then Nixon will regret having invited a black militant to his residence.

E109' If Nixon invites Angela Davis to the Whitehouse and regrets having invited a black militant to his residence, then he will organise a cover-up.

For both of these, one reading of van der Sandt's theory will presumably involve a partial match of the black militant with one of the earlier discourse entities. Nixon may be pragmatically ruled out as the antecedent on a number of grounds, such as common knowledge that he is not a black militant and is not the sort of person to invite himself to the Whitehouse. In that case, the model will predict just the anaphoric connection for which Gazdar argued. But the predictions will be nonetheless bizarre, producing DRSs that may be squibbed as follows:

E95' If Nixon invites Davis and Davis is a black militant, then Nixon will regret having invited a black militant.

E109' If Nixon invites Davis, Davis is a black militant, and Nixon regrets having invited a black militant, then he will organise a cover-up.

Under this claimed interpretation, the speaker is not committed as to whether Davis is a black militant, but if it turned out that she was not, both E95 and E109 would be validated (regardless of Nixon's mental state). This cannot be right. What is worse, we will see shortly that even if the partial match can be prevented in these cases, the remaining interpretations predicted by van der Sandt's model are also inappropriate.

5.6 Intermediate Accommodation

The following examples from Beaver (1994b) are clearly infelicitous. A small group of correspondents were asked to rate eighteen discourses on a five point scale from 'weird' upwards. All informants judged both of these examples weird (with various extra comments, like "I think I'm missing something."):

E139   How many team members and cheerleaders will drive to the match?

⋆ Few of the 15 team members and none of the 5 cheerleaders can drive, but **every team member will come to the match in her car**. So expect about 4 cars.

E140   How many of your employees with company cars had problems with their car radiators last year?

Although few of the sales staff had any problems with their cars last year, **all of the management discovered that their car radiators had sprung a leak**. ⋆ However, most of the management didn't have a single problem with their car radiator the whole year: they are generally quite conscientious about car maintenance.

What is wrong with these discourses? It seems that the only reading available for the bold sentences is the one corresponding to local accommodation. Thus in the first case, every team member must have a car, and in the second case every member of the management must have had problems with their car radiators (the presupposition being triggered by the factive verb 'discover'). In each case, this contradicts information elsewhere in the discourse. Van der Sandt's prediction that a presupposition in the scope of a quantifier can trigger domain restriction is falsified by the oddity of the above examples, since on the domain restriction (or rather, intermediate accommodation) reading there would be no contradiction. Furthermore, it is not open for the defender of van der Sandt's model to claim that some extraneous fact about the discourse would mean that intermediate accommodation would result in an incoherent discourse, as is shown by the following two variant examples:

E141   How many team members and cheerleaders will drive to the match?

Few of the 15 team members and none of the 5 cheerleaders can drive, but **every team member who owns a car will come to the match in her car**. So expect about 4 cars.

E142   How many of your employees had problems with their car radiators last year?

Although few of the sales staff had any problems with their cars last year, **all of the management whose car radiators sprang a leak discovered that their car radiators had sprung a leak.** However, most of the management didn't have a single problem with their car radiator the whole year: they are generally quite conscientious about car maintenance.

In these examples, the crucial sentences from the earlier examples are replaced by new sentences which have exactly the meanings that the earlier sentences would have been predicted to have on van der Sandt's intermediate accommodation reading. Thus 'every team member will come to the match in her car' is replaced by 'every team member who owns a car will come to the match in her car.' Both discourses are clearly felicitous (although only the first was included in the survey). For variety, I also tried versions with an extraposed relative clause as a domain restrictor, like the following:

E143 How many team members and cheerleaders will drive to the match?

Few of the 15 team members and none of the 5 cheerleaders can drive, but **every team member will come to the match in her car, if she owns one.** So expect about 4 cars.

Although informants uniformly rated this example better than E139, some still thought it was "a bit odd", which was only one point above "weird" on the scale that the informants were given. I had more success on the few informants I tested verbally: stress and rhythm appear to be critical. It might be that this extraposed relative construction is just more typical of spoken than written discourse, the sort of after-thought that is quite common in everyday speech, but not normal in the world of white-out fluid and delete keys. But the point remains that the sentence 'Every team member will come to the match in her car' does not have van der Sandt's intermediate accommodation reading in the context set up in E139, and that the felicity of sentences with precisely that meaning shows there to be no independent reason for the reading to be blocked.

Similar comments apply to intermediate accommodation into the antecedent of a conditional. Consider the following two examples:

E144 If the problem was easy, I know that somebody solved it.

E145 What do I know about the problem?
Well, if it was difficult, it's probably still unsolved.
? If it was difficult, then it was Morton who solved it.
That's all I know.[14]

---

[14]I believe that the original "Morton" examples are due to Soames, and suspect that the reference is to my former teacher at the University of Bristol, the wonderfully inspiring Adam Morton.

Regarding E144, let us make the reasonable assumption that everything asserted in the global DRS is known to the speaker, an assumption that could be encoded using meaning postulates. Global accommodation of the proposition that somebody solved the problem is then blocked by the local informativity constraint. So van der Sandt's theory predicts an intermediate accommodation reading whereby the sentence means the same as 'If the problem was easy and it was solved, then I know that it was solved.' However, the only possible reading of E144 seems to correspond to local accommodation: 'If the problem was easy then it was solved and I know that it was solved'. Similarly, with regard to E145, an approach allowing intermediate accommodation predicts that the third sentence has a reading where the presupposition that somebody solved the problem (which is triggered in the consequent) is accommodated in the antecedent. It clearly does not have this reading, for such accommodation would produce the same DRS as the following discourse, which is felicitous:

E146 What do I know about the problem?
Well, if it was difficult, it's probably still unsolved.
If it was difficult and was solved, then it was Morton who solved it.
That's all I know.

Thus we have reached precisely the same conclusion with respect to conditional sentences as was reached earlier with respect to quantificational examples. Indeed, this is hardly surprising, for in DRT quantifiers and conditionals are regarded as being semantically related. Consider the following pair of examples:

E147 If Mary buys a car, she'll sell her Cadillac.

E148 If a woman buys a car, she'll sell her Cadillac.

Whilst in E147 we readily globally accommodate that Mary has a Cadillac, global accommodation of 'x owns a Cadillac' for some x introduced by the NP 'a woman' is blocked in E148, at risk of x becoming unbound. Significantly, E148 seems to imply that any woman who buys a car has (or will have) a Cadillac to sell, despite this being *a priori* implausible. Clearly there is no intermediate accommodation reading (at least not in texts where the set of female Cadillac owners is not already topical) since under such a reading (i.e. 'If a woman who owns a Cadillac buys a car, she'll sell her Cadillac') the implausible consequence would vanish. Once again, a presupposition trigger in the consequent of a conditional is not able to produce accommodation into the antecedent. And this is precisely what we would expect on the basis of consideration of the quantificational analogue of E148, which also lacks an intermediate accommodation reading:

E149 Every woman who buys a car will sell her Cadillac.

Despite all the evidence I have presented to the contrary, there are cases where domain restriction readings like those discussed above occur. Several years ago, my father made the following comment to me:

E150 Everybody takes their pram into the supermarket.

What did he mean? For a start, it seems to be a statement about pram-owners, so that domain restriction has occurred, even though, as I recall, nothing in the previous discourse had explicitly made the set of pram-owning people salient. But specifying the meaning precisely is difficult. Presumably he meant, roughly, that on occasions when people with a pram faced a choice as to whether to take their pram into the supermarket or not, they took it in.[15] Or, to put it another way, he meant that everybody, when finding themselves in a certain type of circumstance follows a certain course of action: the type of circumstance is 'possession of a pram that might be taken into the supermarket', and the course of action is 'taking the pram into the supermarket'. So the sentence might be understood as containing an implicit generic, and given an initial LF something like: every(x,person(x),gen(c, c is a circumstance where x considers taking x's pram into the supermarket, c is a circumstance where x takes x's pram into the supermarket)). Under this interpretation, the trigger 'their pram' is understood as occurring in the restrictor of an implicit generic. Accommodation that x has a pram might occur not in the restrictor of the initial universal, but in the restrictor of the generic. But this would then not be a case of intermediate accommodation, but of local accommodation in the restrictor of an implicit operator.

Whether or not such an analysis seems far-fetched, it should be borne in mind that some explanation must be found for the fact (and I take it to be so) that the claimed intermediate accommodation readings have only been found to occur in sentences that have a distinctly generic flavour. For instance, examples like E151 are sometimes given by van der Sandt:

E151 Every German woman drives her car to work.

The intermediate accommodation reading appears to me to get distinctly less clear when the genericity is removed. For example, consider E152:

E152 Between 9:00 and 9:30 yesterday, every German woman drove her car to work.

---

[15]We were standing outside a supermarket at the time, but it is not entirely clear whether 'the supermarket' referred just to this supermarket, or to supermarkets more generally.

With this variant, I find a clear implication that every German woman has a car, although this implication would not be there on the intermediate accommodation reading. This is not to say that the sentence could not be used in a context where German car owners, or car owning women, were already salient, so that domain restriction would be licensed by the previous context independently of the presence of the presupposition trigger.

Perhaps some will contend that E152 also has an intermediate accommodation reading. Then I would have to accept the need for intermediate accommodation. But I would suggest that it is constrained in such a way that it is only applied when the quantificational domain of a statement is in some sense unclear. For instance, in the discourse 'Ten women work at the company. Every woman drives her car to work', the domain is explicit, and intermediate accommodation (to produce 'Every woman who works for the company and has a car') seems to be difficult or impossible. We could postulate that quantificational statements are always anaphoric on some set which is assumed to be salient, but that when this set has not been introduced explicitly, the hearer must globally accommodate a referent for the set. Then the intermediate accommodation readings would be explained without recourse to intermediate accommodation, but only in terms of global accommodation. Further, such readings would be blocked whenever the domain of a quantificational statement was clearly linked to an explicit antecedent.[16]

Intermediate accommodation is clearly a problematic operation. It is heavily constrained, and is related in some way to genericity. Lacking either suitable constraints, or an account of generics, van der Sandt's theory would make better predictions without intermediate accommodation. The same applies to Heim's theory.

5.7 Conditional Presuppositions

I have taken as a defining characteristic of a theory of presupposition that a function from simple sentences to their elementary presuppositions is given. But this has left open the question of how presuppositional inferences connected with complex sentences are explained. In cancelling and filtering theories, complex sentences have presuppositions which are simply a subset of the elementary presuppositions, whilst in multivalent and dynamic semantic theories complex sentences have presuppositions which need not

---

[16]Good examples (with a decidedly generic flavour) involving domain restriction effects that could be modelled using intermediate accommodation are found in Schubert and Pelletier (1989). Extensive further discussion of the interaction between presupposition and adverbial domain restriction is found in Beaver and Clark (2000). See also the discussions of quantificational domain restriction in Gawron (1995) and Roberts (1995).

come from this set. We may say that in the cancellation and filtering theories the possible presuppositions of complex sentences are structurally predictable from the set of elementary presuppositions, whilst in a theory employing multivalent or dynamic semantics this need not be so. In an accommodation theory, an explanation of presupposition related inferences may be given without any direct definition of what the presuppositions of complex sentences are. This is the case in van der Sandt's recent theory, where accommodation cuts and pastes the elementary presuppositions into the logical form itself, until a logical form is produced containing no further presuppositions. Although we cannot say that the possible presuppositions of complex sentences are structurally predictable, since complex sentences are given no presuppositions, we may still say that van der Sandt has employed a *structural* notion of accommodation: what is accommodated is strictly drawn from amongst the elementary presuppositions.[17]

The problem that I see for a purely *structural* account of accommodation is as follows: it is not possible to predict on structural grounds alone exactly what should be accommodated. In general, the exact accommodated material can only be calculated with reference to the way in which world knowledge and plausibility criteria interact with the meaning of a given sentence. Consider the following George-and-Al example:

E153   Perhaps if George has arrived, none of the press corps. knows that both George and Al are both here.

Here the relevant presupposition trigger is the factive *knows*, and the elementary presupposition is that both George and Al are here. However, there is a clear tendency to come to the conclusion that although the speaker knows Al is here but that George may not be.

In van der Sandt's theory accommodating the presupposition that both George and Al are present is (correctly) blocked, since it would render the antecedent of the conditional vacuous. Accommodating directly under the possibility operator is also (correctly) blocked for the same reason. However, intermediate accommodation of the elementary presupposition in the antecedent of the conditional, which is predicted by van der Sandt, produces the wrong interpretation. The meaning this yields can be paraphrased as 'Perhaps if George has arrived and both George and Al are here, none of the press corps. knows they are here'. This is not the preferred interpretation of E153. Accommodating into the consequent would yield: 'Perhaps if George turns up then both George and Al are here and none of the press corps. knows they are here'. There are occasions of use of E153

---

[17]It could be argued, however, that partial match cases involve a sort of non-structural accommodation, since identity statements are added to the DRS which are not part of the elementary presuppositions themselves.

where this meaning would be reasonable. However, the implication that Al is here remains unexplained. I would not wish to claim that no structural account of accommodation could lead to the correct result, but certainly no existing such account does, and van der Sandt's theory would require apparently *ad hoc* modifications.[18]

The most glaring weak point of a structural account of accommodation concerns the fact that there is no way for it to produce conditional presuppositions, which I have argued are appropriate in many cases.[19] Let us consider one such case:

E154 If Spaceman Spiff lands on Planet X, he will be bothered by the fact that his weight is greater than it would be on Earth.

The 'fact that' construction in this case triggers the presupposition that Spiff's weight is greater than it would be on Earth, and this is further re-enforced by the presence of the factive 'bothered by'. Structural accounts of accommodation suggest that this proposition should be globally accommodated. However, this result is simply wrong: it is not normal to conclude from E154 that Spiff's weight is greater than it would be on Earth. Indeed, it seems natural for this sentence to be uttered under conditions where Spiff is hanging about in space, and completely weightless. It is difficult to argue against a conditional presupposition, that if Spiff lands on X his weight will be greater than on Earth. Can non-global accommodation save the structural account? Accommodation into the antecedent produces something like 'If Spaceman Spiff's weight is greater than it would be on Earth and he lands on Planet X, he will be bothered by the fact that his weight is greater than it would be on Earth.' I do not think this is a possible meaning of E154.

Accommodation into the consequent appears to improve on this, yielding (after charitable adjustment of tense) 'If Spaceman Spiff lands on Planet X, his weight will be greater than it would be on Earth and he will be bothered by the fact that his weight is greater than it would be on Earth.' This provides

---

[18]With regard to an earlier version of this discussion, one reviewer correctly pointed out that I should establish that the relevant effects are connected with presuppositions and not merely with interpretation of conditionals. To see that this is indeed a presuppositional effect, consider the non-presuppositional variant 'Perhaps if George has arrived, George and Al are both here.' This example does not imply that Al is already here. So it is reasonable for us to conclude that the inference that Al is present arises in E153 because of the (partial) projection of a presupposition.

[19]It is ironic, and worrying, that the occurrence of such readings in the CCP account without an accommodation mechanism continues to be taken as one of the most serious objections to Karttunen-derived models (see e.g. Geurts 1994), and the non-occurrence of such readings in other accounts continues to be taken by Karttun-ists (such as myself) to be a serious failing of those theories. It is obviously too soon to say whether the arguments in this book will advance the debate any further, or merely leave the combatants as deeply entrenched as ever.

a reasonable meaning for E154, and suggests that if only some way could be found of removing the two incorrect readings, the structural account might be saved. Now recall the way in which cancellation models were shown to sometimes produce an analogue of a conditional presupposition for the Mc-Cawley type examples, but could not in general produce such readings (in §3.9, p.77). Much the same holds regarding a structural account of accommodation: it can sometimes produce conditional readings, but it is easy to find cases where it cannot. Slight variations on E154 produce examples where the structural account produces multiple incorrect (or, at the very least, non-preferred) readings, and completely fails to yield the preferred reading:

E155 It is unlikely that if Spaceman Spiff lands on Planet X, he will be bothered by the fact that his weight is greater than it would be on Earth.

E156 If Spaceman Spiff lands on Planet X and is bothered by the fact that his weight is greater than it would be on Earth, he won't stay long.

The preferred readings of these sentences still involve the same conditional implication that if he lands on Planet X, Spiff's weight will be greater than it is on Earth. It is clear (given the treatment of *and*) that the Karttunen, Karttunen and Peters and CCP models will make this prediction for E156, and quite natural assumptions about the semantics of the 'it is unlikely' construction would lead to these theories making the same predictions for E155. But in these cases the structural accommodation account no longer yields the right reading after accommodation into the consequent of the conditional. Such accommodation is not even available as an option for E156, and in the case of E155 would yield 'It is unlikely that if Spaceman Spiff lands on Planet X, his weight will be greater than it is on Earth and he will be bothered by it', which does not imply that if he lands on Planet X, Spiff's weight will be greater than it is on Earth. On the contrary, one might expect from this gloss that if Spiff lands on Planet X his weight probably will not be greater than it is on Earth, which is clearly inappropriate.

Example E154 has essentially the same form as the McCawley example E95, a form which I earlier glossed as 'If A then B$_C$'. This being so, it should be clear to the reader how my remarks could be transferred from the Spiff examples to the Nixon/Davis examples, which means that even if van der Sandt's incorrect partial match reading for the Nixon/Davis cases could be avoided, accommodation could still not produce the right results.

It might seem to the reader that the problems I am citing with regard to structural notions of presupposition are rather academic in nature, involving sentences far from the run of everyday conversation. But perhaps the greatest problem with structural accommodation concerns a phenomenon which is quite obviously commonplace. This is the phenomenon of *bridging* whereby a new discourse entity is linked indirectly (i.e. not by identity) to an old one. Consider the following:

E157   Jane sat in the car. She adjusted the rear-view mirror.

E158   If I go to a wedding then the rabbi will get drunk.

E159   An old woman hit me. The knuckle-duster cut deep.

E160   Whenever you remove the head stratifier from a hyperspace drive unit, remember to hold your nose.

In these examples, it seems that the rear-view mirror is connected to the car, the rabbi is connected to the wedding, the knuckle-duster (U.S.: 'brass knuckles') is connected to the hitting event, or the old woman or both, and the head stratifier is connected to the hyperspace drive unit. But what enables us to make these connections? Perhaps it could be claimed that 'rear-view mirror' is an intrinsically relational noun with an argument place for a car, and that the NP 'the rear-view mirror' thus contains the content necessary to make the connection to the car Jane sat in. However, I am not sure that we would wish to analyse 'rabbi' as a relational noun with an argument place for religious ceremonies, or 'knuckle-duster' as having an argument place for an old woman. Furthermore, in the last example, it seems that all that is required to understand that hyperspace drive units have head stratifiers is competence in English and a little common sense, and not competence in hyperspace drive maintenance or a working knowledge of the concepts involved. In all these cases, accommodation might allow us to fill in the missing links. For instance, we might accommodate that a certain knuckle duster is being worn by a certain old woman, or we might accommodate more general rules, say that hyperspace drive units have (/can have) head stratifiers. But we cannot expect the accommodated material to be provided by our knowledge of grammar alone.[20]

---

[20]How crucial to van der Sandt's model is it that accommodation is a structural operation? I think the correct answer, and perhaps the answer van der Sandt would give, is that such structurality is not essential, it is merely a simplifying assumption. There has been some work which, though building on van der Sandt's ideas, drops the assumption that the accommodated material is wholly derived from the trigger. Lorenz (1992) develops an account of presuppositions in the temporal domain which uses default world knowledge to generate the accommodated material, and Bos *et al.* (1995), Krahmer and van Deemter (1998), Piwek and Krahmer (2000) offer accounts of various forms of partial match and bridging descriptions. I find myself very much in sympathy with this direction of research: I think it shows that the gap between the van der Sandtian account of accommodation and the non-structural account which will be proposed in this book may itself, in due course, be bridged.

5.8 Anaphora from Accommodated Material

Now, to provide at least a modicum of balance, I will turn to one aspect of van der Sandt's model which I consider a particular strength. The following two counter-examples to DRT constraints on accessibility of anaphoric antecedents date back to over a decade before DRT was introduced, from Karttunen's influential work on discourse reference (Karttunen 1976, which was only published some years after its first presentation):

E161 a. Bill didn't realise that he had a dime. It was in his pocket.

E162 John knew that Mary had a car, but he had never seen it.

In the first example, not only is 'a dime' embedded within an intensional context, but that context is itself embedded under a negation. In standard DRT, either of these embeddings would normally be sufficient to guarantee anaphoric inaccessibility. Since 'a car' in the second example is embedded within an intensional context, standard DRT incorrectly predicts it to be inaccessible. However, van der Sandt predicts that in both these cases global accommodation occurs. For instance the final DRS for E161a would be something like the following:

E161 b.

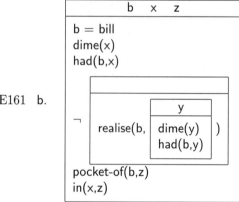

Here global accommodation of a DRS of the form [x][dime(x),had(b,x)] creates an anaphorically accessible dime to which the pronoun in the second sentence can refer.

Such patterns of anaphoric reference can be demonstrated with a wide range of presuppositional constructions embedded in environments that would otherwise block anaphoric reference. Perhaps most significant of these presuppositional constructions are definite descriptions. For instance, in the following discourse, van der Sandt's theory predicts that the presupposition associated with 'the tallest mountain in the world' is globally accommodated, and hence correctly licenses subsequent anaphoric reference:

E163   John believes that he can see the tallest mountain in the world. But in fact it is completely obscured by mist.

What is most notable about this last case is that it shows that given a theory like van der Sandt's, a rather *ad hoc* stipulation in standard DRT, the promotion of proper names and definites, can be dispensed with. More explicitly, this stipulation says that referents introduced by proper names and definite descriptions are automatically promoted to a position in the global DRS regardless of how deeply the sentences in which they occur are embedded. The principle was originally motivated only by the need to account for the special anaphoric accessibility of names and definites. But in van der Sandt's account, the separately motivated theory of presupposition takes care of promotion (under the name of accommodation), and it is only necessary to make the relatively uncontroversial assumption that both definites and names are presuppositional.

5.9   Alternative Accommodation Strategies

Cancellation and filtering might be said to bring the woodsman's axe and hacksaw into the linguistic operation theatre, allowing grisly brute force amputations of unwanted chunks of meaning. By comparison, accommodation is the modern surgeon's toolkit, which in the right hands can enable precision repair of linguistic contexts or major transplants of lexical material across logical forms. As I will attempt to show, accommodation provides one of the great unifying themes of modern presupposition theory, since many theories of presupposition which were not originally proposed as accommodation theories can be thought of in terms of accommodation.

5.9.1   From Amputation to Accommodation

In a sense cancellation is the inverse of global accommodation. After suggesting her enhancement of the CCP model with an account of accommodation, Heim (1983b) makes the following observation:

> Note that by stipulating a *ceteris paribus* preference for global over local accommodation, we recapture the effect of [Gazdar's] assumption that presupposition cancellation occurs only under the threat of inconsistency.

I find this stunning. With one short remark buried in a terse paper Heim offers a simple synthesis between the two antitheses of 1970s presupposition theory, namely the Karttunen 1974 derived model which her paper uses as its base, and Gazdar's cancellation account. Perhaps implicit in

Heim's remark is the idea that global accommodation of an elementary presupposition may be identified with what was termed *projection* in earlier models. In this case whenever accommodation is not global, we have the effect of cancellation. Looked at this way, a preference for global over local accommodation becomes a preference for projection over cancellation, and given an appropriate stipulation of the circumstances in which this preference can be overridden (e.g. in order to avoid inconsistency), the effects of a cancellation theory can be mimicked. In a stroke this shows a way to eliminate the bulk of existing counter-examples to the CCP model, particularly examples where a presupposition associated with an embedded trigger is eliminated by explicit denial. Further, and in common with van der Sandt's cancellation account, Heim's remark introduces a way of thinking about Gazdar's theory that preserves his insight that default reasoning is involved in the processing of presuppositions, whilst restoring the intuition that, in some sense, presuppositions are to do with *what come first*, with definedness conditions on the input rather than preferences on the output. Note that van der Sandt (1988) is explicit in identifying his cancellation analysis as involving an accommodation-like mechanism, although this was not the case in his theory's first incarnation (van der Sandt 1982). Also note that for Heim's analogy between cancellation and accommodation theories to really drive home it is important that in the cancellation account it is assumed that presuppositions are also part of the asserted content, which, as elaborated above, is a reasonable assumption. Entailment of presuppositions is what produces the effect of local accommodation in cases where the presupposition is globally cancelled.

5.9.2 The Transformation from Russell to van der Sandt

Now let us consider a very different type of theory, the neo-Russellian account discussed earlier. Recall that the essential idea of this theory was that alternative presuppositional readings are obtained only as a result of variations in logical scope, or, put another way, as a result of variations in logical form. Strangely, these scopal variations are mirrored by the alternative accommodation readings in van der Sandt's theory, save that Russell's logical forms happened to be expressed in FOPL, whereas van der Sandt's are expressed in the language of DRT. Russell gave few hints as to how his logical forms should be derived, and I see no obvious reason why a Russellian theory of scopal variation should not be developed where scope bearing operators are initially interpreted *in situ* to produce a first logical form, and are then moved about to produce the final logical form in a manner reminiscent of the semantic *move-α* operations of van der Sandt's theory. Thus we see that the transformation from Russell to van der Sandt is surprisingly small. For instance, as regards sentences like E39a, repeated

below, the neo-Russellian and van der Sandt accounts allow essentially the
same two readings.

E39   a'.   Pooh doesn't realise that Eeyore is sad.

      b'. $[x - \text{sad}(e)](\neg\text{realises}(p, x))$

      c'. $\neg([\text{sad}(e)](\text{realises}(p, x)))$

Corresponding to the neo-Russellian narrow scope negation reading in
E39b' is the following van der Sandtian global accommodation reading:

E39   d.

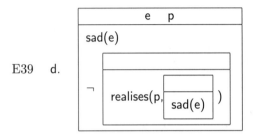

On the other hand the neo-Russellian wide-scope negation reading,
E39c', is analogous to van der Sandt's local accommodation reading:

E39   e.

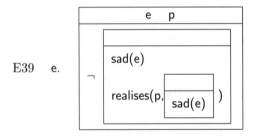

But this is not to deny that van der Sandt's theory incorporates important innovations. First, lack of anaphoricity was mentioned earlier as
being problematic in a purely Russellian account (§1.6, p.25), but van der
Sandt's account includes not only an accommodation component, but also
an anaphoric resolution component completely alien to the Russellian picture of definites. Second, van der Sandt not only allows for presuppositional elements to take different *scopes*, he also provides an account of
which scopes are to be preferred, and this is again something absent from
the Russellian account. Third, and specifically as a result of being situated
in DRT, van der Sandt's model allows for extra possibilities which would
not be available to Russell. For instance, a presupposition α triggered in
the consequent of a conditional may, in van der Sandt's theory, eventually
make its way to the antecedent of the conditional. Such a transformation

would make no sense on the Russellian picture, since an element in the antecedent of a conditional could classically not bind material in the consequent. But are these *extra scopes* in van der Sandt's theory a good or a bad thing? Above I suggested that intermediate accommodation into the antecedent of a conditional or restrictor produced problematic results, so that van der Sandt's theory might actually improve its descriptive coverage by sticking to purely Russellian scopes.

5.9.3   Accommodation as a Journey through Mental Space

Fauconnier (1985) presents a representationalist theory in which meanings are rendered in a structured collection of interconnected *mental spaces*. Mental spaces are akin to Kamp's DRS boxes (or, perhaps even more aptly, Seuren's *discourse domains*). A few remarks should clarify the similarity with DRT:

1. Like DRS boxes, mental spaces can be seen as partial models in which a set of discourse entities bear certain properties and relations to each other, but in which the extensions of many other properties and relations are left undecided.

2. Like DRS boxes, mental spaces are arranged hierarchically, with some boxes being seen as subordinate to others. Properties of objects in subordinate *daughter* spaces may be inherited from their *parent* spaces. However, the links between entities in different spaces are not sustained by variable binding, but by a Lewisian counterpart relation. The inter-space links between entities are analogous to the connections between discourse markers in later versions of DRT (Kamp and Reyle 1993) where objects in intensional contexts are linked to objects outside by *anchoring* functions, these determining which objects are counterparts of which others.

3. Unlike Kamp, Fauconnier does not follow the Montagovian method of fragments. He does not provide a fully formalised method of constructing mental spaces for all the strings produced by a generative grammar.

4. Unlike in DRT, no semantic interpretation or Tarski truth definition is given for mental spaces, and no notion of logical consequence between mental spaces is defined.

5. Fauconnier considers a wide range of syntactic constructions and complications of the interpretation process which have so far eluded DRT. For instance, he discusses the special semantic environment set up by descriptions of pictures or the painting of pictures (sentences like

'In this picture, Kamp and Fauconnier have been painted as the same person') and cases of *perspective shift*, more commonly dealt with in literary theory than in generative linguistics.

In order to see what Fauconnier's theory of presupposition (Fauconnier 1985, pp. 86–87) would look like in a van der Sandtian setting, let us assume that a space is just a DRT box (i.e. a set of discourse markers and a set of conditions), and assume a DRT-like notion of accessibility. Let us say that a proposition is *validated* in a space if it is a consequence of the conditions in that space, and that a proposition is *accessible* from a space if it is a consequence of propositions in accessible (i.e. superordinate) spaces, and let us assume a standard logical definition of *consistency* of a space, meaning consistency of the set of conditions in that space.[21]   In certain cases (generally non-intensional contexts) Fauconnier also employs a notion of *compatibility*, meaning consistency of the set of conditions either in the space or accessible from it. Fauconnier's theory of presupposition can be described as a theory of presupposition flotation, whereby locally triggered presuppositions float up through as many spaces as they can without creating inconsistency.[22] I would characterise the theory as follows:

1. Presuppositions must be validated in the local space of the trigger.

2. If a presupposition is accessible, then nothing further need be done.

3. Otherwise, the presupposition is accommodated into successively more global spaces along the accessibility path, until reaching the highest space where accommodation does not create inconsistency at the accommodation site, or incompatibility of any (non-intensional) subordinate space.[23]

---

[21]The relation *validates* corresponds to Fauconnier's *satisfaction*, but I refrain from using this term here since I have tended to use it elsewhere with a slightly different meaning. For Fauconnier, *satisfaction of a proposition* means that the propositions in the local context entail the proposition, whereas my use means roughly that all the accessible conditions taken together entail the proposition. For exegetical purposes, I have also been rather cavalier with Fauconnier's notion of *accessibility* of a proposition. I have assumed that propositions in all superordinate spaces are accessible, but Fauconnier is interested in a wide variety of intensional contexts such that (consequences of) propositions holding in parent spaces cannot in general be expected to hold locally. The approximation will suffice at least for treatment of logical connectives (provided counterfactuality is not involved).

[22]The flotation metaphor is used by Fauconnier himself. Coincidentally, the same evocative picture is chosen by Geurts (1994; 1999) in a discussion of a *van der Sandtian* accommodation strategy, and it surfaces once more in Geurts (2000). After reading the surreal discussion by Link (1986), some may find it hard to take flotation seriously.

[23]I take the *incompatibility* requirement from Fauconnier's discussion of conflicting presuppositions in disjunctions (Fauconnier 1985, p.92).

It is readily seen that, at least in the van der Sandtian form that I have presented it, Fauconnier's model will make predictions comparable to some of the other models that have been discussed in this chapter. The first clause means that in a sense Fauconnier always locally accommodates, whatever else he does. This produces the effect that in a cancellation account would be derived by assuming presuppositions to be part of the asserted content.[24] The second clause provides for something like van der Sandt's anaphoric resolution of presuppositions. In most cases this will presumably yield filtering of entailed presuppositions as in Karttunen's '73 model. The third clause prevents global accommodation where that would produce inconsistency, thus giving the effect of a cancellation theory in cases of presupposition denial.

There is one important respect in which the version of Fauconnier's theory above makes different predictions from van der Sandt's. Under Fauconnier's accommodation strategy as a presupposition floats upwards, it leaves a shadow behind (i.e. a copy of the presupposition) in every space through which it passes. But van der Sandt's strategy depicts presuppositions as bubbling up without leaving any trace of their journey. In fact Zeevat has compared an accommodation strategy just like Fauconnier's to van der Sandt's, although Zeevat attributes what I call Fauconnier's strategy to Heim. Distinguishing the two strategies Zeevat (1992, p.396) says: "The one remaining difference [i.e. between his version of van der Sandt's theory and his version of Heim's theory] is the question whether we should add the presupposition everywhere between the position of the trigger and the highest position where it can be accommodated, or whether we can be satisfied with adding it just once at that position." So which is the right strategy? Zeevat comes to an interesting conclusion: both are right, but for different classes of presupposition trigger. The two classes Zeevat delimits are what he calls *anaphoric* and *lexical* presuppositions. The anaphoric (or *resolution*) triggers are those "whose primary function is — like anaphora — to collect entities from the environment in order to say new things about them." (Zeevat 1992, p.397) This class, which presumably at least includes definite noun phrases, and discourse particles like *too* and *again*, is the one for which Zeevat supposes the van der Sandtian strategy to be appropriate. The following data back up his point:

E164   a.   Bill called Mary a Republican. And it is clear from Mary's diary that John insulted her too.

---

[24]In a section entitled "Presupposition Transfer" (Fauconnier 1985, pp. 105–108), Fauconnier also discusses cases where a presupposition need not be validated in the local space of its trigger. For example, he discusses the sentence 'Hey, In this painting Gudule is beautiful again.' He allows that that the sentence may be interpreted in a context where Gudule in reality was once beautiful, but is no longer, without committing the speaker to a proposition like 'In the painting Gudule was once beautiful.'

b. It is clear from Mary's diary that Bill insulted her.

E165 a. Bill called Mary a Republican. And it is clear from Mary's diary that Bill thinks that John insulted her too.

b. It is clear from Mary's diary that Bill insulted her.

c. It is clear from Mary's diary that Bill thinks he insulted her.

In Zeevat's terms, the *too* in E164a and E165a is used because the speaker is collecting up a property which he takes to already be realised in the context, the property of insulting Mary, and saying something new about the extension of that property. I would say that on hearing either E164a or E165a a hearer would normally conclude that the speaker thinks that Bill insulted Mary, presumably in the act of calling her a Republican. So it would seem that 'Bill insulted Mary' — or the proposition that the event of Bill calling Mary a Republican is identical to an event of Bill insulting Mary — is globally accommodated. But (and I hope readers can convince themselves of this) I do not think that on the basis of E164a a hearer would conclude that the speaker believes E164b. This is just what would be predicted on van der Sandt's strategy, since the local context to the trigger, the mental space set aside for what is clear in Mary's diary, would not need to contain the presupposition. Similarly, I do not think a hearer of E165a would normally infer that the speaker believes either of E165b or E165c, although these propositions are certainly compatible with what the speaker has said. Thus the presupposition arguably skips over both the space assigned to what Bill thinks in Mary's diary, and the space assigned to what is clear in Mary's diary, just as van der Sandt predicts. On the other hand, on Fauconnier's strategy both E165b and E165c would be inferred.

The *lexical triggers* are those where the presupposition is a condition on the application of a concept, so that the presupposition must hold in any context where the trigger is applied if the application of the concept is to be meaningful. Factive verbs are presumably in this class. From the definition of lexical triggers, we can see that the presupposition should be expected to hold not only at the highest accommodation site, but also locally. Zeevat goes further in requiring lexical presuppositions to hold Fauconnier fashion in all the intermediary contexts, but the following examples perhaps provide some support for this analysis:

E166 a. Bill called Mary a Republican. And it is clear from Mary's diary that she realised that he had insulted her.

b. It is clear from Mary's diary that Bill insulted her.

E167 a. Bill called Mary a Republican. And it is clear from Mary's diary that Bill thinks she realised that he had insulted her.

b.   It is clear from Mary's diary that Bill insulted her.

c.   It is clear from Mary's diary that Bill thinks he insulted her.

That E166b follows from E166a seems indisputable. E167a is obviously a more complicated case, and requires considerably more effort to comprehend. But my feeling is that both E167b and E167c do follow from it, in accordance with Zeevat's prediction that the Fauconnier (or Heim) algorithm is appropriate in this case.[25]

Whilst I have adduced some support for Zeevat's distinction and his choice of accommodation strategies, the data is not clear cut, and there is clearly room for more research on the issue.[26] My aim was not in fact to argue for the distinction *per se*, but to demonstrate that a rather promising vista is opened up when we start comparing different theories in terms of the alternative accommodation strategies they manifest. In turn this suggests that we should strive for a better technical understanding of what accommodation is, and that is one of the main goals of this monograph.[27]

5.10 Accommodation and Projection

What is the relationship between *accommodation* and *projection*? As mentioned in §5.9.1, one could view projection as global accommodation. However, in a theory like Heim's or van der Sandt's, presuppositions play an

[25]Cases like E167 constitute counterexamples not only to van der Sandt's theory, but to any theory where accommodation occurs at only one site. As discussed above, all the cancellation and filtering theories can be thought of as falling into this class. The problem will typically occur whenever a lexical presupposition is embedded under an operator which is itself embedded in an intensional context. For instance, 'Fred thinks Mary doesn't know that she won' involves the lexical presupposition trigger 'know' embedded under a negation operator itself embedded under 'thinks'. The example suggests not only that Mary won, which is predicted by cancellation theories, but also that Fred thinks she won, which is not predicted by these accounts.

[26]For this reason, I will follow the bulk of the presupposition literature in not distinguishing between Zeevat's two classes of presupposition in the main body of this book. But I do believe that the theory to be developed would be compatible with making such a distinction, or indeed further distinctions amongst presuppositional constructions. Goldberg *et al.* (1990) motivate a division between what they term *external* and *internal* presuppositions, the idea being that external presuppositions hold in the model, but internal presuppositions need only be satisfied in the discourse context. At least at a schematic level, it seems natural to equate their term *external* with Zeevat's *lexical*, and their *internal* with Zeevat's *resolution*, although I will not pursue this line any further here.

[27]Other theories of presupposition that compare with van der Sandt's in much the same way as Fauconnier's are Dinsmore (1981; 1992), and Schiebe (1979).   Like the theories of van der Sandt and Fauconnier, these accounts are explicitly procedural, and explicitly representational. Note that although Schiebe talks of worlds of evaluation, one of his uses of the term *world* is akin to Fauconnier's term *mental space*.

important role in determining meaning even if there is no global accommodation. Contemporary presupposition theorists are concerned not merely with whether a presupposition is projected, but also with what happens to the presupposition if it is not projected. Furthermore, it need not be assumed that what is accommodated corresponds directly to an elementary presupposition, and neither Heim's account, nor that to be developed in the second part of this book, require such a correspondence. In van der Sandt's account, resolution of presuppositions with a partially matching antecedent is accompanied by some accommodation of information, but the conditions added, which include equality conditions to bind the presupposition to its antecedent, need not be strictly part of the elementary presupposition. If it is not elementary presuppositions which are accommodated, but something else, then it is hard to see how we could determine when it is appropriate to say that an elementary presupposition has been projected. Perhaps it should be recognised that Langendoen and Savin's *projection problem*, as usually conceived, has outlived its usefulness?

Part II

The Assertion:
What Comes First in
Dynamic Semantics

Overview of Part II

In the second part of the monograph I study how the view presupposition should be accounted for in a dynamic model of utterance interpretation. I limit myself to assertive speech acts, and do not make any formal proposals about the interpretation of other types of utterance, such as questions or imperatives.[1] Given this simplifying restriction, utterance meaning may be broken down into two parts, the presupposition and the assertion. The question then arises as to how this dichotomy, between information which a speaker takes as shared and information which a speaker intends to communicate, should be integrated into a theory of meaning.

The last few years have seen a shift of emphasis in the study of semantics. The traditional job of the natural language semanticist involved relating sentences to truth conditions, or to functions from certain contextual parameters to truth conditions. However, much recent work has concentrated on how the process of understanding itself helps to determine the relevant contextual parameters, and thus to determine the truth conditions. To some researchers, truth conditions have become secondary, the primary object of study being the way in which context changes during language processing. In other words, there has been a shift from a static conception of meaning, through a contextually sensitive but still essentially static conception, leading (finally?) to a radically dynamic view. At the same time as this philosophical shift has occurred, there has also been a tendency for semanticists to import formal approaches to modelling dynamics from the discipline of theoretical computer science.

Heim's Context Change Potential (CCP) model of presupposition, which develops ideas of Stalnaker and Karttunen, is a *dynamic* account of meaning *par excellence*, but its genesis preceded recent technical advances in dynamic semantics. In Part Two of the book, I elaborate and defend the CCP model. I show that by taking advantage of recent technical develop-

---

[1] However, in Chapter 10 there is some discussion of extensions of the formal model which would apply to presuppositional phenomena occurring in speech acts of denial.

ments, most of the outstanding problems with that model can be overcome, and I propose a way in which the CCP account of sentence presupposition may be formally combined with an account of the inferential processes which hearers use when determining the assumptions of the speaker. Furthermore, dynamic theories of presupposition, anaphora, quantification and epistemic modality are integrated into a single compositional grammar fragment. The reason for attempting this integration is twofold. First, it is worth providing an integrated theory with wide empirical coverage just to show that this can be done, and thus that the various theories are compatible. Without such integration, the community of researchers in dynamic semantics would be open to the accusation that they shared only an allegiance to jargon, and no deeper common view on the nature of meaning. Second, the essential details of the theory of information underlying the CCP model can be motivated independently of the study of presupposition, and this can only be demonstrated within an integrated theory that incorporates both presupposition and various other dynamic phenomena.

The formal developments take place within the general framework of dynamic semantics which has been laid out by such researchers as van Benthem (1996; 1991), Dekker (1993), Groenendijk and Stokhof (1991b;a), Muskens (1990) and Veltman (1996). In a dynamic semantic account, sentences of formal and natural languages are understood as providing a means of updating the information state of some agent, or as instructions for an agent to use in order to update. Given a simplified formal model of an information state, it is possible to specify exactly which sentences of a precisely defined formal language correspond to which instructions. A notion of logical consequence can then be defined not in terms of truth or falsity of sentences in a model, but in terms of the information which sentences can provide an agent. The relevance of such notions of consequence to natural language may be demonstrated by providing dynamic semantic interpretations for formal languages which form significant fragments of natural language, and showing that the consequence relation accords with empirical data concerning implications between sentences of natural language. This is essentially the path taken in the first four of the six chapters comprising Part II of the book, with the remaining two chapters serving to draw some formal and empirical comparisons with the approaches to presupposition discussed in Part One. Here is a summary of what is to come:

Chapter 6: "Two Birds and One Stone" Some simple (purely propositional) dynamic systems are presented. It is shown how the context sensitivity of epistemic modality can be modelled in a propositional dynamic logic, and how this same system can be adapted to account for presupposition data.

Chapter 7: "A Bit Like English" A dynamic semantics for predication, quantification and anaphora within a first-order language, ABLE, is developed.

Chapter 8: "Presupposition and Modality" The ABLE semantics is further refined. The refinement is shown to solve some difficult problems occurring in the interaction between quantification and modality on the one hand, and quantification and presupposition on the other.

Chapter 9: "Lets Get Real" It is shown how the semantics developed for ABLE can be used as the basis of a compositional analysis of English, within a system I refer to as Kinematic Montague Grammar (KMG). It is then demonstrated that an adequate treatment of presupposition accommodation must involve a complex interaction between world knowledge and compositionally derived meaning. A formal model of global accommodation based on an extension to KMG is developed, and it is shown that this model has the potential to account for empirical observations which are problematic for other theories of presupposition.

Chapter 10: "Connections and Directions" Some technical connections are made between the theory developed here and some of those theories described in Part One of the book. These connections are shown to open up some promising directions for further research, suggesting solutions to problems both within the theory developed here and within pre-existing theories of presupposition.

Chapter 11: "Conclusion" Coverage of the model proposed here, as compared with that of other models, is summarised, and a final assertion is made.

6

Two Birds and One Stone

6.1 Introduction

In the first part of this monograph I introduced some of the larger theoretical trends in the study of presupposition, concentrating on accounts of presupposition projection. I have pointed out both strengths and weaknesses of all the major frameworks. What we may conclude is that there are a number of frameworks available which show significant promise, but that all of them require further development in order to best the criticisms I have levelled at them. However, to further advance all of the competing theories in one monograph would be absurd, or at least overambitious for me personally. So I will restrict the remainder of the monograph to a detailed development of just one line of inquiry, namely the Context Change model proceeding from the ideas of Stalnaker, Karttunen and Heim.

A number of considerations introduced in the first part of this book motivate my choice of the Context Change account for the remainder, including asymmetric projection from connectives, conditional presuppositions, and failures resulting from cancellation or intermediate accommodation. But I have two additional motivations which are of a more general nature, concerning the relationship between presupposition and other phenomena of language, and the relationship between semantics and pragmatics. First, recent technical developments have made it clear to me how the model can be developed into an integrated compositional account of presupposition, anaphora and epistemic modality that lives up to Montagovian standards of rigour. I will present such an account in the coming three chapters. The second additional motivation concerns a longer term goal of mine, namely the development of a satisfactory account of the semantics-pragmatics interface. As I will show in chapter 9, the context change model can provide the basis of a novel account of accommodation, one that suggests a new way of thinking about how communicative content is influenced by common sense reasoning.

In this chapter I will begin my planned integration of different strands of semantic and pragmatic theory, and show how two apparently disparate aspects of natural language meaning, presupposition and epistemic modality, can be tackled using a single, suitably dynamic, theory of information. The chapter reworks and remotivates the dynamic semantic account of presupposition introduced in chapter 4.1, so preparing the reader for some of the more ambitious formal developments in the following two chapters.

Both in this chapter and in the remainder of the book I will focus on two types of presuppositional construction, definites, which I take to include not only definite descriptions but also pronouns and proper names, and *factives*. I will take as paradigmatic examples like the following, containing the attitude verb 'realise', which is factive and is said to presuppose the truth of its propositional complement:

E168   Anna realises that Bertha is hiding.

Whilst I will occasionally mention presuppositional constructions other than definites and factives,[1] the formal theory as such will be limited to just these two. I will not take the raw data to consist of sentences and their presuppositions, and then present a theory which predicts for each sentence its presuppositions. In a sense I will not specifically be addressing

---

[1] Karttunen (1971c) distinguished between two classes of factive verbs, full factives and semifactives. He suggested that whilst both assertions and denials of sentences with matrix factives require the truth of the factive complement, the two subclasses differ in their behaviour when embedded in hypothetical contexts such as conditionals. Supposedly, whereas a full factive which is embedded in a hypothetical context such as the antecedent of a conditional still requires the truth of the factive complement, this is not the case for a semifactive. However, Stalnaker (1974, pp. 207-210) argued convincingly that the source of the differences Karttunen had observed does not reflect an important taxonomic division, and instead suggested a pragmatic explanation for the original data. Stalnaker's point of view seems to have won the day, for later work rarely mentions the distinction. For instance a cursory inspection of the authoritative collection in Oh and Dineen (1979) revealed only one mention of semifactives, that being in a passage in Gazdar's article (pp. 86–87) where he agrees with Stalnaker that Karttunen's distinction is "otiose", and provides a formalisation of Stalnaker's argument (the same passage is found in Gazdar (1979a, pp. 153–154) modulo minor, mostly typographical alterations and a unit decrement of example numbering). Accordingly, I will not distinguish between subclasses of factive verbs. But the reader should be aware that this monograph is not intended to explain the differences that Karttunen observed, and the compositional grammar to be developed will not predict any such differences. Only in Chapter 10 will it be shown formally how the approach developed in the book could be adapted so as to account fully for the defeasibility of presuppositional inferences, this defeasibility lying at the heart of the Stalnaker/Gazdar account of Karttunen's observations. Note further that the observational differences between classes of factive verbs pointed out by Karttunen concerned first-person uses, and to my knowledge have not been observed in third-person uses. Since the examples I will consider are uniformly third person, there is reason to think that Karttunen's observations do not bear on the data to be discussed.

the Projection Problem for Presuppositions. Instead, I will consider that old and familiar projection problem of which presupposition is but a tiny part, namely the problem of predicting the *meanings* of complex sentences in terms of the *meanings* of their parts, or the problem of *compositionality* as it is best known.

I will attempt to follow a long standing tradition of philosophers and semanticists. The data will consist of implications between sentences of natural language, and to account for the data I will define logics which yield these implications as entailments between formulae, combined with a general way of translating from natural language into the logic. An obvious advantage of using implications as the raw data is that it makes perfect sense to talk of a complex discourse having a particular sentence as an implication, whereas, as I have said, there is no test for presuppositions which applies to multiple sentence texts. In summary, the projection problem for presuppositions forms just one part of a much larger projection problem, and not a very clearly defined part. I will address the larger, better defined problem, but in the process the sub-problem, whatever the details of its definition, should be covered.

The special demands that presuppositional constructions place on a compositional theory of meaning have been discussed at length in part I of this monograph. I will now rapidly run through some of the points that have been made with regard to the projection properties of connectives, using examples that I can easily relate to the speculative account of epistemic modality that follows.

First, and most obviously, are the basic projection properties of negation: utterances of either E168 or its negation E169 would tend to imply that Bertha was hiding:

E169 Anna does not realise that Bertha is hiding.

As I have discussed, it is this characteristic behaviour of presuppositions under negation which most clearly marks them out as different from ordinary entailments. For example an utterance of E170 would also lead to the conclusion that Bertha was hiding, but this would not be the case with an utterance of E171. So E170 is said to entail but not presuppose that Bertha is hiding.

E170 Bertha is hiding in the attic.

E171 Bertha is not hiding in the attic.

An utterance of E172, in which a presuppositional construction is embedded in the antecedent of a conditional, would implicate that Bertha was hiding.[2] Similar predictions seem warranted for embedding under the modality 'might', as seen in E173, and for iterative embedding of presuppositional constructions as in E174.

E172 If Anna realises that Bertha is hiding, then she will find her.

E173 Anna might realise that Bertha is hiding.

E174 Bertha regrets that Anna realises that she is hiding.

However, complex sentences do not uniformly preserve the presuppositions of their parts. For instance, an utterance of E175 would not implicate that Bertha was in the attic, in spite of the occurrence of 'Bertha is in the attic' as the complement of a factive verb. Similarly, neither E176 nor E177 seems to implicate that Bertha is hiding at all, although they both involve a factive verb with complement 'Bertha is hiding'.

E175 If Bertha is not in the kitchen, then Anna realises that Bertha is in the attic.

E176 If Bertha is hiding, then Anna realises that Bertha is hiding.

E177 Perhaps Bertha is hiding and Anna realises that Bertha is hiding.

In the remainder of the chapter I will weave backwards and forwards between the topics of presupposition and epistemic modality. Beginning with presupposition, in §6.2 I focus on a problematic methodological issue concerning the Context Change model. In §6.3 I jump to the semantics of epistemic modality, presenting some data and suggesting informally how a dynamic semantics could improve over more traditional static accounts of modality. A formal presentation of a dynamic system appropriate to the treatment of the data in §6.3 is given in §6.4. In §6.5, it is shown that a minor extension to this system provides us with an account of presupposition, and we see how the account fares with the data presented above.

---

[2]Note that the verb 'realise' which is being used in some of these examples is one that Karttunen classed as semifactive. It has been pointed out to me by Gerald Gazdar that differences between factives and semifactives can surface under the types of embedding being considered here, for instance in conditionals. Thus to be sure of the generality of the inference patterns found in these examples one should consider variants with full factives. The reader should verify that substituting ' be glad' (which Karttunen classed as a full factive) for 'realise' does not affect the relevant presuppositionally derived inferences (or, in some cases, absence of them) in any of the examples considered.

6.2 Descriptive versus Explanatory Adequacy

One objection to Karttunen's account was that the CCPs of complex sentences are defined arbitrarily and with no independent motivation. In early formulations the meanings of lexical items included separate specifications of truth conditions and heritage conditions, where by *heritage* conditions I mean the rules which say how presuppositions will be projected.

Consider the Karttunen (1974) definition for the conditional discussed in §4.2, in which the truth conditions are as for material implication and the heritage conditions are given by: " Context X satisfies-the-presuppositions-of 'If A then B' just in case (i) X satisfies-the-presuppositions-of A, and (ii) X [augmented with] A satisfies-the-presuppositions-of B." Since the truth conditions are specified independently of the heritage conditions, it would be possible to imagine a child mistakenly learning the correct truth conditions of the conditional but the wrong heritage conditions.[3] This does not seem plausible, and we would clearly prefer a theory in which the heritage conditions were not specified separately, but somehow derived from the truth conditions and other general principles.

Heim (1983b) attempted to rescue Karttunen's approach by showing how truth conditions could generally be derived from appropriate specifications of Context Change Potential. On this basis she claimed that the CCP model had at least the explanatory adequacy of its competitors, such as Gazdar's theory. However Mats Rooth (as cited by Heim 1990) and Soames (1989) have noted that whilst the correct truth conditions derive from the CCPs for connectives that Heim specifies, this would also be the case for a number of other specifications of the CCP, and some of these alternative specifications would give incorrect heritage conditions. So we could still imagine a child learning CCPs for some connectives that gave the correct truth conditions but incorrect heritage conditions. On this basis Heim (1990) retracted her claim.

It is impossible to justify any claim to explanatory adequacy without some definition of what it is for a theory to be an explanation for some phenomenon, and previous authors on presupposition have tended to take this notion for granted without actually saying what it is. I will not attempt a definition here. But I will assume that at least one factor determining explanatoriness is independent motivation: if phenomenon X and phenomenon Y are detected through independent observations, then a model motivated by phenomenon X alone can be seen as having some explanatory power with regard to phenomenon Y if it predicts Y without substantive addition. Those who are not prepared to accept that this is what is intended by *explanatory* might simply regard the developments in

---

[3]This is similar to the argument of Heim (1983b).

this chapter as developing an analogy between two disparate phenomena, an analogy that hopefully helps us understand the dynamic model that I use to account for those phenomena.

The key observation I wish to make is that work of Veltman (1996) on the semantics of epistemic modal operators relies on a strikingly similar underlying notion of context change to that utilised by Heim. And indeed this is hardly surprising given that both have taken inspiration from the same philosophical well-springs, for instance from the work of Robert Stalnaker and David Lewis.

I will borrow from Veltman's work to show how the context sensitivity of words like 'might' and 'must' motivates a dynamic semantics. None of the alternative CCPs for connectives that have been suggested by Rooth and Soames would be compatible with this semantics, and it is hard to imagine how a relevantly different dynamic semantics could still get the facts right about the meanings of the epistemic modalities.

I will then show how a simple extension to the logic developed in §6.3 — in fact the addition of a single unary operator — produces a system with all the presupposition inheritance properties we would expect of a CCP model. In the process, the connection between presupposition and the epistemic modalities, and also the logic of presupposition itself, will become transparent.

6.3 Hide and Seek with Epistemic Modalities

Imagine the following situation, which is very like an example considered by Veltman (1986). The difference is that he had misplaced his marbles, whereas I have lost a number of women.

- Anna is seeking Bertha, Clothilde and Daisy, and for our benefit she is recording her thoughts on a small portable cassette recorder.

- Anna has searched almost everywhere, and she knows that the only remaining hiding places are the cupboard (which is not in the attic) and the attic (which is not in the cupboard.)

- Only one person fits in the cupboard.

- Anna, having heard some noises, knows that somebody is in the cupboard.

Let us consider what we would expect to find on Anna's tape, restricting our attention to discourses involving interesting mixtures of connectives and epistemic modalities, as they might occur when Anna tells us what she has found out. First, look at the following two examples involving conjunctions, which I take to include sentence sequencing as well as the particle 'and', the word 'perhaps', which I take to mark epistemic possibility, and 'must' which seems to act as a sort of epistemic necessity operator:

E178 Perhaps it is Bertha in the cupboard and ... it is Clothilde in the cupboard. Got you! So Bertha must be in the attic.

E179 ? It is Clothilde in the cupboard and ... perhaps it is Bertha in the cupboard. So Bertha must be in the attic.

It is quite plausible that we might find E178, but by contrast it is hard to imagine an occurrence of the discourse in E179. The reason for this is clear. As Anna learns about where everybody is hiding, she gradually eliminates possibilities. So what is possible at one point may not be possible after the addition of new information. However, the reverse does not hold. So long as Anna has not been in any way deluded, and provided she is suitably cautious in her reasoning process and does not make any unwarranted eliminations of possibilities, then the addition of new information can never increase the number of open possibilities.

The only significant difference between examples E178 and E179 seems to be in the ordering of conjuncts, and this will motivate the definition of an asymmetric conjunction. We will also need to define epistemic operators that are sensitive to the local context of interpretation. Thus the meaning of a sentence 'A and B', or a sequence of sentences 'A. B.', will be expressed as an update with A followed by an update with B. An occurrence of 'perhaps A' at a particular point in a discourse will mean that *at that point in the discourse* the possibility of A remains, and we will take 'must A' to mean that at the phrase's point of occurrence, the possibility of A being false has been excluded.

Next, consider a case involving a conditional:

E180 ? Daisy might be in the cupboard. So if Daisy is not in the cupboard, then she might be in the cupboard.

We could not account for this data by interpreting the conditional as material implication, and taking 'perhaps' and 'must' to be standard, say S5, modal possibility and necessity operators using the same modal accessibility relation. Under such *static* assumptions the consequents of conditionals would be evaluated with respect to the same context (i.e. the same possible world) as the conditionals as a whole. The intuitively invalid argument in E180 would be valid in the standard picture, since if it was possible that Daisy was in the cupboard, then any conditional with an expression of this possibility in the consequent would be true.[4]

---

[4] I mention S5 merely as an example. In fact, the data given here are not predicted by any of the logics in the standard modal hierarchy, such as K, T or S4. The difference

E181   Clothilde is in the attic. Now although Bertha might be hiding in the cupboard, and might be hiding in the attic, I conclude that if Daisy is not hiding in the cupboard then Bertha must be hiding there, and if Daisy is hiding in the cupboard then Bertha must be hiding in the attic.

By contrast E181 is a valid argument, but would appear invalid on the standard picture. Standardly, E181 would come to imply that:

i.   There are accessible worlds where Bertha is in the cupboard,

ii.   There are accessible worlds where Bertha is in the attic,

iii.   Daisy is in the attic implies that Bertha is in the cupboard in all accessible worlds,

iv.   Daisy is in the cupboard implies that Bertha is in the attic in all accessible worlds.

Suppose that Daisy was in the cupboard. Then (iv) could only be true if Bertha was in the cupboard in all accessible worlds, which contradicts (ii). On the other hand, suppose that Daisy was not in the cupboard. Then (iii) could only be true if Bertha was in the attic in all accessible worlds, which contradicts (i). The relevant cases being thus exhausted, the discourse as a whole would appear logically inconsistent. However, this is at odds with our intuitions, for it seems that E181, although somewhat convoluted, is a perfectly reasonable thing for Anna to say.

---

between examples E178 and E179 is one of ordering. Depending on translation, this may be ordering of conjuncts or ordering of premises in an argument. Either way, the logics K–S5 do not predict a difference, since in these logics permutation of conjunctions and permutation of premises both preserve argument validity or invalidity. As far as E180 is concerned, standard translation into modal logic would produce a valid argument. This is easily seen: translate E180 as having premise ϕ and conclusion $\psi \rightarrow \phi$. This form is classically valid, and remains valid in the all modal logics which are generated from K by addition of axioms. In these logics it is irrelevant to the validity of this inference that the ϕ formula is modalised ('she might be in the cupboard'). Note also that Hintikka's (1962) proposal to translate all sentences as intrinsically epistemic by embedding them under a belief operator has no direct bearing on the issue since it does not introduce any order sensitivity into the logic (two arguments which, like E178 and E179, differ only by permutation are not distinguished) and does not affect the validity of the argument in E180 (since in Hintikka's S4 $B\phi \models B(\psi \rightarrow \phi)$ regardless of whether ϕ is itself a modal statement). Note that Hintikka's motivation for assuming embedding under an extra belief operator arose from *Moore's paradox*, which concerns the oddity of utterances of discourses like 'The cat is on the mat. I don't believe that the cat is on the mat.' Clearly the oddity of such a discourse must be linked to the oddity of 'The cat is on the mat. It might not be on the mat.', which is analogous to the first sentence of E179 (in the special context assumed). However, Moore's paradox does not involve making distinctions between permuted variants like the first sentences of E178 and E179, and thus the literature on Moore's paradox impinges only indirectly on the data analysed here. For recent discussion of Moore's paradox, see e.g. Blok (1993, p.125–128).

Such examples support an analysis of the conditional as an assertion of the consequent under the assumption of the antecedent: this will be stated more formally below. Thus, concerning the conditional in E181, the assumption that Daisy was in the cupboard, would exclude the possibility that she was not there, and the conditional would not be supported by the given assumptions. In E181 whilst Anna is still open to the possibility that Bertha is in the cupboard, under the additional assumption that Daisy is in the cupboard she is prepared to assert that Bertha is not in the cupboard. Similarly, whilst she is open to the possibility that Bertha is in the attic, under the assumption that Daisy is in the attic it would have to be the case — since she would have no other open possibilities — that Bertha is in the cupboard.

I will not discuss the meaning of negation in detail. Suffice it to say that we must define a negation consistent with our picture of an agent gradually eliminating possibilities. It must predict that in a case like E182, when we hear Anna telling us the negation of 'Daisy is in the cupboard', we need no longer consider alternatives where Daisy is in the cupboard. And, considering examples like E183 — I leave the reader to invent some more, or search for counter-examples, according to taste — it should predict that epistemic possibility and necessity behave as logical duals.

E182 ? Daisy is not in the cupboard. Perhaps Daisy is in the cupboard.

E183 Daisy might not be in the cupboard. So it's not the case that Daisy must be in the cupboard.

6.4 Update Logic (UL)

To meet the requirements of the data presented above, I will define a logic along the lines of one presented by Veltman (1986). The significant difference will be syntactic, in that I will allow arbitrarily deep embeddings of the epistemic modalities whereas Veltman prefers to keep his modalities near the surface.

For the moment I will restrict myself to a propositional language defined over some set of atomic formulae, such as the proposition that Bertha is in the cupboard and the proposition that she is in the attic. I will let $\mathcal{P}$ stand for the set of atomic propositions.

Unlike in the Tarskian scheme, where semantics concerns itself with determining the truth or falsity of propositions, the main concern of Update Logic is the potential of a proposition to change an agent's information state. An information state will be identified with the range of open possibilities an agent has with regard to her knowledge of reality. Each open possibility, or *possible world*, will provide a complete picture of reality. To this end a proposition will be identified with a set of possible worlds, intuitively the set of worlds in which the proposition is true, and an information state will be a set of possible worlds.

Definition D20 (Models for UL) A model of UL is a pair $\langle W, F \rangle$ where W is a set of possible worlds and F is an interpretation function mapping propositional constants to sets of worlds.

Definition D21 (Information States in UL) An information state (context) in UL is a subset of W. Thus the minimal information state is W itself, which will also be written $\top$, and the maximal information state is the empty set of worlds, also written $\bot$. Non-maximal information states will be called **consistent**.

Definition D22 (Syntax of UL) The sentences of an Update Logic restricted to the propositions in $\mathcal{P}$ are formed in the usual way from the atomic formulae in $\mathcal{P}$, the unary operators NOT, MIGHT, MUST and the binary connectives AND and IMPLIES. We will use p, q as metavariables over atomic formulae, and ϕ, ψ as metavariables over arbitrary sentences of UL.

The above definitions seem to assume worlds as ontological primitives. However, Veltman's system has a more syntactic flavour, in that worlds are not basic but identified with sets of atomic formulae. To see how a set of atomic formulae can be equated with a possible world think of the atomic formulae in the set as those which are true in that world, and those not in the set as false in that world. Later, when we work through some examples, it will be useful to view worlds in this syntactic light, and the following definition gives a method of constructing the appropriate models:

Definition D23 (Term Models for UL) A term model for UL over the atomic formulae $\mathcal{P}$ is a pair $\langle W, F \rangle$ where W is the powerset of $\mathcal{P}$ and F is a function such that if $p \in \mathcal{P}$ and $w \in W$ then $w \in F(p)$ *iff* $p \in w$.

Now we are in a position to define the semantics of UL. The meaning of an expression ϕ of UL, written $[\![\phi]\!]$ will be defined as a relation, written in infix notation, between two information states, intuitively an input and an output state. In general we should think of this relation as holding between a given pair of states just in case when we are in the first state the new information could leave us in the second state:

Definition D24 (Update) If $\sigma [\![\phi]\!] \tau$ then τ is said to be an **update** of σ with ϕ.

In the following definition all UL formulae will denote relations which are equivalent to total functions on the domain of information states, and I

have diverged superficially from Veltman by specifying the semantics relationally rather than functionally. In this respect, I also differ from Heim
(1983b), as seen in the presentation I gave in chapter 4.1. Heim defines sentential interpretations to to be functional, although her use of restrictions
on definedness means that, unlike in Veltman's work, her context change
potentials are really partial functions. My choice of a relational specification allows encoding of either total or partial functions, and does so without
the complications of partiality — in the coming chapters this facilitates encoding in classical type theory. Hence it also facilitates statement of a
fully compositional fragment without the complications of a partial type
theory.[5]

Definition D25 **(Semantics of UL)** For all models $\mathcal{M}$ and information
states σ, τ, the relation $[\![.]\!]_{UL}^{\mathcal{M}}$ (sub- and super-scripts omitted where unam-
biguous) is given recursively by:

$$
\begin{array}{lll}
\sigma[\![p_{\text{atomic}}]\!]\tau & \textit{iff} & \tau = \{w \in \sigma \mid w \in F(p)\} \\
\sigma[\![\phi \text{ AND } \psi]\!]\tau & \textit{iff} & \exists v \ \sigma[\![\phi]\!]v[\![\psi]\!]\tau \\
\sigma[\![\text{ NOT } \phi]\!]\tau & \textit{iff} & \exists v \ \sigma[\![\phi]\!]v \wedge \tau = \sigma \backslash v \\
\sigma[\![\phi \text{ IMPLIES } \psi]\!]\tau & \textit{iff} & \sigma[\![\text{ NOT } (\phi \text{ AND } (\text{ NOT } \psi))]\!]\tau \\
\sigma[\![\text{MIGHT}\phi]\!]\tau & \textit{iff} & \exists v \ \sigma[\![\phi]\!]v \ \wedge \\
& & \quad (v \neq \perp \rightarrow \tau = \sigma) \ \wedge \\
& & \quad (v = \perp \rightarrow \tau = \perp) \\
\sigma[\![\text{MUST}\phi]\!]\tau & \textit{iff} & \exists v \ \sigma[\![\phi]\!]v \ \wedge \\
& & \quad (v = \sigma \rightarrow \tau = \sigma) \ \wedge \\
& & \quad (v \neq \sigma \rightarrow \tau = \perp)
\end{array}
$$

Let us consider the clauses of definition D25 individually:

(1) Atomic Formulae The base case of the recursion says that to update an information state with an atomic formula, you must remove
all those worlds in that state which are incompatible with the new
proposition, and what remains is the outgoing state.

(2) Conjunction The meaning of a conjunction is defined as a relational
composition between the meanings of the conjuncts. This definition

---

[5]A notational point: iteration of update relations will be allowed, such that $\sigma[\![\phi]\!]\tau[\![\psi]\!]v$
will mean that both $\sigma[\![\phi]\!]\tau$ and $\tau[\![\psi]\!]v$ hold. Note that although this is a common
convention of iteration, for instance being used in statements like "$x \geq y \geq z$", it is not
the only convention used in logic. For example, "$\phi \vee \psi \vee \chi$", although ambiguous, would
never be used to mean "$(\phi \vee \psi) \wedge (\psi \vee \chi)$". Following up on remarks of one referee, I
must make it very clear that the use of this convention does not make the metalanguage
I use in any way *dynamic*: the predicate logical metalanguage is classical and static, and
should hold no surprises to anyone with a basic logical training.

corresponds to the informal analysis above suggesting that to update with a conjunction, you should update with the first conjunct, and then with the second.

(3) Negation This is defined in terms of a set complement operation. We find those worlds in the input state which are compatible with the negated proposition, and the output state is what remains after removing these worlds from the input. Note the similarity to Heimian negation in definition D14.

(4) Implication Implication is defined using a standard equivalence, and it is the fact that a dynamic conjunction is used within that equivalence that gives the implication its dynamic flavour. In particular, the consequent is only evaluated in the context set up by a previous assertion of the antecedent. Again, compare to D14.

(5) Epistemic Possibility There are two cases to be considered in the definition of the MIGHT-operator, which corresponds to Veltman's "might" operator. Either the propositional complement of the MIGHT corresponds to one of the open possibilities in the incoming information state (which is established by attempting to update with the argument and checking that the result is not the absurd state) in which case the outgoing state is identified with the incoming one, or else the complement is already falsified by the incoming state, in which case the result is absurdity.

(6) Epistemic Necessity Again there are two relevant cases. Either adding the complementary proposition would not remove any worlds from the incoming state, in which case the complementary proposition "must" hold in the input state and the outgoing state is again identified with the incoming one, or else the complement would remove some worlds. In this case the complement is not yet established, it is clearly false that the complement "must" be true in the incoming state, and the final result is absurdity.

There are several notions of entailment that can be appropriate to a dynamic logic like UL, and for discussion the reader is referred to Veltman (1996). The definition below says that a sequence of UL premises entails a conclusion just in case the relational composition of the meanings of the premises has in its range only fixed points of the conclusion. In other words, once we have updated any information state with all the premises, updating with the conclusion would add no new information.

Definition D26 (Entailment in UL)

$$\phi_1, \ldots, \phi_n \models \psi \quad \textit{iff} \quad \textit{for all models, } \forall \sigma_0, \ldots, \sigma_n$$

$$\sigma_0[\![\phi_1]\!]\sigma_1[\![\phi_2]\!]\ldots[\![\phi_n]\!]\sigma_n \to \sigma_n[\![\psi]\!]\sigma_n$$

The following clause gives a derivative notion of entailment against a particular background of assumptions:

Definition D27 (Contextual Entailment in UL) If σ is an information state, then:

$$\phi_1, \ldots, \phi_n \models_\sigma \psi \quad \textit{iff} \quad \textit{for all models, } \forall \sigma_1, \ldots, \sigma_n$$
$$\sigma[\![\phi_1]\!]\sigma_1[\![\phi_2]\!]\ldots[\![\phi_n]\!]\sigma_n \to \sigma_n[\![\psi]\!]\sigma_n$$

Examples

We will now consider some simple-minded translations of examples E178 – E183 above. We will confine ourselves to an update language restricted to the six atomic formulae bc, cc, dc, ba, ca and da, which concern who is hiding where. For instance bc is the proposition that Bertha is hiding in the Cupboard, and da is the proposition that Daisy is hiding in the Attic. In the translations below I have ignored the presuppositional component of the it-clefts in some of the examples, and have also ignored the propositional content of 'Got you!'. Further, I have treated discourses of the form 'A. So B.' and 'A. I conclude that B.' as consisting of two parts, an assertion of the content of A, and a *meta-level* assertion that A entails B in the context σ of the given assumptions. In the following discussion, the context σ will correspond to the hide-and-seek situation described at the beginning of §6.3.

First the cases motivating the asymmetric definition of conjunction:

E178 a. Perhaps it is Bertha in the cupboard and ... it is Clothilde in the cupboard. Got you! So Bertha must be in the attic.

     b. MIGHT bc AND cc, (MIGHT bc AND $cc \models_\sigma$ MUST ba)

E179 a. ?It is Clothilde in the cupboard and ... perhaps it is Bertha in the cupboard. So Bertha must be in the attic.

     b. cc AND MIGHT bc, (cc AND MIGHT $bc \models_\sigma$ MUST ba)

In explaining the contrast between these two examples (and also for the discussion of the remaining examples), we will need to consider what would happen to our information state as we heard them playing on Anna's cassette recorder. It will be helpful to construct the relevant information states using the term model over the above six atomic formulae. A world will be a subset of the six atomic propositions, and an information state will be a set of such worlds.

However, since we already know that one person cannot be in two places at once, and that each person is in at least one place, our initial information state need not contain surreal possible worlds like $\{ba, bc, ca, cc\}$, which would depict Bertha and Clothilde as being in both the cupboard and the attic, and Daisy as being nowhere. Furthermore we know that only one person fits in the cupboard, so we can eliminate possible worlds like $\{bc, cc, dc\}$, which would paint a picture of a very crowded cupboard indeed. And one more piece of information: somebody is in the cupboard. The only three possible worlds compatible with all this information are $w_1 = \{ba, ca, dc\}, w_2 = \{ba, cc, da\}$ and $w_3 = \{bc, ca, da\}$, and if we initially have just this information, our information state will be $\{w_1, w_2, w_3\}$.

Now consider the effect of updating this information with the formulae in E178b. The reader should verify that the only possible sequence of information states starting with $\{w_1, w_2, w_3\}$ is:

E178 c. $\{w_1, w_2, w_3\} [\![\text{MIGHT} \, bc]\!] \{w_1, w_2, w_3\} [\![cc]\!] \{w_2\} [\![\text{MUST} \, ba]\!] \{w_2\}$

On the other hand, the only possible sequence of states resulting from an update with the formulae in E179b, and starting from the same initial state is:

E179 c. $\{w_1, w_2, w_3\} [\![cc]\!] \{w_2\} [\![\text{MIGHT} \, bc]\!] \perp [\![\text{MUST} \, ba]\!] \perp$

Thus the oddity of E179 arises because updating a state which does not allow for the possibility of ba with the proposition $\text{MIGHT} \, ba$ yields a contradictory information state.

Regarding the conditionals in E180 and E181, we see that the contextual entailment in the first is not valid, since in the context of $\{w_1, w_2, w_3\}$, $[\![(\text{NOT} \, dc) \, \text{IMPLIES} \, \text{MIGHT} \, dc]\!]$ is not a fixed point, but the contextual entailment in the second is valid since $\{w_1, w_3\}$ is a fixed point of:

$$[\![((\text{NOT} \, dc) \, \text{IMPLIES} \, \text{MUST} \, bc) \, \text{AND} \, (dc \, \text{IMPLIES} \, \text{MUST} \, ba)]\!]$$

E180 a.   ? Daisy might be in the cupboard. So if Daisy is not in the cupboard, then she might be in the cupboard.

      b. $\text{MIGHT} \, dc, \; (\text{MIGHT} \, dc \models_\sigma (\text{NOT} \, dc) \, \text{IMPLIES} \, \text{MIGHT} \, dc)$

      c. $\{w_1, w_2, w_3\} [\![\text{MIGHT} \, dc]\!] \{w_1, w_2, w_3\}$
            $[\![(\text{NOT} \, dc) \, \text{IMPLIES} \, \text{MIGHT} \, dc]\!] \{w_1\}$

E181 a.   Clothilde is in the attic. Now although Bertha might be hiding in the cupboard, and might be hiding in the attic, I conclude that if Daisy is not hiding in the cupboard then Bertha must be hiding there, and if Daisy is hiding in the cupboard then Bertha must be hiding in the attic.

      b. $ca, \; (ca \, \text{AND} \, \text{MIGHT} \, bc \, \text{AND} \, \text{MIGHT} \, ba \models_\sigma$
            $((\text{NOT} \, dc) \, \text{IMPLIES} \, \text{MUST} \, bc) \, \text{AND} \, (dc \, \text{IMPLIES} \, \text{MUST} \, ba))$

c. $\{w_1, w_2, w_3\} \llbracket ca \rrbracket \{w_1, w_3\} \llbracket (\text{MIGHT}\, bc)\ \text{AND MIGHT}\, ba \rrbracket \{w_1, w_3\}$
...$\llbracket ((\text{NOT}\, dc)\ \text{IMPLIES MUST}\, bc)\ \text{AND}\ (dc\ \text{IMPLIES MUST}\, ba) \rrbracket \{w_1, w_3\}$

We have already considered some examples involving negation, so it should by now be clear to the reader why E182 is anomalous. The statement that 'Daisy is not in the cupboard' removes any alternatives in which Daisy was in the cupboard, and the following assertion that there still remains the possibility of Daisy being in the cupboard leads to absurdity.

E182 a.   ? Daisy is not in the cupboard. Perhaps Daisy is in the cupboard.

b.   (NOT dc) AND MIGHT dc

c. $\{w_1, w_2, w_3\} \llbracket$ NOT $dc \rrbracket \{w_2, w_3\} \llbracket\text{MIGHT}\, dc \rrbracket \bot$

However, E183 adds something new to the discussion, since it involves a negation outscoping an epistemic modality:

E183 a.   Daisy might not be in the cupboard. So it's not the case that Daisy must be in the cupboard.

b.   MIGHT NOT dc, (MIGHT NOT $dc \models_\sigma$ NOT MUST dc)

c. $\{w_1, w_2, w_3\} \llbracket\text{MIGHT NOT}\, dc \rrbracket \{w_1, w_2, w_3\}$
$\llbracket$ NOT MUST $dc \rrbracket \{w_1, w_2, w_3\}$

That E183 is consistent follows from the fact that the first and second sentences of E183 translate into equivalent formulae of UL. This, of course, is just one example of a more general equivalence, namely that MIGHT and MUST are logical duals:

Fact 6.1 For any formula ϕ and information states σ , τ:

$$\sigma \llbracket\text{MUST}\phi\rrbracket \tau \quad \textit{iff} \quad \sigma \llbracket \text{NOT}\,(\text{MIGHT}(\,\text{NOT}\,\phi)) \rrbracket \tau$$

Proof: From the definitions of NOT and MIGHT it can be seen that:

$$\sigma \llbracket\text{MIGHT}(\,\text{NOT}\,\phi)\rrbracket \tau \quad \textit{iff} \quad \exists v\ \sigma \llbracket\phi\rrbracket v\ \wedge$$
$$(v \neq \sigma \to \tau = \sigma)\ \wedge$$
$$(v = \sigma \to \tau = \underline{\bot})$$

Using the definition of NOT once more we obtain:

$$\sigma \llbracket \text{NOT}\,(\text{MIGHT}(\,\text{NOT}\,\phi)) \rrbracket \tau \quad \textit{iff} \quad \exists v\ \sigma \llbracket\phi\rrbracket v\ \wedge$$
$$(v \neq \sigma \to \tau = \underline{\bot})\ \wedge$$
$$(v = \sigma \to \tau = \sigma)$$

But this is just the definition of MUST.

To understand how examples like E183 constrain the definition of negation, we need only consider alternative possible definitions which would be consistent with the classical picture of negation, but not preserve the logical duality of the dynamic modal operators. For instance, we could have defined negation by:

Definition D28 (Pointwise Negation)

$$\sigma[\![\natural\phi]\!]\tau \quad \textit{iff} \quad \tau = \{w \in \sigma \mid \{w\}[\![\phi]\!]\bot\}$$

This negation is *pointwise* in that it looks at the individual worlds in the incoming state, and checks which ones are incompatible with the negated proposition. Using such a negation would not have affected examples E178 – E182, since it is easily verified that it is equivalent with the earlier negation provided the negated proposition contains no epistemic modalities. But the entailment in E183 would not have held, since the conclusion would no longer be a fixed point in the context set up by the premise, as is seen from the following sequence of updates:
$\{w_1, w_2, w_3\}[\![\text{MIGHT}\natural dc]\!]\{w_1, w_2, w_3\}[\![\natural\text{MUST}dc]\!]\{w_2, w_3\}$. In fact we would have the unlikely equivalence: $\natural\text{MIGHT}\phi \equiv \natural\text{MUST}\phi \equiv \natural\phi$. The original definition of negation, in which the negated proposition is evaluated with respect to the entire incoming context rather than just its parts, is clearly preferable.

6.5 A Presupposition Operator

The dynamic account above leads to a straightforward characterisation of the CCP notion of presupposition, as introduced in chapter 4.1. A context can only be updated with a sentence if the presuppositions of the sentence are already satisfied in the context. To see this, the reader may like to compare the below definition of admittance with that of "▷" in definition D13, or the below definition of presupposition with that of "≫" in D12.

Definition D29 (Satisfaction) A context σ **satisfies** a formula ϕ *iff* $\models_\sigma \phi$ (or equivalently $\sigma[\![\phi]\!]\sigma$.)

Definition D30 (Admittance) A context σ **admits** (can be updated with) a formula ϕ *iff* there is a context τ such that $\sigma[\![\phi]\!]\tau$.

Definition D31 (Presupposition) A formula ϕ **presupposes** a formula ψ *iff* for all contexts σ, if σ admits ϕ then σ satisfies ψ.

In these terms, the formulae of UL carry no non-trivial presuppositions, since every context can be updated with any formula of UL. This is because the meanings of UL formulae define the equivalent of total functions on the domain of contexts. However, I will now extend UL with a single unary operator which allows us to restrict the incoming contexts for which an update is defined. In the resulting Partial Update Logic (PUL), some formulae will define the equivalent of partial functions on the domain of contexts.

Definition D32 (Models for PUL) As for UL.

Definition D33 (Information States in PUL) As for UL.

Definition D34 (Syntax of PUL) As for UL but with an additional unary operator, ∂, "the presupposition operator".

Definition D35 (Semantics of PUL) As for UL but with the following additional clause:

$$\sigma[\![\partial\phi]\!]\tau \quad \textit{iff} \quad \tau = \sigma \wedge \sigma[\![\phi]\!]\sigma$$

Definition D36 (Entailment and Contextual entailment in PUL) As for UL.

The presupposition operator ∂ is reminiscent of the modal operator MUST defined previously. Given any formula ϕ which itself contains no presuppositions, both $\partial\phi$ and MUSTϕ have the same fixed points as ϕ. That is, for all states σ, if $\sigma[\![\phi]\!]\sigma$ then $\sigma[\![\partial\phi]\!]\sigma$ and $\sigma[\![\text{MUST}\phi]\!]\sigma$. However, the two operators differ with respect to the non-fixed points of ϕ — that is the states σ such that there is a state $\tau \neq \sigma$ for which $\sigma[\![\phi]\!]\tau$. The presupposition operator will not define a transition for such points. That is, if σ is a non-fixed point of ϕ then σ does not *admit* $\partial\phi$. On the other hand, the necessity operator does define a transition for the non-fixed points: for any state σ which is not a fixed point of ϕ, we have that $\sigma[\![\text{MUST}\phi]\!]\bot$. So the ∂-operator is importantly different from the MUST-operator in that all contexts admit MUSTϕ, whereas no consistent context for which updating with MUSTϕ would yield an absurd state admits $\partial\phi$.

I will now show how the presupposition operator can be used to reproduce the CCP treatment of presupposition as it concerns the examples from §6.1. Consider E168a together with the suggested translation in E168b:

E168 a.   Anna realises that Bertha is hiding.

      b. ∂bih AND cb_a_bih

      c. ∂bih AND $cb\_a\_bih \models bih$

I have assumed two atomic formulae in this translation, bih, the proposition that 'Bertha Is Hiding', and cb_a_bih, the proposition that 'Anna' has 'Come-to-Believe' that 'Bertha is Hiding'. The translation is given as a conjunction of the presupposition that Bertha is hiding together with the assertion that Anna has come to believe this. I have used a similar translation scheme for E169:

E169 a.   Anna does not realise that Bertha is hiding.

       b.   NOT $(\partial bih$ AND $cb\_a\_bih)$

       c.   NOT $(\partial bih$ AND $cb\_a\_bih) \models bih$

In these translations I have been intentionally naive with respect to the lexical semantics of 'realises', and I would not wish to defend a general strategy of dividing the meaning of a mentalistic factive verb into one presupposed proposition and one asserted proposition about someone's mental state. The same strategy seems particularly problematic in the case of the verb 'regret', a verb so intrinsically intensional that it is almost impossible to isolate a purely mental component for it in ordinary English. The best I could manage was the strange circumlocution 'negative vibes arising from belief.' But for the moment it will be helpful to assume this division of meaning, as it will make the logical behaviour of presuppositions transparent. In the next chapter I will offer an approach to the lexical semantics of factives which is more abstract, and does not rest upon this assumption.

Crucially, both the entailments in E168c and E169c are valid in Partial Update Logic. If a formula *presupposes* (in the technical sense of definition D31) that Bertha is hiding, then (i) the formula entails that Bertha is hiding, and (ii) the negation of the formula entails that Bertha is hiding. In fact a negated formula always carries precisely the same presuppositions (i.e. the set of propositions which are *presupposed* in the above technical sense) as its positive counterpart. Thus PUL preserves the characteristic behaviour of presuppositions under negation.

Since an understanding of this behaviour is essential to the remainder of the book, I will go though the entailments in E168c and E169c in detail. Given a PUL term model restricted to the two propositions bih and cb_a_bih, information states will be subsets of the following four worlds:

$$A \;=\; \{bih, cb\_a\_bih\}$$
$$B \;=\; \{bih\}$$
$$C \;=\; \{cb\_a\_bih\}$$
$$D \;=\; \emptyset$$

First, let us consider the denotation of the first sub-formula in E168b, ∂bih. From definition D25, the meaning of bih is given by:

$$\sigma[\![bih]\!]\tau \quad \textit{iff} \quad \tau = \{w \in \tau \mid bih \in w\}$$

Definition D35 allows us to calculate from this the denotation of ∂bih:

$$\sigma[\![\partial bih]\!]\tau \quad \textit{iff} \quad \tau = \sigma \ \textit{and} \ \sigma[\![bih]\!]\sigma$$
$$\textit{iff} \quad \tau = \sigma \ \textit{and} \ \forall w \in \sigma \ bih \in w$$

This relation is equivalent to a set of pairs of states, where each state is expressed in terms of the four worlds $A - D$:

$$[\![\partial bih]\!] \quad \equiv \quad \{\langle\{A, B\}, \{A, B\}\rangle, \langle\{A\}, \{A\}\rangle, \langle\{B\}, \{B\}\rangle, \langle\perp, \perp\rangle\}$$

Utilising definition D25 again, we can calculate the denotation of the whole formula:

$$\sigma[\![\partial bih \ \text{AND} \ cb\_a\_bih]\!]\tau \quad \textit{iff} \quad \exists v \ \sigma[\![\partial bih]\!]v[\![cb\_a\_bih]\!]\tau$$
$$\textit{iff} \quad \forall w \in \sigma \ bih \in w \ \textit{and}$$
$$\tau = \{w \in \sigma \mid cb\_a\_bih \in w\}$$

Finally, given the restricted term model, the denotation of E168b can be written out in full as a set of transition pairs:

E168 d. $\{\langle\{A, B\}, \{A\}\rangle, \langle\{A\}, \{A\}\rangle, \langle\{B\}, \perp\rangle, \langle\perp, \perp\rangle\}$

It can be easily verified that the formula in E168b entails both *bih* and *cb_a_bih*, since both of the possible output states (i.e. the right-hand members of the pairs in E168d) $\{A\}$ and $\perp$ are fixed points of *bih* and *cb_a_bih*. Similarly, we can calculate the denotation of the formula in E169b:

$$\sigma[\![\text{NOT} \ (\partial bih \ \text{AND} \ cb\_a\_bih)]\!]\tau \quad \textit{iff} \quad \exists v \ \sigma[\![\partial bih \ \text{AND} \ cb\_a\_bih]\!]v$$
$$\textit{and} \ \tau = \sigma\backslash v$$

The denotation of E169a is expressed as the set of pairs in E169d, below, which shows that the only information states that can result from updating with E169b are $\{B\}$ and $\perp$:

E169 d. $\{\langle\{A, B\}, \{B\}\rangle, \langle\{A\}, \perp\rangle, \langle\{B\}, \{B\}\rangle, \langle\perp, \perp\rangle\}$

The two output states, $\{B\}$ and $\perp$, are once again fixed points of *bih*, so the entailment *bih* is preserved. Indeed, all the possible input states (i.e. the left-hand members of the pairs in E169d) are also fixed points of *bih*, which shows that the formula in E169b *presupposes bih* as well as entailing it. The same holds for E168b — all the possible inputs of the formula are fixed points of *bih*. However, E169b differs from E168b in that the output states of E169b are not fixed points of *cb_a_bih*, but of NOT *cb_a_bih*. Thus E169a is seen to presuppose that Bertha is hiding, and assert that Anna has not come to believe this.

Before proceeding to the remaining examples, a comment is in order about the translations in E168b and E169b. Both of these translations involved an asymmetric conjunction, and derivation of the correct presuppositional behaviour depended crucially on the ordering of the conjuncts. This seems unnatural, for it is not obvious why there should be any preferred ordering of these conjuncts which essentially derive from the lexical semantics of a single verb rather than from any surface ordering of lexical items.

However, it is quite possible to introduce a second, *static* conjunction into PUL:

Definition D37 (Static Conjunction)

$$\sigma[\![\phi \,\&\, \psi]\!]\tau \quad \textit{iff} \quad \exists \rho, \upsilon \; \sigma[\![\phi]\!]\rho \text{ and } \sigma[\![\psi]\!]\upsilon \text{ and } \tau = \upsilon \cap \rho$$

If the dynamic conjunctions in E168b and E169b were replaced with this static conjunction, the same presuppositional behaviour would result, and the ordering of the conjuncts would be irrelevant. With this additional connective, a sensible strategy might be to translate surface occurrences of 'and', 'but' and sentence sequencing in terms of the dynamic conjunction, and to make all other conjunctions static. My reasons for not pursuing this strategy here are pedagogical — one type of conjunction is enough for current purposes.

Let us now consider some more examples from §6.1. The entailments in E172c, E173c and E174c) show that in PUL if a formula contains a presupposed proposition embedded within the antecedent of a conditional, or within an operator of epistemic possibility, or within another presuppositional construction, then the formula as a whole will entail the presupposed proposition. Thus the PUL analysis correctly predicts that all the three examples entail that Bertha is hiding.

In the translations, *awfb* is the proposition that 'Anna Will Find Bertha', and NVB_B_$(\partial\_bih \,\& \, cb\_a\_bih)$ is the proposition that 'Bertha' has 'Negative Vibes' arising from her 'Belief' that Anna realises that Bertha is hiding:

E172 a. If Anna realises that Bertha is hiding, then she will find her.

 b. $(\partial bih \text{ AND } cb\_a\_bih) \text{ IMPLIES } awfb$

 c. $(\partial bih \text{ AND } cb\_a\_bih) \text{ IMPLIES } awfb \models bih$

E173 a. Anna might realise that Bertha is hiding.

 b. MIGHT$(\partial bih \text{ AND } cb\_a\_bih)$

 c. MIGHT$(\partial bih \text{ AND } cb\_a\_bih) \models bih$

E174 a. Bertha regrets that Anna realises that she is hiding.

 b. $\partial(\partial bih \text{ AND } cb\_a\_bih) \text{ AND NVB\_B\_}(\partial\_bih \,\& \, cb\_a\_bih)$

 c. $\partial(\partial bih \text{ AND } cb\_a\_bih) \text{ AND NVB\_B\_}(\partial\_bih \,\& \, cb\_a\_bih) \models$
 $bih \text{ AND } cb\_a\_bih$

As a final illustration of PUL, we consider three examples where an embedded presupposition is not projected. Example E175 shows the standard weak predictions of the CCP model with respect to presuppositions embedded in the consequent of a conditional. As shown in E175c, the conditional in E175a does not entail that Bertha is in the attic. We only have the weaker entailment shown in E175d, that if Bertha is not in the kitchen then she is in the attic. A similar story can be told for E176: the translation in E176b does not entail the embedded presupposition bih. Note that whilst this behaviour seems appropriate for the conditionals in E175a and E176a, as discussed in Part I of this monograph, similar CCP predictions for other conditionals have often been criticised. In chapter 9 it will be shown how this aspect of the CCP model can be defended.

E175   a.   If Bertha is not in the kitchen, then Anna realises that Bertha is in the attic.

      b.   (NOT bc) IMPLIES (∂ba AND cb_a_ba)

      c.   (NOT bc) IMPLIES (∂ba AND cb_a_ba) $\not\models ba$

      d.   (NOT bc) IMPLIES (∂ba AND cb_a_ba) $\models$ (NOT bc) IMPLIES ba

E176   a.   If Bertha is hiding, then Anna realises that Bertha is hiding.

      b. bih IMPLIES (∂bih AND cb_a_bih)

      c. bih IMPLIES (∂bih AND cb_a_bih) $\not\models bih$

Any PUL information state will admit E177b, so that the sentence as a whole carries no presupposition. The reason should by now be familiar. The second clause is evaluated in the context set up by previous evaluation of the first clause. Since updating with the sub-formula bih results in a context containing only worlds in which Bertha is hiding, and since the sub-formula corresponding to the second clause, ∂bih AND cb_a_bih is defined on all such contexts, the whole formula will be admitted by any incoming context. And if a formula is admitted by any context, then it has no presuppositions.

E177   a.   Perhaps Bertha is hiding and Anna realises that Bertha is hiding.

      b.   MIGHT(bih AND ∂bih AND cb_a_bih)

      c.   MIGHT(bih AND ∂bih AND cb_a_bih) $\not\models bih$

6.6   The N-bird Problem

The main aim of this chapter was to provide sufficient introduction to dynamic semantics for the reader to appreciate how that approach may be

applied to presupposition and to other phenomena. Secondarily, I hope to
have shown that, in principle, the theory of interpretation underlying the
CCP model of presupposition can be independently motivated in terms of
extraneous semantic phenomena. I have considered only one of these phenomena, namely the behaviour of epistemic modality. However, the treatment of epistemic modality is far from being the only non-presuppositional
motivation for a dynamic semantics. A far better established motivation
is the treatment of donkey and discourse anaphora, and in the following
chapters I make some attempt at the harder "3-bird" problem, combining
a treatment of presupposition and modality with a Groenendijk & Stokhof-
style treatment of anaphora. An account of presupposition along the lines I
have sketched also has potential for a dynamic treatment of focus, as shown
by Krifka (1992). But the search must continue for the *semanticist's stone*,
that single theory of information with which we could knock any arbitrary
collection of problems in the theory of Natural Language meaning straight
out of the sky.

7

A Bit Like English

7.1 Introduction

The system (ABLE) to be described in this chapter and the next, which will form the basis of the fragment to be defined in Chapter 9, extends the ideas presented in the PUL system in previous chapter. It combines and extends the analysis I gave of presupposition and modality with accounts of predication, quantification and anaphora. ABLE brings together ideas from many sources. The analysis of quantified presuppositions is a further development of that in Beaver (1992), which, like PUL, builds on earlier work of Heim that I described in Chapter 4.1; the theory of anaphora descends from that of Kamp (1981), Heim (1982), Groenendijk and Stokhof (1991b), Dekker (1992); the dynamic approach to quantification is based on the work of Dekker (1992), Chierchia (1992), Groenendijk and Stokhof (1991b;a); and the account of epistemic modality, which extends the Veltman (1996) *might* operator as incorporated in UL and PUL systems of Chapter 6 to the predicate level, arose from collaboration with those of the above who were colleagues of mine at the University of Amsterdam.[1]

I will follow Muskens (1990) in preferring classical type theory over Montague's variant IL as a formalism appropriate to the embedding of dynamic semantics in an otherwise Montagovian theory of meaning. IL is a *designer* logic. Montague's aim was to build a formalism that reflected his Fregean view of meaning, and intertwined ideas from modal logic and type theory so as to reflect that view. Thus the underlying formalism Montague created is inextricably tied to the application Montague had in mind. For that very reason, any attempt to model a qualitatively different account of meaning using IL is fraught with problems. More particularly, in the last decade or so, much effort has gone into theories of meaning which are *partial* and/or *dynamic*, but the theory of meaning Montague had in mind was both *total* and *static*.

---

[1] Thus Dekker, Groenendijk, Stokhof and Veltman.

For this reason, it has been generally recognised that IL was not handed down on stone tablets, and is open to modification or replacement. Thus Muskens (1990) has introduces a variant of type theory to model partiality, and Groenendijk and Stokhof (1991a) utilises a variant of IL developed by Janssen in order to model dynamics. However, I think it is clear that whilst some alternative to IL is required, the needless multiplication of semantic formalisms is to be avoided. Fortunately, one does not have to look far in order to find an existing formalism adequate to my purposes: classical type theory, apart from having a much cleaner logic than IL, is well suited to modelling the dynamics of natural language.

To be more precise, the advantage of classical type theory over IL in the remainder of this book is as follows. I will want to reason formally about information and information states, and possible worlds will be involved in the specification of these states. However, in IL it is difficult to reason explicitly about possible worlds, since *intensional* objects are cloaked by special syntactic restrictions which prevent the use of objects of type s (i.e. possible worlds). In type theory, there is no restriction as to which types can be represented syntactically by constants and variables, and the full apparatus of functional abstraction and application is available over all types. Thus, in type theory, it is possible to be explicit about possible worlds (and other aspects of information states) where in IL one would have to use *ad hoc* and round-about trickery.

This chapter will be taken up with an initial definition of the semantics for a language A Bit Like English, or ABLE. ABLE is a first order language in the tradition of DPL, EDPL and KPL.[2] That is to say, it is a dynamic logic based around a language sufficiently close to English that those with imagination and faith can easily believe that formulae are compositionally derivable from the English sentences they are supposed to represent.

Definition D38 (Syntax of ABLE) Given a set of predicates $\mathcal{P}$ consisting of unary predicates $\mathcal{P}^1$, binary predicates $\mathcal{P}^2$ and attitude predicates $\mathcal{P}^a$, a language $\mathcal{L}_{\text{ABLE}}{}^{\mathcal{P}}$ is given by recursion over the following set of rewrite rules, where all brackets are optional:

$$
\begin{aligned}
dm &\implies 1 \mid 2 \mid \ldots \\
det &\implies \text{SOME} \mid \text{THE} \mid \text{EVERY} \mid \text{NO} \mid \text{MOST} \mid \text{FEW} \mid \text{EXACTLY-ONE} \\
form &\implies \mathcal{P}^1.dm \mid \mathcal{P}^2.dm.dm \mid \mathcal{P}^a.dm.(form) \mid \\
&\quad (dm \text{ IS } dm) \mid (det.dm.form.form) \mid \\
&\quad (form \text{ AND } form) \mid (form \text{ OR } form) \mid (form \text{ IMPLIES } form) \mid
\end{aligned}
$$

---

[2]These abbreviations are for, respectively, the Dynamic Predicate Logic of Groenendijk and Stokhof (1991b), the Eliminative Dynamic Predicate Logic of Dekker (1993), and finally my Kinematic Predicate Logic Beaver (1992).

$$(\text{NOT}\ form)\ |\ (\text{MIGHT}\ form)\ |\ (\text{MUST}\ form)$$

In the following sections of this chapter I will first discuss some general and meta-theoretical considerations, before tackling the various basic components of ABLE one at a time. In Chapter 8 it will be shown how this basic apparatus can be applied to the study of presupposition and epistemic modality. Those who lack imagination or faith will hopefully be appeased by Chapter 9, where it will be shown how ABLE can be utilised in the definition of a compositional grammar fragment.

7.2 Some Metatheory

Throughout Chapters 7–9, classical type theory will play much the same role as IL does in PTQ: it will be the vehicle for the formal expression of meaning. In Chapters 7 and 8 it will be used to specify the semantics of ABLE, and in Chapter 9 it will be used to specify the semantics of a fragment of English. The motivation for having used type theory to give the semantics of ABLE will be made clear in Chapter 9.

Definition D39 **(Three Sorted Type Theory)** Ty_3 is a three sorted type theory along the lines of Gallin's Ty_2[3] Gallin (1975), which itself is a reformulation of Russell's Theory of Types, having the normal apparatus of abstraction, function application, existential and universal quantification over objects of every type, and standard truth functional connectives, as well as a number of distinguished constants to be introduced in the remainder of the book. The symbol ".", which will be used left-associatively, will denote function application.

The types are given by the category TYPE in the following recursion, in which d, e, w and t are, respectively, the types of discourse referents, individuals, possible worlds and truth values:

$$\text{BASIC} \implies d\ |\ e\ |\ w\ |\ t$$
$$\text{TYPE} \implies \text{BASIC}\ |\ \langle \text{TYPE}, \text{TYPE} \rangle$$

Definition D40 **(Models)** A Model $\mathcal{M}$ for Ty_3 is a tuple $\langle W, E, \|.\| \rangle$ where W and E are non-empty. Each type α is associated with a domain $\mathcal{D}_\alpha$, with $\mathcal{D}_w = W$, $\mathcal{D}_d = \mathbb{N}$ (the natural numbers), $\mathcal{D}_e = E$, $\mathcal{D}_t = \{true, false\}$ and domains for the complex types being built up recursively from the basic domains such that for all types α and β, the domain $\mathcal{D}_{\langle \alpha, \beta \rangle}$ is the set of functions from $\mathcal{D}_\alpha$ to $\mathcal{D}_\beta$. The interpretation function $\|.\|$ is a mapping from constants of type α to elements of the domain $\mathcal{D}_\alpha$, with the distinguished

---

[3]Also see Groenendijk and Stokhof (1984) for an application of Ty_2, and yet another motivating discussion.

constants $\top$ and $\bot$ of type t mapped onto *true* and *false* respectively, and any discourse marker i (where i must be in $\mathbb{N}$) mapped to i.

Rather than independently defining models for ABLE, I will simply let Ty$_3$ models also be ABLE models. Using Ty$_3$ models for such a simple language might be felt to be overkill, but will be formally adequate.

ABLE formulae are to be interpreted dynamically, as functions from information states to information states. Following Stalnaker (1979) and Veltman (1996), factual information will be encoded in terms of shrinking sets of possible worlds. At a given point in a conversation the information state of a participant will be partially characterised by a set of worlds, intuitively those worlds which are compatible with everything that has been established up until that point.

A conversational participant must do a certain amount of bookkeeping in order to keep track of what is being talking about. For current purposes it will be assumed that what is being talked about — the topics of conversation — are individuals or groups of individuals, and not, for instance, properties or propositions. Further, as the reader might have expected, it will be assumed that each participant keeps track of the conversation using a set of *discourse markers*. On encountering a new discourse topic, for instance introduced by an indefinite noun phrase, a conversational participant assigns a discourse marker to that topic.

I will take a discourse *referent* or *topic* to be a public entity, something shared by all the conversational participants.[4] By contrast I will treat discourse *markers* as personal record-keeping devices private to each conversational participant. In fact, discourse markers, as the reader may have gathered from the above definition of Ty$_3$ models, will simply be natural numbers. Thus the privacy of discourse markers amounts only to the absence of any assumption that different participants use the same markers.

The relationship between discourse markers and the objects in the model is mediated by what I will call an *extended sequence*, a simple development of the notion of a *sequence* employed by Heim: where no ambiguity is introduced I will used the terms *sequence* and *extended sequence* interchangeably. A Heimian sequence is a partial function from discourse markers to objects.[5] An extended sequence is just a total function from

---

[4]The reader is also referred to Groenendijk *et al.* (1995; 1997) and Dekker (1993; 1997), Dekker and van Rooy (1998) for some indication of how a dynamic semantics lends itself to an account of discourse referents as public objects.

[5]In Heim's work there is some variation as to whether partial or total assignments are used. Heim (1982; 1983b) uses total assignments, but with a distinguished referent to indicate which entities are already in the domain of discourse, whilst Heim (1983a) uses partial assignment functions. Dekker (1993) recognises that using partial assignments could be of technical benefit in defining logics which deal both with anaphora and modality, and so my use of partial assignments could be traced to his work as much as to Heim's.

discourse markers to sets of objects, and this set will be referred to as the *sequence valuation* of the discourse marker by the sequence.

Definition D41 (Extended Sequences) Any object of type $\langle d, \langle e, t \rangle \rangle$ is an extended sequence, and the type of such an object will be abbreviated as σ.

The sequence valuation of an unused marker is the empty set, and other markers are mapped onto singleton or larger sets according to whether they represent one or many objects. Strictly I should not talk of sets of objects, since the standard interpretation of type theory would make these entities functions from individuals to truth values rather than sets, but I find that some things are best understood in terms of functions, and some in terms of sets. So I will continue to talk about sets of this or that, but when I do so I will usually mean not *sets of this or that* but rather *the characteristic function corresponding to a set of this or that*, that is, a function from the domain of *this* or *that* into the domain of truth values. There will be similar latitude in my use of the word relation: commonly what I will refer to as relations between *this* and *that* will be coded up in type theory as functions from *this* into functions from *that* to truth values.

Extended sequences can be equated with the *states* of Groenendijk and Stokhof's (1991a) Dynamic Montague Grammar (DMG) or Muskens' (1990) Logic of Change (LoC), since in these systems the only function of an information state is to keep track of the values of discourse markers. A first difference to note is that in DMG and LoC, *states* are total assignment functions, whereas here extended sequences are to be interpreted as partial assignment functions (i.e. a marker being mapped onto the empty set is interpreted as equivalent to the marker not being in the domain of the function) albeit encoded in a space of total functions. A second significant difference is that in both DMG and LoC states rather than discourse markers are ontologically primary: there is a basic domain of states in the models (type s), and discourse markers are interpreted as functions from states to individuals (type $\langle s, e \rangle$, although in DMG this is the *intensional* type corresponding to a discourse marker, and its *extension* simply has type e).[6]

---

[6]The motivation for states being basic in DMG and LoC does not appear to be philosophical but technical, and stems from consideration of anaphora to objects of types other than that of individuals, although neither DMG nor LoC provides any treatment of non-individual-typed anaphora. If discourse markers are basic, then, in order to keep track of information about high-typed objects in a completely general way, the notion of a state has to be complicated so as to provide mappings from discourse markers to the high-typed domains. Indeed, if we really want the potential to keep track of arbitrarily typed objects, then there will be no single type of state up to the job, since the type hierarchy is infinite but individual types are finite. DMG and LoC utilise a solution suggested by Janssen (1984), which is to assume a basic type of states, and

Some distinguished constants for talking about extended sequences will
now be defined. Note that the Ty$_3$ quantifiers $\forall$ and $\exists$ are taken to outscope
connectives, so that for instance $\exists x\ \phi \wedge \psi$ will mean $\exists x\ (\phi \wedge \psi)$. In case of
ambiguity I will use round brackets to demarcate the scope of quantifiers,
but the scope of lambda abstracts will always be indicated with square
brackets.

Meaning Postulate MP1

$$\odot_\sigma = \lambda D_d \lambda x_e\ [\bot]$$
$$domain_{\langle \sigma, \langle d,t \rangle \rangle} = \lambda f_\sigma \lambda D_d\ [\exists x_e\ f.D.x]$$
$$\succeq_{\langle \sigma, \langle \sigma,t \rangle \rangle} = \lambda f_\sigma \lambda g_\sigma\ [\forall D_d\, domain_{\langle \sigma, \langle d,t \rangle \rangle}.g.D \rightarrow$$
$$g.D = f.D]$$

This meaning postulate, and those that follow, should be thought of as
constraints which Ty$_3$ models should obey if they are to suit the purpose
of defining a semantics for ABLE. Note that whereas meaning postulates
are Ty$_3$ formulae, and Ty$_3$ validity of these formulae constrains Ty$_3$ models, other definitions (which are labelled Dxy rather than MPxy) are not
Ty$_3$ formulae (although they may contain Ty$_3$ formulae). A model which
obeys all the meaning postulates to be given I will call a *suitable* model.
Thus in any suitable model $\odot_\sigma$ is interpreted as the empty sequence, that
is the function mapping every discourse marker onto the empty set of in-
dividuals, and $domain_{\langle \sigma, \langle d,t \rangle \rangle}$ is a function from any sequence onto the set
discourse markers in its domain. Thus we have that $domain.\odot = \lambda D_d\ [\bot]$.
The constant $\succeq_{\langle \sigma, \langle \sigma,t \rangle \rangle}$ can be thought of as a binary relation: using infix
notation, $f \succeq g$ can be read as "f is an extension of g", meaning that for
all discourse markers in the domain of sequence g, the two sequences give

make discourse markers do the work. In order to keep track of objects of some type α,
simply use discourse markers having (intensional) type $\langle s, \alpha \rangle$. The solution is general,
but requires an awkward construction to make sure that there are enough states to
distinguish arbitrarily high typed discourse referents.

One consideration that should be taken into account is the fact that in English not only
individual anaphora, but also kind anaphora, VP anaphora and propositional anaphora
can be mediated by noun-phrases, typically pronominal. Thus the NP 'one' can be
anaphoric to a kind, and the NP 'it' can be anaphoric to a VP (e.g. 'Do it!') or a
proposition (e.g. 'Believe it!'). In order to analyse such anaphora some type shifting
operation might be required for relating properties and propositions to their individual
correlates. And if, at the point of anaphoric resolution, the individual correlate of a
previously mentioned property or proposition is invoked, then why not simply assume
that the anaphoric information concerned the individual correlate all along? Although I
do not claim to present a theory of abstract entity anaphora in this monograph, I think
it possible, and even sensible, to defend an account of anaphoric information in which
no types other than that of individuals (or sets of them) are involved. In this case, the
motivation for making states basic in DMG and LoC would no longer apply.

the same interpretation, but f may also assign values to some additional discourse markers.

Since infix form often makes binary relations more perspicuous, I will adopt the following convention: if $+$ is a binary operation of type $\langle \alpha, \langle \alpha, t \rangle \rangle$, where α is any type except t, and if A and B are of type α, then $A + B$ will be used to mean $+.A.B$. Furthermore, iteration will be allowed, such that if C is also of type α then $+.A.B \wedge +.B.C$ may be abbreviated as $A + B + C$. Sometimes the notation $A\{+\}B\{+\}C$ will be used to show that $+$ is being treated as an infix operator. For the truth-functional connectives in Ty$_3$, as for the ABLE connectives, the standard notational conventions will be assumed, which is the reason for the exceptive clause saying that α cannot be t.

Information states are defined as mappings from possible worlds onto sets of extended sequences. Ignoring for a moment the differences between my definition of an extended sequence and other authors' definitions of sequences, assignments or partial assignments, there remains only a superficial difference between making information states into sets of pairs of worlds and sequences as in Heim's work, or into functions from worlds to sets of extended sequences as here, or into functions from worlds to total assignments as in van Eijck and Cepparello (1994). The additional slight variation on Heim's original notion of a context is of course just a by-product of the use of functional type theory as a meta-language. In fact I will sometimes prefer to talk of a pair of a world w and an extended sequence f being contained in some state I, rather than saying that I maps w to a set containing f, and I will sometimes talk of one such pair being an extension of another, meaning that each pair involves the same possible world, but that the sequence in one pair is an extension of the sequence in the other pair.

Definition D42 **(Information States in ABLE)** Any object of type $\langle w, \langle \sigma, t \rangle \rangle$ is an information state, and the type of such objects will be abbreviated as ι.

It might be of mathematical interest to explore the structure of the space of ABLE information states in detail, but I refrain from doing so here since my intention is to provide only as much formal theory as is necessary for the applications which are to follow.[7] However, I will introduce some constants which make ABLE information easier to manipulate:

Meaning Postulate MP2

$$\cap_{\langle \iota, \langle \iota, \iota \rangle \rangle} = \lambda I_\iota \lambda J_\iota \lambda w_w \lambda f_\sigma \left[I.w.f \wedge J.w.f \right]$$

---

[7]But the reader may wish to refer to the discussion of Dekker (1993), where the algebra of a closely related state space, that of Dekker's EDPL, is examined more fully.

$$\cup_{\langle \iota, \langle \iota, \iota \rangle \rangle} = \lambda I_\iota \lambda J_\iota \lambda w_w \lambda f_\sigma \, [I.w.f \lor J.w.f]$$

$$\backslash_{\langle \iota, \langle \iota, \iota \rangle \rangle} = \lambda I_\iota \lambda J_\iota \lambda w_w \lambda f_\sigma \, [I.w.f \land \neg J.w.f]$$

$$\sqsubseteq_{\langle \iota, \langle \iota, t \rangle \rangle} = \lambda I_\iota \lambda J_\iota \, [\forall w \forall f \, J.w.f \to I.w.f]$$

$$\overline{\top}_\iota = \lambda w_w \lambda f_\sigma \, [f_\sigma = \odot_\sigma]$$

$$\underline{\bot}_\iota = \lambda w_w \lambda f_\sigma \, [\bot]$$

$$\omega\text{-}set_{\langle \iota, \langle w, t \rangle \rangle} = \lambda I_\iota \lambda w_w \, [\exists f_\sigma \, I.w.f]$$

$$p\text{-}domain_{\langle \iota, \langle d, t \rangle \rangle} = \lambda I_\iota \lambda D_d \, [\exists w_w \exists f_\sigma I.w.f \land domain_{\langle \sigma, \langle d, t \rangle \rangle}.f.D]$$

$$t\text{-}domain_{\langle \iota, \langle d, t \rangle \rangle} = \lambda I_\iota \lambda D_d \, [\forall w_w \forall f_\sigma I.w.f \to domain_{\langle \sigma, \langle d, t \rangle \rangle}.f.D]$$

The interpretation of the first four constants, for which infix notation will be used, should be obvious: thinking of states as sets of world-sequence pairs, $\cap$, $\cup$, $\backslash$ and $\sqsubseteq$ are just the standard set-theoretic operators. The constants $\overline{\top}$ and $\underline{\bot}$ represent respectively the *zero* information state, which may be thought of as the established common ground at the beginning of a conversation, and the *absurd* information state, which is reached whenever an information state is updated with contradictory propositions. The function $\omega\text{-}set$ associates with each information state a set of possible worlds, intuitively those worlds which are compatible with all the information up to that point in the discourse. Thus $(\omega\text{-}set.\overline{\top})$ is the set of all possible worlds, and $(\omega\text{-}set.\underline{\bot})$ is the empty set of worlds — for there are no possible worlds that are compatible with contradictory information.

The constants $p\text{-}domain_{\langle \iota, \langle d, t \rangle \rangle}$ and $t\text{-}domain_{\langle \iota, \langle d, t \rangle \rangle}$ are analogues of $domain_{\langle \sigma, \langle d, t \rangle \rangle}$, which was introduced above. Given a state I, $p\text{-}domain.I$ denotes the set of discourse markers which are at least partially defined in I. If D is a discourse marker, then $p\text{-}domain.I.D$ will hold just in case there is some world associated with a sequence which has D in its domain. The total domain of I, the set of discourse markers which have a value in every world-sequence pair in I, is given by $t\text{-}domain.I$. This book will mostly concern itself with totally-defined discourse markers, so that regarding most information states which arise in examples, the partial and total domains will be identical. However, the possibility of partially defined discourse markers do arise.

Following Heim, I will call the denotation of an ABLE formula a *context change potential*:

Definition D43 **(Context Change Potentials)** Any object of type $\langle \iota, \langle \iota, t \rangle \rangle$ is a context change potential (CCP), and the type of such objects will be abbreviated as π.

ABLE formulae are thus relations between information states, and have denotations of the form $\lambda I \lambda J \, [p_t]$. Such expressions have the by now obvious interpretation that λI is an abstraction over possible input states, and λJ over possible outputs.

Definition D44 **(ABLE Update)** If an ABLE formula has denotation F and it holds for some I and J that $I\{F\}J$, we say that in state I the formula provides an *update* to state J.

In fact it will hold that no ABLE formula denotes more than one update from a given input state, but it will be argued that expressions of natural language should be thought of as having such relational meanings, for the ambiguity and underspecificity of natural language often means that there is more than one way in which a given expression could be used to update an information state.

In effect this non-determinism will be built into the translation from natural language into ABLE formulae, so that ABLE could be viewed, to use hackneyed terminology, as a disambiguated language of logical form. However, I have Montagovian pretensions: a type logic is used here, as for Montague, in order to make the business of defining a compositional semantics easier, and not because type theory is claimed to bear any special relationship to any language of mental representation. Similarly, the disambiguated LFs of ABLE are not intended to be thought of as mental representations (although, equally, none of the formal developments here preclude ABLE being thought of in this way). The motivation for putting the non-determinism into the translation function, or more properly the translation *relation*, is methodological. Keeping ABLE denotations deterministic permits the definition of a relatively clean logic over the ABLE language, and thus facilitates the process of turning what I think is the semanticist's primary source of data, namely natural language entailments, into intuitions about how natural language expressions must be translated. So we now turn to the problem of defining a notion of entailment for a language which claims to describe not facts about the world, but information change in agents. Consider a notion of entailment discussed by Veltman (1996):

> A formula entails another if after updating any state with the first, updating with the second adds no new information.

In ABLE, as in Heim's File Change Semantics and Dekker's Eliminative Dynamic Predicate Logic, there are two ways in which information can grow. First, extra constraints can be learnt concerning the interpretation of predicates and whatever discourse markers are in use, and second new discourse markers may be added. It seems that it is the first type of information and not the second which is relevant to our intuitive notion of natural language entailment, as is shown in the following example discourse:[8]

---

[8]This discourse is reminiscent of Partee's *marble* examples.

E184 a.   There are three frogs, and exactly two are in the water.

       b.   Therefore one of the frogs is out of the water.

       c.   Obviously, it is not swimming.

The argument from a to b is valid, since in any world in which the first is true the second will also be true. However, E184b also introduces a new discourse referent. This is shown by considering E184a followed directly by E184c, a strange discourse indeed. It is clear that E184a does not by itself license the pronoun in E184c. However, the full discourse of E184a+b+c is quite natural. Thus E184b augments the context set up by E184a even though E184b is entailed by E184a, and more generally we must conclude that an entailed sentence can introduce certain types of new information.[9] A suitably modified version of Veltman's entailment, which is essentially that used by Groenendijk and Stokhof (1991b) and Dekker (1992), is thus:

> A formula entails another if after updating with the first, up-dating with the second adds no new information except for the possible introduction of new discourse referents.

The formalisation of this notion hinges on the possibility of differentiating between different types of information. The following postulate defines a notion of *closure* with respect to anaphoric potential. The anaphoric closure of a CCP F, written $\downarrow F$, is a purely eliminative CCP: it may remove some of the states in the input, but it will not introduce any new discourse markers. Given states I and J, and a CCP F, the formula $I\{\downarrow F\}J$ will be true if and only if some state K can be obtained by updating I with F, and the output, J, is that subset of the world-sequence pairs in the input, I, which have extensions in K:

Meaning Postulate MP3

$$\downarrow_{\langle \pi,\pi \rangle} \;=\; \lambda F_\pi \lambda I_\iota \lambda J_\iota \; [\exists K_\iota \; I\{F\}K \; \wedge$$
$$J = \lambda w_w \lambda f_\sigma \; [I.w.f \; \wedge \; \exists g_\sigma \; g \succeq f \; \wedge \; K.w.g]]$$

Such a notion of closure does not make sense for arbitrary CCPs. For instance, if a CCP were to denote a *downdate* (a loss of information), such that the w-*set* of the output could be a strict superset of the w-*set* of the input, then the anaphoric closure of the CCP would not preserve

---

[9]It does not matter to the current discussion whether the argument from E184a to E184c is sound. Even if it is not sound, it remains the case that (1) anaphora between premises and conclusions in arguments is possible, and (2) a notion of consequence which fails to take anaphoric information into account is inadequate for modelling argument in natural language.

this property: the anaphoric closure of a CCP always denotes an update, whereby the output ω-*set* is a (not necessarily strict) subset of the input ω-*set*. Thus, to be sure that the notion of anaphoric closure is appropriate to ABLE CCPs, in Appendix A the following fact will be proved:

Fact 7.1 (Eliminativity) For any ABLE formula, ϕ, and states I and J, $I[\![\phi]\!]J$ if and only if J contains only extensions of world-sequence pairs in I.

If updating a context with the closure of some CCP would have no effect, then the context will be said to *satisfy* the CCP:

Meaning Postulate MP4

$$satisfies_{\langle \iota, \langle \pi, t \rangle \rangle} \quad = \quad \lambda I \lambda F \, [I\{\downarrow F\}I]$$

Infix notation will be used for relations between states and CCPs, producing formulae like I *satisfies* F. It is now simple to define a binary relation *entails* which holds between two CCPs just in case any update with the first produces a state which *satisfies* the second, and in terms of this constant to define an entailment relation holding directly between ABLE formulae, as opposed to their denotations.

Meaning Postulate MP5

$$entails_{\langle \pi, \langle \pi, t \rangle \rangle} \quad = \quad \lambda F_\pi \lambda F'_\pi \, [\forall I_\iota \forall J_\iota$$
$$I\{F\}J \rightarrow J \, satisfies \, F']$$

Definition D45 (Entailment in ABLE)

$$\phi \models_{\text{able}} \psi \quad \textit{iff} \quad [\![\phi]\!]\{entails\}[\![\psi]\!] \text{ is valid on}$$
$$\text{the class of suitable models.}$$

This book is largely concerned with the entailments of presupposing formulae, and it is to the notion of presupposition that we now turn. The denotations of ABLE formulae are functions from input states to sets of output states, and there may be some input states which are mapped onto the empty set of output states. For such inputs, the ABLE formula provides no update. Those states for which an ABLE formula does provide an update will be said to *admit* the formula, and in terms of this property *presupposition* is defined. One ABLE formula *presupposes* another when the only states from which the first formula provides an update are those in which the second is satisfied:

Meaning Postulate MP6

$$admits_{\langle \iota, \langle \pi, t \rangle \rangle} \quad = \quad \lambda I_\iota \lambda F_\pi \, [\exists J_\iota \, I\{F\}J]$$
$$presupposes_{\langle \pi, \langle \pi, t \rangle \rangle} \quad = \quad \lambda F \lambda F' \, [\forall I_\iota \, I \, admits \, F \; \rightarrow \; I \, satisfies \, F']$$

Definition D46 (Presupposition) An formula ϕ presupposes a formula ψ if and only if $presupposes_{\langle \pi, \langle \pi, t \rangle \rangle}.[\![\phi]\!].[\![\psi]\!]$ is true in every suitable model.

The ABLE notions of presupposition and entailment are logically independent, in the sense that not all presuppositions of a formula are entailments, and not all entailments are presuppositions. However, for the class of nonmodal formulae (i.e. the sub-language of ABLE not involving MIGHT), the presuppositions of a formula will form a strict subset of the entailments: this is shown in appendix A.

To finish this section I will introduce one last meta-theoretic notion, *consistency*. MP7 says that a state I is *consistent-with* a CCP F just in case it is possible to update I with F and not end up in the absurd information state. A *consistent* formula is just one for which there is some state which it is *consistent-with*.

Meaning Postulate MP7

$$consistent\text{-}with_{\langle \iota, \langle \pi, t \rangle \rangle} = \lambda I_\iota \lambda F_\pi \left[\exists J_\iota \; I\{F\}J \wedge \neg (J = \perp) \right]$$

$$consistent_{\langle \pi, t \rangle} = \lambda F_\pi \left[\exists I_\iota \; consistent\text{-}with_{\langle \pi, \langle \iota, t \rangle \rangle}.I.F \right]$$

Definition D47 (Consistency) An ABLE formula ϕ is **consistent** if and only if $consistent_{\langle \pi, t \rangle}.[\![\phi]\!]$ is true in some suitable model. An ABLE formula ϕ is **consistent with** an information state I if and only if in some suitable model it holds that $consistent\text{-}with_{\langle \pi, \langle \iota, t \rangle \rangle}.[\![\phi]\!].I$.

Having now introduced all the major types of objects to be used, sequences, states and so forth, the presentation can be simplified by ceasing to decorate every variable and constant with its type, and instead using a simple set of typing conventions: these are given in Table 7.1. For all the symbols given in the table, it will be assumed that the same symbol with subscripted numbers or superscripted dashes is of the same type.

The following sections will be concerned with providing a semantics for ABLE formulae. But this semantics will be given only indirectly, via an embedding into the language of Ty_3, the embedding function being denoted $[\![.]\!]$. Not surprisingly, the rules that result will look suspiciously reminiscent of standard semantic definitions.[10] For any ABLE formula ϕ I will refer to the corresponding Ty_3formula $[\![\phi]\!]$ as the semantics of ϕ.

---

[10]Of course, standard semantic definitions are also embeddings of a certain sort, namely embeddings of a formal language into our semantic metalanguage. The only difference here is that the "meta-language" is type theory.

Symbol	Type	Interpretation
d	d	discourse markers
D	d	variables over discourse markers
a, b, c	e	individual constants
x, y, z	e	variables over individuals
A, B, C	ε $= \langle e, t \rangle$	group constants
X, Y, Z	ε	variables over groups
w	w	variables over worlds
f, g, h	σ $= \langle d, \langle e, t \rangle \rangle$	variables over extended sequences
I, J, K	ι $= \langle w, \langle \sigma, t \rangle \rangle$	variables over information states
F	π $= \langle \iota, \langle \iota, t \rangle \rangle$	variables over the denotations of ABLE formulae (CCPs)
$\mathcal{P}$	ρ $= \langle d, \pi \rangle$	variables over dynamic properties
$\mathcal{Q}$	$\langle \rho, \pi \rangle$	variables over dynamic generalised quantifiers

Table 7.1: Types of Meta-variables

7.3 Predication and Identity

What will be presented in this section is not so much a theory of predication as a place for such a theory to go. ABLE predicates will be interpreted directly as higher order constants of Ty3, mapping arguments onto CCPs, and without additional constraints on Ty3 models these CCPs do not reflect any intuitive notion of the information which is given by a predication.

It will be assumed that for every unary ABLE predicate there is a corresponding identically named Ty3 constant which has the type of a function mapping the denotation of an ABLE discourse marker to the denotation of an ABLE formula. Constants of this type will be called *dynamic unary predicates*. ABLE discourse markers correspond directly to Ty3 discourse markers, that is to say objects of type d, and ABLE formulae denote CCPs, which have the type π, so dynamic unary predicates have the type $\langle d, \pi \rangle$. The symbol P^1 will be used as a metavariable over ABLE unary predicates and the corresponding Ty3 dynamic unary predicate constants. Similarly, every binary ABLE predicate (metavariable P^2) will correspond to a *dynamic binary predicate* of type $\langle d, \langle d, \pi \rangle \rangle$, and every ABLE attitude predicate (metavariable P^a) will correspond to a *dynamic attitude predicate* of type $\langle d, \langle \pi, \pi \rangle \rangle$ — a function from discourse markers to a function from the denotation of an ABLE formula to the denotation of an ABLE formula. The clauses for the semantics of ABLE predications are thus trivial, and given by the following schema:

Definition D48 **(Semantics of Predication in ABLE)**

$$
\begin{aligned}
[\![P^1.i]\!] &= P^1.i \\
[\![P^2.i.j]\!] &= P^2.i.j \\
[\![P^a.i.\phi]\!] &= P^a.i.[\![\phi]\!]
\end{aligned}
$$

It is arguable that such a *minimalist* approach to the interpretation of predications leaves a bit too much unsaid, for ABLE predicates are intended in the first place to correspond to the predicates of natural language, and there are many functions in the denotation spaces of the dynamic predicate constants which have no intuitive interpretation in terms of natural language. As things stand, it is possible for an ABLE predication to denote, for example, an information downdate, or the introduction of every prime numbered discourse marker into the context, or perhaps some sort of complement operation leaving only worlds in the ω-*set* of the output which were not in the ω-*set* of the input. To exclude such possibilities I will put some constraints on the denotations of dynamic predicates, although the job of creating particular entries within the remaining denotation space I see as the role of the lexical semanticist, and I will do no more in that respect than give a couple of examples.

The following set of meaning postulates radically restricts the behaviour of ABLE predications by relating the dynamic predicate constants to objects of lower, static types such as might be found in a more conventional Montague grammar. The traditional, Fregean intension of a one place predicate is, of course, a function from worlds to a function from individuals to truth values, which in the current framework would be an object of type $\langle w, \langle e, t \rangle \rangle$. Similarly, the Fregean intension of a two-place predicate can be correlated with a Ty$_3$ object of type $\langle w, \langle e, \langle e, t \rangle \rangle \rangle$. Given that ABLE concerns not only individuals (type e) but also groups of individuals (type ε), it will come as no surprise that in the first of the following clauses dynamic unary predicate constants are related to objects of type $\langle w, \langle \varepsilon, t \rangle \rangle$, whilst in the second clause dynamic binary predicate constants are related to objects of type $\langle w, \langle \varepsilon, \langle \varepsilon, t \rangle \rangle \rangle$. I will call objects of these types static unary predicates and static binary predicates, respectively.

The first postulate says that for every dynamic unary predicate constant there must be some static unary predicate, such that whenever the CCP obtained by application of the constant to a discourse marker provides an update from some input state, the input state must have the discourse marker in its domain, in which case the output state can be calculated in terms of the static predicate.[11] In particular, the output must be the set of world-sequence pairs in the input such that the extension of the static predicate at the world includes the sequence valuation of the discourse marker.

The second postulate follows the first closely, and presumably requires no further explanation. The third postulate concerns dynamic attitude predicates, but it does not simply relate them to Fregean intensions of attitude verbs, the reason being that it is difficult to find a single such postulate appropriate to the needs of both factive and non-factive attitude verbs. Instead, for any given formula which serves as the propositional complement of a dynamic attitude predicate, the combination of the dynamic attitude predicate and the denotation of the formula is related to a static unary predicate. In effect the translations of complete verb phrases involving attitude verbs, like 'realises that she is surrounded' and 'doubts that Shakespeare will ever write another best-seller', are constrained to behave like intransitive verbs. Note the use in the following postulates of the type ε, which is simply an abbreviation for $\langle e, t \rangle$:[12]

---

[11] Note that the formula in the postulate is not strictly a formula of Ty$_3$ but a schema over such formulae, since P^1 is not a constant of Ty$_3$ but a metavariable over dynamic unary predicate constants. Similar comments apply to other meaning postulates.

[12] As noted by one of the referees of this monograph, the implications in MP8 could be strengthened to bi-implications. This seems reasonable, and even desirable, but the one way implications I use are sufficient to establish the properties that follow in the text.

Meaning Postulate MP8

If P^1 is a dynamic unary predicate constant then:

$$\exists V_{\langle w, \langle \varepsilon, t \rangle \rangle} \quad \forall I \forall J \forall D \; I\{P^1.D\}J \rightarrow$$
$$t\text{-}domain.I.D \; \wedge$$
$$J = \lambda w \lambda f \; [I.w.f \wedge V.w.(f.D)]$$

If P^2 is a dynamic binary predicate constant then:

$$\exists V_{\langle w, \langle \varepsilon, \langle \varepsilon, t \rangle \rangle \rangle} \quad \forall I \forall J \forall D \forall D' \; I\{P^2.D.D'\}J \rightarrow$$
$$t\text{-}domain.I.D \wedge t\text{-}domain.I.D' \wedge$$
$$J = \lambda w \lambda f \; [I.w.f \wedge V.w.(f.D).(f.D')]$$

If P^a is a dynamic attitude predicate constant, and F of type π is the denotation of some ABLE formula, then:

$$\exists V_{\langle w, \langle \varepsilon, t \rangle \rangle} \quad \forall I \forall J \forall D \; I\{P^a.D.F\}J \rightarrow$$
$$t\text{-}domain.I.D \wedge$$
$$J = \lambda w \lambda f \; [I.w.f \wedge V.w.(f.D)]$$

On the basis of these postulates some general characteristics of unary and binary ABLE predications can be given. If an ABLE formula ϕ is of the form $P^1.i$ or $P^2.i.j$ then the following will hold:

Partiality There may be some states from which ϕ does not produce an update. For instance ϕ will only provide an update from states which have the discourse markers in ϕ in their domain. That is to say:
$$\exists I \; \neg(I \; admits \; [\![\phi]\!])$$

Determinism ϕ is functional, so that for every input state there is at most one possible output state. Formally:
$$\forall I \forall J (I[\![\phi]\!]J \rightarrow \neg(\exists K I[\![\phi]\!]K \wedge \neg(K = J)))$$

Distributivity An update with ϕ can be calculated pointwise on the individual world-sequence pairs in the input, a property which is discussed by Groenendijk and Stokhof (1990). Thus if $\langle\langle w, f \rangle\rangle$ denotes the *singleton* information state having only one sequence-world pair in it, namely the pair consisting of w and f, then for any states I and J:
$$I[\![\phi]\!]J \rightarrow J = \lambda w \lambda f \; [\exists K \exists w' \exists f' \; I.w'.f' \wedge \langle\langle w', f' \rangle\rangle[\![\phi]\!]K \wedge K.w.f]$$

Eliminativity If $I[\![\phi]\!]J$ then J contains only a subset of the world-sequence pairs in I. This property, which like *distributivity* is discussed by Groenendijk and Stokhof (1990), excludes the possibility of ϕ being a downdate, and also excludes the possibility of ϕ introducing new discourse markers. If I and J are states then:
$$I[\![\phi]\!]J \; iff \; \forall w \forall f \; J.w.f \rightarrow I.w.f$$

Relevance Only the discourse markers mentioned in ϕ are relevant to the calculation of an update with ϕ. More formally, if $I - k$ denoted a state differing from I only by the sequences in I being *shrunk* so as not to give a value to k, then we would have for any states I, J and K:

$$(I[\![\phi]\!]J \wedge (I - k)[\![\phi]\!]K) \rightarrow J = \lambda w \lambda f[I.w.f \wedge \exists g\ f \succeq g \wedge K.w.g]$$

Alpha-invariance The names of the discourse markers in ϕ do not matter, except to the extent that they determine sequence valuations. Let us say that $\phi[i/k]$ denotes the formula obtained by substituting k for i in ϕ, and that $I[i/k]$ denotes the information state obtained by *swapping* the values given to i and k in every sequence in I. Then if k is not mentioned in ϕ and is not in the domain of the state I we would have that for any states I and J:

$$I[\![\phi]\!]J \leftrightarrow I[i/k][\![\phi[i/k]]\!]J[i/k]$$

These six properties could, of course, have been stated as meaning postulates in the first place, and would have replaced the above postulate MP8. However, I have not attempted any proof that this alternative would yield precisely the same denotation space for the dynamic predicate constants.

To illustrate the working of ABLE predication, I will first consider the definition of ABLE predicates MALE^u, FEMALE^u, ANIMATE^u, NEUTER^u, SINGULAR^u and PLURAL^u. We begin with a simple theory about the meaning of the predicates, expressed in terms of simple static predicates:

Meaning Postulate MP9

$$
\begin{aligned}
\forall w \forall x\ male_{\langle \omega, \langle \epsilon, \tau \rangle \rangle}.w.x &\rightarrow \neg female_{\langle \omega, \langle \epsilon, \tau \rangle \rangle}.w.x \\
\forall w \forall x\ female_{\langle \omega, \langle \epsilon, \tau \rangle \rangle}.w.x &\rightarrow \neg male_{\langle \omega, \langle \epsilon, \tau \rangle \rangle}.w.x \\
\forall w \forall x\ \neg(neuter_{\langle \omega, \langle \epsilon, \tau \rangle \rangle}.w.x) &\rightarrow (male_{\langle \omega, \langle \epsilon, \tau \rangle \rangle}.w.x\ \vee \\
&\qquad female_{\langle \omega, \langle \epsilon, \tau \rangle \rangle}.w.x) \\
\forall w \forall x\ male_{\langle \omega, \langle \epsilon, \tau \rangle \rangle}.w.x &\rightarrow animate_{\langle \omega, \langle \epsilon, \tau \rangle \rangle}.w.x \\
\forall w \forall x\ female_{\langle \omega, \langle \epsilon, \tau \rangle \rangle}.w.x &\rightarrow animate_{\langle \omega, \langle \epsilon, \tau \rangle \rangle}.w.x \\
\forall X\ singular_{\langle \epsilon, \tau \rangle}.X &\rightarrow \exists x\ (X.x \wedge \forall y\ (X.y \rightarrow x = y)) \\
\forall X\ plural_{\langle \epsilon, \tau \rangle}.X &\rightarrow \exists x \exists y\ (X.x \wedge X.y \wedge \neg(x = y))
\end{aligned}
$$

I take it that these postulates do not require much explanation, save for noting that I allow objects to be both neuter and sexed. This might be appropriate in the case of animals, for instance, since we can refer to an animal as 'it' even though it has a sex.[13] In the following postulate, dynamic

---

[13] Of course, in many languages it would be completely inappropriate to conflate sex and grammatical gender. For such a language it would be more sensible to class the dis-

unary predicates are defined in terms of the static predicates introduced above. Note that the first postulate defines *distributive* predicates, so that a group of individuals can only be animate if all the members of the group are animate. It would, however, make no sense for the predicates SINGULAR^u and PLURAL^u to be distributive.[14]

Meaning Postulate MP10

If P^1 is one of the dynamic unary predicate constants MALE^u, FEMALE^u, NEUTER^u and ANIMATE^u then:

$$P^1 = \lambda D \lambda I \lambda J \, [t\text{-}domain.I.D \,\wedge$$
$$J = \lambda w \lambda f \, [I.w.f \wedge \forall x \, (f.D.x \to P_{\langle w, \langle \epsilon, \tau \rangle \rangle}.w.x)]]$$

If P^1 is either of the dynamic unary predicate constants SINGULAR^u and PLURAL^u then:

$$P^1 = \lambda D \lambda I \lambda J \, [t\text{-}domain.I.D \,\wedge$$
$$J = \lambda w \lambda f \, [I.w.f \wedge P_{\langle \epsilon, \tau \rangle}.(f.D)]]$$

Identity, although not introduced as one of the predication clauses syntactically, behaves as a two place predicate, and would obey a version of postulate MP8, above. The following semantic clause makes an ABLE identity statement i IS j provide an update only if both discourse markers are in the domain of the input state, in which case the output is the set of world-sequence pairs from the input such that the sequence valuation of the two discourse markers is identical. Note that identity is effectively a *collective* predicate, since the condition for identity of two groups is not that every member of the first group is equal to every member of the second, but that the two groups consist of the same set of individuals.

---

course markers themselves as having gender, number and so on, so that the number and sex of the discourse referents could be irrelevant for the purposes of the grammar. There are several ways in which ABLE could be extended so as to allow for this possibility, for instance by using predicates like *female*$_{\langle d,t \rangle}$ to provide a permanent sortal structure on the domain of discourse markers, or by using predicates like *female*$_{\langle w, \langle d,t \rangle \rangle}$ to make the sortal categorisation of discourse markers contingent; in this case an information state could be updated with the fact that a given discourse marker fell into a particular grammatical category. And of course, mixed strategies are also possible, whereby gender and number of markers is related to sex and number of referents, but this relation is not one-to-one. I will not pursue any of these possibilities any further here since for the fragment of English with which I will be concerned, there is a systematic relation between grammatical and semantic categorisations.

[14]Although plurals are incorporated in the fragment I develop, I make no claim to theoretical innovation with respect to the standard problems of plurality, such as the collective/distributive distinction and how it arises in grammar. The semantic type used for discourse referents allows plurals to have a simple algebraic structure as is standard in the literature, and ABLE would be compatible with further development of the account of plurals along standard lines. For a recent general discussion of plurals and further references, see Lönning (1997). For development of a theory of plurals in a specifically dynamic setting, see van der Berg (1994; 1996).

Definition D49 **(Semantics of Identity in ABLE)**

$$[\![i \text{ IS } j]\!] \;=\; \lambda I \lambda J\, [t\text{-}domain.I.i \wedge t\text{-}domain.I.j \,\wedge$$
$$J = \lambda w \lambda f\, [I.w.f \wedge f.i = f.j]]$$

So far we have only seen ABLE predicates which provide an update on a context whenever the context has the predicated discourse markers in its domain. However, a predicate may involve more complex presuppositions. Presuppositions may be stated as meaning postulates explicitly stating what formulae must be satisfied by the input state of a predication in order for the predication to provide an update. For instance the following postulate would restrict the predicate WALK^u so that it could only apply to markers the values of which were already established to be animate entities:

$$\forall I \forall D\, (\exists J\, I\{\text{WALK}^u.D\}J) \;\leftrightarrow\; I\, \textit{satisfies}\,(\text{ANIMATE}^u.D)$$

Here a selectional restriction on a predicate is encoded as a presupposition. I will not argue the point as to whether all such selectional restrictions may appropriately be considered presuppositional, although, from a technical perspective, it is attractive that we have this option. As indicated earlier, I will concentrate on the presuppositions of factive verbs like those found in all the presuppositional examples considered in the previous chapter of this book, verbs like 'realise' and 'regret'. These may be understood as two place verbs which place selectional restrictions on both arguments: the subject argument must be animate (a restriction which will be ignored), and the object must be a proposition which is satisfied in the local context. To ensure that the corresponding ABLE predicates REGRET^a and REALISE^a have appropriate presuppositional properties, it is simply stipulated that they have the property of *factivity*, defined below:[15]

Definition D50 **(Factivity)** A dynamic attitude predicate denoted by the constant ATT^a is factive if

$$\forall I \forall D \forall F \quad I\, \textit{admits}\, \text{ATT}^a.D.F \;\leftrightarrow$$
$$t\text{-}domain.I.D \,\wedge\, I\, \textit{satisfies}\, F$$

Meaning Postulate MP11 The dynamic attitude predicate constants REGRET^a and REALISE^a are factive.

In what follows, it will often be useful to ignore presupposition altogether. For this purpose a class of distributive, and almost presupposition-free predicates is now introduced:

---

[15]As discussed earlier in footnote 1, I do not divide between factive and semifactive verbs, the evidence which originally motivated Karttunen to make such a distinction being best explained in terms of conversational implicature than in terms of a bifurcation of lexical semantics.

Definition D51 (Simple Predicates)

A dynamic unary predicate denoted by the constant P^u is **simple** if there is a constant P of type $\langle w, \langle e, t \rangle \rangle$ such that:

$$\forall I \forall J \forall D \quad I\{\mathrm{P}^u.D\}J \leftrightarrow$$
$$(t\text{-}domain.I.D \wedge$$
$$J = \lambda w \lambda f \, [I.w.f \wedge \forall x \, (f.D.x \rightarrow P.w.x)])$$

A dynamic binary predicate denoted by the constant P^b is **simple** if there is a constant P of type $\langle w, \langle e, \langle e, t \rangle \rangle \rangle$ such that:

$$\forall I \forall J \forall D \forall D' \quad I\{\mathrm{P}^b.D.D'\}J \leftrightarrow$$
$$(t\text{-}domain.I.D \wedge t\text{-}domain.I.D' \wedge$$
$$J = \lambda w \lambda f \, [I.w.f \wedge$$
$$\forall x \forall y \, ((f.D.x \wedge f.D'.y) \rightarrow P.w.x.y)])$$

The reason for calling the simple predicates *almost* presupposition free is that there remains a presupposition that the predicated discourse markers are in the domain of the input. However, if this condition is met in some input state, then it is clear that the definition of a simple predicate defines what the output is, so a predication involving a simple predicate is guaranteed to provide an update. Note that on the above definition, all the predicates MALE^u, FEMALE^u, ANIMATE^u and NEUTER^u are simple.

In the language PUL introduced in the previous chapter (as in Beaver 1992), the operator ∂ was used to express presuppositions, and the non-logical constants of the language were assumed to be presupposition free. On the other hand, ABLE predicate constants can incorporate presuppositions directly, such that when combined with arguments they produce the relational equivalent of a partial function, so there is no need for a separate presupposition operator. However, as is shown later, the operator could have been incorporated in ABLE and used as the basis of the definition of any ABLE predicate.

The presupposition operator, while helpful in developing intuitions about the logic of presuppositions, has no direct formal (morphological, lexical or syntactic) counterpart in natural language. This is why it is not particularly useful in this chapter or the next, where the goal is to introduce an artificial language that is close to English, and use that artificial language as the basis of a fragment. The decision not to use the presupposition operator is a matter of convenience: adapting a propositional operator to place selectional restrictions on all sub-propositional arguments would expand many of the formulae below without clarifying their meaning.

7.4 Connectives

The definitions of the connectives given below are natural generalisations of those presented in the first part of this book, and furthermore differ little from the definitions found in Dekker (1992) and Beaver (1992), which in turn are close to those of Heim (1983b).

Conjunction is defined as relational composition, and negation is defined as a set complement operation, although the anaphoric closure of the negated formula is taken so as to avoid problems which would be caused by the introduction of discourse markers in the negated formula. Implication is defined using the same standard equivalence as in Chapter 6, and disjunction is also defined using a standard equivalence.

Definition D52 (Semantics of Connectives in ABLE)

$$[\![\phi \text{ AND } \psi]\!] = \lambda I \lambda J \, [\exists K \, I [\![\phi]\!] K [\![\psi]\!] J]$$

$$[\![\text{ NOT } \phi]\!] = \lambda I \lambda J \, [\exists K \, I \downarrow [\![\phi]\!] K \wedge \\ J = I \backslash K]$$

$$[\![\phi \text{ IMPLIES } \psi]\!] = [\![\text{ NOT } (\phi \text{ AND } \text{ NOT } \psi)]\!]$$

$$[\![\phi \text{ OR } \psi]\!] = [\![\text{ NOT } (\text{ NOT } \phi \text{ AND } \text{ NOT } \psi)]\!]$$

7.5 Determiners

The treatment of determiners to be given is related to earlier dynamic accounts such as Heim (1982; 1983a), Chierchia (1992), Groenendijk and Stokhof (1991b;a). I hope I will be able to demonstrate that within a dynamic setting an analysis of determiners is possible which begins to parallel that of Barwise and Cooper (1981) in its uniformity, and yet encompasses a much broader view of meaning than is found in their by now standard account of generalised quantifiers.

Historically we could attribute to Russell (1905) the first serious attempt at a uniform analysis of determiners. But although the tradition of quantificational analysis extending from his work has fared well in the treatment of relatively exotic determiners, it has faced much criticism closer to home, in particular regarding the treatment of the humblest determiners of all, 'the' and 'a'. The two best known philosophical challenges to the uniform quantificational analysis of determiners, namely that of Strawson (1950) with respect to definites, and that of Geach (1962) with respect to the interaction of indefinites and definites, have both been met with non-quantificational solutions in the work of Heim and Kamp in the early eighties. It is not until Groenendijk and Stokhof (1991b), building on the work of Barwise (1987) and Rooth (1987), that the possibility of bringing indefinites back into the quantificational fold — given a suitably broad conception of quantification — became readily apparent. Chierchia (1992) shows a way to extend the approach developed by Groenendijk and Stokhof (1991b;a) to a wider range of determiners, and this monograph is intended to further this line of development, attempting to bring out the similarities between the dynamic analyses not only of indefinites and paradigmatically quantificational determiners, but also of definites.

7.5.1 Indefinites

The semantics of the ABLE determiner SOME will follow the standard dynamic analysis, which holds that the meaning of an indefinite resides in its ability to introduce a new referent into the discourse context. When an indefinite is used in a conversation the speaker may or may not intend to refer to a particular object which he or she has in mind. But regardless of whether the indefinite is being used *specifically* or *non-specifically*, it will not generally be the case that the other conversational participants are able to pinpoint a particular object to which the indefinite refers, and thus each participant's information state must leave the reference of the indefinite phrase underspecified. In fact, given that in this chapter an information state is being conceived of only as a model of the common ground, and that other aspects of a participant's knowledge are being ignored, even the speaker's information state must leave the reference of an indefinite noun-phrase underspecified. The process of updating an information state so as to incorporate an underspecified referent begins with the assignment of a completely underspecified value to a previously unused discourse marker, which is defined in terms of the constants *add* and +:

Meaning Postulate MP12

$$add \;=\; \lambda D \lambda f \lambda g \left[\exists x \; g = \lambda D' \lambda y \left[\begin{array}{l} D' = D \to x = y \;\wedge\; \\ (\neg D' = D) \to f.D'.y \end{array} \right] \right]$$

$$+ \;=\; \lambda D \lambda I \lambda J \left[\neg p\text{-}domain.I.D \;\wedge\; \right.$$
$$\left. J = \lambda w \lambda f \left[\exists g \; I.w.g \;\wedge\; g\{add.D\}f \right] \right]$$

A Ty$_3$-formula $f\{add.i\}g$ says that sequences f and g agree on the values they assign to all discourse markers apart from i, and that g maps i to a set containing one, arbitrary object. The constant + is defined in terms of *add*, and says something similar at the level of information states instead of sequences. A formula $I\{+.i\}J$, "J is an *arbitrary extension* of I with a value for i", means that i is not in the domain of state I, and that any pair of a world and a sequence in J differs from some pair in I only by the sequence being extended with some arbitrary valuation for i.

In ABLE, determiner clauses are of the form *det.dm.form.form*. I will call the discourse marker at the head of such a clause the *determined* marker, and, following standard conventions, I will call the first subformula the *restrictor* and the second the *scope*. The interpretation of a formula SOME.$i.\phi.\psi$ can be thought of procedurally as an instruction to perform the following sequence of modifications to an input state: arbitrarily extend the input with a value for the determined marker, then add first the information in the restrictor, and second the information in the scope. This is captured by the following definition:

Definition D53 (Semantics of SOME— First Version)

$$[\![\text{SOME}.i.\phi.\psi]\!] \quad = \quad \lambda I \lambda J \, [\exists I_{\text{in}} \exists I_{\text{res}} \, I\{+.i\} I_{\text{in}} [\![\phi]\!] I_{\text{res}} [\![\psi]\!] J]$$

In E185 a simple example of an indefinite sentence and its ABLE translation is given. The translation defines (the relational equivalent of) a partial function from input states which give no valuation for the determined marker 1, to output states containing only world-sequence pairs which are defined on 1 and map it onto an individual from the domain which is a walking woman in the given world. The output pairs are thus extensions of elements of that subset of the input pairs involving a world where there is a walking woman.

E185   a.   A woman is walking.

        b.   SOME.1.(WOMAN^u.1).(WALK^u.1)

7.5.2 Definites

Beaver (1992) analyses definite descriptions in a similar way to Heim (1983b). It was assumed that a definite description presupposed the existence of an object which satisfied the description. However, the analysis I will present for the ABLE determiner THE will be closer to the treatment given by Heim (1982). The difference is as follows: in her thesis Heim argues not that a definite presupposes the existence of an object satisfying the description, but that it presupposes there to be a salient discourse marker whose value satisfies the description. Thus a formula THE.$i.$(WOMAN^u.i).(WALK^u.i) will provide an update only from those contexts in which the determined marker is established to refer to a woman.

The analysis has the advantage, as will be seen later, that it can yield a uniform treatment of various sorts of definite noun phrase — the semantics of proper names and pronouns will all be defined in terms of the semantics of THE. On the other hand, there are many uses of definite descriptions for which the analysis given here will be inadequate, for instance when the referent has been introduced but the fact that it satisfies the given description has to be be inferred, or when the referent has not been explicitly introduced but only implicitly made salient by its relevance to other topics of conversation. I believe, in agreement with views expressed by Heim, that such uses of definites should be dealt with by supplementing the theory with an account of *accommodation* — the process whereby a context which does not satisfy the presuppositions of a sentence is adjusted so as to allow update with that sentence. In Chapter 9 I will show how such a mechanism may be formalised.

The following definition restricts input states from which a formula $[\![\text{THE}.i.\phi.\psi]\!]$ provides an update to those which both have the determined marker in their domain and support the proposition in the restrictor. If these conditions are met then the output state is simply the input updated sequentially with the restrictor and the scope.

Definition D54 (Semantics of THE)

$$[\![\text{THE}.i.\phi.\psi]\!] \quad = \quad \lambda I \lambda J \left[t\text{-}domain.I.i \ \wedge \ I \ satisfies \ [\![\phi]\!] \ \wedge \right.$$
$$\exists K \ I [\![\phi]\!] K [\![\psi]\!] J]$$

Examples E186–E188, which provide an inane continuation to E185, illustrate the effects of the above definition:

E186   a.   The woman is talking.

       b.   THE.1.(WOMAN^u.1).(WALKING^u.1)

E187   a.   Butch is barking.

       b.   THE.2.(NAMED-BUTCH^u.2).(BARK^u.2)

E188   a.   She regrets that he is barking.

       b.   THE.1.(FEMALE^u.1 AND SINGULAR^u.1).
                (REGRET^a.1.(THE.2.(MALE^u.2 AND SINGULAR^u.2).(BARK^u.2)))

The scene was set, the reader will recall, by the introduction of a walking woman, for whom a corresponding ABLE discourse marker 1 was introduced. Such a context can be updated with E186b, which provides an update from any input state in which 1 is determined to be a woman, to that subset of input world-sequence pairs in which the referent of 1 is talking. Occurrences of discourse markers outside of the syntactic scope of the quantificational determiner that introduced them, as in E186b, will sometimes be referred to as being *unquantified*. E187b does not provide an update from all possible outputs of the conjunction of E185b and E186b, but only from those in which the unquantified marker 2 is totally defined, and only takes *butch* values. Supposing this condition — which will be turned to in a moment — is met, E187 adds the information that 2 is barking, and thus provides an appropriate input to E188b, which is only defined on contexts in which 1 is female, 2 is a barking male. Of course, this input will only be fully appropriate on the assumption that being named Butch entails masculinity.

Meaning Postulate MP13

NAMED-BUTCH^u is **simple**

$\forall w \forall x \; named\text{-}butch_{\langle \omega, \langle \epsilon, \tau \rangle \rangle}.w.x \rightarrow male_{\langle \omega, \langle \epsilon, \tau \rangle \rangle}.w.x$

Failing the existence of such a postulate, accommodation would be needed, enabling the addition of the information that 2 was male as and when this was presupposed. Accommodation should also provide the answer to the problem of satisfying the presupposition of E187, that the discourse marker 2 corresponded to Butch. However, as will be seen in Chapter 8, even without describing a general mechanism of accommodation, presupposing formulae like E187b can still play an interesting role in the logic of ABLE.

To end this section on definites, here are some obvious abbreviations for ABLE formulae:

$$
\begin{aligned}
\text{SHE}.i.\phi &= \text{THE}.i.(\text{SINGULAR}^u.i \text{ AND FEMALE}^u.i).\phi \\
\text{HE}.i.\phi &= \text{THE}.i.(\text{SINGULAR}^u.i \text{ AND MALE}^u.i).\phi \\
\text{IT}.i.\phi &= \text{THE}.i.(\text{SINGULAR}^u.i \text{ AND NEUTER}^u.i).\phi \\
\text{THEY}.i.\phi &= \text{THE}.i.(\text{PLURAL}^u.i).\phi
\end{aligned}
$$

7.5.3 Dynamic Generalised Quantifiers

According to the standard generalised quantifier analysis of Barwise and Cooper (1981), the quantificational determiners of natural language correspond to binary quantifier relations, a binary quantifier relation being able to combine with some set to produce a generalised quantifier, which is a property of sets. With which sets should the quantifier relations combine? The restrictor and scope of the quantifier appear to be properties of individuals, so that the sets are simply the sets of individuals in the extensions of the properties. But here the classic problem of donkey anaphora arises, as discussed by Geach (1962). Consider the following examples:

E189   a.   Every farmer owns a donkey.

     b.   EVERY.i.
         (FARMER$^u.i$).
         (SOME.j.(DONKEY$^u.j$).(OWNS$^b.i.j$))

E190 a.   Every farmer who owns a donkey beats it.

  b.   EVERY.i.
       (FARMER^u.i AND SOME.j.(DONKEY^u.j).(OWNS^b.i.j)).
       (IT.j.(BEATS^b.i.j))

The generalised quantifier analysis for E189 will be familiar: the quantifier relation corresponding to *every* must hold between the set of farmers and the set of donkey owners. Equally familiar will be the difficulties that the analysis faces with E190. The denotation of the restrictor is obvious — it is just the property of being a farmer who owns a donkey. But the scope does not seem to denote an absolute property: the property of being a *beater of it* must be relativised to some interpretation for the pronoun *it*.

This problem concerns the *internal dynamism* (cf. Groenendijk and Stokhof 1991b) of quantificational constructions, by which is meant the fact that the dynamic effects of updating the input context with the restrictor of a quantifier help determine the context of evaluation for the scope. To begin with I will present an analysis which makes quantifiers internally dynamic, but makes them *externally static*. The final ABLE semantics, however, will make quantifiers both internally and externally dynamic, thus both allowing for internal anaphoric links within the quantificational construction, and allowing whole quantificational constructions to introduce discourse markers so that they may support later anaphoric reference.

To introduce internally dynamic quantifiers, it will be helpful to consider a restricted set of worlds: in this way the relevant information states become more easily visualisable. In figure 7.1 the characteristics of eight individuals (a – h) in four different worlds (W1 – W4) are pictured. It should be clear that in world W2, for instance, one farmer who owns three donkeys beats only one of them, whilst the two other farmers own one donkey each, and in each case beat it. Note that I am also assuming the predicates FARMER^u, DONKEY^u, OWNS^b and BEATS^b to be *simple* (i.e. both presupposition free and distributive) in the sense of §7.3 above, thus allowing the denotation of a predication involving one of these to be calculated in terms of underlying lower typed predicates like $farmer_{\langle w, \langle e, t \rangle \rangle}$: it is the denotation of these lower typed predicates which is pictured in figure 7.1.

Suppose that we wish to update the information state which has only these four worlds in its ω-set, and which has no discourse markers in its domain, with the formula in E190b, the ABLE representation of the classic donkey sentence. We begin the analysis of the universal in the same way as for an indefinite, calculating the effect of introducing the determined marker i into the input context, and then updating with the restrictor followed by the scope. Let us call the information state in which the discourse marker i has been initialised *init*, the state reached after updating with the restrictor

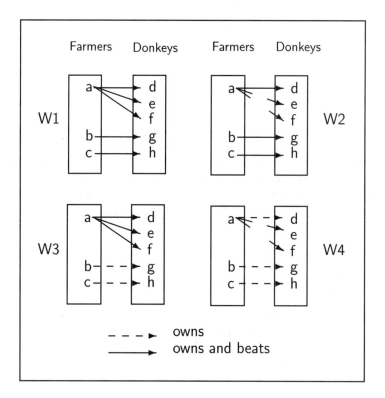

Figure 7.1: Some Worlds

res, and the state reached after updating with the scope *sco*.

Given that, for the moment, it is being assumed that the complete quantificational construction introduces no discourse markers, the output state must contain a subset of the world-sequence pairs in the input, namely all those world-sequence pairs which are compatible with the information in the quantificational formula. To discern whether a given world-sequence pair from the input should be in the output, it is necessary to look at the extensions of that pair in the contexts *res* and *sco*, and check what values the determined discourse marker takes in these extensions.

Let us represent sequences in such a way that, for example, a sequence in which the discourse marker i is mapped onto the single individual a, and the discourse marker j is mapped onto the group containing b and c becomes: $\langle i \mapsto \{a\}, j \mapsto \{b, c\}\rangle$. Thus the example input state, which contains no information about discourse markers, simply consists of the following set of pairs:

$$
\left\{
\begin{array}{ll}
W1 & \langle\rangle \\
W2 & \langle\rangle \\
W3 & \langle\rangle \\
W4 & \langle\rangle
\end{array}
\right\}
$$

The four worlds pictured in figure 7.1 do not vary with respect to the denotation of the underlying predicates *farmer*, *donkey* and *owns*: in each world there are five ways in which i and j can be mapped respectively onto a farmer and a donkey which that farmer owns. This means that update of the input state with the restrictor introduces only five different sequences, so that *res* consists of each of the four worlds paired with each of the five sequences:

$$
\left\{
\begin{array}{ll}
W1 & \langle i \mapsto \{a\}, j \mapsto \{d\}\rangle \\
W1 & \langle i \mapsto \{a\}, j \mapsto \{e\}\rangle \\
W1 & \langle i \mapsto \{a\}, j \mapsto \{f\}\rangle \\
W1 & \langle i \mapsto \{b\}, j \mapsto \{g\}\rangle \\
W1 & \langle i \mapsto \{c\}, j \mapsto \{h\}\rangle \\
W2 & \langle i \mapsto \{a\}, j \mapsto \{d\}\rangle \\
W2 & \langle i \mapsto \{a\}, j \mapsto \{e\}\rangle \\
\vdots & \qquad \vdots
\end{array}
\right\}
$$

For a given world-sequence pair wf from the input and a given *res*, let us call the set of sequences which extend f, and are paired with w in *res*, the *restrictor sequence set* of wf. Formally the restrictor sequence set will be given by the expression: $\lambda h\,[h \succeq f \ \wedge \ res.w.h]$. A similar expression can be used to determine the *scope sequence set* of a given world-sequence pair from the input.

The state *sco*, which includes not only information about farmer-donkey ownership, but also about cruelty to animals, associates different sets of sequences with each world:

$$
\left\{
\begin{array}{ll}
W1 & \langle i \mapsto \{a\}, j \mapsto \{d\}\rangle \\
W1 & \langle i \mapsto \{a\}, j \mapsto \{e\}\rangle \\
W1 & \langle i \mapsto \{a\}, j \mapsto \{f\}\rangle \\
W1 & \langle i \mapsto \{b\}, j \mapsto \{g\}\rangle \\
W1 & \langle i \mapsto \{c\}, j \mapsto \{h\}\rangle \\
W2 & \langle i \mapsto \{a\}, j \mapsto \{d\}\rangle \\
W2 & \langle i \mapsto \{b\}, j \mapsto \{g\}\rangle \\
W2 & \langle i \mapsto \{c\}, j \mapsto \{h\}\rangle \\
W3 & \langle i \mapsto \{a\}, j \mapsto \{d\}\rangle \\
W3 & \langle i \mapsto \{a\}, j \mapsto \{e\}\rangle \\
W3 & \langle i \mapsto \{a\}, j \mapsto \{f\}\rangle
\end{array}
\right\}
$$

Here W1 is the only world which is paired with the same sequences as in *res*, all three farmers being hideously cruel in this world. By contrast, each of W2 and W3 remain paired with only three of the original five sequences, whilst the utopian W4 is no longer even in the ω-*set* of *sco*: there are no beatings in W4.

One way to define internally dynamic quantifiers would be to preserve in the output those world-sequence pairs from the input for which the restrictor sequence set and scope sequence set are satisfied by the given quantifier relation. Thus, in the current example concerning the quantifier *every*, only the pair $W1\langle\rangle$ would be in the output, since this is the only pair for which every extension in *res* is also in *sco*. However, as is shown by Rooth (1987), this sequence counting approach will not work in general. Consider the following simple variation on E190:

E191   a.   Most farmers who own a donkey beat it.

b.   MOST.i.
FARMER^u.i AND (SOME.j.(DONKEY^u.j).(OWNS^b.i.j)).
(IT.j.(BEATS^b.i.j))

Intuitively this sentence should be true only in worlds W1 and W2, since in both of the other worlds less than half of the farmers are malign. However, counting sequences would leave not only W1 and W2 in the output, but also W3. In this world, one farmer happens to own and beat three donkeys whilst the other two farmers do not beat their single donkeys, which means that three out of the five sequences from *res* are preserved in *sco*, and, 3/5 being more than half, this in turn means that the quantifier relation *most* is satisfied. The conclusion to be drawn is that the quantification involves counting farmers and not sequences.

It is easy to calculate the relevant set of individuals from a given restrictor sequence set or scope sequence set. Suppose that for some pair wf the restrictor sequence set is G_{res}, and the determined marker is i. Then the set of values of i in *res* extensions of wf will be: $\lambda x\,[\exists h\,G_{\mathrm{res}}.h \wedge h.i.x]$, and similarly for the scopal values.

In the example we have been looking at, each of the four world-sequence pairs in the input will yield the same set of values for the determined marker in the restrictor, namely the set: $\{a,b,c\}$. The scopal values will of course differ. The input pairs $W1\langle\rangle$ and $W2\langle\rangle$ yield values $\{a,b,c\}$, whilst $W3\langle\rangle$ yields the set $\{a\}$, and $W4\langle\rangle$ yields the empty set. Clearly using these sets will be an improvement in the case of E191, since it will only hold for the pairs $W1\langle\rangle$ and $W2\langle\rangle$ that over half the members from the restrictor extensions are still in the scope extensions.

There are other consequences of the decision to count individuals rather than sequences, to which we will come shortly. First, let us see what the upshot of the above discussion is in terms of a general semantics for internally dynamic quantificational determiners. In the definition below, *init*, *res* and *sco* are assumed to be variables of type ι, and have the same interpretation as in the above discussion. The output state J is obtained by calculating for each wf in the input state the corresponding restrictor and scope sequence sets (G_{res} and G_{sco}, which are each of type $\langle \sigma, t \rangle$), then calculating from these the sets of values taken by the determined marker in the restrictor and the scope (these sets being given by X_{res} and X_{sco}, each of type $\varepsilon = \langle e, t \rangle$), and finally checking whether the relevant underlying quantifier relation holds between two sets. The definition we arrive at is essentially the same as that of Chierchia (1992), although tailored to ABLE's needs:

Definition D55 (Non-existential Determiners — First Version)
If $\mathcal{D}$ is one of EVERY, MOST, FEW or NO, and $\mathcal{D}'$ is a corresponding quantifier relation of type $\langle\langle e, t \rangle, \langle\langle e, t \rangle, t \rangle\rangle$, then:

$$
\llbracket \mathcal{D}.i.\phi.\psi \rrbracket = \lambda I \lambda J
\begin{bmatrix}
\exists init \, \exists res \, \exists sco \\
I\{+.i\} init \llbracket \phi \rrbracket \, res \llbracket \psi \rrbracket \, sco \ \wedge \\[6pt]
J = \lambda w \lambda f \\
\begin{bmatrix}
\exists G_{\text{res}} \, \exists G_{\text{sco}} \, \exists X_{\text{res}} \, \exists X_{\text{sco}} \\
I.w.f \ \wedge \\
G_{\text{res}} = \lambda h \, [h \succeq f \ \wedge \ res.w.h] \ \wedge \\
G_{\text{sco}} = \lambda h \, [h \succeq f \ \wedge \ sco.w.h] \ \wedge \\
X_{\text{res}} = \lambda x \, [\exists h \, G_{\text{res}}.h \wedge h.i.x] \ \wedge \\
X_{\text{sco}} = \lambda x \, [\exists h \, G_{\text{sco}}.h \wedge h.i.x] \ \wedge \\
\mathcal{D}'.X_{\text{res}}.X_{\text{sco}}
\end{bmatrix}
\end{bmatrix}
$$

The following postulate ensures that the underlying quantifier relations have appropriate denotations. The definitions for EVERY' and NO' should be clear. I have made the simplifying assumption that MOST' means *more than half*, and FEW' means *less than half*. The definition for MOST' says that two sets of individuals X and Y stand in the relation MOST' if and only if there is no function with domain $Y \setminus X$ (i.e. the set containing only members of Y that are not in X) and range $X \cap Y$: this implies that the cardinality of $X \cap Y$ is greater than the cardinality of $X \setminus Y$, and thus that more than half of the elements of X are in Y. The definition for FEW' runs along similar lines.

Meaning Postulate MP14

$$
\text{EVERY}' = \lambda X \lambda Y \, [\forall x \, (X.x \rightarrow Y.x)]
$$

$$\text{NO}' \;=\; \lambda X \lambda Y \;[\neg\exists x \;(X.x \wedge Y.x)]$$

$$\text{MOST}' \;=\; \lambda X \lambda Y \;[\neg\exists F_{\langle e,e\rangle}$$
$$\forall x \;((X.x \wedge Y.x) \to \exists y \;(X.y \wedge \neg Y.y \wedge F.y = x))]$$

$$\text{FEW}' \;=\; \lambda X \lambda Y \;[\neg\exists F_{\langle e,e\rangle}$$
$$\forall x \;((X.x \wedge \neg Y.x) \to \exists y \;(X.y \wedge Y.y \wedge F.y = x))]$$

Before going on to consider externally dynamic quantifiers, we will briefly consider how the account given so far bears on the problem of *weak* and *strong* readings for donkey sentences. In the case of E190, the strong reading — that obtained on Lewis's case-quantification analysis, in Kamp's DRT and in Heim's FCS — is the reading where every donkey owning farmer beats every donkey he owns. This is *strong* in the sense that it entails the so-called *weak* reading, where every donkey owning farmer beats at least one of the donkeys he owns. There is, to the best of my knowledge, as yet no conclusive evidence as to which reading is appropriate for E190, or whether, indeed, both readings are present. However, intuitions are clearer with regard to donkey sentences involving right downward monotone quantifiers such as 'no':

E192 a.   No farmer who owns a donkey beats it.

   b.   NO.i.
   (FARMER^u.i AND SOME.j.(DONKEY^u.j).(OWNS^b.i.j)).
   (IT.j.(BEATS^b.i.j))

Regarding this example it is difficult to justify the existence of a weak reading — the reading where no farmer beats all of his donkeys although some farmers may beat some of their donkeys. It seems that the existence of a single example of a farmer owning a donkey but not beating it would be enough to falsify the statement in E192.

In general the definition in D55 yields *existential* readings. Thus E190 comes to have the weak reading where every donkey-owning farmer beats at least one donkey, and E192 comes to have the strong reading (which as I have indicated seems to be the only plausible one) where no farmer beats any of his or her donkeys. However, both Chierchia (1992) and Kanazawa (1994) indicate that it is best to allow for the possibility of right upward monotone quantifiers having both strong and weak readings. To this end I note that we at least have the option of making the upward monotone quantifiers ambiguous, simply by introducing two new ABLE quantifiers EVERY* and MOST*. I leave it to the reader to verify that the following definitions would introduce strong right upward monotone determiners:

Definition D56 (Strong upward monotone determiners)

$$[\![\text{EVERY} * .i.\phi.\psi]\!] \;=\; [\![\text{NO}.i.\phi.(\text{NOT }\psi)]\!]$$

$$[\![\text{MOST}* .i.\phi.\psi]\!] \quad = \quad [\![\text{FEW}.i.\phi.(\text{NOT}\,\psi)]\!]$$

One final point about the limits of the current strategy for defining internally dynamic quantifiers: as discussed by Chierchia, the strategy is only appropriate for *conservative* quantifiers. This property holds of a quantifier, roughly speaking, if in calculating the truth of a quantificational statement, it is only necessary to consider how many of the individuals satisfying the restrictor also satisfy the scope, and it is irrelevant whether individuals not satisfying the restrictor satisfy the scope. Thus in evaluating whether it is true that 'every girl is hiding', it is irrelevant whether boys and other non-girls are hiding. It seems possible to maintain that this property holds for all English determiners: the only putative exception with which I am familiar is the word 'only'. However, it is quite plausible that 'only' is not a determiner at all, since, from the point of view of a naive syntactician, it has a quite different distribution than would be expected. For instance, 'only' can modify not only nouns, but also noun-phrases, as in 'only me', as well as commonly occurring outside of noun-phrases. On the other hand, even if 'only' is not a determiner, this does not excuse us from the task of giving it a semantics. But my feeling is that this job belongs within a more general theory of the dynamics of focus-sensitive constructions (see, for instance, Krifka 1992) and not here.

We now move on to the external dynamics of quantifiers. Consider the following examples:

E193 a.   Most farmers own a donkey.

  b.   MOST.i.   (FARMER^u.i).
        (SOME.j.(DONKEY^u.j).(OWN^b.i.j))

E194 a.   They ride to the pub.

  b.   THEY.i.(RIDE-TO-PUB^u.i)

E195 a.   Most of the donkeys are alcoholics.

  b.   MOST.k.   (THE.j.(DONKEY^u.j AND PLURAL^u.j).(OF^b.k.j))
        (ALCOHOLIC^u.k)

The fact that E193a–E195a constitute a coherent discourse shows that it is a simplification to assume that quantificational determiners have no anaphoric potential. It seems that E193a introduces at least two new topics of conversation: the set of donkey owners, and the set of donkeys that people own. In fact, there may well be other new topics, such as the set of all farmers and the set of all donkeys, but I will ignore these, although it seems plausible that the approach that will be described could be extended appropriately.

To make matters more tangible, the desired dynamic effects of E193b can be relativised to the example input state used earlier, consisting of the four worlds from figure 7.1 paired with empty sequences. Given this input, the following update would leave (in each world) i mapped to the set of all farmers, and j mapped to the set of donkeys owned by farmers:

$$\left\{ \begin{array}{ll} W1 & \langle\rangle \\ W2 & \langle\rangle \\ W3 & \langle\rangle \\ W4 & \langle\rangle \end{array} \right\} [\![\text{E193b}]\!] \left\{ \begin{array}{ll} W1 & \langle i \mapsto \{a,b,c\}, j \mapsto \{d,e,f,g,h\}\rangle \\ W2 & \langle i \mapsto \{a,b,c\}, j \mapsto \{d,e,f,g,h\}\rangle \end{array} \right\}$$

In the earlier definition of internally dynamic quantifiers, D55, extensions of a given input pair compatible with both the restrictor and scope were collected in the scope sequence set. Let us say that some input pair wf has a scope sequence set G_{sco}, and that wf would have been in the output state according to the earlier definition of internally dynamic quantifiers, D55. Then the output of an externally dynamic quantifier might be expected to contain the pair consisting of w together with the sequence g defined as follows:

$$g = \lambda D \lambda x \, [\exists h \, G_{\text{sco}}.h \wedge h.D.x]$$

This formula defines g as a function which maps each discourse marker onto the set of all values which it is assigned by the member sequences of the scope sequence set: we can call this the *scope sequence union*. However, although this approach would lead to an acceptable definition for E193b above, it would not be appropriate for right downward monotone quantifiers. For instance, the input world-sequence pairs which satisfy a quantification with the determiner 'few' may sometimes be associated with empty scope sequence sets since, on standard assumptions, there being few farmers who own a donkey is compatible with there being none at all. Thus calculating output sequences from scope sequence sets alone will sometimes yield only empty output sequences, and so fail to preserve the anaphoric information present in the input state.

One strategy for avoiding this problem would be to use different definitions for the semantics of upward and downward right monotone quantifiers. However, a single definition for both upward and downward monotone quantifiers is possible, provided the output sequence corresponding to a given input pair is calculated in terms of a combination of the input sequence and the scope sequence set. For a given input pair wf, having a scope set G_{sco}, the relevant output sequence associated with w will be calculated using the following formula:

$$g = \lambda D \lambda x \left[\begin{array}{l} f.D.x \; \vee \\ \exists h \, G_{\text{sco}}.h \wedge h.D.x \end{array} \right]$$

This makes the output sequence map each discourse marker onto the set of values which it is assigned either by the initial sequence f, or by member sequences of the scope sequence set. The problem is thus avoided, since if the scope sequence set is empty, the output sequence will be the same as the input, and if the scope sequence set is nonempty, then the output sequence will just be the scope sequence union, as before. We thus finally arrive at a semantics for non-existential determiners which incorporates both internal and external dynamism:

Definition D57 (Non-existential Determiners — Second Version)

If $\mathcal{D}$ is one of EVERY, MOST, FEW or NO, and $\mathcal{D}'$ is a corresponding quantifier relation of type $\langle\langle e, t\rangle, \langle\langle e, t\rangle, t\rangle\rangle$, then:

$$
[\![\mathcal{D}.i.\phi.\psi]\!] = \lambda I \lambda J
\left[
\begin{array}{l}
\exists init\, \exists res\, \exists sco \\
I\{+.i\}\,init[\![\phi]\!]\,res[\![\psi]\!]\,sco \ \wedge \\[2mm]
J = \lambda w \lambda g \\
\quad \left[
\begin{array}{l}
\exists f\, \exists G_{\mathrm{res}}\, \exists G_{\mathrm{sco}}\, \exists X_{\mathrm{res}}\, \exists X_{\mathrm{sco}} \\
I.w.f \ \wedge \\
G_{\mathrm{res}} = \lambda h\, [h \succeq f \ \wedge \ res.w.h] \ \wedge \\
G_{\mathrm{sco}} = \lambda h\, [h \succeq f \ \wedge \ sco.w.h] \ \wedge \\
X_{\mathrm{res}} = \lambda x\, [\exists h\, G_{\mathrm{res}}.h \wedge h.i.x] \ \wedge \\
X_{\mathrm{sco}} = \lambda x\, [\exists h\, G_{\mathrm{sco}}.h \wedge h.i.x] \ \wedge \\
\mathcal{D}'.X_{\mathrm{res}}.X_{\mathrm{sco}} \ \wedge \\
g = \lambda D \lambda x \left[
\begin{array}{l}
f.D.x \ \vee \\
\exists h\, G_{\mathrm{sco}}.h \wedge h.D.x
\end{array}
\right]
\end{array}
\right]
\end{array}
\right]
$$

In the recent semantic literature, indefinites have typically been distinguished from other quantificational determiners by virtue of their anaphoric potential. Having given, in D57, a definition that forms externally dynamic ABLE determiners from arbitrary quantifier relations, an obvious question arises: is the same definition appropriate for indefinites? Consideration of the following two classic examples shows that although extending D57 to include indefinites opens up a promising vista, it is not tenable:

E196   a.   ? There is a doctor in London. He is Welsh.

   b.   SOME.i.(DOCTOR^u.i).(IN-LONDON^u.i)
       AND HE.i.(WELSH^u.i)

E197   a.   If a farmer owns a donkey then he beats it.

   b.   SOME.i.(FARMER^u.i).(SOME.j.(DONKEY^u.j).(OWNS^b.i.j))
       IMPLIES HE.i.(IT.j.BEATS^b.i.j)

It has been argued by Evans (1977) that E196a is odd or incoherent, and that this oddity arises from the fact that the first sentence does not uniquely pick out a single individual to which the singular pronoun in the second sentence can refer. The judgement that the discourse is incoherent is not clear cut: there is at least one reading of E196a on which it is coherent, namely the so-called *specific* reading, as would be more obvious if the noun phrase 'a doctor' were replaced with 'a certain doctor'. However, let us assume for the moment that E196a is indeed incoherent, and consequently that explaining this incoherence would be a desirable goal for a semantic theory. Extending D57 to include the determiner SOME, and translating E196a in the obvious way as E196b, would immediately satisfy this desideratum. The translation of the first sentence would no longer introduce a discourse marker which ranged over alternative individual doctors in each world, but instead would introduce a marker assigned to the set of all London doctors in each world. Since an ABLE formula HE.$i.\phi$ carries the presupposition that i is established to be both male and singular, presupposition failure would follow unless the input state guaranteed that there was only one London doctor, and that this individual was male.

Regarding E196a, then, the extension of D57 to indefinites would have acceptable, or even desirable results. However, the same strategy would have significant effects for the treatment of quantificational donkey sentences, and disastrous effects for the treatment of conditional donkey sentences like E197a. In the case of quantificational donkey sentences like the prototypical E190a, the important consequence would be the introduction of a presupposition that every farmer had at most one donkey. But the translation of E197a would carry a far stronger uniqueness presupposition, namely that there was only one farmer, and that that this farmer had only one donkey. In effect Lewis's insight that the donkey conditional can be seen in terms of *case-quantification* would have been lost, since under such an analysis there could only be one case. Furthermore, it does not seem that an alternative semantics for the pronouns in E197a could save the analysis of indefinites. The translation of 'a farmer owns a donkey' would introduce markers corresponding to the complete set of farmers and the complete set of donkeys owned by farmers, and it would not preserve information about which farmers owned which donkeys. Clearly extensive further modifications would be needed in order to provide a compositional semantics for the conditional which entailed only that farmers beat their own donkeys.

Thus it seems that it would be wiser to stick with the original semantics for indefinites given in D53 than to use the same semantics as for the non-existential determiners. However, it remains somewhat disconcerting that D53 bears so little resemblance to D57, and I think it reasonable to wonder whether the ABLE determiner SOME, as defined in D53, in any sense qualifies as a quantifier. I will now show that D53 can be reformulated in more obviously quantificational terms, and this reformulation will have the advantage that it is also appropriate to other related quantifiers like EXACTLY-ONE.[16]

In terms of internal dynamics, the following definition for the existential quantifiers SOME and EXACTLY-ONE is identical to D58, which defined the semantics of EVERY, MOST, FEW and NO. However, the external dynamics is quite different. Instead of collecting together members of the scope sequence set to produce group referents, as in D57, the definition in D58 puts all members of relevant scope sequence sets directly into output world-sequence pairs.

I leave it to the reader to verify that the new definition is equivalent to D53 with regard to the determiner SOME. We can now say in precisely what sense the definition for SOME is quantificational: the output of a formula SOME.$i.\phi.\psi$ is determined in terms of an underlying quantifier relation. In particular, the set of input pairs of which extensions survive in the output of such a formula can be determined by checking whether the relation SOME$'$ holds between the set of values taken by i after update with the restrictor and the set of values taken by i after update with the scope.

Definition D58 (Existential Determiners — Second Version)

If $\mathcal{D}$ is SOME or EXACTLY-ONE, and $\mathcal{D}'$ is a corresponding quantifier relation of type $\langle\langle e,t\rangle,\langle\langle e,t\rangle,t\rangle\rangle$, then:

$$
[\![\mathcal{D}.i.\phi.\psi]\!] = \lambda I \lambda J
\begin{bmatrix}
\exists init \, \exists res \, \exists sco \\
I\{+.i\} init [\![\phi]\!] res [\![\psi]\!] sco \ \wedge \\[6pt]
J = \lambda w \lambda g
\begin{bmatrix}
\exists f \, \exists G_{\mathrm{res}} \, \exists G_{\mathrm{sco}} \, \exists X_{\mathrm{res}} \, \exists X_{\mathrm{sco}} \\
I.w.f \ \wedge \\
G_{\mathrm{res}} = \lambda h \, [h \succeq f \ \wedge \ res.w.h] \ \wedge \\
G_{\mathrm{sco}} = \lambda h \, [h \succeq f \ \wedge \ sco.w.h] \ \wedge \\
X_{\mathrm{res}} = \lambda x \, [\exists h \, G_{\mathrm{res}}.h \wedge h.i.x] \ \wedge \\
X_{\mathrm{sco}} = \lambda x \, [\exists h \, G_{\mathrm{sco}}.h \wedge h.i.x] \ \wedge \\
\mathcal{D}'.X_{\mathrm{res}}.X_{\mathrm{sco}} \ \wedge \\
G_{\mathrm{sco}}.g
\end{bmatrix}
\end{bmatrix}
$$

---

[16]In natural languages, quantifiers are sometimes not lexicalised, but still expressible. 'Exactly one' may be such a quantifier. In common with much recent literature on generalised quantifiers (see e.g. Keenan 1992), it is assumed here that we require logical analysis of both lexicalised and non-lexicalised quantifiers, and that an analysis which is mathematically uniform across both classes is desirable.

It remains only to specify the quantifier relations relevant to the determiners SOME and EXACTLY-ONE:[17]

Meaning Postulate MP15

$$
\begin{aligned}
\text{SOME}' &= \lambda X \lambda Y\, [\exists x\, (X.x \wedge Y.x)] \\
\text{EXACTLY-ONE}' &= \lambda X \lambda Y\, [\exists x\, (X.x \wedge Y.x \wedge \\
&\quad \forall y\, ((X.y \wedge Y.y) \rightarrow x = y))]
\end{aligned}
$$

7.6 PUL and ABLE

As stated above, presuppositions could have been introduced into ABLE using the presupposition operator of PUL, but I elected not to do so in order to keep ABLE more English-like. The presuppositions of definite descriptions are encoded in the semantics of the definite description operator. It would have been easy to translate definite descriptions of English into a compound of ABLE: instead of using THE.$i.\phi.\psi$, I could have used $\partial(\text{SOME}.i.\phi.phi)$ AND ψ. The presuppositions of predicates are located in the model: to impose a selectional restriction on a particular predicate, one adds an appropriate meaning postulate. It will now be shown that without loss of generality predicates could instead have been defined in terms of separate presuppositional and assertional components, and the ∂ operator used to combine them.

Let the language ABLE+∂ be ABLE with the addition of the presupposition operator:

Definition D59 **(Presupposition Operator in ABLE)**

$$
\partial F \quad \equiv_{\text{defn}} \quad \lambda I \lambda J[I = J \wedge I \text{ satisfies } F]
$$

Let us consider two sources of presuppositions in ABLE, predicates and definite descriptions, and let us say that an ABLE formula is *factive presupposition free* iff there is some set of discourse markers such that every state having these discourse markers in its domain admits the formula.

Fact 7.2 (Componential breakdown of ABLE+∂ predications) If ϕ is a predicational formula of ABLE, then there exist formulae ψ and χ which are factive presupposition free such that $\phi \equiv \partial\psi$ AND χ.

Proof: Define a singleton information state as $\langle\langle w, f\rangle\rangle \equiv \lambda w' \lambda f'[w' = w \wedge f' = f]$.

Now set $\psi = \lambda I \lambda J\, [J = \lambda w \lambda f\, [\langle\langle w, f\rangle\rangle \text{ admits } \phi]]$, and $\chi = \lambda I \lambda J\, [J = \lambda w \lambda f\, [\langle\langle w, f\rangle\rangle \text{ satisfies } \phi]]$.

---

[17]For another recent discussion of dynamic generalised quantifiers, see the work of van der Berg, e.g. van der Berg (1994).

Both ψ and χ are factive presupposition free, since they are defined on any input state. Furthermore the formula ϕ is predicational, so it is distributive, and by inspection of its definition the formula $\partial\psi$ AND χ is also distributive. So in establishing the equivalence, it suffices to consider whether for any singleton information state I, and for any state J, $\phi.I.J = (\partial\psi$ AND $\chi).I.J$. From right to left, there are three cases to consider:

1. Suppose there is no J such that $\phi.I.J$ is true. Then I does not admit ϕ, I does not satisfy ψ, and I does not admit $\partial\psi$ AND χ, so there is no J such that $(\partial\psi$ AND $\chi).I.J$.

2. Suppose $\phi.I.I$. Then I admits ϕ, so I satisfies ψ, and $\partial\psi.I.I$. Furthermore I satisfies ϕ, so I satisfies χ, and $\chi.I.I$ holds, whence, by definition of conjunction, $(\partial\psi$ AND $\chi).I.I$.

3. Suppose $\phi.I.\langle\rangle$, where $\langle\rangle$ is the absurd information state. As in (ii), I admits ϕ, so I satisfies ψ, and $\partial\psi.I.I$. Since I does not satisfy ϕ, it does not satisfy χ either, so $\phi.I.\langle\rangle$, and hence $(\partial\psi$ AND $\chi).I.\langle\rangle$

The reverse direction of the equality proceeds similarly.

What the above establishes is that ABLE predications behave just as if they were broken down into presuppositional and non-presuppositional components, as in the translations used in the previous chapter.[18]

---

[18]Beaver (1993b) contains an additional detailed technical discussion of the relationship between PUL and ABLE, showing a convergence between the logical properties of the two systems.

8

Presupposition and Modality in ABLE

8.1 Introduction

In this chapter the dynamic framework developed so far will be adapted to allow for an adequate treatment of presupposition and epistemic modality. I will begin, in §8.2, by detailing the projection behaviour of presuppositions in the system as so far defined, showing some advantages of the approach, but also revealing a problem in the interaction between presupposition and quantification. The problem is one familiar from Heim's (1983b) development of the CCP model. §8.3 will be spent ignoring the problem, and instead concentrating on the semantics of epistemic modality. It will be shown that essentially the same definition of the *might* operator as was given for the system UL, in Chapter 6, is also appropriate for ABLE, and that this definition leads immediately to a satisfying treatment of modal identity. However, it will also be shown that difficulties occur when quantifiers outscope the *might* operator, and this will motivate some tinkering with definitions from Chapter 7. Having dealt appropriately with the semantics of epistemic modality, we will return, in §8.4, to presupposition, only to find that the earlier problems concerning the interaction of presupposition and quantification have miraculously vanished.

8.2 Presupposition Projection in ABLE

It will now be shown that, regarding the projection of presuppositions, the system developed in Chapter 7 is comparable with Heim's 1983 account.[1] It will also be shown, in §8.2.2, that the ABLE treatment of proper names

---

[1] That is to say, the system is comparable with the more formally developed aspects of Heim's 1983 account, since including Heim's informal description of a mechanism of *accommodation* would lead to a quite different set of predictions. In Chapter 9, I will consider ways in which the process of accommodation might be formalised.

and definites, combined with ABLE's presupposition projection properties, lead to DRT-like anaphoric accessibility.

8.2.1 Projection from Connectives

With regard to the connectives, ABLE manifests much the same presupposition projection behaviour as PUL, or any other CCP account. This is most obviously seen by considering ABLE translations of the simple examples from Chapter 6, for which the following abbreviations will be useful:

$$\begin{aligned}
\text{BERTHA}.D.\phi &= \text{THE}.D.(\text{NAMED-BERTHA}^u.D).\phi \\
\text{ANNA}.D.\phi &= \text{THE}.D.(\text{NAMED-ANNA}^u.D).\phi \\
bih &= \text{BERTHA}.7.(\text{HIDING}^u.7)
\end{aligned}$$

We begin with simple cases of presuppositions embedded under negations or in the antecedents of conditionals:

E198   a.   Bertha is hiding

      b. bih

E168'   a.   Anna realises that Bertha is hiding

      b. $\text{ANNA}.3.(\text{REALISES}^a.3.bih)$

E169'   a.   Anna does not realise that Bertha is hiding.

      b. $\text{NOT}\,(\text{ANNA}.3.(\text{REALISES}^a.3.bih))$

E172'   a.   If Anna realises that Bertha is hiding, then she will find her.

      b. $(\text{ANNA}.3.(\text{REALISES}^a.3.bih))\ \text{IMPLIES}\ (\text{FIND}^b.3.7)$

It is easily shown that all of E168b, E169b and E172b *presuppose* (and also entail) E198b. Indeed, these are just instances of the following general property:

Fact 8.1 If ϕ presupposes ψ, then $\text{NOT}\,\phi$, $\phi\,\text{AND}\,\chi$ and $\phi\,\text{IMPLIES}\,\chi$ all presuppose ψ.

Proof: Simple. First, show by inspection of the clause for NOT (AND, IMPLIES) that if I *admits* $\text{NOT}\,\phi$ (etc.) then I *admits* ϕ. Thus the set of contexts which admit ϕ is a superset of those which admit $\text{NOT}\,\phi$ (etc.), and if all contexts which admit ϕ satisfy ψ (the condition for ϕ to presuppose ψ), then it must be the case that all contexts which admit $\text{NOT}\,\phi$ (etc.) satisfy ψ.

Next a case of one presuppositional construction embedded within another:

E174 a. Bertha regrets that Anna realises that she is hiding.

  b. BERTHA.7.(REGRETS^a.7.(ANNA.3.(REALISES^a.3.bih)))

E174b presupposes E198b, and once again this is an instance of a more general principle:

Fact 8.2 If ϕ presupposes ψ, and ψ presupposes χ, then ϕ presupposes χ.
Proof: The result follows directly from the definitions of presupposition and satisfaction. If ϕ presupposes ψ then every context which admits ϕ must satisfy ψ, but ψ can only be satisfied in contexts which admit it, and all these contexts satisfy χ. Thus every context which admits ϕ satisfies χ.

What really marks the CCP model out from other theories is the occurrence of Conditionalised presuppositions, as in the following case:

E175 a. If Bertha is not in the kitchen, then Anna realises that Bertha is in the attic.

  b. NOT (BERTHA.7.(IN-KITCHEN^u.7)) IMPLIES
      (ANNA.3.(REALISES^a.3.(IN-ATTIC^u.7)))

  c. NOT (BERTHA.7.(IN-KITCHEN^u.7)) IMPLIES
      (IN-ATTIC^u.7)

As might be expected, E175b presupposes the conditional E175c, i.e. that if Bertha is not in the kitchen, then she's in the attic. Conditionalised presuppositions are probably the single most controversial aspect of the CCP model, and the paradigmatically CCP behaviour of ABLE in this respect, as witnessed by the following fact, will be explored in more detail in Chapter 9.

Fact 8.3 If ϕ presupposes ψ, then χ AND ϕ and χ IMPLIES ϕ each presuppose χ IMPLIES ψ.
Proof: It suffices to show that under the assumption that $I\ admits\,(\chi$ AND $\phi)$ (or $I\ admits\,(\chi$ IMPLIES $\phi))$ it follows that $I\ satisfies\ [\![\chi$ IMPLIES $\psi]\!]$. Here is the reasoning for the conjunctive case, that for implication being similar:

$I\ admits\,(\chi$ AND $\phi)$	assumption
$\exists J\ I[\![\chi]\!]J \wedge J\ admits\,[\![\phi]\!]$	defns. of AND, $admits$
$\exists J\ I[\![\chi]\!]J \wedge J\ satisfies\,[\![\psi]\!]$	ass., defn. of $\gg$
$\exists J\ I[\![\chi]\!]J \downarrow [\![\psi]\!]J$	defn of $satisfies$
$\exists J\ I[\![\chi]\!]J[\![$ NOT $\psi]\!]\bot$	defn. of NOT
$I[\![\chi$ AND NOT $\psi]\!]\bot$	defn. of AND
$I[\![$ NOT $(\chi$ AND NOT $\psi)]\!]I$	defn. of NOT
$I[\![\chi$ IMPLIES $\psi]\!]I$	defn. of IMPLIES
$I\ satisfies\,[\![\chi$ IMPLIES $\psi]\!]$	defn. of $satisfies$

8.2.2   The Projection of Proper Names

The projection of presuppositions from embedded contexts, combined with the fact that proper names presuppose the presence of an appropriately named discourse marker, leads to proper names having very special anaphoric properties. Consider the following example:

E199 a.   If Butch is happy, then he is barking. He is happy. Therefore he is barking.

   b. $\text{THE}.2.(\text{NAMED-BUTCH}^u.2).(\text{HAPPY}^u.2)$ IMPLIES
           $\text{THE}.2.(\text{MALE}^u.2 \text{ AND SINGULAR}^u.2).(\text{BARK}^u.2)$

   c. $\text{THE}.2.(\text{MALE}^u.2 \text{ AND SINGULAR}^u.2).(\text{HAPPY}^u.2)$

   d. $\text{THE}.2.(\text{MALE}^u.2 \text{ AND SINGULAR}^u.2).(\text{BARK}^u.2)$

   e.   E199b,E199c $\models_{\text{able}}$ E199d

On its most obvious reading, that in which all the pronouns refer to Butch, E199a is an intuitively valid argument involving one application of *modus ponens*. Correspondingly, the ABLE entailment in E199e holds — that is to say, the translations of the first two sentences (i.e. E199b,c) entail the translation of the third (i.e. E199d). Yet E199b carries the same presupposition as E187b ('Butch is barking'), namely that 2 is established to refer to an individual named Butch. So even without specifying ways in which contexts satisfying the presuppositions of a formula may be generated, the formula can still appear in the premises of arguments. This is because the notion of entailment given in D45 does not depend on the premises being defined on all contexts, but only says that for all *suitable* contexts which satisfy the presuppositions of the premises, updating with the premises yields a state which satisfies the consequent.

It may surprise some readers that the ABLE translations of E199 can sustain the anaphoric linkage between the proper name Butch, which occurs within the antecedent of a conditional, and later pronouns beyond the scope of the conditional. In effect, ABLE manifests accessibility conditions for proper names and other definites reminiscent of Kamp's Discourse Representation Theory. The fact that a presuppositional analysis for proper-names can account for their distinctive anaphoric properties is discussed by Zeevat (1991), but this awkward detail of Kamp's work had generally been ignored in earlier reformulations of DRT, such as Groenendijk and Stokhof (1991a) and Muskens (1990).

Looked at from a slightly different angle, the projection behaviour of definites in ABLE tells us something about the relationship between DRT and File Change Semantics. The special mechanism for dealing with accessibility of names appears to be one of the few ways in which DRT and FCS differ significantly. Yet the ABLE analysis of definites, which I have shown leads to DRT-like anaphoric accessibility conditions, is basically that found in the original manifestation of FCS, namely Heim's thesis. Thus FCS contains the core of an idea that not only reproduces, but also explains the special behaviour of definites and names in DRT. One can imagine adding an ABLE-like notion of entailment to FCS, something along the lines of "one sentence entails another if after updating a file set with the file change potential (FCP) of the first, updating with the FCP of the second has no effect". It remains a matter of speculation whether such a line of research could lead to a more concrete demonstration that DRT-like behaviour of definites can be derived within FCS.

8.2.3 Quantificational Projection: A Problem

The following example shows that a problem which appeared in Heim's 1983 paper (and discussed in §4.4) has resurfaced:

E200 a. A man discovered that he owned a priceless Modigliani.

b. $\text{SOME}.i.(\text{MAN}^u.i).(\text{DISCOVER}^a.i.(\text{OAPM}^u.i))$

E201 a. Every man owned a priceless Modigliani.

b. $\text{EVERY}.j.(\text{MAN}^u.j).(\text{OAPM}^u.j)$

After updating with the restrictor of E200b, a state would be reached in which i was known to be a man. Assuming that the dynamic attitude predicate DISCOVER^a is constrained to be *factive*, this state could only be updated with the scope of E200b if the formula $\text{OAPM}^u.i$ was satisfied. However, this formula would only be satisfied if all the values of i were already established to correspond to priceless Modigliani owners. Thus a state could only be updated with E200b if in that state every man was established to be a priceless Modigliani owner. Thus E200b *presupposes* E201b. The problem is that E200a certainly does not presuppose (or entail) E201a.

Heim's account also predicts overly strong, universal presuppositions from existential sentences, and for essentially the same reason: quantified markers represent *arbitrary objects*. Thus at the point where the factive verb in E200b is reached, the discourse marker plays the role of an *arbitrary man*, and updating can only continue if it is established that any arbitrary man satisfies the factive's presupposition. The provisional semantics for ABLE's determiner's presented in Chapter 7 is uniform in this respect, so that the semantics for all the quantificational determiners is based on the same approach as for indefinites, which can be summed up as "add an arbitrary object, and check what effect updating with the restrictor and scope will have". Thus the occurrence of universal presuppositions is not restricted to indefinites alone, as is shown by the following examples:

E202 a.   Every woman regrets that she is married

  b. $\text{EVERY}.i.(\text{WOMAN}^u.i).(\text{REGRET}^a.i.(\text{MARRIED}^u.i))$

E203 a.   No woman regrets that she is married

  b. $\text{NO}.i.(\text{WOMAN}^u.i).(\text{REGRET}^a.i.(\text{MARRIED}^u.i))$

E204 a.   Every woman who regrets that she is married is sane

  b. $\text{EVERY}.i.(\text{WOMAN}^u.i \text{ AND REGRET}^a.i.(\text{MARRIED}^u.i)).(\text{SANE}^u.i)$

E205 a.   Every woman is married

  b. $\text{EVERY}.i.(\text{WOMAN}^u.i).(\text{MARRIED}^u.i)$

According to the Chapter 7 semantics, each of E202b, E203b and E204b presuppose E205b. This may be defensible for E202a, though I will later argue that even in this case the universal presupposition is inappropriate, it seems harder to justify the presence of such a strong presupposition for E203a and E204a. Intuitively, E203a is true just in case there are no married women who regret being married, and E205a is true just in case every married woman who regrets being married is sane. Such truth conditions are, of course, compatible with the existence of unmarried women.

The following fact summarises the problem with the *arbitrary object* analysis of quantification, showing that, as things stand, whenever a presupposing construction is bound within the scope of a quantifier, a universal presupposition arises:

Fact 8.4 If $\phi \gg \psi$, $\mathcal{D}$ is any quantificational determiner (i.e. not THE), and *true* of type π is interpreted as the trivial CCP $\lambda I \lambda J[I = J]$, then under the temporary definitions D58 and D57 the following hold:

1. $\mathcal{D}.i.\phi.\chi \gg \text{EVERY}.i.true.\psi$, and

2. $\mathcal{D}.i.\chi.\phi \gg \text{EVERY}.i.\chi.\psi$

Sketch of proof for (1): inspection of definitions D58 and D57 shows that if I *admits* $[\![\mathcal{D}.i.\phi.\chi]\!]$ then $\exists J\ I\{+i\}J \wedge J\ admits\ [\![\phi]\!]$, and thus that $\exists J\ I\{+d\}J \wedge J\ satisfies\ [\![\psi]\!]$. By the definition of satisfaction it follows that $(+i) \circ [\![\psi]\!]$ (where $\circ$ is relational composition) is satisfied in I, and thus that $(+i) \circ true \circ [\![\psi]\!]$ is satisfied in I, from which the result follows by the semantics of EVERY. The reasoning is similar for (2).

The above problem motivates an alteration to the semantics of quantification, but, as will be seen in the next section, such a change can to some extent be motivated by independent considerations.

8.3 Epistemic Modality

8.3.1 Modal Identity Problems

In this section I will provide a semantics for the unary ABLE operator MIGHT, extending the account of epistemic modality from the previous chapter to the first-order language of ABLE. In fact the PUL definition D25 requires little modification, except for adjustment to the Ty_3 format of ABLE semantic clauses:

Definition D60 **(Epistemic Modalities in ABLE)**

$$
\begin{aligned}
[\![\text{MIGHT}\phi]\!] \quad &= \quad \lambda I \lambda J\, \exists K\, I[\![\phi]\!]K \;\wedge \\
&\qquad (\neg(K = \bot) \;\rightarrow\; J = I) \;\wedge \\
&\qquad (K = \bot \;\rightarrow\; J = \bot) \\
[\![\text{MUST}\phi]\!] \quad &= \quad [\![\, \text{NOT}\,(\text{MIGHT}(\,\text{NOT}\,\phi))]\!]
\end{aligned}
$$

This definition for MIGHT, which clearly preserves the intuitions behind the operator in Veltman's original work and in the UL/PULsystems from Chapter 6 of this book, is essentially that used by Dekker (1992; 1993). In discussing the general properties of these operators, it is helpful to introduce Veltman's notion of a *test*. Tests are a special class of formulae which have, in terms of ABLE, the following property:

Definition D61 **(Tests)** A formula ϕ is a test if and only if:

$$\forall I \forall J\, I[\![\phi]\!]J \;\rightarrow\; (J = I \;\vee\; J = \bot)$$

This means that updating with a test is either uninformative, the output state being the same as the input state, or *over-informative*, the output being the absurd state. It is now possible to get a formal grasp on the interpretation of ABLE's epistemic modalities:

Fact 8.5 The MIGHT-operator defines a consistency test. Thus for any non-absurd state I which admits an ABLE formula ϕ:

1. MIGHTϕ is a test.

2. $I[\![\text{MIGHT}\phi]\!]I$ *iff* I *consistent-with* $[\![\phi]\!]$

3. $I[\![\text{MIGHT}\phi]\!]\bot$ *iff* $\neg I$ *consistent-with* $[\![\phi]\!]$

Proof of (1): Simply observe that if a pair I, J are in the denotation of MIGHTϕ, then by the definition of MIGHT there must be some state K for which $I[\![\phi]\!]K$ holds, and since K either is or is not the absurd state, at least one of the two conditional antecedents in the definition must be met, from which it follows that at least one of the consequents holds, namely that $J = I$ or $J = \perp$, but this is the condition for test-hood.

Proof of (2) and (3). The condition for $I[\![\text{MIGHT}\phi]\!]I$ is that updating with ϕ does not lead to the absurd state, and this is also the condition for consistency of ϕ with I. On the other hand, the condition for $I[\![\text{MIGHT}\phi]\!]\perp$ is that updating with ϕ does lead to the absurd state, and this is both necessary and sufficient for consistency to fail.

The following lemma helps to clarify the interpretation of the MUST-operator:

Lemma 8.6 *For any state I which admits a formula ϕ:*

I satisfies $[\![\phi]\!]$ iff $\neg I$ consistent-with $[\![\text{NOT }\phi]\!]$

Proof: By the definition of satisfaction, I satisfies $[\![\phi]\!]$ iff $I[\![\phi]\!]I$, and by the definition of negation this holds iff $I[\![\text{NOT }\phi]\!]\perp$, which in turn, by the definition of consistency, holds iff $\neg I$ consistent-with $[\![\text{NOT }\phi]\!]$.

Fact 8.7 The MUST-operator defines a test for satisfaction. Thus for any non-absurd state I which admits an ABLE formula ϕ:

1. MUSTϕ is a test.

2. $I[\![\text{MUST}\phi]\!]I$ iff I satisfies $[\![\phi]\!]$

3. $I[\![\text{MUST}\phi]\!]\perp$ iff $\neg I$ satisfies $[\![\phi]\!]$

Proof of (1): Since for any ϕ, MIGHTϕ is a test, it follows that MIGHT(NOT ϕ) is also a test, and so if a pair I, J is in the denotation of MIGHT(NOT ϕ), then $J = I$ or $J = \perp$. From the semantics of negation it follows that if $I[\![\text{MIGHT(NOT }\phi)]\!]I$ then $I[\![\text{NOT (MIGHT(NOT }\phi))]\!]\perp$, and if $I[\![\text{MIGHT(NOT }\phi)]\!]\perp$ then $I[\![\text{NOT (MIGHT(NOT }\phi))]\!]I$. Since this is exhaustive, the result follows.

Proof of (2):

$$\begin{aligned} I \text{ satisfies } \phi \quad &\textit{iff} \quad \neg(I \text{ consistent-with } [\![\text{NOT }\phi]\!]) &\text{lemma 8.6} \\ &\textit{iff} \quad I[\![\text{MIGHT(NOT }\phi)]\!]\perp &\text{defn. consistency} \\ &\textit{iff} \quad I[\![\text{NOT (MIGHT(NOT }\phi))]\!]I &\text{defn. negation} \end{aligned}$$

Proof of (3): Similar to (2).

I will not discuss the MUST operator in detail here, but the reader is invited to verify that it behaves appropriately with respect to the hide-and-seek examples from Chapter 6. Even without examining the applications of the MUST operator, it is at least comforting that the dual of a consistency test should be a test for satisfaction. On the basis of this interpretation, one could think of MUST as corresponding not to the English modal 'must', but as one of the sentential operators which could be called *argument connectives*, for example 'so' or 'therefore'. It is also comforting that the definitions of the modalities preserve the standard CCP presupposition inheritance properties of modals:

Fact 8.8 If ϕ presupposes ψ, then (1) MIGHTϕ and (2) MUSTϕ also presuppose ψ.

Proof: From the definition of MIGHT it can be seen that I *admits* MIGHTϕ only if I *admits* ϕ, from which the first result follows by the definition of presupposition. The same result for MUST follows from the proof of (1), the duality of the modalities, and the inheritance properties of NOT (Fact 8.1).

To see that in general this projection behaviour is appropriate — counter-examples being discussed in Chapter 9 — recall the following example from Chapter 6, which was argued to presuppose that Bertha is hiding:

E173 Anna might realise that Bertha is hiding.

Although there remain some problems, to which we will turn shortly, the account of epistemic possibility already has significant applications. In particular, some intuitive results arise when epistemic uses of the English modals 'possible' and 'perhaps' are translated using the MIGHT operator, as will now be shown with reference to examples E206–E209:

E206 a. It is possible there is a happy farmer, but, then again, it is possible that there are no happy farmers.

     b. MIGHT.(SOME.i.(FARMER^u.i).(HAPPY^u.i)) $\wedge$
        MIGHT.(NO.i.(FARMER^u.i).(HAPPY^u.i))

E207 a. No farmer is happy.

     b. NO.i.(FARMER^u.i).(HAPPY^u.i))

E208 a. Perhaps the spy is the president.

     b. MIGHT.(THE.i.(SPY^u.i).(THE.j.(PRESIDENT^u.j).($i = j$)))

E209 a. The spy is not the president.

     b. THE.i.(SPY^u.i).(THE.j.(PRESIDENT^u.j).(NOT ($i = j$))))

If my proposal for research into depression amongst farmers were to include E206a, and if, having obtained funding and done the relevant field-work, I were later to produce a report including E207a, I think I would feel justified in taking a certain pride in the fruitfulness of my research. In spite of an initial dearth of data, I would have made an important discovery about the distribution of agriculture-related emotional disorders. On the other hand, if my research proposal were to include E207a, and my final conclusions included E206a, I think DARPA would be justified in questioning whether I deserved further funding. For, quite apart from the limited military potential of my results, it would seem that my proposals tended to be rather unreliable. The conclusion that some farmer might be happy is simply inconsistent with the previous assertion that no farmer is happy.

The contrast between E206a followed by E207a on the one hand, and E207a followed by E206a on the other, is mirrored by the fact that the ABLE formula E206b AND E207b is consistent, whereas the formula E207b AND E206b is not. This holds if definition D60 is, and it holds according to the final definition for the semantics of MIGHT to be given below. The predictions with regard to examples E208 and E209 are similarly sensible on either definition. In particular, the formula E208b AND E209b is consistent, but swapping the order of the two conjuncts would yield an inconsistent formula. The success of ABLE in dealing with this last pair of examples shows that a serious problem with another recent attempt to combine DPL and update semantics, namely the Dynamic Modal Predicate Logic (DMPL) of van Eijck and Cepparello (1994), has been circumvented. In DMPL it would make little sense to give a definition like D60. The reasons are technical: the DMPL notions of entailment and negation require that DMPL formulae can be calculated pointwise over assignment functions (recall the property of *distributivity* introduced in §7.3). However, D60 cannot be calculated pointwise over assignment functions (sequences), as consistency of a formula is evaluated with respect to the full set of world-sequence pairs in the input. To give a flavour of the DMPL semantics for epistemic possibility, it must be translated into ABLE terms. This is not difficult given the technical proximity of DMPL to ABLE:

Definition D62 (Epistemic Possibility: DMPL Version)

$$[\![\text{MIGHT}\phi]\!] \;=\; \lambda I \lambda J \, [\exists K \, I \downarrow [\![\phi]\!] K \;\wedge$$
$$J = \lambda w \lambda f \, [I.w.f \wedge \exists w' \; K.w'.f]]$$

This definition can be seen as being in terms of equivalence classes of world-sequence pairs in the input: each class contains only pairs involving the same sequence. Given some input state I, the (anaphorically closed) output of MIGHTϕ will be the union of all the equivalence classes for which at least one world-sequence pair would survive in an update with ϕ. Put another way, a given world-sequence pair in the input will survive just in case there is some relevant world where the values that the sequence gives to discourse markers are consistent with ϕ. Unfortunately the use of a definition like

D62 means that in DMPL the following entailment is valid:[2]

$$\exists x \exists y \Diamond(x = y) \models x = y$$

Thus if the above examples were to be translated into DMPL with 'the spy' as x and 'the president' as y, then the validity of the pattern above would mean that learning that the spy might be the president would be equivalent to learning that the spy was the president. Furthermore, there is no obvious alternative translation which would solve the problem. For instance, translating the definite descriptions as constants would not help, since in DMPL updating with MIGHT($a = b$) for separate constants a and b always yields absurdity. Besides this, the problem is not restricted to definite descriptions but applies also to pronominals:

E210 a. The first lady is not spying

     b. THE.j.(FL^u.j).(NOT SPYING^u.j)

E211 a. I can see a woman in the Whitehouse

     b. SOME.i.(WOMAN^u.i).(I-SEE-IN-W^u.i)

E212 a. She might be spying.

     b. SHE.i.MIGHT(SPYING^u.i)

E213 a. However, she might be the first lady.

     b. SHE.i.(THE.j.(FL^u.j).MIGHT(i IS j))

This discourse consisting of E210a–E213a seems perfectly consistent, and, indeed, the formula (E210b AND E211 AND E212 AND E213) is consistent in ABLE. Yet there is a single discourse referent which might be spying, and also might be the first lady, even though the first lady is apparently above suspicion. Thus the sub-formula MIGHT(SPYING^u.i) in E212b should not — as would be the case in DMPL — remove sequences which map i onto the first lady, even though such sequences considered in isolation lead to values which are inconsistent with the assertion of spyhood.

It should be realised that identity problems like those found in DMPL are not altogether new, and not essentially dynamic in nature: many static systems of modal predicate logic have comparable properties. Indeed Kripke (1972) has argued persuasively that identity is a non-contingent property, so that if two things are identical then they are necessarily so. Given the logical duality of necessity and possibility, it immediately follows

---

[2]Note that in DMPL, as in DPL or ABLE, quantifiers take non-standard scope, so that a quantifier in the premise of an argument is able to bind a variable in the conclusion.

that things which might not be identical are not identical, and thus that things which might be identical are identical. However, it is clear that Kripke's arguments (which have remained controversial) could not be applied in defence of the properties of DMPL, for those arguments concern metaphysical contingency within total logics, and do not extend into the epistemic realm.[3]

In summary, whilst DMPL could well be an interesting object of logical investigation, it lacks any intuitive interpretation. In most respects the $\Diamond$ operator behaves comparably to Veltman's MIGHT: learning what *is* the case restricts what merely *might* be. However, with regard to questions of identity the $\Diamond$ behaves not as a *Veltmanesque* epistemic modality but as a *Kripkean* metaphysical modality: learning that things *might* be identical determines that they *are* identical. The reason is technical. An epistemic operator must be sensitive to all aspects of a referent's identity, but DMPL's entailment (and also negation) is not compatible with such a sensitive operator. On the other hand, the entailment used in ABLE or in Dekker's EDPL (from which much of the inspiration for ABLE derives), is compatible with the definition of an identity-sensitive operator. Finally, and without going into details, I should point out the *sequence semantics* for DPL introduced by Vermeulen (1992) provides yet another route to an identity-sensitive modality, but, as with DMPL and ABLE, would also be technically compatible with a DMPL-style insensitive operator.

8.3.2 The Dynamics of Quantifying-in.

Unfortunately, the definition of MIGHT given in D60 does not interact appropriately with quantificational determiners. For example, it is clear

---

[3]Kripke's main argument, which, as I must stress again, is applied within a metaphysical rather than an epistemic setting, involves consideration of which pairs of objects could falsify the open formula $\Diamond(x = y) \rightarrow x = y$. Substituting distinct values for x and y into the implication would falsify the antecedent, whereas substituting one value for both x and y would validate the consequent. But, if the formula is not falsifiable, then $=$ is not metaphysically contingent. Within an epistemic setting, the argument loses its force, for although it is impossible to simultaneously locate a pair of objects in the world which would obviously falsify the implication, it seems that the objects of thought and discourse, which may not even have a location in the exterior world, behave differently. There is manifestly no contradiction in positing that the objects referred to by two different descriptions, perhaps even in different languages, are in fact identical, nor is there necessarily any certainty about the question of whether a person seen in one guise is the same person as was separately seen in another guise. This is why it is consistent, albeit unwise in the wrong company, to assert that 'the spy might be the president', and still allow that they may later be discovered to be different. So even if data like that discussed here is reminiscent of data discussed in the philosophical literature, it is even so distinct data, since it concerns epistemic and not metaphysical modality, and the Kripkean arguments would seem to be irrelevant to a defence of the DMPL account of quantifying-in.

that E214a and E215a express quite different propositions, but the formula E214b differs from E215b only in terms of its anaphoric potential. That is to say, E214b and E215b are satisfied by exactly the same set of states.

E214 a. Most politicians might be spying.

   b. MOST.i.(POLITICIAN^u.i)(MIGHT(SPYING^u.i))

E215 a. Some politician might be spying.

   b. SOME.i.(POLITICIAN^u.i)(MIGHT(SPYING^u.i))

The definition for the semantics of ABLE's quantificational determiners is based on the principle of adding a discourse marker which in different sequences takes each single object as its value, and then checking what new information about the possible value of the marker is obtained by updating with the restrictor and scope. Thus the privileged marker stands proxy for the entire set of objects onto which it is mapped by different sequences associated with the various intermediate information states involved in updating with a quantificational formula. However, the interpretation of discourse markers outside of the scope of their introductory quantifier is quite different. An unquantified marker may also have several alternative valuations, but the interpretation is essentially disjunctive rather than conjunctive. Rather than standing proxy for the entire set of objects which it can take as values, an unquantified marker is understood as standing for just one of the alternative values: the presence of alternative values represents not multiplicity but underspecificity.

This difference in interpretation becomes crucial when quantifying into a modal context. MIGHT must check separately for consistency of its argument with regard to each of the alternative values for the quantified markers. Thus in E214b and E215b, where i is a quantified discourse marker, the effect of updating with MIGHT(SPYING^u.i) should be to remove all those sequences which map i onto an object which is known not to be spying. However, the same sub-formula should have a quite different effect when it occurs in E212b, above.

In order to define a notion of epistemic possibility which preserves the positive traits of that given in D60 and also gives a sensible account of the behaviour of quantified markers which distinguishes appropriately between E214b and E215b, the semantics of ABLE quantification will be altered. Note, however, that this is not the only way to proceed: in an earlier version of this chapter (appearing as Beaver 1993a), a special mechanism was added for keeping track of quantified markers, and the semantics of MIGHT was altered so as to interact differently with quantified and unquantified markers. Here I will formulate things more along the lines of Groenendijk et al. (1995). The motivation, however, differs somewhat from theirs. My reason for following their formulation is not simply that it eliminates the above-mentioned problem with epistemic modality, but that it will also lead to an elegant solution of some longstanding problems in the treatment of presupposition.

As I have said, under the semantics above, a quantified marker at some point in a formula stands proxy for the entire set of individuals which are compatible with the formula up to that point. So, although the semantics of MIGHT is only appropriate when multiplicity of interpretations represents underspecificity of reference, this is not the case with a quantified marker. The solution is to alter the semantics of quantification so that rather than considering all the different possible values of the quantified marker simultaneously, they are considered one at a time. By evaluating the restrictor and scope of a quantification separately for each value of the quantified marker, operators in the restrictor and scope become insensitive to the multiplicity of different values. To this end, a special way of interpreting a formula is defined. Given an ABLE formula, ϕ, and a discourse marker, d, $[\![\phi]\!]_d$ will define that relation between information states such that after splitting up the first state with respect to each different value of the marker d, and updating each of the resulting states using the normal interpretation $[\![\phi]\!]$, the outputs can be recombined to yield the second state. $[\![\phi]\!]_d$ is defined using a constant *distribute*, where *distribute.F.d* will be referred to as the distributive re-interpretation of the CCP F with respect to the marker d.

In the definition below, *distribute* is defined in two stages. First, a function *unfold* is given, where *unfold.F.d* defines a relation between two information states holding just in case there is a value of d such that after restricting the input to sequences which give that valuation, updating with F yields the output. Here, the process of *restricting* an information state with respect to values taken by some discourse marker is easily defined: if I is a state and d is a marker, then the restriction of i with respect to the value X for d is given by $\lambda w \lambda f[I.w.f \wedge f.d = X]$. The constant *distribute* is then defined such that a formula *distribute.F.d* denotes a CCP having as inputs only states which admit *unfold.F.d*, and having as output the union of the outputs of $\|\phi\|_d$. Here, given an input I, the union of the outputs of a CCP F is just $\lambda w \lambda f[\exists K\ I\{F\}K \wedge K.w.f]$.

Meaning Postulate MP16

$$
\begin{aligned}
\textit{unfold} \;=\; & \lambda F \lambda D \lambda I \lambda J \,[\exists X\, (\lambda w \lambda f\, [I.w.f \,\wedge\, f.d = X])\{F\}J] \\
\textit{distribute} \;=\; & \lambda F \lambda D \lambda I \lambda J \,[I \,\textit{admits}\,(\textit{unfold.F.D}) \,\wedge \\
& J = \lambda w \lambda f\, [\exists K\, I\{\textit{unfold.F.D}\}K \,\wedge\, K.w.f]]
\end{aligned}
$$

Definition D63 (Distributive Interpretation of ABLE Formulae)

$$[\![\phi]\!]_{\mathrm{d}} \;=\; distribute.[\![\phi]\!].d$$

The definition allows for a relatively conservative alteration to the quantifiers. It can be seen from the following two properties that the use of $[\![\phi]\!]_{\mathrm{d}}$ in place of $[\![\phi]\!]$ will only have an effect in a very restricted range of circumstances:

Fact 8.9 If ϕ does not contain the discourse marker d then $[\![\phi]\!]_{\mathrm{d}} = [\![\phi]\!]$
Sketch of proof: ABLE predicates have the property of *relevance* (cf. §7.3), which is easily shown (by induction over formula complexity) to be preserved by all ABLE's operators. Thus we need only consider states I, J which do not have d in their domain. For such states it is clear that $I[\![\phi]\!]J \leftrightarrow I[\![\phi]\!]_{\mathrm{d}}J$ (Note that the definition of $[\![\phi]\!]_{\mathrm{d}}$ is compatible with the input state only giving d the value $\lambda x\,[\bot]$.)

Fact 8.10 If $I\,admits\,[\![\phi]\!]$ and ϕ does not contain any occurrences of the epistemic modality, MIGHT, then $I[\![\phi]\!]J \leftrightarrow I[\![\phi]\!]_{\mathrm{d}}J$
Sketch of proof: ABLE predicates have the property of *distributivity* (cf. §7.3), and this can be shown (another induction) to be preserved by ABLE's connectives and determiners. Thus we need only consider singleton states (those with only one world-sequence pair), and for these the result is trivial, since distributing over a single world-sequence pair has no effect.

Having given a definition of $[\![\phi]\!]_{\mathrm{d}}$, amending the semantics of quantifiers is easy. Where before the passage from input to output was mediated by a sequence of updates $I\{+.i\}init[\![\phi]\!]res[\![\psi]\!]sco$, we simply replace the occurrences of $[\![.]\!]$ by $[\![.]\!]_i$ to get the new definitions, given below as D64 and D65 for completeness.

What is the reason for the definedness condition, $I\,admits\,(unfold.F.D)$ in postulate MP16? It is easy to see that with no such condition some rather strange effects would arise. For instance, if the formula F was the denotation of a simple predication $P(d')$ for some discourse marker d' not in the domain of the input, then $unfold.F.D$ would have no outputs, and the effect of taking the *union* of the outputs would be to produce the absurd state. Whereas, for such an input, $[\![P(d')]\!]$ would not define an output, $[\![P(d')]\!]_{\mathrm{d}}$ would define an update to the absurd state. Thus undefinedness would cease to propagate through formulae involving distributive updates, leading to a rather strange inconsistency, and consequently strange logic.

Clearly, some definedness condition is needed. However, it would be possible to use a stronger definedness condition, say insisting not just that there is at least one value of the distributed marker for which there is an update, but requiring that for every value an update was defined. Such a condition would still be sensible as far as the interaction of quantification and modality was concerned, but would lead to different predictions regarding the projection of presuppositions from quantified contexts. In fact, such a strong definedness condition would yield the same predictions for presupposition projection as were obtained with the earlier definitions of quantification in Chapter 7. However, in the next section it will be shown that whereas the earlier definitions of quantification give the same undesirable presupposition projection effects as plagued the system of Heim (1983b), the new definitions provide quite attractive projection properties.

Definition D64 (Non-existential Determiners — Final Version)

If $\mathcal{D}$ is one of EVERY, MOST, FEW or NO, and $\mathcal{D}'$ is a corresponding quantifier relation of type $\langle\langle e, t\rangle, \langle\langle e, t\rangle, t\rangle\rangle$, then:

$$
[\![\mathcal{D}.i.\phi.\psi]\!] = \lambda I \lambda J
$$

$$
\left[
\begin{array}{l}
\exists init\, \exists res\, \exists sco \\
I\{+.i\}\, init[\![\phi]\!]_i\, res[\![\psi]\!]_i\, sco\ \wedge \\[2mm]
J = \lambda w \lambda g \\
\left[
\begin{array}{l}
\exists f\, \exists G_{\mathrm{res}}\, \exists G_{\mathrm{sco}}\, \exists X_{\mathrm{res}}\, \exists X_{\mathrm{sco}} \\
I.w.f\ \wedge \\
G_{\mathrm{res}} = \lambda h\, [h \succeq f\ \wedge\ res.w.h]\ \wedge \\
G_{\mathrm{sco}} = \lambda h\, [h \succeq f\ \wedge\ sco.w.h]\ \wedge \\
X_{\mathrm{res}} = \lambda x\, [\exists h\, G_{\mathrm{res}}.h \wedge h.i.x]\ \wedge \\
X_{\mathrm{sco}} = \lambda x\, [\exists h\, G_{\mathrm{sco}}.h \wedge h.i.x]\ \wedge \\
\mathcal{D}'.X_{\mathrm{res}}.X_{\mathrm{sco}}\ \wedge \\
g = \lambda D \lambda x\ \left[
\begin{array}{l}
f.D.x\ \vee \\
\exists h\, G_{\mathrm{sco}}.h \wedge h.D.x
\end{array}
\right]
\end{array}
\right]
\end{array}
\right]
$$

Definition D65 (Existential Determiners — Final Version)
If $\mathcal{D}$ is SOME or EXACTLY-ONE, and $\mathcal{D}'$ is a corresponding quantifier relation
of type $\langle\langle e,t\rangle,\langle\langle e,t\rangle,t\rangle\rangle$, then:

$$\llbracket \mathcal{D}.i.\phi.\psi \rrbracket = \lambda I \lambda J$$

$$\left[\begin{array}{l} \exists init\, \exists res\, \exists sco \\ I\{+.i\}init\llbracket\phi\rrbracket_i res\llbracket\psi\rrbracket_i sco\ \wedge \\[6pt] J = \lambda w \lambda g \\ \left[\begin{array}{l} \exists f\, \exists G_{\mathrm{res}}\, \exists G_{\mathrm{sco}}\, \exists X_{\mathrm{res}}\, \exists X_{\mathrm{sco}} \\ I.w.f\ \wedge \\ G_{\mathrm{res}} = \lambda h\, [h \succeq f\ \wedge\ res.w.h]\ \wedge \\ G_{\mathrm{sco}} = \lambda h\, [h \succeq f\ \wedge\ sco.w.h]\ \wedge \\ X_{\mathrm{res}} = \lambda x\, [\exists h\, G_{\mathrm{res}}.h \wedge h.i.x]\ \wedge \\ X_{\mathrm{sco}} = \lambda x\, [\exists h\, G_{\mathrm{sco}}.h \wedge h.i.x]\ \wedge \\ \mathcal{D}'.X_{\mathrm{res}}.X_{\mathrm{sco}}\ \wedge \\ G_{\mathrm{sco}}.g \end{array}\right] \end{array}\right]$$

8.4 Presupposition in ABLE Revisited

Fact 8.4, which says that universal presuppositions arise from the Chapter 7
definitions of quantification, would fail under the amended definitions. To
see this it suffices to give a counter-example, so constructing an information
state which admits E200b but does not satisfy E201b will be adequate:

E200   a.   A man discovered that he owned a priceless Modigliani.

        b.   SOME.i.(MAN^u.i).(DISCOVER^a.i.(OAPM^u.i))

E201   a.   Every man owned a priceless Modigliani.

        b.   EVERY.j.(MAN^u.j).(OAPM^u.j)

    Let us assume MAN^u and OAPM^u to be simple, and DISCOVER^a to be fac-
tive. Here is a definition of an appropriate information state in a simplified
model:

- The state I contains the single world sequence pair $w, \langle\rangle$

- The domain D_e consists of only two individuals, a and b

- w is a man's world (i.e. both a and b are men)

- In w, a owns a priceless Modigliani and has discovered that he owns
  it, whilst b does not own a priceless Modigliani. Note that ownership
  of a priceless Modigliani is assumed to be a basic property, so that
  the object corresponding to the Modigliani can be ignored.

That I does not satisfy E201b should be clear, since in I there is a man who does not own a priceless Modigliani. Inspection of the semantics for existential determiners D65 shows that the condition for I to admit E200b is that there exist states J, K, L such that:

$$I\{+.i\}J[\text{MAN}^u.i]_i K[\text{DISCOVER}^a.i.(\text{OAPM}^u.i)]_i L$$

It is easy to find the appropriate values for J and K. J must consist of two world sequence pairs mapping i onto a and b, respectively. Furthermore, since both a and b are men, we should expect the update with $[\text{MAN}^u.i]_i$ not to remove any world-sequence pairs from J: since MAN^u is simple, J must admit $[\text{MAN}^u.i]$, and 8.10 means that we can ignore the fact that $\text{MAN}^u.i$ is evaluated distributively with respect to i. Thus:

$$J = K = \{w : \langle i \mapsto a\rangle, w : \langle i \mapsto b\rangle\}$$

By the definition of distributive update D63, L is calculated by taking the union of all the states M (provided that there is at least one state M) such that:

$$K\{\text{unfold.}[\text{DISCOVER}^a.i.(\text{OAPM}^u.i)].i\}M$$

Since of the two values for i, only a corresponds to an individual satisfying the factive presupposition of $\text{DISCOVER}^a.i$, there will only be one appropriate M:

$$M = \{w : \langle i \mapsto a\rangle\}$$

The existence of this single value for M is enough to guarantee that E200b is admitted in I, as required. Further, it can be seen that L will take the same value, i.e. the singleton set containing the pair of w and a sequence mapping i onto the individual a, and, by inspection of the semantics for SOME, that this will also be the output of the whole formula E200b.

So given that Fact 8.4 is no longer appropriate, what are the presuppositions of quantificational formulae involving a bound presuppositional expression? The following fact shows that under the new semantics for quantifiers, although the universal presuppositions associated with the Chapter 7 definitions have gone, there remain at least existential constraints:

Fact 8.11 If $\phi \gg \psi$, $\mathcal{D}$ is any quantificational determiner (i.e. not THE), and *true* of type π is interpreted as the trivial CCP $\lambda I \lambda J\ [I = J]$, then under the final definitions D64 and D65:

    1. $\mathcal{D}.i.\phi.\chi \;\gg\; \text{SOME}.i.true.\psi$, and

2. $\mathcal{D}.i.\chi.\phi \gg \text{SOME}.i.\chi.\psi$

Sketch of proof for (1): From D64 and D65, $\mathcal{D}.i.\phi.\chi$ is admitted by any state for which:

$$\exists init \exists res \exists sco \; I\{+.i\} init[\![\phi]\!]_i res[\![\chi]\!]_i sco$$

Given the assumption that ϕ presupposes ψ, it follows that a necessary condition for the formula to be admitted by I is that there is some state *init* such that:

$$I\{+.i\} init \;\wedge\; init \, admits \, [\![\phi]\!]_i$$

From the definition of distributive update, it follows that:

$$init \, admits \, [\![\phi]\!] \quad iff \quad init \; admits \; (unfold.[\![\phi]\!].i)$$

Using the definition of *unfold* gives us:

$$init \, admits \, [\![\phi]\!] \quad iff \quad \exists X \; ((\lambda w \lambda f \; [init.w.f \;\wedge\; f.d = X]) \; admits \; [\![\phi]\!])$$

But by assumption ϕ presupposes ψ, so:

$$init \, admits \, [\![\phi]\!] \quad iff \quad \exists X \; ((\lambda w \lambda f \; [init.w.f \;\wedge\; f.d = X]) \; satisfies \; [\![\psi]\!])$$

Thus for I to admit $\mathcal{D}.i.\phi.\chi$, it must be the case that there is some individual in a singleton set X such that if I is extended with the marker i, and is then restricted by removing all the world sequence pairs where i is not mapped onto X, the resulting state satisfies ψ. This existential requirement is enough to force the required condition, that $\text{SOME}.i.true.\psi$ is satisfied in the input, but I omit the remaining details. The proof of (2) would be similar.

So whilst E200b does not presuppose E201b, it does presuppose E216b:

E216 a. Some man owned a priceless Modigliani.

     b. $\text{SOME}.j.(\text{MAN}^u.j).(\text{OAPM}^u.j)$

Similar results are obtained for the other quantificational examples considered earlier, and it will now be argued that these results are not only reasonable, but represent an advance over previous analyses. First, a case with a presupposition in the restrictor of a quantifier:

E204 a. Every woman who regrets that she is married is sane

     b. $\text{EVERY}.i.(\text{WOMAN}^u.i \text{ AND REGRET}^a.i.(\text{MARRIED}^u.i)).(\text{SANE}^u.i)$

E217 a. Some woman is married

    b.   SOME.i.(WOMAN^u.i).(MARRIED^u.i)

As pointed out earlier, the prediction of a universal presupposition for E204 is quite clearly inappropriate. On the current analysis, E204b presupposes E217b, and this existential presupposition is certainly to be preferred. Although there can be no question that analyses[4] which predict a universal presupposition for this case are inappropriate, there must remain a question as to whether the existential analysis is correct. I think it quite possible to defend a view that such sentences should have no presuppositions, but only implicate that there are some individuals which satisfy the restrictor conditions, and thus implicate that there are some individuals which satisfy the restrictor's presuppositions. It could be that variations on the definition of distributive update used within the semantics of quantifiers would lead to such results, but in this book I will not attempt any further development along these lines.[5]

Much more controversial are cases where a presupposition occurs in the scope of a quantificational construction. Unfortunately, there is, to my knowledge, no intellectually rigorous analysis of such sentences in the existing presuppositional literature, and most authors have been happy to advocate whatever claims about the data pose fewest problems for their own theory. There is thus no consensus concerning the presuppositions of the following examples, the first being repeated from above:

E202' a.   Every woman regrets that she is married

      b.   EVERY.i.(WOMAN^u.i).(MARRIED^u.i)

E218 a.   Every man discovered that he owned a priceless Modigliani

      b.   EVERY.i.(MAN^u.i).(DISCOVER^a.i.(OAPM^u.i))

I find the lack of consensus surprising, since there is no reason why standard presuppositional tests should not be applied in order to resolve the issue. I will only consider one such test, embedding under negation.

First, consider E219a below, which I consider to be true: there are women who do not regret that they are married. Given that not every woman is married, we have a situation (the real world) where E219a is true, but it is false that every woman is married. It is clear that this contradicts any claim that E219a entails that every woman is married. Now, although the negation in E219a is syntactically realised within the subject NP, there is good reason to analyse it as semantically having scope

---

[4]E.g. Heim (1983b) without her suggested addition of a mechanism for accommodation.

[5]Yet another option would be to produce a defeasible presupposition, along the lines to be sketched for the propositional case in Chapter 10.

over the whole sentence.[6] Thus, it seem reasonable to accept that E219a functions semantically as the negation of E202a, and thence that E202a does not presuppose that every woman is married.

E219 a.   Not every woman regrets that she is married.

   b.   NOT $(\text{EVERY}.i.(\text{WOMAN}^u.i).(\text{REGRETS}^a.i.(\text{MARRIED}^u.i)))$

Now consider E220a, which I take to be a slightly strange thing to say unless there is previous reason to think that there have been some discoveries of Modigliani ownership. I think it indisputable that the sentence could be true in worlds where some, but not all, men had discovered that they owned Modigliani's. This is sufficient to show that E218 does not presuppose universal Modigliani ownership.

E220 a.   Not every man discovered that he owned a priceless Modigliani.

   b.   NOT $(\text{EVERY}.i.(\text{MAN}^u.i).(\text{DISCOVER}^a.i.(\text{OAPM}^u.i)))$

These observations are completely in line with the predictions obtained within ABLE: none of the above four examples (E202a, E218a, E219a, E220a) carry universal presuppositions. However, this is not the end of the story. My intuition is that, knowing that not all women are married, E202a is a slightly strange thing to say, and, given that not every man owns a Modigliani, E218 is an even stranger thing to say. However, even knowing that not all women are married, E203 does not seem in the least odd. My intuition is that it is simply false, since there are married women who regret being married:

E203 a.   No woman regrets that she is married

   b.   NO.$i.(\text{WOMAN}^u.i).(\text{REGRET}^a.i.(\text{MARRIED}^u.i))$

Similarly, E221 is quite compatible with there being some non-Modigliani owners:[7]

---

[6]I would offer two arguments that negations like that in E219a function semantically as sentential operators. First, an argument from truth conditions: 'Not every chameleon has a crest' is intuitively true if and only if it is not the case that 'Every chameleon has a crest.' Second, from licensing of negative polarity items (NPI's): 'Not every chameleon has any friends', containing the NPI 'any', is notably more felicitous than 'Every chameleon has any friends', suggesting that in the first of these the 'not' has semantic scope including the object NP. Beaver (1994b) utilises another embedding test, embedding in the antecedent of a conditional, to determine the presuppositions of sentences with elementary presuppositions bound by universal quantifiers. This is shown to lead to the same conclusions as reached here. One advantage of the conditional embedding is that the syntactic form more obviously correlates with the semantic interpretation, the semantic scope of the conditional not being at issue.

[7]Some would doubtless go further, and say that E221 is compatible with there being no Modigliani owners. As mentioned above, I think this is a tenable viewpoint, although

E221 a. No man discovered that he owned a priceless Modigliani

     b. $\text{NO}.i.(\text{MAN}^u.i).(\text{DISCOVER}^a.i.(\text{OAPM}^u.i))$

In ABLE these contrasts are explained straightforwardly. Although none of the above regretful-wife examples are predicted to presuppose that every woman is married, E202 is predicted to entail that every woman is married, although this is not the case with E219 or E203. Likewise, none of the Modigliani-discovery examples are predicted to presuppose that every man owns a Modigliani, although E218 is predicted to entail this proposition. Thus, what seems to me rather a strong contrast between occasions in which 'every' and 'no' are appropriate,[8] is explained not in terms of any difference in presupposition, but in terms of entailments.

It may seem that the contrasts are too vague to merit the sharp semantic division which ABLE predicts. However, I believe that the apparent blurriness of the contrasts is explained solely by the failure to specify the context of utterance in sufficient detail, which means that regarding the above examples it is not *a priori* clear exactly which sets of individuals are being talked about. The contrasts become much stronger when more of the preceding context of utterance is given:

E222 a. Ten girls were playing hide-and-seek.

     b. Every girl discovered that she could hide in the attic.

     c. No girl discovered that she could hide in the attic.

Suppose that Clothilde, one of the ten girls mentioned in E222a, is for some reason unable to pass through the trap-door to the attic, and thus cannot possibly hide there. The discourse consisting of E222a followed by E222b is not appropriate: it simply contradicts the assumption about Clothilde's limitations. On the other hand, E222a followed by E222c could conceivably be true under the assumptions about Clothilde. The contrast is very sharp. Once again, it will be explained quite readily in ABLE, since E222b will entail that every girl could hide in the attic, but E222c will not entail this.

However, this contrast is not predicted by either Heim or van der Sandt's accommodation based theories of presupposition, as described in Chapter 5. In both of these theories, presuppositions bound in either the scope of a quantificational construction are able to trigger restriction of the quantificational domain through the mechanism of *intermediate accommodation*.

I will not attempt to adjust ABLE's semantics accordingly. Note also that although there may be effects with this type of example related to Karttunen's division of verbs into factives and semifactives (as indicated to me by Gerald Gazdar) the conclusions I draw are made on the basis of examples with both types of verbs (a factive in E203 and a semifactive in E221), and therefore should be safe.

[8]Hans Kamp (p.c.) drew my attention to this contrast.

But, as was shown in §5.6, intermediate accommodation produces incorrect predictions, and the problems discussed there resurface in the case of the above discourses.

Let us see how van der Sandt's account fares with E222b. Assume that previous knowledge of Clothilde and the explicit addition of E222a have produced the following simplified DRS (where chia = 'could hide in attic'):

E222 d.

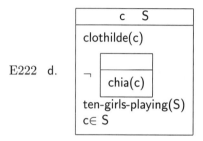

On parsing E222b, and assuming resolution of 'she' to the locally quantified marker, an initial DRS like the following would presumably be produced:

E222 e.

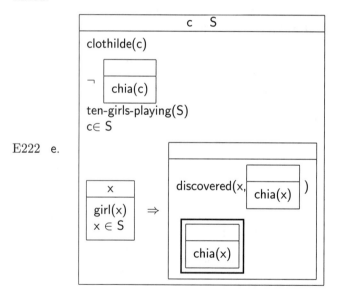

Global accommodation of the presupposition is not possible because of van der Sandt's *trapping* constraint, which prevents markers in presuppositions from becoming unbound in the accommodation process. So the preferred option will be the next most global form of accommodation, intermediate accommodation of the presupposition in the restrictor of the quantifier:[9]

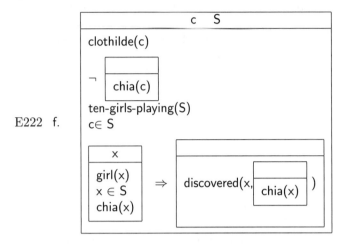

E222 f.

This DRS would be true (embeddable) in a model just in case Clothilde could not hide in the attic, ten girls of whom Clothilde was one were playing, and every one of those girls who could hide in the attic had discovered that she could. But this set of requirements is consistent. Therefore no anomaly is predicted for the discourse ending in E222b (and similarly for the discourse ending in E222c). I take it that Heim's earlier but less explicitly formulated account of accommodation would produce the same effect.[10]

These examples show that presuppositions in the scope of a quantification do not automatically trigger domain restriction, and that any theory of accommodation which says they do, is wrong. Given this, and given that some women are single, does it then follow that it is never correct to say 'Every woman regrets that she is married.'? No, it does not. Rather, the contexts in which this can be appropriately uttered are those in which marriage and the set of married women are already salient, and the previous salience of the set of married women licences domain restriction, as is argued in detail in Beaver (1994a). I will not attempt to describe formally

---

[9]I am not positive whether van der Sandt would wish to term this an instance of resolution or accommodation, but resolution of the presupposition would produce identical results so the choice is not relevant to current concerns.

[10]However, the reasoning producing those results in Heim's account might be different. Global accommodation that every girl in the given set could hide in the attic would be possible in Heim's account, except that in this case it would produce inconsistency and presumably be ruled out. Likewise, purely local accommodation would be ruled out, also on pain of producing inconsistency. But intermediate accommodation would remain a feasible option, and presumably yield similar results to van der Sandt's model if it was clear exactly what material to accommodate, this not being explicitly stated in Heim's papers.

a mechanism whereby previous context could trigger domain restriction, but it is clear that the basic apparatus is present in ABLE to allow such a development. In particular, the fact that plural referents can be generated means that it would be straightforward to add a clause to the semantics of quantificational determiners to allow quantification to be restricted to a set demarcated by some existing plural referent. Neither would this be an *ad hoc* addition to the system: it is uncontroversial that some mechanism of quantificational domain restriction is present in natural language, and that the process of domain restriction is heavily dependent on previous context.[11]

In conclusion, ABLE offers a semantic solution to many problems that arise when quantifiers and presuppositions interact, and a solution that is to some extent independently motivated by a consideration of the semantics of epistemic modality. However, there remain many outstanding problems of both an empirical and technical nature. I have indicated that I have doubts about whether even a prediction of an existential presupposition is appropriate in the above cases. But I will finish this section by noting yet another potential problem. The reader may like to verify that in the above cases where a presupposition is bound by a quantifier, ABLE predicts not only an existential presupposition, but a presupposition that there is at least one rigidly designated individual that has the presupposed property. Thus for E203 to be admitted, there would have to be an element of the domain of individuals such that in every world in the input that individual was married. This technical artifact has little obvious empirical support, and it is clear to me that further work is required.[12]

---

[11]Further discussion of these issues is found both in Beaver (1994a) and von Fintel (1995).

[12]In fact the slight differences in the version of this work presented in Beaver (1993a) mean that the system given there does not suffer from the rigid-designator problem, so clearly we should not give up hope.

9

Let's Get Real!

9.1 Introduction

The language ABLE is all very well as a means for developing intuitions about the dynamics of determiners, presuppositions and so forth, but ABLE is only a bit like English. The aim of this chapter is to develop a more realistic model of the process of natural language interpretation, in particular providing answers to the following two questions:

1. How can the meanings of English sentences be derived compositionally?

2. How does world knowledge constrain utterance interpretation?

9.2 Kinematic Montague Grammar

In Chapters 7 and 8, ABLE was set up as an independent language, which merely happened to have its semantics defined in terms of another formal language, namely Ty_3. The choice of type theory as a meta-language certainly did not enhance readability, a fact of which the reader is presumably painfully aware, and it is probably of little consolation that using type theory in this way did not enhance *writability* either. But now we come to the pay-off.

The pay-off is that it is straightforward to embed ABLE in Ty_3, as a mere sub-language, and then use the apparatus of type theory to relate expressions of ABLE to the meanings of expressions of English. I say *straightforward*, but what I really mean is that Montague did the hard work, by showing how (a modified form of) type theory can be used to specify the semantics of natural language.

9.2.1 ABLE in Ty_3

In this section it will be shown how to define Ty_3 constants AND, NOT, IMPLIES, THE, EVERY, NO, MOST, FEW, EXACTLY-ONE, IS, MIGHT and MUST: the embedding of ABLE into Ty_3 enriched with these constants will then be unproblematic. Consider the definitions for the semantics of the ABLE connectives, given originally in Chapter 7:

$$[\![\phi \text{ AND } \psi]\!] \;=\; \lambda I \lambda J \, [\exists K \, I[\![\phi]\!] K [\![\psi]\!] J]$$

$$[\![\text{ NOT } \phi]\!] \;=\; \lambda I \lambda J \, [\exists K \, I \downarrow [\![\phi]\!] K \wedge \\ J = I \backslash K]$$

$$[\![\phi \text{ IMPLIES } \psi]\!] \;=\; [\![\text{ NOT } (\phi \text{ AND NOT } \psi)]\!]$$

These definitions can be used as the basis of three Ty_3 constants AND, NOT, and IMPLIES, of types $\langle \pi, \langle \pi, \pi \rangle \rangle$, $\langle \pi, \pi \rangle$ and $\langle \pi, \langle \pi, \pi \rangle \rangle$, respectively, where AND and IMPLIES will be used in infix form. In the following postulate ϕ and ψ are taken to be Ty_3 variables of type π:

Meaning Postulate MP17

$$\text{AND} \;=\; \lambda\phi\lambda\psi\lambda I\lambda J \, [\exists K \, I\{\phi\} K\{\psi\}J]$$

$$\text{NOT} \;=\; \lambda\phi\lambda I\lambda J \, [\exists K \, I\{\downarrow \phi\}K \wedge \\ J = I \backslash K]$$

$$\text{IMPLIES} \;=\; \lambda\phi\lambda\psi \, [\text{ NOT } (\phi \text{ AND NOT } \psi)]$$

The general recipe for producing an appropriate Ty_3 constant from an ABLE semantic clause runs as follows: first wipe out all the semantic brackets (but replacing formulae $[\![\phi]\!]_{\text{D}}$ with $distribute.\phi.D$), and then remove the argument expressions one at a time from left to right in the *definiendum*, adding them from right to left together with a preceding lambda at the beginning of the *definiens*.

Given the enrichment of Ty_3 with these constants, it can be seen that any sentence of ABLE is also a sentence of Ty_3. Furthermore, since the postulates restricting the interpretation of the Ty_3 constants are based on the same definitions as for the original ABLE semantics, it is clear that for any formula ϕ, in the ABLE fragment of Ty_3, the embedding function $[\![.]\!]$ will map ϕ onto a Ty_3 formula which is Ty_3-equivalent to ϕ. That is, if $[\![\phi]\!] = \psi$, then $\psi \equiv_{\text{Ty}_3} \phi$.

9.2.2 Indexed English in Ty_3

It will now be shown how indexed trees of English can be given a direct interpretation in type theory. Trees may be represented as bracketed strings, such that E223b is a tree for the indexed English discourse in E223a:

E223 a. $\quad$ A_1 woman realises John$_2$ owns a$_3$ donkey. She$_1$ is angry.

     b. $\quad$ *((((a 1) woman)(realises ((John 2)*
$\quad\quad\quad$ *(owns ((a 3) donkey)))))∘)*
$\quad\quad\quad$ *((she 1) is-angry)*

     c. $\quad$ SOME.1.(WOMAN^u.1)(REALISES^a.1.
$\quad\quad\quad$ (THE.2.(NAMED-JOHN^u.2).
$\quad\quad\quad$ (SOME.3.(DONKEY^u.3).(OWNS^b.2.3)))
$\quad\quad\quad$ AND (SHE.1.(IS-ANGRY^b.1))

Note that E223b is the tree not for a sentence of indexed English, but for a discourse, the ∘ representing a sentence sequencing operator. If words of English are defined to be constants of the right types, and if some simple notation conventions are used, such trees become formulae of type theory. We will now see how such constants can be defined, and in a way which yields intuitively reasonable meanings — at least intuitive for those who accept that the meaning of E223a is given by the ABLE formula E223c.

First, let us say that simple nouns and intransitive verbs correspond directly to the dynamic unary predicate constants that were used for ABLE's semantics, which were constants of type $\langle d, \pi \rangle$:

Meaning Postulate MP18

$$
\begin{aligned}
woman &= \text{WOMAN}^u \\
donkey &= \text{DONKEY}^u \\
is\text{-}angry &= \text{IS-ANGRY}^u
\end{aligned}
$$

Propositional verbs, of course, correspond to ABLE's dynamic attitude predicate constants, except that the ABLE attitudes combined first with the subject marker and then with the propositional argument, whereas it will be more natural here to assume that an attitudinal predicate combines first with a proposition to form a verb phrase. Thus an argument swap is required:

Meaning Postulate MP19

$$
realises = \lambda F \lambda D \left[\text{REALISES}^a.D.F \right]
$$

In ABLE, determiners combined with a discourse marker and two propositions to form a proposition. Clearly a determiner of indexed English ought to combine with a discourse marker and two dynamic properties. Variables $\mathcal{P}$ and $\mathcal{P}'$, of type $\rho = \langle d, \pi \rangle$, will be used to range over dynamic properties, of which dynamic unary predicates are examples.

Meaning Postulate MP20

$$
\begin{aligned}
a &= \lambda D \lambda P \lambda P' \left[\text{SOME}.D.(P.D).(P'.D) \right] \\
the &= \lambda D \lambda P \lambda P' \left[\text{THE}.D.(P.D).(P'.D) \right]
\end{aligned}
$$

Noun phrases now correspond to Ty$_3$ formulae of type $\langle \rho, \pi \rangle$, and variables $\mathcal{Q}$ and $\mathcal{Q}'$ range over objects of this type. For instance $a.1.woman$ is a formula of type $\langle \rho, \pi \rangle$. A transitive verb should combine with an noun phrase to form a verb phrase, so transitive verbs must have the type $\langle \langle \rho, \pi \rangle, \rho \rangle$. This means that in order to define constants for transitive verbs in terms of ABLE's dynamic binary predicate constants, which have type $\langle d, \rho \rangle$, a little type raising is necessary:

Meaning Postulate MP21

$$
owns = \lambda \mathcal{Q} \lambda D \left[\mathcal{Q}.(\text{OWNS}^b.D) \right]
$$

The sequencing operator $\circ$ is to be interpreted as conjunction:

Meaning Postulate MP22

$$
\circ = \text{AND}
$$

We now turn to pronouns and proper names. As with ABLE, these may be interpreted in terms of the determiner *the*:

Meaning Postulate MP23

$$
\begin{aligned}
john &= \lambda D \left[the.D.\text{NAMED-JOHN}^u \right] \\
she &= \lambda D \left[the.D.(\lambda D \left[\text{SINGULAR}^u.D \text{ AND } \text{FEMALE}^u.D \right]) \right.
\end{aligned}
$$

Let us adopt the following notation conventions for Ty$_3$:

Reversibility: If X is of type α and Y is of type $\langle \alpha, \beta \rangle$ then $(XY) = (YX) = Y.X$

Parsimony: For any Ty$_3$ expressions X, Y and Z, if $X(YZ)$ is a sentence of type theory, and $(XY)Z$ is not, then XYZ will be understood as equivalent to $X(YZ)$, and *vice versa* if $(XY)Z$ is a sentence of type theory but $X(YZ)$ not. If neither or both of these bracketings are sentences of type theory, then the unbracketed string will not be understood as a sentence of type theory.

Indexing: If X is of type $\langle d, \alpha \rangle$ and Y is of type d, then $X_Y = X.Y$.

Given the first of these conventions, E223b can be taken as a well-formed sentence of type theory. More importantly, given the above postulates, we have that E223b = E223c. Here is a small part of the proof, the rest being left up to the reader:

$$
\begin{aligned}
a &= \lambda D \lambda P \lambda P' \left[\text{SOME}.D.(P.D).(P'.D) \right] \\
(a\ 3) &= \lambda P \lambda P' \left[\text{SOME}.3.(P.3).(P'.3) \right] \\
donkey &= \text{DONKEY}^u \\
((a\ 3)\ donkey) & \\
&= \lambda P' \left[\text{SOME}.3.(\text{DONKEY}^u.3).(P'.3) \right] \\
owns &= \lambda Q \lambda D \left[Q.(\text{OWNS}^b.D) \right] \\
(owns\ ((a\ 3)\ donkey)) & \\
&= \lambda Q \lambda D \left[Q.(\text{OWNS}^b.D) \right]. \\
&\quad (\lambda P' \left[\text{SOME}.3.(\text{DONKEY}^u.3).(P'.3) \right]) \\
&= \lambda D \left[(\lambda P' \left[\text{SOME}.3.(\text{DONKEY}^u.3).(P'.3) \right]).(\text{OWNS}^b.D) \right] \\
&= \lambda D \left[\text{SOME}.3.(\text{DONKEY}^u.3).(\text{OWNS}^b.D.3) \right] \\
john &= \lambda D \left[the.D.\text{NAMED-JOHN}^u \right] \\
the &= \lambda D \lambda P \lambda P' \left[\text{THE}.D.(P.D).(P'.D) \right] \\
john &= \lambda D \lambda P' \left[\text{THE}.D.(\text{NAMED-JOHN}^u.D).(P'.D) \right] \\
(john\ 2) &= \lambda P' \left[\text{THE}.2.(\text{NAMED-JOHN}^u.2).(P'.2) \right] \\
((John\ 2)\ (owns\ ((a\ 3)\ donkey))) & \\
&= \lambda P' \left[\text{THE}.2.(\text{NAMED-JOHN}^u.2).(P'.2) \right]. \\
&\quad (\lambda D \left[\text{SOME}.3.(\text{DONKEY}^u.3).(\text{OWNS}^b.D.3) \right]) \\
&= \text{THE}.2.(\text{NAMED-JOHN}^u.2). \\
&\quad (\text{SOME}.3.(\text{DONKEY}^u.3).(\text{OWNS}^b.2.3))
\end{aligned}
$$

The last two of the above notation conventions allow even more English-like structures to be interpreted in type theory. The convention of *parsimony* means that brackets are only needed where they disambiguate, and the *indexing* convention allows indices to be subscripted. Given these conventions,

"$(a_1$ *woman realises John*$_2$ *owns* a_3 *donkey* $\circ$) *she*$_1$ *is-angry*", for example, becomes a Ty$_3$ formula.

Next I will consider a classic example from the presupposition literature:

E224 a. Somebody managed to succeed George V on the throne of England.

The infamous E224a appeared in an endnote to Karttunen and Peters (1979). It will be recalled from part one of this book that the basis of Karttunen and Peters' extension to Montague Grammar is the division of meaning into two components, which for current purposes can be labelled as *assertive* and *presuppositional*, with rules of composition being separately specified for each component.

The fact that assertions and presuppositions are specified independently means that the ordinary assertive meaning of an expression places no constraints on what the presupposition might be, so that at first sight their approach appears to be of great generality. However, it is this very independence of assertion and presupposition which ultimately must force us to reject such an approach, for it makes it impossible to specify scope and binding relations between the assertion and presupposition. This is essentially what Karttunen and Peters observed with respect to E224a. They assume that the control verb 'manage' carries a presupposition (or conventional implicature) to the effect that the subject of the verb has difficulty in achieving whatever is specified by the verb's infinitival complement. Thus, for example, 'I managed to complete my monograph' should presuppose that I had difficulty in doing so.

That 'manage' displays classically presuppositional behaviour can be seen from the fact that the 'difficulty' inference tends to survive from certain embedded contexts. For instance 'I *might* manage to complete my monograph' still seems to suggest that I would find completion difficult.

Karttunen and Peters argue that it is natural to infer from E224a that the person who succeeded George V had difficulty in doing so, and that it is the fact that the successor did not in fact have any difficulty succeeding which makes the sentence seem odd to those with a little historical knowledge. Thus it seems that it is presupposed that some individual had difficulty, and it is asserted of the same individual that he eventually succeeded, so that there must be some binding relation between the presupposition and the assertion. To repeat: such a binding relation cannot obtain in Karttunen and Peters' system, which yields a presupposition that somebody had difficulty succeeding George V, and a quantificationally independent assertion that somebody succeeded George V. As Karttunen and Peters observe, there are many people who would have found it difficult to succeed George V, so that the predicted presupposition is trivially satisfied, and no account of the example's oddity is provided.[1]

In the second half of this book I have attempted to develop an integrated account of presuppositional and assertive aspects of meaning, following Heim in relating the peculiar behaviour of presupposition to extraneous semantic phenomena. Within the integrated account it is possible to describe binding relations between presuppositions and assertions, or *vice versa*. Let us consider a translation into type theory of (the relevant aspects of) E224a:

---

[1]C.f. the discussion of 'Somebody curtsied' in §2.3, which was shown to be problematic for Karttunen and Peters in precisely the same way as the George V example discussed above.

E224 b.   *Somebody$_6$ managed to succeed George-V$_5$*

Of course, this does not look much like a formula of type theory, but if the right constants are defined then, according to the above notational conventions, it will be. There is a minor problem in treating this example, in that ABLE does not contain the equivalent of control verbs, although there is no obvious reason why ABLE should not be extended in this respect. For the moment it will suffice to make the crass assumption that control verbs are interpreted in terms of underlying dynamic attitude predicates. The following postulate restricts the denotation of an ABLE attitude predicate MANAGED^a such that MANAGED^a.D.F can only provide an update if it is established that the proposition F 'is problematic for' the individual represented by D, in which case the output is calculated by simply updating with the proposition F.

Meaning Postulate MP24

$$\forall I \forall J \forall D \forall F \quad I\{\text{MANAGED}^a.D.F\}J \leftrightarrow$$
$$(t\text{-}domain.I.D \ \wedge$$
$$I \ satisfies \ \text{PROBLEMATIC-FOR}^a.D.F \ \wedge \ I\{F\}J)$$

The definition of the constants appearing in E224b is now straightforward. The noun phrase *somebody*, which has the same type as for a name or pronoun, is defined in terms of the ABLE determiner SOME and a unary predicate PERSON^u, such that *somebody$_7$* is equivalent to *a$_7$ person*:

Meaning Postulate MP25

$$somebody \ = \ \lambda \mathcal{P} \lambda D \ [\text{SOME}.D.(\text{PERSON}^u.D).(\mathcal{P}.D)]$$

The constants *George-V*, *succeed* and *to* do not require much thinking about, names and transitive verbs having been dealt with above, and *to* being assumed semantically trivial:

Meaning Postulate MP26

$$George\text{-}V \ = \ \lambda D \lambda \mathcal{P} \ [\text{THE}.D.(\text{NAMED-GEORGE-V}^u.D).(\mathcal{P}.D)]$$
$$to \ = \ \lambda \mathcal{P} \ [\mathcal{P}]$$
$$succeed \ = \ \lambda \mathcal{Q} \lambda D \ [\mathcal{Q}.(\text{SUCCEED}^b.D)]$$

Finally, *managed* of type $\langle \rho, \rho \rangle$ is defined in terms of the attitude predicate MANAGED^a, so that for any marker D and dynamic property $\mathcal{P}$, *managed.D.$\mathcal{P}$* defines the same CCP as MANAGED^a.D.($\mathcal{P}$.D):

Meaning Postulate MP27

$$managed \;=\; \lambda P \lambda D \,[\text{MANAGED}^a.D.(\mathcal{P}.D)]$$

Given these postulates, it is easily verified that the formulae in E224b and E224c denote the same CCP:

E224   c.   SOME.6.(PERSON^u.6).(MANAGED^a.6.
(THE.5.(NAMED-GEORGE-V^u.5).(SUCCEED^b.6.5)))

    ABLE formulae of this form were discussed in §8.4, and on the basis of that discussion it is clear that E224c will (only) be admitted by contexts in which at least one individual is established to find his succession to the throne problematic, and it will provide an update to a context where such an individual actually has succeeded George V.[2]

    The above *ad hoc* translations of indexed English discourses into type theory serve for illustrative purposes, but it is more useful to specify general procedures for the interpretation process. This will make the theory easier to extend or attack, according to taste. Here, then, is an *official* definition of the syntax of the language of indexed, bracketed English (Indexed Bracklish):

Definition D66 (Syntax of Indexed Bracklish) Given sets of names, nouns, intransitive, transitive and attitude verbs, occupying the categories Name, N, IV, TV, and AV respectively, and that the category i consists of the integers, the language of Indexed Bracklish is defined by the following rewrite rules:

det	$\Rightarrow$	*the* | *a* | *exactly one* | *every* | *no* | *most* | *few*
PN	$\Rightarrow$	*he* | *she* | *it* | *they*
NP	$\Rightarrow$	((det i) N) | ((det i) (N (*who* VP))) | (PN i) | (Name i)
VP	$\Rightarrow$	IV | (TV NP) | (AV S)
S	$\Rightarrow$	(NP VP) | (NP (*do(es)n't* VP)) | (NP (*might* VP)) | (*perhaps* S) | ((*if* S) S) | (S *and*) S
D	$\Rightarrow$	S | ((D ∘) D)

---

[2]In fact I have reservations about the basic analysis of 'managed' advocated by Karttunen and Peters, and have used more or less the same analysis simply in order to bring out the difference in the binding mechanisms of the two theories. The point that the Karttunen and Peters theory does not yield an adequate account of binding could have been made with the Modigliani ownership examples which I considered above, and I refrained from doing this only because Karttunen and Peters do not consider these examples. My own preference would be for analysing the presuppositions of 'managed' not in terms of a simple proposition about the subject having had difficulty, but in terms of the hearer's expectations. However, I will not attempt to justify this here.

Below I present a schema for defining constants for the terminal symbols of a language of Indexed Bracklish: all underlined expressions are to be understood as replaceable by constants representing elements of the relevant categories.

Definition D67 (Schema for constants of Indexed Bracklish)

$$\underline{n} \;=\; \underline{\mathrm{N}}^u$$

$$\underline{iv} \;=\; \underline{\mathrm{IV}}^u$$

$$\underline{tv} \;=\; \lambda Q \lambda D \,[Q(\underline{\mathrm{TV}}^u.D)]$$

$$av \;=\; \lambda F \lambda D \,[\underline{\mathrm{ATTITUDE}}^a.D.F]$$

$$det \;=\; \lambda D \lambda \mathcal{P} \lambda \mathcal{P}' \,[\underline{\mathrm{DET}}.D.(\mathcal{P}.D).(\mathcal{P}'.D)]$$

$$name \;=\; \lambda D \lambda \mathcal{P} \,[\mathrm{THE}.D.(\mathrm{NAMED\text{-}\underline{NAME}}^u.D)(\mathcal{P}.D)]$$

$$pronoun \;=\; \lambda D \lambda \mathcal{P} \,[\mathrm{THE}.D.(\underline{\mathrm{CONDITIONS\ ON\ D}}^u)(\mathcal{P}.D)]$$

$$who \;=\; \lambda \mathcal{P} \lambda \mathcal{P}' \lambda D \,[\mathcal{P}.D \text{ AND } \mathcal{P}'.D]$$

$$might \;=\; \lambda \mathcal{P} \lambda D \,[\mathrm{MIGHT}.(\mathcal{P}.D)]$$

$$perhaps \;=\; \lambda F \,[\mathrm{MIGHT}.F]$$

$$and \;=\; \lambda F \lambda F' \,[F \text{ AND } F']$$

$$\circ \;=\; \lambda F \lambda F' \,[F \text{ AND } F']$$

$$if \;=\; \lambda F \lambda F' \,[F \text{ IMPLIES } F']$$

$$do(es)n't \;=\; \lambda \mathcal{P} \lambda \mathcal{Q} \,[\,\mathrm{NOT}\,(\mathcal{Q}.\mathcal{P})]$$

The only definitions introduced which are not of types familiar from the earlier example derivations are those for *who, might, perhaps, don't* and *doesn't*. The first of these, *who*, is defined as the conjunction of two properties. The reason for including both *perhaps* and *might* is one of convenience, in that the discussion of epistemic modality in §8.3 involves both examples where the subject noun phrase appears within the scope of a modality, and examples where the subject takes scope over the modality. It seems reasonable to assume that the sentential operator *perhaps* always takes wide scope, and this is reflected in the above definition. However, whereas the 'might' of English can appear in either scope configuration, I have assumed here that *might* is semantically just a verb phrase modifier, so that the subject takes wide scope. The reader may like to verify that the Indexed Bracklish sentence *(((most 1) politicians) (might be-spying))* (cf. E214) is given the meaning discussed in §8.3. In contrast, the constants *don't* and *doesn't* are both defined so as to take wide scope over the subject noun phrase in the interpretation of Indexed Bracklish. There is no fundamental reason why *might* should not be defined similarly, such that it also took wide scope. However, to extend the interpretation of Indexed Bracklish with a systematic way of accounting for such scope ambiguities, for instance using a type polymorphism approach as developed by Emms (1990) or Hendriks (1989), would take us beyond the scope of the current work.

9.3 A Plea for Common Sense

9.3.1 Mutual Ignorance

What is the common ground? What, for example, is the common ground between you and me? To answer this question, you need to know something about my beliefs. But what do you know about my beliefs? Can you specify even one proposition which you are sure I believe in?[3]

In short, no participant in a conversation knows what the common ground is. This truism ought to be rather disturbing to those who would associate the information states of dynamic semantics with the common ground of the conversational participants, a conflation which I always found attractive. But if states are identified with the common ground and nobody knows what the common ground is, then the states could not be states *of* anybody. A state which is not a state of something or someone, is not of much use to anything or anyone.

Of course, the intuition that information states be *associated* with some notion of common ground need not force us to accept that the relationship is one of identity. In what follows, I will try to show that once the proper relationship between information states and the common ground is established, the very intangibility and unknowability of the common ground can become a source of inspiration rather than despair.

Consider the case of a doctoral thesis: it is doubtful that there is any determinate notion of a common ground between author and readers. Unless the examiners recommend that every copy be burnt, the thesis will remain for an indefinite number of years in a dusty university archive. There always remains the possibility that somebody will accidentally stumble across the thesis, and begin to read. But if the common ground is not only unknowable by the author, but arguably completely indeterminate, then the candidate, as with any author, is forced to make assumptions about the knowledge of the eventual readers. These assumptions may even end up partially determining who the readership is. Thus, although the real common ground is indeterminate, an operational definition could be given: the common ground is (modulo rewrite requests of the examiners) whatever the candidate decides it will be.

Unfortunately, this operational definition is of only limited assistance to the reader of a doctoral thesis, for, as has already been established,

---

[3]A tautology, perhaps? As it happens, I never accept tautologies, although I am quite partial to contradictions. You too? Well, then we certainly have a lot in common.

the reader knows nothing about the author with any certainty. But the operational definition does tell us about the nature of the problem facing the readers: the readers do not know what the author assumed about the common ground, but they know that if they had information corresponding to that assumed common ground, then they could safely update this state with the content of the thesis. In effect, readers are forced to reason abductively from the presuppositions of the text to calculate the assumptions of the writer.

Those familiar with Stalnaker's work (e.g. Stalnaker 1974) will recognise something like his theory of pragmatic presupposition in my description up to this point of the difficulties facing those writing and reading theses — my operational definition of the common ground coincides with his definition of *speaker's presuppositions*. Now, however, I want to ask a question that will take us beyond Stalnaker's account. Given that the readers never know what information the author assumed them to have before they started reading, how can we represent the information that a reader has after reading an arbitrary initial chunk of thesis?

In terms of KMG, the obvious answer would run as follows. The relevant aspect of a reader's information state at any point is an object of type ι, such that at the beginning of the thesis the reader has information corresponding to the state of minimal information $\overline{\top}$, and later states are obtained by updating this state successively with the content of the thesis. Such an answer is clearly naive, for as soon as the reader reached a presupposition which had not been previously justified in the text, the rules of KMG would give no indication as to how to continue updating. Could the reader simply have started with a more informed state and updated that? Yes, of course, but which one? Unfortunately, no single information state is appropriate, if the term *information state* is taken simply to mean the objects of type ι introduced in the previous chapters. An example should clarify the point.

Suppose that as you read this book, you do not know whether it was Montague or Kahlish, or perhaps even Carnap who first started using the term *pragmatics* to describe what is now commonly called *indexical semantics*. But you guess that the author of the book will know which it was, and furthermore is quite likely to take for granted that readers also know. Thus, as far as you know, the author may choose to use the presuppositional phrase 'the well-known fact that Carnap first used the term 'pragmatics' to refer to what we now call indexical semantics'. If you had simply assumed that the author's model of the common ground involved Carnap having made the introduction, then you could safely update with a sentence containing this phrase. On the other hand, you know that the author may use the same phrase with 'Kahlish' or 'Montague' substituted for 'Carnap'. If you happen to choose the right assumption you will have no problem, but ι-typed information states leave no room for sitting on the fence. For if you simply choose to begin reading the book with a disjunctive state in which it is not established who actually was responsible, then as soon as you come across the use of one of the above presuppositional phrases you will be sunk: your information state will not satisfy the presupposition, and, at least according to the theory of the last few chapters, there will be no way to continue updating.

Thus we are faced with a conundrum. If we interpret an information state realistically, in terms of the information the reader might conceivably have about the writer, then KMG will often fail to provide an update when it clearly should. On the other hand, interpreting information states as the assumed common ground of the writer is of no use in providing a realistic model of how a reader's information state develops, since a reader cannot know in advance what the writer has assumed. Conclusion? The notion of updating developed in this book so far is incorrect. Could the definition of an information state be preserved, but an alternative notion of update be used? If so, then the new notion will have to be defined with great caution, for I have gone to considerable lengths in this monograph to motivate a theory of information independently of presuppositional data. Thus, there is little leeway for making major changes to the relations between contexts defined by English sentences, without actually reformulating the definition of a context. Neither is it possible simply to weaken the constraints on the incoming context due to presuppositional constructions. For instance, it would not be appropriate to alter the definition of factivity such that the incoming context was only constrained to be consistent with the presupposition rather than to satisfy it, whilst making the output of a factive verb satisfy the presupposition. This would yield the right entailment patterns for unembedded factives, but would destroy projection properties: the negation of a factive would no longer entail the truth of the factive complement.

9.3.2 Information Sets

The Carnap/Kahlish/Montague story above is suggestive. Suppose that you maintained in parallel a number of ι-typed states, such that in some Carnap redefined pragmatics, in others it was Kahlish or Montague, and perhaps in some it was not established that any of them redefined anything. Then you could try updating each state separately with the content of the book, and see which structures survived. That way, whatever assumptions the author had made concerning the redefinition of pragmatics, at least one state would satisfy the assumptions, and would thus produce an output. This idea is easily formalised. If states are to be maintained in parallel, then updating must be framed in terms of sets of states, where each state in the set corresponds to a possibly correct model of the speaker's assumptions about the common ground:

Definition D68 **(Information Sets)** An information set is any object of type $\langle \iota, \tau \rangle$, and variables S, T will range over objects of this type.

Now a new set-update operator, $+$, can be defined. This operator maps information sets onto functions from CCPs to information sets, and is thus of type $\langle\langle \iota, \tau \rangle, \langle \pi, \langle \iota, \tau \rangle\rangle\rangle$. Note that the definition of the update function "$+$" is related to the ordinary update relation by a standard 'lifting' technique, the so-called *subset* construction (c.f. the discussion in Fernando 1995). If S is an initial information set, then the set-update of S with a CCP ϕ is denoted by $S + \phi$, which is simply the set of outputs obtained by updating (in the KMG sense) the elements of the set S with ϕ:

Meaning Postulate MP28

$$+ = \lambda S \lambda \phi \lambda I \, [\exists J \; S.J \, \wedge \, J\{\phi\}I]$$

To make sense of information sets, it helps to relate them to familiar logical notions. The following postulate defines a constant *supports*. Support is an analogous notion to satisfaction, but defined at the level of information sets rather than states:

Meaning Postulate MP29

$$supports = \lambda S \lambda \phi \, [\forall I \; S.I \to I \; satisfies \, \phi]$$

In terms of *supports*, a notion of entailment can be defined. The following fact shows that defining ϕ to entail ψ as "updating the *minimal* information set with ϕ yields an information set supporting ψ" just yields the earlier definition of entailment from Chapter 7.[4]

Fact 9.1 (Support-based Entailment) If ϕ and ψ are eliminative CCPs, then:

$$\phi \models \psi \quad iff \quad (\lambda I \, [\top] + \phi) \; supports \, \psi$$

Proof: By the definition of *supports* and $+$, $(\lambda I \, [\top] + \phi) \; supports \, \psi$ *iff* every possible output of ϕ satisfies ψ, but this is just the definition of entailment in MP5.

As it happens yet another standard dynamic notion of entailment in terms of information sets reduces to the same old definition:

---

[4]Naturally, what I am calling a *minimal* information set is in another sense maximal, in that it contains every possible information state.

Fact 9.2 (Another support-based Entailment) If ϕ and ψ are eliminative CCPs, then:

$$\phi \models \psi \quad \textit{iff} \quad \forall S \forall S' \ S + \phi = S' \rightarrow S' \ \textit{supports} \ \psi$$

Proof: The definition of $+$ shows that update is distributive across the component states of an information set. That is, if S is the union of $S_1, \ldots, S_n$ (i.e. that function from information states that returns true for any state for which one of $S_1, \ldots, S_n$ would return true) then $S + \phi$ is the union of $S_1 + \phi, \ldots S_n + \phi$). So it suffices to consider singleton information sets. But for these the requirement $\forall S \forall S' \ S + \phi = S' \rightarrow S' \ \textit{supports} \ \psi$ reduces to $\forall I \forall I' \ I\{\phi\}I' \rightarrow I' \ \textit{satisfies} \ \psi$, which again is just the earlier definition of entailment in MP5.[5]

Since lifting the semantics up to the level of information sets has no effect on entailment, it is clear that the presupposition projection properties established in Chapter 8 will be maintained. The only difference is that whereas at the level of states, presuppositions can cause undefinedness, at the level of information sets a CCP always yields an update. In fact, 9.1 combined with the fact that (non-modal) presuppositions of CCPs are also entailments, shows that updating the minimal information set with a CCP which presupposes some (non-modal) proposition will always yield a set which supports that proposition.

Let us see how information sets help with a simple example, based on the earlier 'who redefined pragmatics?' story. First, here are some constants of Indexed Bracklish and some relevant states:

- All constants are defined using the schema in D67: *carnap*, *montague* and *pragmatics* are names, *redefine=redefined* is a TV, *realised-that* is a factive AV, and *didn't* uses the same semantics as *doesn't*.

- A *satisfies* ($carnap_1$ *redefined* $pragmatics_2$)

- A *satisfies* ($montague_3$ *didn't redefine* $pragmatics_2$)

- B *satisfies* ($montague_3$ *redefined* $pragmatics_2$)

- B *satisfies* ($carnap_1$ *didn't redefine* $pragmatics_2$)

- $C = A \cup B$

- $A\{montague_3$ *didn't realise-that* $carnap_1$ *redefined* $pragmatics_2\}A'$

---

[5]Both of these support based notions of entailment correspond to definitions proposed in Veltman (1996), who also observes that they collapse for distributive systems.

Neither B nor C admits the proposition *montague₃ didn't realise-that carnap₁ redefined pragmatics₂*. However, representing an information set containing iotas $I, J, \ldots$ as $(I, J, \ldots)$, we have the following update:

(A, B, C) + *montague₃ didn't realise-that carnap₁ redefined pragmatics₂* = (A')

Thus an information state which does not support the proposition that Carnap redefined pragmatics can still be updated with a sentence in which the proposition is presupposed. More generally, by being realistic about what a hearer knows of the speaker's assumptions about the common ground, an obvious difficulty with the CCP model has been resolved. Once it is recognised that the states of ABLE and KMG semantics are not to be identified with the common ground, but are to be thought of as possible models of the common ground, the awkward fact that presuppositions can be informative becomes unproblematic.

9.3.3 Information Orderings

Information sets provide a model of an agent's uncertain knowledge of the common ground, but there is good reason to consider more sophisticated models. It is intuitively clear that not all assumptions that a writer/speaker might make are equally plausible. For instance, it is more plausible that Carnap redefined pragmatics than that Carnap's dog redefined pragmatics, and it seems reasonable that a reader's model of the writer's assumptions about the common ground should reflect this difference. But it is not appropriate merely to assume that some states are in the context and some not, since there is no obvious place to draw the line. If it is implausible that Carnap's dog redefined pragmatics, is it plausible that Carnap's grandmother redefined pragmatics?

One can imagine various more structured notions of context than simple sets of states that might be used to encode the difference in plausibility of different assumptions. For example we might consider adding a type p of probabilities to the type theoretic setup, and defining a context to be a function of type $\langle \iota, p \rangle$ — something like a *vague* set. The more plausible states would be mapped onto higher probabilities. Such a notion of context would allow very fine-grained distinctions between states to be made: in fact, although the vague set analysis seems intuitive to me, I do not have applications in mind which would require quite such a fine grain. It will suffice if a context provides a measure of the relative plausibility of different states, such as to answer to questions like whether state I is more plausible than state J. In other words, what is needed is some sort of ordering over states:

Definition D69 (Information Ordering) Any object O of type π which has the property of transitivity is an information ordering. An *initial information ordering* is additionally reflexive.

Reflexivity: $\forall I \quad I\{O\}I$

Transitivity: $\forall I \forall J \forall K \quad (I\{O\}J \wedge J\{O\}K) \rightarrow I\{O\}K$

An *information ordering* O is a set of pairs of states, such that if a pair of states I and J is in the ordering relation, represented as $I\{O\}J$, then both I and J could correspond to the generator's assumptions, and I is at least as plausible as J. Note that information orderings have the same type as CCPs, which are also relations between states. However, orderings and KMG CCPs are quite different slices of π. For instance, whereas KMG CCPs are not in general transitive relations, orderings are by definition always transitive, and whilst the only pairs in the denotation of KMG CCPs are those in which the output is more informative than the input, there is no corresponding restriction on information orderings.

The use of orderings to represent default information of various kinds is becoming well-established, as in Veltman (1996), although Veltman's *expectation frames* involve orderings over possible worlds rather than over ι-typed states. It is clear that there must be many more states than there are worlds, and thus that information orderings provide a more fine-grained notion of preference than expectation frames. Indeed, it is clear that any ordering over worlds can be expressed using an ordering over states, if we simply associate the sub-part of an information ordering containing only single-world states with the corresponding expectation frame. I will not make any attempt to account for how preference orderings over states are formed, but simply take as given that the common sense of an agent provides him or her with such an ordering. It is clear that an underlying ordering over worlds could be used to induce a (very partial) ordering over states, and thus that mechanisms like those discussed by Veltman to provide orderings over worlds could be reinterpreted so as to generate information orderings. We could then add some additional general preference criteria, like specifying that if two states differ only by one having a larger domain of discourse markers than the other, then the smaller-domained state is *a priori* more plausible.

Updating can be defined along similar lines to the information-set based definition above, using a constant $*$, of type $\langle \pi, \langle \pi, \pi \rangle \rangle$. The update operation proceeds by taking all pairs of states in the denotation of the initial ordering, and trying to update each element of the pair with the CCP. If both states can be successfully updated, then the resulting states are paired in the output ordering. Thus if one state is initially at least as plausible as another, and both states admit the CCP, then in the final ordering the output from the first state will be at least as plausible as the output from the second.

Meaning Postulate MP30

$$* \; = \; \lambda O \lambda \phi \lambda I \lambda J \, [\exists I' \exists J' \; I'\{O\}J' \; \wedge \; I'\{\phi\}I \; \wedge \; J'\{\phi\}J]$$

A reader who had forgotten or never knew who redefined pragmatics, and was taken in by my story, might now be surprised by the fact that it was Bar Hillel who first defined pragmatics to be indexical semantics. Yet even if you were surprised by this fact, or surprised that I knew it, the surprise does not mean that you had any difficulty updating with the previous sentence. This is what would be expected if the structures which you updated were like information orderings, and the mechanism of update was something like the $*$ operation: even apparently unlikely alternatives should be represented somewhere in an information ordering, albeit rather low down.

However, orderings need not *contain* every state, in the sense that for some states I it will neither be the case that $\exists J \; I\{O\}J$ nor that $\exists J \; J\{O\}I$. In particular, an ordering produced by updating with a CCP will only contain states which are possible outputs of the CCP, and it need not even contain all of those. Thus, an information ordering registers two kinds of information. First, it says which states are possible models of the speaker's assumptions, and, second, it says what the preferences are amongst those states. Since an initial ordering is *reflexive*, which means that every state is at least as plausible as itself, it is clear that every state will be contained in an initial ordering. The set of states which a non-initial ordering registers as being possible models of the speaker's assumptions will be precisely those which the ordering says are at least as plausible as themselves:

Meaning Postulate MP31

$$contains \; = \; \lambda O \lambda I \, [I\{O\}I]$$

The constant *contains* relates information orderings to information sets: if O is an information ordering, then *contains*.O is an information set. Thus *contains* can be used to apply the above definition of *support* to information orderings: an ordering O supports a CCP ϕ *iff* (*contains*.O) *supports* ϕ. Clearly this possibility combined with 9.1 and 9.2 shows that some natural notions of entailment in terms of information orderings would correspond to the original definition in terms of ι-typed states. It is also clear that the potential informativeness of presuppositions is accounted for in just the same way as with information sets. But, as will be demonstrated shortly, there is more to the processing of presuppositions than can be naturally explained in terms of strict entailment, and this is where the additional structure of information orderings comes into play.

In an information ordering, there are some *optimal* states, in the sense that they are at least as plausible as all the other states which the ordering contains. Sometimes it will be the case that the optimal states are also minimal, by which I mean that all the non-preferred states are extensions of a preferred state. In this case, the set of propositions supported by the set of optimal states will be just the same as the set of propositions supported by the entire set of states which the ordering contains. However, it may also be the case that the optimal states are non-minimal. In that case, there will be propositions supported by the optimal states that are not supported by the ordering as a whole. If updating some ordering O with a CCP ϕ leads to an ordering in which the set of optimal states supports another CCP ψ, then I will say that relative to O, ϕ *implicates* ψ. The formal definitions of *optimal* and *implicates* are straightforward:

Meaning Postulate MP32

$$
\begin{aligned}
optimal &= \lambda O \lambda I \left[contains.O.I \ \wedge \ \forall J \left[J\{O\}I \rightarrow I\{O\}J \right] \right] \\
implicates &= \lambda O \lambda \phi \lambda \psi \left[\left(optimal.(O * \phi) \right) supports \, \psi \right]
\end{aligned}
$$

Let us consider a case where strict entailment seems too weak:

E52   If I go to London, my sister will pick me up at the airport.

As shown in §8.2, in ABLE (and the same clearly holds for KMG) presuppositions in the consequent of a conditional yield conditional presuppositions. Thus the CCP corresponding to E52 presupposes that if I go to London then I will have a sister. The occurrence of these weak, conditionalised presuppositions is one of the most strongly criticised aspects of the CCP model (see e.g. Gazdar 1979a). It seems intuitively obvious that somebody hearing E52 would conclude not only that if the speaker were to go to London he would have a sister, but that the speaker actually has a sister. In terms of information orderings, this inference pattern might lead us to come to a certain conclusion about a hearer's typical information ordering. For the inference to go through, some states in which it was definitely established that the speaker had a sister would have to be more plausible than all states in which the existence of a sister was conditionalised on the speaker's journeying to London. Here, by saying that one state is *more plausible than* another, I mean that the first is at least as plausible as the second, but not *vice versa*. Relative to such an ordering, E52 would *implicate* that the speaker had a sister, since updating the ordering with E52 would lead to an ordering in which the optimal states all satisfied the existence of a sister.

But why should it be the case that states in which the speaker has a sister are more plausible than certain states in which this proposition is conditionalised? This is a difficult question to answer completely, but I can imagine some potential lines of explanation. In the first place, note that although the CCP corresponding to E52 will only conditionally presuppose the existence of a sister, it will unconditionally presuppose the presence of a discourse marker in the input state. The input state will admit the CCP just in case in the world-sequence pairs where the speaker goes to London, the discourse marker is constrained to be the speaker's sister.

Suppose that the speaker acted as if their was no uncertainty about the identity of immediate family members. This would amount to treating them as rigid designators, a variant of Kripke's (1972) account of metaphysical constancy of named individuals. Suppose further that there were a general principle to the effect that states where assumed discourse markers corresponded to rigid designators were more plausible than those where assumed markers are non-rigid. In that case, of all the states which contained a marker that corresponded to the speaker's sister in any world-sequence pair, those in which the marker corresponded to the speaker's sister in every world-sequence pair would be most plausible, and this would lead to the observed inference pattern.

Whether or not the reader finds this convincing, it should be clear what I am aiming for: I would like to justify the particular inference pattern relevant to E52 in terms of more general principles. In fact, I think that the above markers-are-rigid line of reasoning is still not general enough, for there are many cases not involving the assumption of a new marker but where KMG's prediction of a conditional presupposition seems too weak. Consider the following example (repeated from §5.7):

E153   Perhaps if George has arrived, none of the press corps. knows that George and Al are both here.

Any state in which it is established that if George turns up then both George and Al will be here would admit the above sentence. However, in a situation where it is known that George and Al's arrival is independent (or even that they generally try to avoid each other) there is a clear tendency to come to a stronger conclusion on hearing E153, namely that Al is already here. For this result to be predicted, it would have to be the case that a state where Al's presence is established is more plausible than every state where Al's presence is conditional on George' arrival. The source of such orderings must be connected with the nature of explanation and justification, in particular the fact that George's arrival does not help explain Al's presence (especially if George and Al habitually avoid each other). On the other hand, it is clear that George's arrival does help explain George's presence, so it is not surprising that E153 does not implicate that George is definitely here.

When reading each of the following two examples, ask yourself whether there actually is any more hot water:

E225 If Jane takes a bath, Bill will be annoyed that there is no more hot water.

E226 If Jane wants a bath, Bill will be annoyed that there is no more hot water.

There is a clear contrast between these two examples. An utterance of E225 does not suggest that there actually is no more hot water, but only that if Jane takes a bath, there will be no more hot water. On the other hand, E226 suggests strongly to me that there is no more hot water. Put another way, E225 is compatible with the standard CCP prediction of a conditional reading, E226 has an interpretation (for me it is the favoured interpretation) which departs from that prediction. It is clear that there exist information orderings that would lead to precisely these predictions. Any ordering satisfying the following two conditions would suffice:

1. At least one state in which it is established that there is no hot water is more plausible than all states in which it is not known whether there is hot water, but in which it is known that if Jane wants a bath then there will be no hot water.

2. A state in which it is not known whether or not there is hot water but in which it is established that if Jane has a bath then there will be no more hot water must be at least as plausible as all states where it is definitely established that there is no hot water.

The general question is, why would it be reasonable to expect information orderings to have such properties? My answer to this question is on the one hand both simple and obvious, and on the other hand both awkward to implement and incompatible with many contemporary theories of presupposition. I know some linguists who will find it unhelpful or unpalatable. The answer is: common sense.

Let me expand on this. The contrast between E225 and E226 results from our ability to find a common-sensical explanation of the lack of hot water in terms of somebody having taken a bath, but in our inability to fully explain a lack of hot water in terms of somebody simply wanting a bath. The simple assumption that there is a finite amount of relevant hot water — about a bathful — is sufficient to allow justification of there being no more hot water in situations where Jane has just taken a bath. However, the same simple assumption would not suffice in the case of E226, and a number of other assumptions would be needed, such as the assumption that if Jane wants a bath then she will definitely take one. Thus it is the relative plausibility of assumptions not explicitly mentioned in the text of the example sentences that determines what is implicated. Here are four more examples (the first two of which were discussed in Part One of this book) which illustrate the same point:

E95   If Nixon invites Angela Davis to the Whitehouse, then Nixon will regret having invited a black militant to his residence.

E154   If Spaceman Spiff lands on Planet X, he will be bothered by the fact that his weight is greater than it would be on Earth.

E227   If John has an exam today, Mary will notice that he is smoking more than usual.

E228   If Jane goes into the cave without a light, she will be annoyed that she cannot see much.

In all of these cases, the standard CCP prediction of a conditional presupposition seems unobjectionable. These predicted presuppositions are, respectively, that if Nixon invites Davis he will have invited a black militant, that if Spaceman Spiff lands on Planet X then his weight will be greater than it would be on Earth, that if John has an exam today then he is smoking more than usual, and that if Jane goes into the cave without a light then she will not be able to see much. I would argue that in all four cases, what makes the conditional presuppositions reasonable is the possibility of finding a deeper explanation.

In the first case (E95) the deeper explanation is that Davis is a black militant. I take it that I am not a terribly unusual Englishman in having constructed this explanation for myself when I first read the example E95 some years ago, although I had no previous knowledge of Angela Davis.

In the second case (E154) the reason why the conditional presupposition makes sense is that it can be justified in terms of common sense physics. We suppose that Planet X is a planet, but we do not know whether Planet X is a big planet or a little planet. The simple assumption that Planet X is big (some readers may have more sophisticated views on the relationship between planets and their gravitational field strength) is sufficient to tell us that if Spiff lands on X then his weight will be greater than it would be on Earth.

I leave it to the reader to construct explanations for the implications of the other two examples. Of course, it might be that the reader deems E227 to implicate that John actually is smoking more than usual, or perhaps thinks E228 is most naturally uttered in a situation where Jane is known to be blind. Yet this would by no means be problematic. On the contrary, it would be grist to my mill, as it indicates something that is quite natural within the current account, namely that the reader's plausibility criteria differ somewhat from my own.

The predictions of the model introduced here stand in sharp contrast to those of various theories that were discussed in Part 1 of this book. The accounts which have occupied centre-field in formal presupposition theory, be they multivalent, partial, filtrationalist, cancellationist, dynamic or accommodational, are generally conceived of as solving the presupposition projection problem without any reference to common sense reasoning, whereas I would argue that in principle a theory lacking common sense cannot solve the projection problem. In particular, in Part 1 a number of the examples considered in this section were considered in detail, and it was shown that they are problematic for existing accounts (c.f. especially §2.4.3, §3.7, §5.5 and §5.7). Even if some authors have been aware that interaction with common sense reasoning is needed in order to account for all the data of presupposition projection, this has generally not resulted in formal models.

Here I would like to mention one prominent research group, namely that of Hobbs, which has provided formal models where common-sense reasoning helps determine presuppositional inferences. The work of this group was not discussed in the first part of this book, partly because it is not usually presented as a theory of presupposition *per se*, but as a complete theory of interpretation. In a series of papers (see e.g. the bibliography of Hobbs *et al.* 1990) Hobbs and colleagues have offered a view of interpretation as abduction, whereby grammar provides only limited absolute constraints on meaning, and a system of weighted abduction allows domain knowledge to supplement grammatical information so as to determine a most plausible interpretation. Systems of abduction typically allow reasoning backwards from some formula to sets of formulae which deductively entail that formula, and also provide some way of selecting the most appropriate such set. Given some observation, an explanation (or set of alternative explanations) for that observation may be generated. In the case of Hobbs' model of interpretation, the observation is an utterance, and the explanation amounts to a theory of the relevant beliefs and intentions of the speaker. And this is just the idea behind the proposal presented in the latter half of the current chapter, albeit that my technical realisation of that idea is quite different from that of Hobbs.

The goals of this book have been more modest than those of Hobbs and his co-workers, in that I have maintained a relatively conservative Frege-derived Montagovian line on the syntax-semantics interface, with compositional rules determining a semantic interpretation (or set of them) for each syntactic constituent in terms of the interpretations of sub-constituents, and in that I have not attempted to provide a computer implementation. The novelty of the current proposal consists principally in two departures from the Frege-Montague tradition. First, I have followed a recent trend in semantic theory by suggesting (in Chapters 6–8) that the traditional static view of what meanings are is inadequate, and I have proposed a dynamic alternative. Second, in this chapter, a model of the semantics-pragmatics interface has been proposed which allows both common-sense reasoning and semantic content to determine the information which a hearer derives from a particular utterance. Thus I have not gone so far as Hobbs, in that common sense reasoning does not determine content in the model I have developed. But I have shown a way in which a mechanism operating very much in the spirit of Hobbs' proposals can be built on top of a compositional theory of meaning.[6]

---

[6]There remain many respects in which the model of plausibility orderings developed here requires further development. A good example (pointed out by a referee of this book) is that if a state A is ranked as more plausible than a state B, then after update with a sentence S, A+S will be ranked as a more plausible state than B+S. I can easily conceive of counterexamples to this property. Suppose B encoded the presence of an umbrella, and A encoded the absence of an umbrella, and S carried the information that it was raining. Presumably B+S should then be more plausible than A+S, since, having mentioned that it is raining, it is quite *de rigeur* to refer presuppositionally to 'someone's umbrella' without first introducing the existence of such an object. What this example shows is that, in general, the plausibility ordering must be recalculated after each sentential update. The assumption made in the model I have presented, in which all plausibility ranking is *a priori*, set by factors that must be known prior to conversation, is simply an approximation. In other work I have considered how the use of preferential rankings over information states may be taken further (Beaver 1999a; 2001), bringing in factors other than world knowledge to determine relative rankings of states.

10

Connections and Directions

10.1 Introduction

In this chapter I will attempt to forge some theoretical links between the model that has been developed in the second part of this book and some of the theories discussed in the first part. These links suggest directions that might be taken to tackle phenomena not so far incorporated in the model presented here, but also directions that might be taken to resolve problems which arise in other theories of presupposition.

10.2 Multivalence

The thesis, descending from the work of Frege and Strawson, that presupposition projection should be explained as inheritance of semantic undefinedness, seems to find an antithesis in the suggestion that presupposition projection arises from (pragmatically justified) principles of context change. However, Peters (1977) provided a synthesis, observing that the presupposition inheritance properties derived by Karttunen (1974) could be duplicated in a system with a trivalent semantics, and thus do not depend on the dynamicity of Karttunen's account. The connectives in Peters trivalent system, which I will refer to as the *Peters connectives* (but which Krahmer 1993 terms the *Middle Kleene* connectives), can be used to show the relationship between the dynamic logics developed in the current work and trivalent logics.[1] Having made such a connection, it becomes easier to see how insights might be transferred from a trivalent to a dynamic setting or *vice versa*.

---

[1]The suggestion of drawing a formal connection between a PUL-like system and one based on Peters' semantics was first made to me by Marcus Kracht after a talk I gave in Amsterdam in 1992, and this resulted in the proof presented here. Willem Groeneveld, who was also at the talk, provided a proof of essentially the same property, and his proof runs along similar lines.

10.2.1 A Trivalent Semantics for the Non-epistemic Sub-language of PUL

The Peters connectives may be likened to the strong Kleene connectives, except that if the left-hand formula under a binary Peters connective is undefined, then the whole formula is undefined:

Definition D70 (Peters Connectives) The 3 valued interpretation of a complex formula ϕ relative to a world w, written $[\![\phi]\!]^3_w$, is given by recursion over the following truth tables:

$\phi \wedge \psi$	t	f	$\star$
t	t	f	$\star$
f	f	f	f
$\star$	$\star$	$\star$	$\star$

$\phi \vee \psi$	t	f	$\star$
t	t	t	t
f	t	f	$\star$
$\star$	$\star$	$\star$	$\star$

$\phi \rightarrow \psi$	t	f	$\star$
t	t	f	$\star$
f	t	t	t
$\star$	$\star$	$\star$	$\star$

ϕ	$\neg\phi$
t	f
f	t
$\star$	$\star$

The intuition behind the presupposition operator ∂ that I have utilised is that a formula $\partial\phi$ only defines an update if ϕ is true. A natural three valued analogue of this semantics would make $\partial\phi$ undefined whenever ϕ is not true, but true otherwise:

Definition D71 (Trivalent Presupposition Operator)

ϕ	$\partial\phi$
t	t
f	$\star$
$\star$	$\star$

The result proved in this section will concern two presentations of the semantics for the language of propositional logic with the addition of the unary ∂-operator. This language will be referred to as PL+∂. We assume models $\langle W, F \rangle$, where W is a set of worlds and F is an interpretation function mapping atomic formulae onto sets of worlds.[2] The first presentation is the trivalent semantics given by the above truth tables, the meaning of a formula ϕ in a world w being denoted by $[\![\phi]\!]^w_3$, and atomic formulae ϕ having interpretation given by $[\![\phi]\!]^w_3 = t$ if $w \in F(\phi)$, and f otherwise. We may then define trivalent entailment as the following relation between

---

[2] Atomic formulae are thus effectively bivalent: every world is either in the extension of a given atomic formula, or it is not, and there is no third possibility. I will not consider the case where atomic formulae themselves have a *fuzzy* extension, whereby worlds could fall neither either into the extension nor the anti-extension, or could fall into both.

formulae in the language:[3]

Definition D72 (Entailment in the 3-valued system)

$$\phi \models_3 \psi \quad \textit{iff} \quad \textit{for all models, } \forall w \in W, \llbracket \phi \rrbracket_3^w = t \; \Rightarrow \; \llbracket \psi \rrbracket_3^w = t$$

The second presentation of the semantics is just the update semantics introduced in Chapter 6 (as it applies to the non-epistemic sublanguage of PUL), the update semantics of a formula ϕ being denoted $\llbracket \phi \rrbracket_u$. For this language, the update notion of entailment from PUL adapted to the single premise case is easily shown to be equivalent to the following (which says that all fixed points of the premise are fixed points of the conclusion):

Definition D73 (Entailment in the Update System)

$$\phi \models_u \psi \quad \textit{iff} \quad \textit{for all models, } \forall \sigma \; \sigma \llbracket \phi \rrbracket_u \sigma \; \rightarrow \; \sigma \llbracket \psi \rrbracket_u \sigma$$

It will now be shown that the trivalent and update notions of entailment define exactly the same logic (i.e. the same binary relation between formulae). First, *truth* and *falsity* of a formula in a world will be defined for the trivalent and update systems, and an equivalence between these notions established. Truth in a world is analogous to the property of satisfaction in a set of worlds defined for PUL earlier. For truth of ϕ in a world w in the trivalent system $w \models_3 \phi$ will be written, with $w \not\models_3 \phi$ being used to indicate that this property is lacking, and $w \nVdash_3 \phi$ for falsity of ϕ in w in the trivalent system. Similar notation is used for these notions in the update system.

Definition D74 (Trivalent Truth in a World)

$$w \models_3 \phi \quad \textit{iff} \quad \llbracket \phi \rrbracket_3^w = t$$

Definition D75 (Trivalent Falsity in a World)

$$w \nVdash_3 \phi \quad \textit{iff} \quad \llbracket \phi \rrbracket_3^w = f$$

Definition D76 (Update Truth in a World)

$$w \models_u \phi \quad \textit{iff} \quad \{w\}\llbracket \phi \rrbracket_u \{w\}$$

---

[3]The definition of trivalent entailment is non-standard insofar as it is adapted for an interpretation of the language in terms of PUL models. Standardly entailment in trivalent propositional logics would be defined using models that gave a single valuation for each atomic proposition, rather than models involving possible worlds. However, this non-standardness in the definition is not significant, since it is clear that the double universal quantification over models and over worlds could be replaced with a single quantification over standard world-like models without affecting which formulae stand in the entailment relation.

Definition D77 (Update Falsity in a World)

$$w \not\models_u \phi \quad \text{iff} \quad \{w\}[\![\phi]\!]_u \emptyset$$

Lemma 10.1 *For all contexts w and propositions ϕ:*
$w \models_u \phi \iff w \models_3 \phi$ **and** $w \not\models_u \phi \iff w \not\models_3 \phi$

> **Proof:** By induction over the complexity of ϕ. Note that since disjunction and implication may be defined in terms of conjunction and negation identically in both systems, it is only necessary to consider the clauses for atomic formulae, the presupposition operator, conjunction and negation. As examples, I give (A) the truth clause for the presupposition operator, and (B) the truth clause for negation.
>
> (A) We want to show that, on the assumption that the above properties hold for some ϕ, then for any w, $w \models_u \partial\phi \iff w \models_3 \partial\phi$. First from left to right. We assume $w \models_u \partial\phi$, from which we obtain $\{w\}[\![\partial\phi]\!]_u\{w\}$ and, by the semantics of ∂, $\{w\}[\![\phi]\!]_u\{w\}$, i.e. $w \models_u \phi$. By the inductive hypothesis, $w \models_3 \phi$, and, by definition of $\models_3$ and the truth table for ∂, $w \models_3 \partial\phi$.
>
> From right to left, $w \models_3 \partial\phi$ gives us $[\![\partial\phi]\!]_3^w = t$, and by inspection of the truth table $[\![\phi]\!]_3^w = t$. The inductive hypothesis gives $\{w\}[\![\phi]\!]_u\{w\}$, from which $\{w\}[\![\partial\phi]\!]_u\{w\}$ follows by update semantics of ∂, and thence, by definition of $\models_u$, the result $w \models_u \partial\phi$.
>
> (B) We want to show that for any w, $w \models_u \neg\phi \iff w \models_3 \neg\phi$. From right to left, $\{w\}[\![\neg\phi]\!]_u\{w\}$ gives us $\{w\}[\![\phi]\!]_u\emptyset$, by update semantics of $\neg$. From this $w \not\models_u \phi$, and by the inductive hypothesis, $w \not\models_3 \phi$, $[\![\phi]\!]_3^w = f$ and thence $[\![\neg\phi]\!]_3^w = t$.
>
> All these steps are reversible, so from left to right, we simply get from $[\![\neg\phi]\!]_3^w = t$ that $w \not\models_3 \phi$, using the inductive hypothesis derive $w \not\models_u \phi$, thence $\{w\}[\![\phi]\!]_u\emptyset$, and $\{w\}[\![\neg\phi]\!]_u\{w\}$.

It must now be shown that the update notion of entailment is equivalent to a definition in terms of update truth and update falsity for this system:

Lemma 10.2 $\phi \models_u \psi$ *iff for all models, $\forall w[w \models_u \phi \to w \models_u \psi]$*

> **Proof:** From left to right, definition of $\models_u$ gives us that for any model $\forall\sigma \; \sigma[\![\phi]\!]_u\sigma \to \sigma[\![\psi]\!]_u\sigma$. It follows that this must hold for singleton sets of worlds σ, i.e. $\forall w \; \{w\}[\![\phi]\!]_u\{w\} \to \{w\}[\![\psi]\!]_u\{w\}$. But now definition of update truth gives us the left hand side.

The proof from right to left is more involved. Definition of update truth again gives us that (1) $\forall w \quad \{w\}[\![\phi]\!]_u\{w\} \rightarrow \{w\}[\![\psi]\!]_u\{w\}$. Now, it may be shown that this system has a distributivity property: (2) $\forall \sigma \ [\sigma[\![\phi]\!]_u\sigma$ *iff* $\forall w \in \sigma \ \{w\}[\![\phi]\!]_u\{w\}]$ (the proof requires another induction over formula complexity). Now define $W_\phi = \{w \mid \{w\}[\![\phi]\!]_u\{w\}\}$. From the distributivity property it follows that (3) $\forall \sigma \subseteq W_\phi \ \sigma[\![\phi]\!]_u\sigma$, and it also follows that (4) $\forall \sigma \nsubseteq W_\phi \ \neg(\sigma[\![\phi]\!]_u\sigma)$. 1 and 3 give that (5) $W_\phi \subseteq W_\psi$. We now know that for any σ, if it is a subset of W_ϕ, then it is a fixed point of both ϕ and ψ, and if it is not a subset it is not a fixed point of ϕ. It follows that all fixed points of ϕ are fixed points of ψ, which is the required result.

Fact 10.3 The trivalent and dynamic entailment notions are extensionally equivalent for the language of PL+∂: $\phi \models_u \psi$ *iff* $\phi \models_3 \psi$

Proof:
By Lemma 2, $\phi \models_u \psi$ is equivalent to $\forall M, w[w \models_u \phi \rightarrow w \models_u \psi]$. This is equivalent to $\forall M, w[w \models_3 \phi \rightarrow w \models_3 \psi]$ by Lemma 1. Now according to the definition of truth in the trivalent system this is in turn equivalent to $\forall M, w[[\![\phi]\!]_3^w = t \rightarrow [\![\psi]\!]_3^w = t]$, which is just the right-hand side of the definition of three valued entailment.

This establishes the main result. Now it is easily shown that according to the definition of presupposition given for PUL, and given the restriction to the non-epistemic sub-language, the presuppositions of a formula are all and only those formulae which are update-entailed both by the formula and by its negation. Furthermore, a standard definition of presupposition in a trivalent logic would be entailment by both the formula and its negation. But given that the notion of update entailment is extensionally equivalent to the notion of trivalent entailment for this system, it follows as a corollary that the notions of presupposition in the two systems are equivalent, which is essentially Peters' result. Another corollary is that for the sub-language without the ∂-operator, the logic is classical. This follows since, by assumption, atomic formulae have bivalent interpretations, and for all of the remaining connectives in the trivalent system, if their arguments are bivalent then they return the classical value.

Clearly there is a tight correspondence between the dynamic systems which have been introduced in Part II of this book and trivalent logics. Although I doubt whether for the epistemic and first-order systems such a strong extensional equivalence could easily be demonstrated, the equivalence demonstrated here is highly suggestive of a general similarity between the traditional semantic approach to presupposition and the dynamic semantic approach.

10.2.2 Assertion and Denial in Dynamic Logic

The operators in the following table are Bochvar's assertion operator (A), Bochvar's (presupposition-cancelling) external negation $(\sharp)$, and Seuren's presupposition-denying negation (S):

Definition D78 (Assertion and Denial Operators)

ϕ	$A\phi$	$\sharp\phi$	$S\phi$
t	t	f	f
f	f	t	f
$\star$	f	t	t

Both the external negation and Seuren's negation can be defined in terms of the assertion operator and connectives from the Peters system above. Thus $\sharp\phi \equiv \neg A\phi$ and $S\phi \equiv \sharp\phi \wedge \sharp\neg\phi$. The following definition provides an appropriate dynamic interpretation for the assertion operator, and thus in the process enables the negation operators to be defined[4]:

Definition D79 (Assertion in PUL)

$$\sigma[\![A\phi]\!]\tau \quad \text{iff} \quad \tau = \{w \in \sigma \mid \{w\}[\![\phi]\!]\{w\}\}$$

Fact 10.4 The trivalent and dynamic entailment notions are extensionally equivalent for the language of PL+∂ + A.

> **Sketch of Proof:** The proof requires us to check that the induction in lemma 10.1 still goes through, and that the A-operator does not affect the distributivity property used in the proof of lemma 10.2.

If an A-operator could be defined as an extension to ABLE, then it would be possible to augment the account given here with a Linkian floating-A type theory as described in §2, which would allow presupposition-denying negation to be analysed without direct postulation of an ambiguous negation. Alternatively, it would be possible to define negation to be ambiguous between internal and external interpretations, or between internal and Seuren negation.

---

[4]One could, of course, define the external negation and Seuren negation directly in the dynamic setting:

$$\sigma[\![\sharp\phi]\!]\tau \quad \text{iff} \quad \tau = \{w \in \sigma \mid \neg\{w\}[\![\phi]\!]\{w\}\}$$
$$\sigma[\![S\phi]\!]\tau \quad \text{iff} \quad \tau = \{w \in \sigma \mid \neg\exists v\{w\}[\![\phi]\!]v\}.$$

10.2.3 Formalising Backward Suppletion

As mentioned in Part One of this book (§2.4), Seuren has suggested that his trivalent logic (Kleene's strong logic with Seuren's presupposition-denying negation) should be augmented with an accommodation-like mechanism which he termed *backward suppletion*, although some details of this mechanism have remained unformalised (Seuren 1985). It will now be shown that the approach to accommodation developed in this book could also be applied to a trivalent system like Seuren's.[5]

Let us define an *epistemic alternative*, a view of what the speaker takes to be the common ground, to be a set of worlds. Then we may approximate the hearer's knowledge of the speaker's assumptions by a set of epistemic alternatives, that is, a set of sets of worlds. Suppose the speaker utters a sentence with meaning ϕ. Let us take it that the presuppositions of ϕ reflect the speaker's assumptions about the common ground, so that if in some epistemic alternative there is a world for which ϕ is undefined, then that alternative is not a good picture of the speaker's assumptions. On the other hand, if an alternative is compatible with the speaker's presuppositions, it can be updated simply by taking the intersection of the worlds in the alternative with the set of worlds for which ϕ is true.

Definition D80 (Updating an Information Set with a Trivalent Meaning)

$$I + \phi = \{\sigma \mid \exists \sigma' \in I$$
$$\forall w \in \sigma' \; [\![\phi]\!]_3^w \neq \star \; \wedge$$
$$\sigma = \{w \in \sigma' \mid [\![\phi]\!]_3^w = t\}\}$$

One can think of the above definition as comprising two principles, a principle of update and a principle of accommodation. The principle of update says that (a) the information which the speaker takes to be established is modelled as a set of worlds and (b) an appropriate assertive utterance should divide this set cleanly into two disjoint covering subsets, such that the utterance is true in all worlds in the first, and false in all worlds in the second. Just this view on how trivalent meanings should determine updates is espoused by Stalnaker (1979, pp. 325–326). On his view, such a principle "connects semantic presupposition with pragmatic speaker presupposition", and he gives the following rationale: "The point of an assertion is to reduce the context set in a certain determinate way. But if

---

[5]However, I have my doubts as to whether the system to be described is true to Seuren's intentions, since the architecture of the semantics-pragmatics interface which I propose differs from that of Seuren. Seuren envisages quite general inferential mechanisms operating at a level of mental representation and has used such devices to explain, for instance, instances of implicature denial. The divergence from this picture in the current work could be thought of as resulting from simplifications made so as to facilitate formalisation.

some proposition is not true or false at some possible world, then it would be unclear whether that possible world is to be included in the reduced set or not." The second principle, the principle of accommodation, carries Stalnaker's view one stage further. It states that (a) the hearer's knowledge of what the speaker takes to be established is modelled as a set of sets of worlds, and (b) an assertive utterance divides this set cleanly into two disjoint covering subsets, such that the utterance is appropriate in the sets of worlds in the first set and inappropriate in the sets of worlds in the second. The two principles combine into a single principle of hearer's context incrementation: given an utterance, update those sets of worlds where it is appropriate, and discard those where it is not.

A more sophisticated approach to modelling incrementation of a hearer's information states is to use *information orderings* like those discussed earlier. An ordering can be defined as a set of pairs of epistemic alternatives. Intuitively, a pair $\langle \sigma, \tau \rangle$ will be in the ordering just in case σ is considered at least as plausible a model of the speaker's assumptions as τ. Update proceeds by filtering out those pairs for which at least one of the alternatives is incompatible with the speaker's presuppositions, and otherwise updating both members of each pair with the new proposition, again simply by intersection with the set of worlds where the proposition is true:

Definition D81 (Updating Information Orderings with Trivalent Meanings)

$$
\begin{aligned}
O + \phi \;=\; & \{ \langle \sigma, \tau \rangle \mid \exists \langle \sigma', \tau' \rangle \in O \\
& \forall w \in (\sigma' \cup \tau')\ \llbracket \phi \rrbracket_3^w \neq \star \ \wedge \\
& \sigma = \{ w \in \sigma' \mid \llbracket \phi \rrbracket_3^w = t \} \ \wedge \\
& \tau = \{ w \in \tau' \mid \llbracket \phi \rrbracket_3^w = t \} \}
\end{aligned}
$$

One characteristic of the strong Kleene connectives is their tendency to yield conditional presuppositions. For instance, the following example (reproduced from the previous chapter) is predicted (on a standard Strawsonian definition of presupposition) to presuppose that if I go to London then I have a sister:

E52'   If I go to London, my sister will pick me up at the airport.

Now we can apply the same argumentation as used earlier to allow for the tendency to come to a stronger conclusion, namely that I have a sister. If it were the case that alternatives containing only worlds where I have a sister were higher in the plausibility ordering than states where it is not established whether I have one but it is established that in all the going-to-London worlds I have a sister, then the stronger inference would be predicted. Of course, whether the model actually does predict strengthening will depend on the particular common sense theory of the world underlying the information ordering.

Note that the same argumentation need not produce strengthening of a non-presuppositional conditional as in 'If I go to London then I have a sister.' Provided that there are some alternatives which are more plausible than all those where I assume that I have a sister (say, for instance, alternatives where nothing at all is assumed), then strengthening need not be predicted.[6]

In conclusion, I hope to have shown how, as an alternative to the dynamic semantic model presented in this book, it would be possible to combine a static (albeit non-bivalent) semantics with a dynamic pragmatics. This line of thinking is carried much further in recently completed work with Emiel Krahmer (Beaver and Krahmer 2001).[7]

10.3 Part-time Presupposition

As mentioned earlier (§3.4), one of the motivations for Karttunen's theories was a desire to avoid postulating what Karttunen termed *part-time* presupposition. Karttunen's intuition was that presuppositions are, to extend the metaphor, always on duty, but that sometimes the local context embedding the presupposition trigger hides the presupposition's work from the global context of interpretation. The cancellationist point of view, on the other hand, is that there are many cases where the presupposition has no apparent effect on the global context, but where a Karttunen type explanation, that the presupposition is there but hidden, is untenable. In this section I will not argue the point either way, but show will how in principle, and from a purely technical perspective, insights from the dynamic model offered in this book may be combined with insights from cancellation theories.

Previously I have assumed that presuppositions must always be satisfied in their local context: Geurts (1996) caricatures this type of model as offering *Local Satisfaction Guaranteed*. I will first introduce a cut-down cancellation theory of presupposition, where (1) presuppositions place con-

---

[6]One could add an extra constraint preventing strengthening of non-presuppositional conditionals by ruling out alternatives which already support the conditional, or, more generally, by ruling out uninformative utterances à la van der Sandt. One would simply need to add extra constraints $\sigma' \subset \sigma$ and $\tau' \subset \tau$ to definition D81.

[7]It would be natural to use the above notion of update as the basis of a definition of defeasible entailment relative to an ordering. For instance, we could say that one formula ϕ entailed another ψ relative to an ordering O if and only if ψ was true in all the worlds in maximal states in the ordering $O + \phi$. In the case of a trivial ordering (where no state is preferred to any other), it is clear that this would simply collapse onto the more standard definition of trivalent consequence discussed above. I leave it to further work to determine what further properties such a notion of entailment would have.

straints not on the local context, but on the global context, and (2) these constraints are defeasible. One could say that this was a model of *Global Satisfaction Preferred*. I will then show how the cancellation model can be altered so that presuppositions place defeasible constraints not on the global context, but on their local context of evaluation. This would presumably be a *Local Satisfaction Preferred* model of presupposition (*Local Satisfaction Guaranteed or Your Money Back*, perhaps.). The model that results is perhaps closest in philosophy to that of Soames (1982). Soames' model not only generates fewer presuppositions than Karttunen derived models, it also generates logically weaker presuppositions than in cancellation models. As a result, it could be argued that Soames' theory needs to be shored up with a pragmatic account of how weak presuppositions may be strengthened. The theory of accommodation presented in the previous chapter provides a natural way of achieving this strengthening, and I will briefly show how the Local Satisfaction Preferred model may be combined with an account of global accommodation.

10.3.1 Global Satisfaction Preferred

A system will now be defined in which presuppositions are interpreted as providing global preferences, which is essentially the idea of cancellationist accounts. I will use the language of PL+∂. The goal is to define a notion of inference that combines classical entailments with just those presuppositional inferences that are consistent with other information.

Models are just as for PUL, pairs $\langle W, F \rangle$, where W is a set of worlds and F is an interpretation function mapping atomic formulae onto sets of worlds. It may be assumed that $[\![.]\!]$ is an essentially classical valuation, mapping formulae onto the set of worlds where they would be classically true, and giving formulae $\partial\phi$ the same valuation as ϕ. An information state will just be a set of worlds, and the update of an information state σ with a formula ϕ, written $\sigma + \phi$ will just be given by $\sigma \cap [\![\phi]\!]$, and as previously in this book, σ will be said to satisfy ϕ, written $\sigma \models \phi$, if σ is a fixed point of ϕ, i.e. $\sigma + \phi = \sigma$. If μ is a pair of states $\langle \sigma, \tau \rangle$, I will write $\mu + \phi$ to mean $\langle \sigma + \phi, \tau + \phi \rangle$.

The preferences of a formula ϕ, written $\uparrow \phi$, will be defined in terms of an information ordering, which, as before, is a set of pairs of states (epistemic alternatives). Definition D82 below specifies the set of *good orderings* (GO) relative to some model. First, the minimally constrained ordering $\odot$, which is the set of pairs of any two non-absurd states, is a good ordering (the set of non-absurd states defined over a set of worlds W being written W^*). Second, an ordering $\omega(\phi)$, which is one where there is a preference for states where ϕ holds, is a good ordering. For a pair $\langle \sigma, \tau \rangle$ to be in $\omega(\phi)$, it must be the case that if τ satisfies ϕ, then σ does too.

Third, the intersection of any two good orderings is also a good ordering. I will not explore the algebraic structure of the Good Orderings here.

Definition D82 (Good Orderings) The set of good orderings is the smallest set GO such that (1) $\odot$ is in GO, (2) for any ϕ, $\omega(\phi)$ is in GO, and (3) for any O and O' in GO, $O \cap O'$ is in GO, where $\odot$ and $\omega(\phi)$ are defined by:

$$
\begin{aligned}
W^* &= \wp(W) \backslash \emptyset \\
\odot &= W^* \times W^* \\
\omega(\phi) &= \{\langle \sigma, \tau \rangle \in \odot \mid \tau \models \phi \rightarrow \sigma \models \phi\}
\end{aligned}
$$

It is natural to write $\sigma \geq_O \tau$ for $\langle \sigma, \tau \rangle \in O$, and $\sigma > \tau$ to mean that $\sigma \geq_O \tau$ but $\tau \not\geq_O \sigma$.

Since any non-modal formula which is satisfied by the minimally informative state W is also satisfied by every other state, it follows that every non-absurd state is at least as preferable as W in any ordering $\omega(\phi)$ for non-modal ϕ. Indeed, a comparable property holds for any good ordering O: $\forall \sigma \in W^*, \sigma \geq_O W$.

For each formula ϕ an associated set of preferences $\uparrow \phi$ will now be recursively stipulated. Here the only clause which actually introduces preferences is that for presuppositional formulae, a formula $\partial \phi$ setting up a preference for states where ϕ holds. Atomic formulae carry the trivial preference ordering $\odot$, which means that no state is strictly preferred to any other. The negation of a formula carries the same preferences as its argument, and the conjunction of two formulae carries a combination of the input preferences of the two conjuncts. Here two orderings are combined simply by taking their intersection.

Definition D83 (GSP Orderings)

$$
\begin{aligned}
\uparrow \phi &= \odot \quad \text{for atomic } \phi \\
\uparrow \neg\phi &= \uparrow \phi \\
\uparrow (\phi \wedge \psi) &= \uparrow \phi \cap \uparrow \psi \\
\uparrow (\phi \rightarrow \psi) &= \uparrow \neg(\phi \wedge \neg\psi) \quad [= \uparrow \phi \cap \uparrow \psi] \\
\uparrow (\phi \vee \psi) &= \uparrow \neg(\neg\phi \wedge \neg\psi) \quad [= \uparrow \phi \cap \uparrow \psi] \\
\uparrow \partial\phi &= \omega(\phi)
\end{aligned}
$$

When defining a notion of entailment it will be important to consider the case of formulae containing explicitly denied presuppositions. So the set of preferred inputs for a formula ϕ, written $\Uparrow\phi$ will be defined as the set of the preferred inputs out of those that are actually consistent with ϕ. I write $c(\phi)$ for the set of states which are consistent with ϕ, and $\sigma \not\leq_O \tau$ to mean that τ is not higher in the ordering O than σ:

Definition D84 (Consistency, Non-Preference, and Preferred Inputs)

$$c(\phi) \quad = \quad \{\sigma \mid (\sigma + \phi) \supset \emptyset\}$$
$$\sigma \not<_O \tau \quad \textit{iff} \quad \tau \geq_O \sigma \rightarrow \sigma \geq_O \tau$$
$$\Uparrow\phi \quad = \quad \{\sigma \in c(\phi) \mid \forall \tau \in c(\phi) \; \sigma \not<_{\uparrow\phi} \tau\}$$

We have now reached the main goal of this subsection and can make precise a notion of inference in which presuppositions are defeasible. In the following definition one formula ϕ can be defined to another ψ, written $\phi \rightsquigarrow \psi$, if and only if with respect to all of ϕ's preferred inputs ϕ contextually entails ψ:

Definition D85 (Presupposition-defeasible Entailment)

$$\phi \rightsquigarrow \psi \quad \textit{iff} \quad \forall \sigma \in \Uparrow\phi \; (\sigma + \phi) \models \psi$$

A logician peering at this definition for the first time might perhaps be worried. What strange newfangled relation is $\rightsquigarrow$, and why is it being described as a notion of logical consequence? I believe it could be termed a *conservative* notion of consequence in at least two senses.

First, for the sublanguage without the ∂-operator, $\rightsquigarrow$ is equivalent to the classical relation of consequence. This is so because none of the operators apart from ∂ introduce non-trivial preferences if their arguments have only trivial preferences, so that the set of preferred inputs for a consistent non-presuppositional formula is just the set of all states. In that case $\phi \rightsquigarrow \psi$ holds if and only if the set of worlds in the extension of ϕ is a subset of those in the extension of ψ, which is just the condition for classical entailment. Inconsistent formulae have an empty set of preferred states, and will presuppositionally entail all other formulae, just as in classical propositional logic.

Second, under this consequence relation all classical entailment patterns should remain valid for the full language of PL+∂ with entailment defined by $\rightsquigarrow$. To see this, initially let us consider the conclusion. Observe that since the preference ordering associated with the conclusion is not involved in the definition of $\rightsquigarrow$, and since the valuation of $\partial\phi$ is just that for ϕ, we may safely erase all occurrences of ∂ on the right of an entailment. Now the premise. Suppose that some formula ϕ has a sub-formula ψ. Clearly replacing ψ by $\partial\psi$ will not affect the semantic interpretation of ϕ, and *a fortiori* will not affect the set of states with which ϕ is consistent. Now suppose that ϕ is classical, i.e. does not contain any instances of the ∂-operator. Then, as shown above, all its classical consequences will also be presupposition-defeasible entailments. Now modifying any number of sub-formulae by enclosing them in (any number of) ∂-operators can only restrict the set of preferred inputs to ϕ. It is easily seen that the set of entailments of the modified premise must be a strict superset of the entailments of the original premise. So, $\leadsto$ is a strictly weaker notion of consequence than classical entailment, in that more formulae are presuppositionally entailed than classically entailed.

Next we consider how the presuppositions of a formula may be defined using the ideas underlying presupposition-defeasible entailment. The following definition says that one formula presupposes another if and only if all preferred states of the first satisfy the second:

Definition D86 (GSP Presupposition)

$$\phi \gg_{\mathrm{GSP}} \psi \quad \textit{iff} \quad \forall \sigma \in \Uparrow\phi \ \ \sigma \models \psi$$

If ϕ is consistent (i.e. $c(\phi) \supset \emptyset$) then for any state σ in $\Uparrow\phi$, $\sigma + \phi$ must be nonempty. Further, since $+$ is defined in terms of intersection, and since the set of propositions which are satisfied in $\sigma \cap \tau$ is just the union of those which are satisfied in σ and those which are satisfied in τ, it follows that the earlier definition of presupposition-defeasible entailment could be rewritten: $\phi \leadsto \psi$ $\textit{iff}$ $\forall \sigma \in \Uparrow\phi$ $(\sigma \models \psi$ or $[\![\phi]\!] \models \psi$. Given that additionally $[\![\phi]\!] \models \psi$ holds if and only if $\phi \models \psi$, where $\models$ is the classical entailment notion (extension of consequent containing extension of premise), it follows that $\leadsto$ can here be expressed in terms of preferential presupposition and classical entailment: $\phi \leadsto \psi$ $\textit{iff}$ $\phi \gg_{\mathrm{GSP}} \psi$ or $\phi \models \psi$[8] The following relatively weak properties of the system show that it is natural to think of ∂-formulae as *potential presuppositions* in Gazdar's sense, for they emerge as presuppositions when nothing conflicts, and disappear otherwise:

1. The presupposition operator yields presuppositions even when embedded: if ϕ contains a subformula $\partial\psi$ and no other ∂-formulae, and the conjunction of ϕ and ψ is consistent, then $\phi \gg_{\mathrm{GSP}} \psi$.

2. Presuppositions persist if there is no conflict: if $\phi \gg \psi$ and χ is a non-presuppositional formula such that the conjunction of ϕ, ψ and χ is consistent, then $\phi \wedge \chi \gg_{\mathrm{GSP}} \psi$.

3. Presuppositions disappear when conflicting material is added: if $\phi \gg \psi$, and although the conjunction of ϕ and χ is consistent, that of ϕ, ψ and χ is inconsistent, then $\phi \wedge \chi \not\gg_{\mathrm{GSP}} \psi$.

What this shows is how a cancellationist account of presupposition can be developed using preference orderings over information states. Of course, much would need to be shown before we could really be confident about this system, and much needs to be added (e.g. cancellation by implicatures)

---

[8]This provides another demonstration that $\leadsto$ is conservative with respect to classical entailment in the senses discussed above.

before the system would be very potent as a theory of presupposition. But the system still manifests at least the most basic property of a cancellationist theory. That is, presuppositions project if there is no conflict and are cancelled otherwise. This development is only intended to be a proof of concept, illustrating how in principle various strands of the presupposition literature might be drawn together. But the formalisation of presupposition-defeasible entailment does provide sufficient foundation to move on to the next stage, of showing how a preference for global satisfaction can be replaced by a preference for local satisfaction.

10.3.2   Local Satisfaction Preferred

In the Global Satisfaction Preferred (GSP) system above, conjunction is symmetrical, its preferences not reflecting any ordering of the conjuncts. The only change now made to that system is an alteration of these preferences associated with conjunction.[9] In the following definition, whilst the presuppositions of the left conjunct become preferences of the whole conjunction, those of the right conjunct only impose a preference for satisfaction in a context which has been first augmented with the left conjunct:

Definition D87 (Local Satisfaction Preference for Conjunction)

$$\uparrow (\phi \operatorname{AND} \psi) \;=\; \{\langle \sigma, \tau \rangle \in \uparrow \phi \mid \langle \sigma + [\![\phi]\!], \tau + [\![\phi]\!]\rangle \in \uparrow \psi\}$$

It is easily checked that this operation does not introduce any non-good orderings.[10]

Let the relation of presupposition in the earlier PUL system be denoted by $\gg_{\mathrm{PUL}}$, and presupposition in the LSP system ($\gg_{\mathrm{LSP}}$) be defined as for

---

[9] The preferences associated with implication and disjunction are taken to be still defined in terms of the equivalences with conjunction and negation used above. Thus disjunction becomes asymmetric once conjunction is asymmetric. But in this system it might make sense to define the preferences for disjunction symmetrically, as the intersection of the preferences of the disjuncts. For now, problematic cases of cancellation of presuppositions occurring in a disjunct need not be handled by defining disjunction so as to enforce local satisfaction, but can instead be handled by the cancellation mechanism.

[10] Define the localisation of O to ϕ as $L(O, \phi) \;=\; \{\langle \sigma, \tau \rangle \in \odot \mid \langle \sigma + \phi, \tau + \phi \rangle \in O\}$. Now the above clause for conjunction may be written: $\uparrow (\phi \text{ and } \psi) \;=\; \uparrow \phi \cap L(\uparrow \psi, \phi)$.

To determine whether this produces only good orderings, we need to check that if O is a good ordering then $L(O, \phi)$ is a good ordering. But if O is a good ordering then either $O = \odot$, or $O = \omega(\chi)$ for some χ, or O is an intersection of two other good orderings O_1 and O_2. Analysing these three cases as follows shows that the preferences associated with the LSP system are good orderings:

1. If $O = \odot$ then $L(O, \phi) = \odot$

2. If $O = \omega(\chi)$ then $L(O, \phi) = \omega(\phi \to \chi)$

3. If $O = O_1 \cap O_2$ then $L(O, \phi) = L(O_1, \phi) \cap L(O_2, \phi)$

the GSP system excepting that the preferences associated with conjunction are altered. The following should now hold:

1. When there is no inconsistency, PUL presuppositions are LSP presuppositions: if ϕ has just one presuppositional subformula, $\phi \gg_{\text{PUL}} \psi$, and the conjunction of ϕ and ψ is consistent, then $\phi \gg_{\text{LSP}} \psi$.

2. Non-PUL presuppositions are not LSP presuppositions: if ϕ has just one presuppositional subformula, and $\phi \not\gg_{\text{PUL}} \psi$, then $\phi \not\gg_{\text{LSP}} \psi$.

3. Inconsistency with presuppositions causes cancellation: if ϕ has just one presuppositional subformula, $\phi \gg_{\text{LSP}} \psi$, and although the conjunction of ϕ and χ is consistent, that of ϕ, ψ and χ is inconsistent, then $\phi \wedge \chi \not\gg_{\text{LSP}} \psi$.

These results, which I hope with further study could be strengthened, show that the LSP system is PUL-like when there is no inconsistency, and thus typically produces weaker presuppositions than the cancellationist GSP model. However, under threat of inconsistency, LSP presuppositions vanish into thin air, in the manner of a cancellationist rather than a dynamic semantic account of presupposition.[11]

There are a number of modifications that it might be of interest to make to the LSP system, such as adding a treatment of implicatures, or replacing the notion of a context with a more constructive notion, such as a set of formulae. One possibility that might be quite significant would be replacing the classical interpretation of $\sigma + \phi$ with a dynamic interpretation. One question that arises is whether we can now extend the proposal

---

[11]One rather puzzling aspect of LSP concerns the fact that whilst the presuppositions of a formula may be cancelled by explicitly denying them, denying the truth of the actual arguments of ∂-operators can still leave non-trivial conditional presuppositions. For instance, let α be $(\phi \rightarrow \neg(\partial(\psi) \wedge \chi)) \wedge \neg\psi$. The left-hand conjunct introduces a preference for states where $\phi \rightarrow \psi$ holds. But this preference is not cancelled by the conjunction with $\neg\psi$. So the formula still ends up presuppositionally entailing more than it would classically entail. In particular α presuppositionally entails $\neg\phi$.

An example may clarify. Consider the discourse 'If Mary closed her eyes then she did not realise that Bill was smiling. He wasn't.', which I find rather odd. If we take the two sentences to be conjoined, and we understand the 'realise' clause as $(\partial(\text{bill-is-smiling}) \wedge \text{mary-realises-bill-is-smiling})$, then the discourse has the logical form of α, and LSP predicts that it entails that Mary did not close her eyes. Given the oddity of this discourse, I am not sure whether this result is problematic. But it does show that there may be cases where LSP predicts *stronger* presuppositions than GSP, for in this case LSP predicts a conditional presupposition, and GSP predicts no presupposition. I would note that, at least in this case, the inference could presumably be removed by stipulating, as is standard, that the conditional introduced an implicature that the truth of its antecedent was unresolved. Whether we could then produce a variant of LSP that did produce strictly weaker presuppositions than (some similar variant of) GSP, and whether this would be desirable, I cannot say.

from a propositional to a first-order setting. In this case, presupposed open propositions would place preferences on their local contexts, but preferences which could be cancelled. I believe the approach I have developed in this section offers a promising line of research for such an extension, and suggests that we may be able to develop a cancellationist model of presupposition which, unlike the models of Gazdar (1979a), van der Sandt (1988), Mercer (1987; 1992), Soames (1982), would allow a treatment of the interaction of presupposition and quantification. However, I will not investigate this possibility here, so my contention remains entirely speculative. Rather, I will consider another line of development, the addition of a mechanism of accommodation which can allow the weak presuppositions of the Soames-like LSP model to be strengthened.

10.3.3 Adding Common Sense to LSP

This monograph is not about common sense. But it does provide a method for a theory of common sense reasoning to interact with a theory of presupposition, this being based on the assumption that whatever method is used to say that one theory is more in line with common sense than another, the output of that method can be encoded in an information ordering. It must now be determined how such a plausibility ordering may be combined with the LSP system, which involves its own ordering determined not by common sense but by a preference for satisfaction of conventionally stipulated presuppositions. This combination will take the form of a definition of presuppositional entailment which is sensitive to an external plausibility ordering, so that $\phi \leadsto_O \psi$ if ψ is a presuppositional consequence of ϕ relative to the ordering O.

One obvious possibility would be to take the intersection of the two orderings, and use that in the new definition of consequence. But I do not think this would give the right results empirically. Suppose that states are preferred where Mary does not own a rhinoceros, and I say 'I didn't realise that Mary owned a rhinoceros.' Taking the intersection of an ordering encoding a preference for states where Mary owns a rhinoceros with one where there is a preference for states where Mary does not own a rhinoceros will have a cancelling effect. The set of maximal states in the resulting ordering would contain both states where Mary had a rhinoceros and states where she did not, and so there would be no net preference for states where Mary did own a rhinoceros. However, my strong impression is that even though it is *prima facie* unlikely that Mary owns a rhinoceros, if I say 'I didn't realise that Mary owned a rhinoceros' and do not explicitly mention any caveat, then I am committed to Mary's having a rhinoceros. Thus, when interpreting what someone has said, satisfaction of the presuppositional defaults could be said to have a higher priority than satisfaction of common sense preferences about how the world ought to be.

We can model this by first finding the maximal states associated with the presuppositions of the utterance, and then using the plausibility ordering to select amongst the resulting states.

Definition D88 **(Plausible Presuppositional Entailment)**

$$max(O, S) \quad = \quad \{\sigma \in S \mid \forall \tau \in S \; \sigma \not< \tau\}$$
$$\phi \leadsto_O \psi \quad \textit{iff} \quad \forall \sigma \in max(O, \Uparrow\phi) \;\; (\sigma + \phi) \models \psi$$

This defines a notion of entailment which allows for filtering of entailed presuppositions, cancellation of presuppositions that are explicitly denied, and strengthening of weak presuppositions such as those generated when a presupposition is located in the consequent of a conditional.

10.4 Non-determinism and Local Accommodation

Although PUL, ABLE and KMG each involve a relationally specified semantics, none of them take full advantage of that denotation space. In particular, in none of these systems is it possible for a formula to be non-deterministic, in the sense that for a given input there is more than one output. Yet I can conceive of a number of potential applications for such non-determinism. One such application was presented in the version of KMG appearing in Beaver (1993a), in which fully relational CCPs are used to model DRT style non-deterministic pronoun resolution. On this basis a semantics is given for a fragment of unindexed English. In the system presented there, given an input state which has two discourse markers in its domain, both of which are established to correspond to singular females, update with the relational CCP corresponding to the unindexed sentence 'she is walking' could yield either of two output states, one in which the first discourse marker was asserted to be walking, and one in which the second was. This is an attractive approach to pronoun resolution, since the assumption that syntax somehow determines pre-indexed logical forms always struck me as unsatisfying. It is clear that syntax imposes strong constraints on coreference, but it is equally clear that syntax does not completely determine the issue.

Non-determinism could also be used in the modelling of local and intermediate accommodation. The trouble is that it is clearly inappropriate to allow arbitrary local accommodation, so the question is, how can it be constrained. One way of constraining it is by restricting what can be accommodated structurally, as in van der Sandt's model of accommodation. However, this account on the one hand is still too unconstrained (witness the inappropriate readings which intermediate accommodation was shown to generate in §5.6) and on the other hand is too constrained. For instance structural accounts fail to generate conditional presuppositions when appropriate (c.f. §5.7) and cannot possibly account for the phenomenon of bridging:

E158' If I go to a wedding then the rabbi will get drunk.

This example has a reading where the rabbi is understood to be somehow related to the wedding mentioned in the antecedent, rather than being a globally salient rabbi. The nature of the conceptual bridge that can be built between a wedding and a rabbi is essentially non-structural, and relies on world-knowledge rather than any detail of the form of the sentence. I leave to further work the job of describing in detail how my common-sense reasoning based approach to accommodation applies to such examples, and how it relates to other theories of bridging using common-sense reasoning such as Asher and Lascarides (1999). The point I want to make here is just that bridges are not always built globally, but, as in E158', are sometimes local.

Most importantly, local accommodation supplies solutions to (amongst many others) the following traditional presuppositional riddles:

E229 The King of France is not bald because there is no King of France.

E230 Either the King of Buganda will open parliament or the President of Buganda will.

In the first case, local accommodation of the existence of a King of France (and an appropriate discourse marker) within the scope of the first negation would allow for the fact that the sentence does not implicate that there is a King of France.[12] In the second case, local accommodation of the existence of a King of Buganda in the first disjunct and the existence of a President in the second would allow the sentence to be used in cases where it was not established whether Buganda was a monarchy or a republic. However, accepting that there is such a thing as local accommodation is only part of what is needed. I believe that local accommodation is a highly constrained process, and there is still no adequate theory of precisely what the constraints are.

Let me indicate briefly how we might introduce a non-structural notion of local accommodation using a radical alteration to the simple PUL system from Chapter 6 (radical in terms of traditional semantic theory rather than with respect to natural language processing systems from Artificial

---

[12]But see van der Sandt (ms) for an alternative view of how this type of example should be treated.

Intelligence research). Suppose that we replaced the PULdefinition of a context as a set of worlds with a notion of a context as a pair of a set of worlds and a cost: the cost will be used to constrain local accommodation. For a context σ, let us say that σ_0 is a set of worlds and σ_1 is a cost. The cost is supposed to represent the implausibility of a given accommodated piece of information, so that the more implausible the propositions that have to be accommodated, the greater the cost.[13] Let us then say that there is some relation of *plausible extension* between contexts, $\mapsto$, which is determined by world knowledge, and which has at least the following properties:

1. If $\sigma \mapsto \tau$, then $\tau_0 \subseteq \sigma_0$.
   Plausible extension cannot cause a downdate.

2. If $\sigma \mapsto \tau$ and $\tau_0 \subset \sigma_0$, then $\tau_1 > \sigma_1$.
   Plausible extension increases the cost.

3. If $\sigma \mapsto \tau$ then there is no υ such that $\sigma \mapsto \upsilon$, $\upsilon_0 = \tau_0$ and $\upsilon_1 \neq \tau_1$.
   Extending some initial state with any given proposition has only one cost.

4. $\forall \sigma \ \sigma \mapsto \sigma$.
   Extending with a tautology (i.e. not at all) is free.

Here are the first few clauses showing what the semantics might look like:

$$\sigma[\![p_{\text{atomic}}]\!]\tau \quad \textit{iff} \quad \tau_1 = \sigma_1 \wedge \tau_0 = \{w \in \sigma_0 \mid w \in F(p)\}$$
$$\sigma[\![\phi \text{ AND } \psi]\!]\tau \quad \textit{iff} \quad \exists \upsilon \ \sigma[\![\phi]\!]\upsilon[\![\psi]\!]\tau$$
$$\sigma[\![\text{ NOT } \phi]\!]\tau \quad \textit{iff} \quad \exists \upsilon \exists \upsilon' \ \sigma \rightsquigarrow \upsilon[\![\phi]\!]\upsilon'$$
$$\wedge \ \tau_1 = \upsilon_1' \wedge \tau_0 = \sigma_0 \backslash \upsilon_0'$$
$$\sigma[\![\phi \text{ IMPLIES } \psi]\!]\tau \quad \textit{iff} \quad \sigma[\![\text{ NOT }(\phi \text{ AND } (\text{ NOT } \psi))]\!]\tau$$

For atomic propositions the cost of the input is simply identified with the cost of the output, whilst conjunction and implication are defined in the normal way. The interesting clause is that for NOT ϕ, which allows for plausible extension before update with ϕ.

Normally, the fact that not accommodating anything is cheaper than accommodating something will mean that the cheapest update with a given

---

[13]C.f. the use by Sperber and Wilson (1984) of *relevance*, there described as a *processing* cost. The cost utilised above measures *unexpectedness* (of extra assumptions). I have sometimes surmised that this cost might be measured in millimetres, a cost of, e.g., 2 mm. corresponding to a surprisingness which would cause raising of the eyebrows by this amount.

formula is equivalent to the standard PULupdate. However, in some circumstances, failure to accommodate would yield presupposition failure. Consider the following example:

E231 Perhaps Bertha is hiding. However, if Anna discovers that Bertha is not hiding, then she will be upset.

The input context to the second sentence will not satisfy the proposition that Bertha is not hiding, and thus updating can only proceed if extra information is accommodated into the antecedent of the conditional, a possibility which arises from the definition of implication in terms of the new negation. On quite reasonable assumptions about the nature of plausible extension, the cheapest update with the sentence will be one corresponding to the local accommodation into the antecedent of the proposition that Bertha is not hiding.

This is a far from complete story, but it does suggest at least the possibility that the theory of meaning described in this paper could be extended with an account of local accommodation. Personally, I would be happier with an account that did not involve postulation of explicit costs and relied instead on a preference ordering mechanism like that invoked to describe global accommodation in Chapter 9. However, in the absence of any detailed proposal, I think it wise to keep an open mind, with there being clear potential for solutions using orderings, costs, or probabilities. Given recent formal convergence in the field of non-monotonic reasoning, it seems likely that a solution depending on any one of these might eventually be recast in terms of either of the others.

10.5   A Note on Presupposition Denial

In making various connections in this chapter, my eye has been on one phenomenon in particular. This is the cancellability of presuppositions when the trigger is embedded under a negation — what could be called the problem of presupposition denial. In the CCP systems introduced in Chapters 6–9 of this book, if a sentence (formula) carries some presupposition, then the negation of the sentence will carry that same presupposition. Yet numerous examples have been cited in the first part of this book for which this result seems inappropriate. One of the goals of this chapter has been to illustrate that there is no reason why insights from elsewhere in the presupposition literature should not be drawn into the kinematic model so as to resolve this difficulty. It is clear that there is no shortage of solutions to the problem of presupposition denial but rather an embarrassment of riches.

First, there is the possibility of adding an extra presupposition-cancelling negation. Then there are three approaches which are more general in their scope, applying not only to cases of cancelled presuppositions embedded under negations, but also cancelled presuppositions under other operators. These three are: introducing assertion operators (plus some pragmatic mechanism for determining when to use them), making presuppositions defeasible, and adding mechanisms of local and intermediate accommodation. The connection between the last two options has already been discussed in §5.9.1, and it is clear that the assertion operator approach is not that distant. All three have the effect that the constraint associated with a presupposition is not absolute, whether what removes that constraint is *co-assertion* (in the terminology of Link 1986), cancellation, or local accommodation.

However, it is not clear to me that any of these yet provide the proper way to deal with cases of presupposition denial. The following data is drawn from Beaver (1992), but Horn (1989; 1985) and Burton-Roberts (1989a) provide voluminous quantities of similar data:

E232   John doesn't *know* that Bill is happy, since Bill is not happy.

E233   John doesn't *know* that Bill is happy, he merely *believes* it.

E234   John doesn't *think* that Bill is happy, he is *totally* convinced.

E235   John doesn't *believe* that Bill is happy, he *knows* it.

The various approaches outlined above provide a treatment of the first two of these examples, but not the last two. Indeed, the last two examples present a major problem for such approaches since if the negation is taken to map true onto false, then they are semantically inconsistent. I believe that an account which offers a treatment of the first two examples, but not the last two (e.g. the presuppositional theories of Mercer, Link or Heim) has not really got to the heart of the problem. My gut feeling is that all of these examples pattern together and should have a uniform explanation.[14] One quite straightforward fact might explain where this feeling comes from: none of E232–E235 would normally be encountered in monologue. It is quite clear that they are intended as rebuttals of some previous utterance. If an *assertive* utterance is taken to be one that is intended to provide a strict increase of the set of propositions held by all parties to be in the common ground, then these sentences are not assertive. As such it

---

[14]Whether or not the examples pattern together (a claim that Seuren, in particular, has devoted much time to argue against), I have no original insight to offer as to what the correct explanation is. The reader must seek solace in a properly considered account of negation, for instance in the work of Horn (1989; 1985), van der Sandt (1991; ms), Seuren (1985; 1988b), Burton-Roberts (1989a).

is hardly surprising that the model proposed in this book is unable to deal with them without significant modification, for the Stalnakerian model of conversational information on which I build takes as one of its basic simplifying assumptions that the common ground is extended monotonically through a conversation. Simply adding mechanisms such as discussed in this chapter to the CCP model without any general theory of non-assertive speech acts would allow treatment of some problematic examples, but it would not, I feel, be a very satisfying treatment. Consider the following quote:

> "It would be natural for a pragmatic presuppositional analyst
> to respond that there are canceling mechanisms of either an
> implicit or an explicit nature, and that when such cancellations
> take place the presupposition must be regarded not as violated,
> with resulting infelicity, but simply removed with no resulting
> defects at all. My reply to this would be that in the first place
> this places him in a totally unassailable position, since there
> are no conceivable counterexamples which cannot be handled
> by such machinery, and second, that it does not explain what I
> take to be a crucial feature of these suggestions: namely, that
> if the speaker denies either that he believes what his sentence
> suggests, or that what he has suggested is in fact true, the sug-
> gestion is *not* simply removed from consideration, but is rein-
> terpreted as coming from someone else, or believed by someone
> else, or reflecting someone else's opinions." (Wilson 1975, p.137)

If we take the type of theory Wilson was discussing to be something like Gazdar's cancellation account, then I must agree with Gazdar (1979a, p. 134) that Wilson was wrong with respect to her "first place" reply. All of the cancellation accounts considered in the first part of this book are not only falsifiable, but falsified, numerous counterexamples having been presented both in this monograph and elsewhere. For that matter, there are clear counterexamples to every existing theory of presupposition which is formally detailed enough to make definite predictions, and I am unable to see why Wilson felt that cancellation type accounts would differ; perhaps hindsight has obscured the point she was trying to make. In his presentation Gazdar chose to excise the final part of the above passage, that concerning the "coming from someone else" suggestion arising in cases of cancellation, but it is this part to which I wish to draw attention.[15] It seems to me that Wilson is absolutely right that an adequate theory of cancellation is not merely one which allows presuppositions to be cancelled,

---

[15]Prince (1978) also discusses the way in which presuppositions can appear to be suspended when they are attributed to someone other than the speaker.

but one which indicates in what circumstances cancellation can occur. If a theory does not distinguish between assertive and non-assertive utterances, but certain types of cancellation are typically or entirely restricted to just one of those, then the theory is inadequate.[16] In this sense all of the extensions to the dynamic semantic model which I have proposed in this chapter would fail, in and of themselves, to produce an adequate theory. In principle any of the three extensions, introducing assertion operators, making local presuppositional constraints defeasible, and adding local accommodation, could produce a model in which denied presuppositions did not project, but this would not make sense of what it is *to deny*, would not explain or account for the distribution of such denials in discourse, and further would not account for the observation that what can be denied is not limited to presuppositions and assertions.

I think it a promising start that from a technical point of view there are methods of extending the coverage of the dynamic semantic model such that cases of presupposition denial are treated at least as well as in presuppositional theories which take the possibility of such denial as their central datum (e.g. the cancellation theories). But it is clear that the revisions called upon in order to adequately treat the types of discourse in which denial occurs are of such a fundamental nature, including a move from monologue to dialogue and a rejection of the simplifying assumption that discourse contexts are incremented monotonically, that it would be premature to champion any one of the extensions I have proposed, for it remains unclear which extension will fit in with the final picture most felicitously.

---

[16]Whilst the cancellation theories I described in part I do not account for dialogue and do not account for variation in speech act type, it should be mentioned that Blok (1993) has proposed extensions in both these directions, and his model of presupposition denial might well answer Wilson's objection.

11

Conclusion

Gazdar (1979a) concludes of Karttunen's "plugs, holes and filters" account of presupposition, the theory which formed the basis of the CCP model:

> The... theory... has had a long and distinguished career. First formulated in 1971, published in 1973, modified and reconceptualized in 1974, and formalised and reterminologized in 1975. But the theory as of 1978 is in poor shape, enmeshed in its own epicycles, beset by counterexamples and constantly in need of "conversational implicatures" to unclog the filters and explain the leakage from its plugs. The time for euthanasia has arrived.

Fifteen years later, the CCP model is alive and kicking, and although it has developed considerably from Karttunen's original proposals, it seems to me that many of the central ideas of the current account are already to be found in Karttunen's work. In this light, one could say that as of 1979 Karttunen's account of presupposition was not a theory five years past its prime, but one fifteen years ahead of its time. Much the same could be said of Karttunen's even earlier account of discourse referents Karttunen (1976). For it is only in the last few years that the technical methods have been developed with which to give adequate expression to the essentially dynamic model that Karttunen was advocating.

In the first part of this book I examined previous literature on presupposition. In doing so I occasionally reformulated theories to enhance clarity and improve predictiveness, and sometimes exposed systematic relationships between apparently opposed theories. An example of reformulation is my presentation of van der Sandt's informativity and consistency constraints, which is more explicit than any in prior published work. An example of finding systematic relationships between theories can be seen in my discussion of the relationship between Gazdar's cancellation model and Karttunen's filtration theory. Improving (at least in terms of simplicity) on earlier work of Soames, I showed how these models could be combined to yield a system that produced better predictions than either of the originals. Yet my main goal in the first part of this book was not reformulation or comparison, but critical evaluation. I showed that there remain many empirical and theoretical problems with existing accounts of presupposition. This critical discussion provided the foundation for the second half of the book, where I went on to provide solutions to various of these problems, such as interaction with quantification, and context dependence of accommodation.

The combination of Heim's work with the further developments in this monograph have provided solutions to many difficulties with Karttunen's 1974 account. Yet the resulting theory is not an *ad hoc* collection of repairs. On the contrary, I have shown that the solutions are form part of a cogent and general account of linguistic interpretation. The same analysis of internal sentence dynamics which is appropriate to the requirements of quantification, anaphora and epistemic modality, is also at the heart of the CCP theory of presupposition. Furthermore, I showed that this integrated analysis can be stated with formal precision for a fragment of natural language. I have presented a system in which CCP meanings may be derived in a fully compositional Montagovian fashion.[1]

I will now summarise some of the developments in this book, and then end with a return to the philosophical backdrop of the theory I have developed, and the intuition that is at its core.

11.1   Presupposition and Quantification

In Chapters 7 and 8 a solution was given for the projection problem for presuppositions arising within compound and quantified sentences, and it was argued that the results with respect to quantified sentences improve on those found in the existing literature.

To begin with, as discussed in Chapter 3, none of the cancellation accounts (e.g. Gazdar 1979a, Mercer 1992, van der Sandt 1988) have offered any account of the interaction of presupposition and quantification, nor is it obvious how this might be done (but c.f. one possible direction for research mentioned in §10.3.1). Thus no comparison with these accounts is possible.

With regard to theories which do account for this interaction, relevant examples are the following:

E236   Somebody curtsied.

E113   A fat man was pushing his bicycle.

---

[1]The approach to compositionality should be compared with those of Chierchia (1995) or Krifka (1992).

E203a No woman regrets that she is married

E204a Every woman who regrets that she is married is sane

E134b? If the Pope fails to appear then he has measles. But every protestant who realises that the Pope has measles is converting.

E139 How many team members and cheerleaders will drive to the match?

> ⋆ Few of the 15 team members and none of the 5 cheerleaders can drive, but every team member will come to the match in her car. So expect about 4 cars.

In §2.3, it was shown that for examples like E236 and E113 Karttunen and Peters (1979) make incorrect predictions because they do not allow for binding between presupposition and assertion. On the other hand, as discussed in §4.4, Heim (1983b) does allow for such binding, but mistakenly predicts a universal presupposition. Although she suggested avoiding this problem using a mechanism of accommodation, it has been shown (Soames 1989) that such a solution would be problematic. The developments in Chapter 8 yielded a system where binding is not only possible, but produces intuitively reasonable results: these examples produce existential rather than universal presuppositions.

As discussed further in Chapter 8, the Heimian system without accommodation also produces incorrect results for sentences like E204a and E203a. Once again the presuppositions she predicts are far too strong. In Chapter 8 it was shown how a modification to the Heimian semantics produces a system with intuitively reasonable existential presuppositions for these examples, and this modified system provided the basis of the KMG fragment.

Van der Sandt's DRT based account was first discussed in Chapter 4.1 and more fully in Chapter 5. Unlike his earlier cancellation account, it does allow for a treatment of the interaction between presupposition and quantification, and indeed it behaves quite respectably. The presuppositional inferences predicted for all of E236, E113, E204a and E203a are uniformly weak. However, it was shown in §5.4 that the DRT accommodation model fails to predict the oddity of E134b due to the presence of an underconstrained mechanism of local accommodation. On the other hand this type of example should be no problem for KMG, which lacks such a mechanism. In the case of E139, it was shown in §5.6 that van der Sandt's model incorrectly predicts domain restriction to the set of car-owning team members, and does not predict any oddity for the example. KMG does not allow this type of accommodation, and will successfully predict incoherence of E139, this incoherence arising from a truth conditional inconsistency.[2]

---

[2]See Beaver (1994b) for a more detailed discussion of data concerning presupposition and quantification.

11.2 Accommodation and Common Sense

It was shown in Chapter 9 how global accommodation can be formalised within an account which is both dynamic and pragmatic, by using preference orderings over information states, and has been demonstrated that this resolves both the general problem of how presuppositions can be informative, and one particular problem with the CCP model concerning the prediction of overly weak conditional presuppositions from compound sentences. It was argued in §9.3 that all purely semantic theories of presupposition, and all theories of presupposition involving structural accounts of accommodation or cancellation make systematically incorrect predictions by failing to account for the importance of common sense in determining exactly what is accommodated (c.f. also §2.4.3, §3.9, §5.5 and §5.7). Here is some relevant data:

E237   We regret that children cannot accompany their parents to commencement exercises.

E52   If I go to London, my sister will pick me up at the airport.

E225   If Jane takes a bath, Bill will be annoyed that there is no more hot water.

E226   If Jane wants a bath, Bill will be annoyed that there is no more hot water.

E238   If Jane takes a bath and Bill is annoyed that there is no more hot water, he won't let her have a towel.

E95   If Nixon invites Angela Davis to the Whitehouse, then Nixon will regret having invited a black militant to his residence.

E154   If Spaceman Spiff lands on Planet X, he will be bothered by the fact that his weight is greater than it would be on Earth.

Karttunen's example E237 demonstrates informativity of presuppositions. The model he proposed their provided no direct treatment of these cases, which he explained as being deviant, arising from imperfections in the functioning of natural discourse. Heim (1983b) does provide a line of explanation for these cases, by adding a mechanism of global accommodation to the CCP model. In this monograph it has been seen how this explanation may be further formalised.

Example E52 is the type of case where a conditional presupposition is generated in the dynamic models of Karttunen (1974) and Heim (1983b), in multivalent accounts based on Kleene's strong logic and a conventional

Strawsonian definition of presupposition, and also in the two dimensional model of Karttunen and Peters (1979) and the hybrid account of Soames (1982). This type of claimed presupposition, here that if I go to London then I have a sister, has been widely attacked. It is clear that an utterance E52 would normally only occur in situations where the speaker actually has a sister, and that a hearer would be able to infer this even if unfamiliar with the speaker's family background. Karttunen and Peters provided a pragmatic explanation for the strengthening of conditional presuppositions, but this justification has come under attack — see especially Geurts (1994) — and is anyway informal. I have offered a formal model of global accommodation whereby the form of an utterance places minimal semantic constraints on what must be accommodated, but does not determine what is accommodated: world knowledge and plausibility criteria determine this. It has been shown that this can yield the appropriate strengthening. Furthermore, the method is of sufficient generality that it can be applied not only to the dynamic semantic model presented in this book, but also, as shown in Chapter 10, to other models, such as those based on a multivalent semantics.

The next two examples, E225 and E226, demonstrate why the interaction with world knowledge is so important. Hearers may come to quite different conclusions when encountering the two sentences. If knowing that there are many households where having a bath tends to exhaust available hot water supplies, a hearer may conclude from E225 that the speaker is referring to such a household, and that if Jane takes a bath the hot water reservoir will indeed be emptied. But a hearer faced with the structurally similar example E226 will generally not be able to conclude that there is a general rule linking the antecedent of the conditional ('Jane wants a bath') to the presupposition that there is no hot water. The most plausible explanation of why the speaker is able to take for granted that there is no hot water in the local context of the consequent of E226 is that he also takes it to be globally true that there is no hot water, and takes this to be an uncontroversial assumption. So in the case of E225 a hearer will tend not to conclude that there is a lack of hot water, but in the case of E226 the hearer will tend to conclude this. The global accommodation mechanism which I have proposed provides a way in which common sense knowledge of what is plausible, encoded as an information ordering, can interact with the CCP model of presupposition so as to yield just this difference.

No model of presupposition which fails to detail the mechanism by which knowledge of plausibility can affect what is accommodated will be able to predict the contrast. Multivalent semantic theories (e.g. van Fraassen 1975, Hausser 1976, Seuren 1985, Burton-Roberts 1989a) cannot predict the difference without an extra pragmatic component, and up until now there has been no serious attempt to formalise such a pragmatic component. Cancellation theories (e.g. Gazdar 1979a, van der Sandt 1988, Mercer 1992) and existing theories of structural accommodation (e.g. van der Sandt 1992a, Zeevat 1992) fail on two counts. First, there is what might be called the *inconsistency problem*: it is determined whether or not a presupposition is projected/globally accommodated using a consistency test. But I have argued that the difference between E225 and E226 concerns plausibility and not consistency. Both examples could consistently be uttered when the speaker was assuming that there was an absence of hot water, so cancellation and structural accommodation theories will uniformly predict projection of this presupposition.

Second, the cancellation theories and the structural accommodation theories do not allow for the fact that what is accommodated is in general not a simple yes-no proposition, but an explanation, a theory which incorporates the conventionally signaled presupposition as just one element. Information orderings provide many such alternative explanations, encoded abstractly in terms of CCP states. In cases such as E225, and also E238–E154, I have argued that the CCP model is right in predicting that a local constraint for presupposition satisfaction yields a global constraint that a conditional holds, e.g. that if Spiff lands on our planet then his weight will be greater than on Earth in the case of E154. Further, I have shown how given that the form of the utterance places such a constraint, the information ordering mechanism allows an appropriate explanation containing that conditional to be accommodated. Conditional presuppositions are thus at the core of the explanations accommodated not only for E225, but also for the remaining examples E238–E154. But current cancellation and structural accommodation theories cannot in general generate conditional presuppositions. Thus, as was shown at length in §3.9 and §5.7, cancellation and structural accommodation theories not only predict overly strong presuppositions in cases like E225 and E238–E154, because of the *inconsistency problem* (i.e. that in these models inconsistency is what causes cancellation or non-accommodation, and not implausibility), they also lack any method for producing appropriate presuppositions if the *inconsistency problem* was overcome.

11.3   A Return to Intuitions

The main premise of the account I have presented is that meaning concerns change of information, and the intuition that has guided my analysis is that we should take seriously the *pre* in presupposition.

Taking the *pre* seriously has allowed me to state simply and formally what the difference is between the presuppositions of an expression and the content. Presuppositions of an expression were defined as all the information which use of the expression gives about the incoming context, and the content (entailment) comprised information about how that context should be changed.

Let me put that definition explicitly in its own context, as regards its philosophical relation to other accounts of presupposition. It may be recalled from the first part of this monograph that accounts of presupposition are divided into purely semantic theories, whereby presupposition is a binary relation between linguistic expressions, and pragmatic accounts. The pragmatic accounts are themselves of two varieties, following either Strawson or Stalnaker (whose use of *presupposition* is not dissimilar to Frege's original use of *voraussetzung*). In Strawsonian theories presupposition is a three place relation between two sentences and a context (i.e. the utterance of sentence X in context Y presupposes sentence Z). Stalnaker's account, following non-technical usage of the term *presupposition*, makes presupposition a relation between individuals and propositions. The philosophical views of Strawson and Stalnaker permeate most recent accounts of presupposition.

The CCP account finesses the problems which lead Strawson, Stalnaker and a majority of theorists since to give up on directly defining presuppositions of linguistic expressions. Those problems concerned the fact that presuppositional inferences are heavily dependent on context and on the intentions of speakers. Yet in this respect, presuppositions are similar to other aspects of meaning.

If contextual variability of presuppositional inferences are enough to prevent definition of the presuppositions of an expression, then similar arguments should convince us that we can never define a notion of the conventional meaning of an expression. All study of meaning would become pragmatics, the study of the presuppositions and assertions of language users when they use expressions, not of the presuppositions and content of the expressions themselves.

Of course, Stalnaker did not argue for replacing the notion of linguistic content with that of assertion, but was prepared to let content and assertion live side by side. What, after all, allows the hearer to recognise the assertion being made if not some conventional notion of content? Likewise, I claim that the notions of conventionalised linguistic presupposition and speaker presupposition should co-exist. Hearers can recognise the speaker's presuppositions a good deal of the time, and one of the ways they do this is by identifying the conventional linguistic presuppositions of what the speaker says.

What I have presented in this work is an account of two sorts of presupposition, albeit that I have not used the term *presupposition* for one of them. First, I have have formalised the relation between conventionalised elementary presuppositions and presuppositions of complex linguistic expressions. In this respect the proposal is closest to semantic accounts of presupposition, in that presupposition is directly defined on the linguistic expression without any separate context parameter. What makes this direct definition of presupposition possible is a broadening of the notion of semantics beyond that in traditional (pre 1980) philosophical and linguistic work. Second, I have formalised the pragmatic relation between conventional presuppositions and the assumptions of the speaker about the common ground. Such sets of assumptions of the speaker can be aligned with Stalnaker's notion of speaker presupposition.

What my variant of the CCP model does not incorporate is a notion of Strawsonian presupposition. According to Strawson presupposition was, in part, a function of context. But in the model I have proposed, presuppositions are constraints on context, not functions from context. It is the presuppositions that help the hearer decide what the speaker thinks the context is, not *vice versa*. This is not to say that Strawson's view of presupposition was not cogent. For Strawson, as for Frege and many other theorists I discussed in Chapter 2, presuppositions of sentences were conditions on definedness of truth value. It is entirely appropriate that definedness of truth value be conditioned on context. But should presupposition be equated with definedness of truth value?

Although I wish to account for some of the same inference patterns as Strawson, I have not sought to do so in terms of definedness of truth value, but in terms of definedness of update. Neither do I find the term *presupposition* particularly apt for the role of capturing truth-conditional definedness. For *presupposition* carries with it an implicit directionality, a before and an after. To the extent that Strawson intended presupposition to model directionality of interpretation, he did not build that into his theory in any substantive way. Neither did anyone else prior to Karttunen in 1974. That is when the *pre* of presupposition started to make sense, although, as I have discussed, it was ignored in a great deal of later work.

If you convert the intuitive idea that presuppositions come *before* other aspects of meaning into the technical claim that presuppositions are constraints on input contexts in dynamic semantics, what results, broadly, is the CCP model. In this book I have extended that model in terms of formalisation and empirical coverage, and have shown various ways in which the result improves upon alternative theories. Yet this entire book has been driven by one idea, an idea which, expressed in other terms, has been present in the CCP model since Karttunen, Stalnaker and Heim laid the groundwork, an idea which even its detractors must accept is attractively simple: Presupposition is what comes first in dynamic semantics.

A

Properties of ABLE

The main facts demonstrated in this appendix are:

1. All ABLE formulae are eliminative. Without this property the definitions of satisfaction and entailment would not be appropriate.

2. The non-modal presuppositions of an ABLE formula are also entailments.

Definition D89 **(Extension)** A state I is an extension of a state J *iff* :

$$\forall w \forall f \; I.w.f \; \rightarrow (\exists g \; f \succeq g \wedge J.w.g)$$

Definition D90 **(Eliminativity)** A CCP F is eliminative *iff* for any states I and J, if $I\{F\}J$ then J is an extension of I.

Fact A.1 All ABLE formulae are eliminative.
Proof: An induction over ABLE formulae. The most difficult cases are the quantificational determiners, which I will leave until last. Firstly, the postulate on the denotation of ABLE predicates, MP8, forces the output to be a subset of the input, from which eliminativity follows. Conjunction is defined as relational composition, and it is clear that if two CCPs are eliminative then their composition will be. Negation is defined such that the output is the input minus some other set, which means that once again the output must be a subset of the input. The output of a definite determiner, if defined, is the input updated with the scope condition, so it suffices that, by the induction hypothesis, the scope condition will be eliminative. Since tests are eliminative, the output either being the input or the absurd state, facts D61 and 8.7 guarantee that the epistemic modalities are eliminative.

The definition of the semantics of existential determiners, D65, is of the following form:

$$[\![\mathcal{D}.i.\phi.\psi]\!] = \lambda I \lambda J$$

$$\begin{bmatrix} \ldots \wedge \\ J = \lambda w \lambda g \\ \begin{bmatrix} \exists f \exists sco \exists G_{\text{sco}} \ldots \\ I.w.f \;\wedge \ldots \wedge \\ G_{\text{sco}} = \lambda h \; [h \succeq f \;\wedge sco.w.h] \;\wedge \\ \ldots \wedge G_{\text{sco}}.g \end{bmatrix} \end{bmatrix}$$

Thus we have that for existential determiners $\mathcal{D}$, if $I[\![\mathcal{D}.i.\phi.\psi]\!] J$, then:

$$\forall w \forall g \; [J.w.g \;\rightarrow\; \exists f \exists sco \exists G_{\text{sco}} \; I.w.f \;\wedge$$
$$G_{\text{sco}} = \lambda h \; [h \succeq f \;\wedge sco.w.h] \;\wedge$$
$$G_{\text{sco}}.g$$

From this it follows that:

$$\forall w \forall g \; [J.w.g \;\rightarrow\; \exists f \; I.w.f \;\wedge g \succeq f$$

This is the required result.

Similarly, it follows from definition D64 that if $\mathcal{D}$ is a non-existential determiner and $I[\![\mathcal{D}.i.\phi.\psi]\!] J$, then:

$$\forall w \forall g \; [J.w.g \;\rightarrow\; \exists f \exists sco \exists G_{\text{sco}} \; I.w.f \;\wedge$$
$$G_{\text{sco}} = \lambda h \; [h \succeq f \;\wedge sco.w.h] \;\wedge$$
$$g = \lambda D \lambda x \begin{bmatrix} f.D.x \;\vee \\ \exists h \; G_{\text{sco}}.h \wedge h.D.x \end{bmatrix}$$

Once again, it is straightforward to verify that g must be an extension of f, and the result follows. This completes the proof.

Definition D91 (Singleton)

$$\langle\langle w, f \rangle\rangle = \lambda w' \lambda g \; [w' = w \;\wedge\; f = g]$$

Definition D92 (Distributivity) A CCP F is distributive *iff*

$$\forall I \forall J \; I\{F\}J \;\leftrightarrow\; J = \lambda w \lambda f \; [$$
$$\exists g \; I.w.g \;\wedge\; \langle\langle w, g \rangle\rangle\{F\}\langle\langle w, f \rangle\rangle]$$

Fact A.2 The non-modal formulae of ABLE are distributive.
Sketch of Proof: Another induction on (non-modal) formula complexity, starting with the fact that MP8 guarantees that ABLE predications are interpreted distributively.

Definition D93 **(Persistence)** A CCP F is persistent *iff*

$$(I \text{ satisfies } F \ \wedge \ J \text{ is an extension of } I) \ \rightarrow \ J \text{ satisfies } F$$

Fact A.3 Non-modal ABLE formulae are persistent.
Proof: ABLE predicates have the property of *relevance*, so that their denotation is only sensitive to the values the input state gives to the predicated markers. Thus if an ABLE predication is satisfied in a state, then adding new discourse markers to the state will produce another state in which the predication is satisfied. Since predications are distributive, it holds that if a predication F is satisfied in some state I, then it must be satisfied in every subset of I. It follows that ABLE predications are persistent.

Inspection of the remaining semantic clauses show that they all preserve relevance, so that if any ABLE formula is satisfied in a state then adding new discourse markers will yield another state which satisfies the formula. Since all non-modal formulae are distributive, it follows that all non-modal formulae are persistent.

Fact A.4 If ϕ is a non-modal formula and ψ presupposes ϕ, then $\psi \models \phi$.
Proof: Since ϕ is non-modal, it must be persistent, so that if it is satisfied in a state then it must be satisfied in any extension of the state. Since ψ presupposes ϕ, it follows that every state that admits ψ satisfies ϕ. Since all ABLE formulae are eliminative, it follows that an output of ψ must be an extension of the input. Thus if an input of ψ satisfies ϕ, then the output must also satisfy ϕ. This yields the required result, since every output of ψ satisfying ϕ is the condition for $\psi \models \phi$.

References

Abusch, Dorit and Mats Rooth, 2000. "Empty-domain effects for presuppositional and non-presuppositional determiners." To appear in Hans Kamp and Barbara Partee (eds), Context Dependency in the Analysis of Linguistic Meaning.

Aristotle, 1950/350 BC. "Categories." In W. D. Ross (ed.), *The Works of Aristotle Translated into English*, vol. 1, Oxford University Press. Translated by E.M. Edghill.

Asher, Nicholas, 1993. *Reference to Abstract Objects in Discourse*, vol. 50 of *Studies in Linguistics and Philosophy*. Kluwer, Dordrecht.

Asher, Nicholas and Alex Lascarides, 1999. "Bridging." *Journal of Semantics* 15, pp. 83–113.

Atlas, Jay, 1976. *On the Semantics of Presupposition and Negation: an Essay in Philosophical Logic and the Foundations of Linguistics*. Ph.D. thesis, University of Princeton.

Atlas, Jay, 1977. "Negation, ambiguity and presupposition." *Linguistics and Philosophy* 1, pp. 321–336.

Atlas, Jay, 1989. *Philosophy Without Ambiguity: A Logico-Linguistic Essay*. Clarendon Press, Oxford.

Atlas, Jay and Stephen Levinson, 1981. "It-clefts, informativeness and logical form: Radical pragmatics." In Peter Cole (ed.), *Radical Pragmatics*, pp. 1–61, Academic Press.

van der Auwera, Johan, 1993. "Already and Still: Beyond duality." *Linguistics and Philosophy* 16, pp. 613–663.

Barwise, Jon, 1987. "Noun phrases, generalised quantifiers and anaphora." In Peter Gardënfors (ed.), *Generalized Quantifiers*, Reidel, Dordrecht.

Barwise, Jon and Robin Cooper, 1981. "Generalized quantifiers and natural language." *Linguistics and Philosophy* 4, pp. 159–219.

Beaver, David, 1992. "The kinematics of presupposition." In Paul Dekker and Martin Stockhof (eds.), *Proceedings of the Eighth Amsterdam Colloquium*, ILLC, University of Amsterdam.

Beaver, David, 1993a. "Kinematic Montague Grammar." In Hans Kamp (ed.), DYANA-2 *deliverable R2.2A, Presupposition*, University of Amsterdam.

Beaver, David, 1993b. "What comes first in dynamic semantics." Tech. Rep. LP-93-15, ILLC, University of Amsterdam.

Beaver, David, 1994a. "Accommodating topics." In Rob van der Sandt and Peter Bosch (eds.), *The Proceedings of the IBM and Journal of Semantics Conference on Focus*, IBM, Heidelberg.

Beaver, David, 1994b. "When variables don't vary enough." In Mandy Harvey and Lynn Santelmann (eds.), *Semantics and Linguistic Theory 4*, CLC Publications, Cornell.

Beaver, David, 1995. *Presupposition and Assertion in Dynamic Semantics*. Ph.D. thesis, University of Edinburgh.

Beaver, David, 1997. "Presupposition." In Johan van Benthem and Alice ter Meulen (eds.), *The Handbook of Logic and Language*, pp. 939–1008, Elsevier, Amsterdam.

Beaver, David, 1999a. "The logic of anaphora resolution." In Paul Dekker (ed.), *Proceedings of the Twelfth Amsterdam Colloquium*, pp. 55–60, ILLC Publications, Amsterdam.

Beaver, David, 1999b. "Presupposition: A plea for common sense." In Lawrence Moss, Jonathan Ginzburg and Maarten de Rijke (eds.), *Logic, Language and Computation*, vol. 2, pp. 21–44, CSLI Publications, Stanford. Revised version of Beaver, D. (1994) "An Infinite Number of Monkeys", Acta Linguistica Hungarica 42:3, pp. 253–270.

Beaver, David, 2001. "Pragmatics, and that's an order." In David Barker-Plummer, David Beaver, Johan van Benthem and Patrick Scotto di Luzio (eds.), *Logic, Language and Visual Information*, CSLI Publications, Stanford.

Beaver, David and Brady Clark, 2000. "'Always' and 'Only': Why not all focus sensitive operators are alike." Ms., Stanford University.

Beaver, David and Emiel Krahmer, 2001. "A partial account of presupposition projection." *Journal of Logic, Language and Information* 10, pp. 147–182.

Belnap, Nuel, 1969. "Questions, their presuppositions, and how they can arise." In Kirk Lambert (ed.), *The Logical Way of Doing Things*, Yale University Press, Connecticut.

van Benthem, Johan, 1991. *Categories, Lambdas and Dynamic Logic*. North-Holland, Amsterdam.

van Benthem, Johan, 1996. *Exploring Logical Dynamics*. Studies in Logic, Language and Information, CSLI Publications, Stanford.

van der Berg, Martin, 1994. "A direct definition of generalised dynamic quantifiers." In Paul Dekker and Martin Stokhof (eds.), *Proceedings of the Ninth Amsterdam Colloquium*, vol. 1, pp. 121–140, ILLC University of Amsterdam.

van der Berg, Martin, 1996. *Some Aspects of the Internal Structure of Discourse: The Dynamics of Nominal Anaphora*. Ph.D. thesis, University of Amsterdam.

Bergmann, Merrie, 1981. "Presupposition and two-dimensional logic." *Journal of Philosophical Logic* 10, pp. 27–53.

Blackburn, Patrick and Johan Bos, ms. "Representation and inference for natural language. A first course in computational semantics." To appear with CSLI Publications, Stanford.

Blackburn, Patrick, Johan Bos, Michael Kohlhase and Hans de Nivelle, 1999. "Inference and computational semantics." In Harry Bunt and Elias Thijsse (eds.), *Third International Workshop on Computational Semantics (IWCS-3)*, pp. 5–21, University of Tilburg.

Blamey, Steven, 1989. "Partiality." In Dov Gabbay and Franz Guenther (eds.), *The Handbook of Philosophical Logic*, vol. IV, pp. 553–616, Reidel, Dordrecht.

Blau, Ulrich, 1978. *Die Driewertige Logik der Sprache: Ihre Syntax, Semantik und Anwendung in der Sprachanalyse*. Walter de Gruyter, Berlin.

Blok, Peter, 1993. *The Interpretation of Focus: An Epistemic Approach to Pragmatics*. Ph.D. thesis, University of Groningen. Groningen Dissertations in Linguistics 6.

Bochvar, Dmitrii Anatoljevich, 1939. "Ob odnom trehznachom iscislenii i ego primeneii k analizu paradoksov klassicskogo rassirennogo funkcional 'nogo iscislenija'." *Matematiciskij Sbornik* 4, pp. 87–112. English Translation: *History and Philosophy of Logic* 2, 1981, "On a Three-valued Calculus and Its Applications to the Analysis of the Paradoxes of the Classical Extended Functional Calculus".

Böer, Steven E. and William G. Lycan, 1976. "The myth of semantic presupposition." In Arnold Zwicky (ed.), *Papers in nonphonology*, vol. 21 of *Working Papers in Linguistics*, Department of Linguistics, Ohio State University, Columbus, Ohio.

Bos, Johan, 1994. "Presupposition as anaphora in the verbmobil semantic formalism." Tech. rep., Universität des Saarlandes.

Bos, Johan, Paul Buitelaar and Anne-Marie Mineur, 1995. "Bridging as coercive accommodation." In Ewan Klein, Suresh Manandhar, Werner Nutt and

Jorg Siekmann (eds.), *Working Notes of the Edinburgh Conference on Computational Logic and Natural Language Processing*, Human Communications Research Centre, University of Edinburgh.

Bridge, Derek, 1991. *Computing Presuppositions in an Incremental Natural Language Processing System*. Ph.D. thesis, University of Cambridge Computer Laboratory. Available as Technical Report No. 237.

Burton-Roberts, Noel, 1989a. *The Limits to Debate: A Revised Theory of Semantic Presupposition*, vol. 51 of *Cambridge Studies in Linguistics*. Cambridge University Press.

Burton-Roberts, Noel, 1989b. "On Horn's dilemma, presupposition and negation." *Journal of Linguistics* 25, pp. 95–125.

Burton-Roberts, Noel, 1989c. "Theories of presupposition." *Journal of Linguistics* 25, pp. 437–454.

Burton-Roberts, Noel, 1990. "Trivalence, gapped bivalence, and ambiguity of negation: A reply to Seuren." *Journal of Linguistics* 26, pp. 455–470.

Chierchia, Gennaro, 1992. "Anaphora and dynamic binding." *Linguistics and Philosophy* 15, pp. 111–183.

Chierchia, Gennaro, 1995. *Dynamics of Meaning*. University of Chicago Press, Chicago.

Chomsky, Noam, 1971. "Deep structure, surface structure and semantic interpretation." In Danny Steinberg and Leon Jacobovits (eds.), *Semantics: an Interdisciplinary Reader in Philosophy, Linguistics and Psychology*, pp. 183–216, Cambridge University Press, Cambridge.

Clark, Herbert and Catherine Marshall, 1981. "Definite reference and mutual knowledge." In Aravind Joshi, Bonnie Webber and Ivan Sag (eds.), *Elements of Discourse Understanding*, pp. 10–63, Cambridge University Press, Cambridge.

Cooper, Robin, 1983. *Quantification and Syntactic Theory*. Reidel, Dordrecht.

Cresswell, Maxwell, 1973. *Logics and Languages*. Methuen, London.

Dekker, Paul, 1992. "An update semantics for dynamic predicate logic." In Paul Dekker and Martin Stokhof (eds.), *Proceedings of the Eighth Amsterdam Colloquium*, ILLC, University of Amsterdam.

Dekker, Paul, 1993. *Trans-sentential Meditations, Ups and Downs in Dynamic Semantics*. Ph.D. thesis, University of Amsterdam.

Dekker, Paul, 1997. "On first order information exchange." In Anton Benz and Gerhard Jaeger (eds.), *Proceedings of Mundial '97 — Munich Workshop on the Formal Semantics and Pragmatics of Dialogue*, CIS, Munich.

Dekker, Paul and Robert van Rooy, 1998. "Intentional identity and information exchange." In Robin Cooper and Thomas Gamkrelidze (eds.), *Proceedings of the Second Tbilisi Symposium on Language, Logic and Computation*, Tbilisi State University, Tbilisi.

Delacruz, Enrique, 1976. "Factives and propositional level constructions in Montague Grammar." In Barbara Partee (ed.), *Montague Grammar*, pp. 177–199, Academic Press, New York.

Delin, Judy, 1989. *Cleft Constructions in Discourse*. Ph.D. thesis, Centre for Cognitive Science, University of Edinburgh.

Delin, Judy, 1992. "Properties of *it*-cleft presupposition." *Journal of Semantics* 9(4), pp. 289–306.

Dinsmore, John, 1981. *The Inheritance of Presuppositions*. John Benjamins, Amsterdam.

Dinsmore, John, 1992. *Partitioned Representations: A Study in Mental Representation, Language Understanding and Linguistic Structure*. Kluwer, Dordrecht.

van Eijck, Jan, 1993. "The dynamics of description." *Journal of Semantics* 10, pp. 239–267. Earlier version appeared in Ton van der Wouden and Wietske Sijtsma (eds), *Computational Linguistics in the Netherlands; Papers from the first CLIN-meeting*, 1990.

van Eijck, Jan, 1994. "Presupposition Failure: a Comedy of Errors." *Formal Aspects of Computing* 3.

van Eijck, Jan, 1995. "Presuppositions and dynamic logic." In Makoto Kanazawa, Christopher Piñon and Henriette de Swart (eds.), *Papers from the Second CSLI Workshop on Logic, Language and Computation*, CSLI Publications, Stanford.

van Eijck, Jan and Giovanna Cepparello, 1994. "Dynamic modal predicate logic." In Makoto Kanazawa and Christopher Piñon (eds.), *Dynamics, Polarity, and Quantification*, pp. 251–276, CSLI Publications, Stanford.

Emms, Martin, 1990. "Polymorphic quantifiers." In Martin Stokhof and Leen Torenvliet (eds.), *Proceedings of the Seventh Amsterdam Colloquium*, University of Amsterdam.

Evans, Gareth, 1977. "Pronouns, quantifiers and relative clauses." *The Canadian Journal of Philosophy* 7.

Fauconnier, Gilles, 1985. *Mental Spaces: Aspects of Meaning Construction in Natural Language*. MIT Press, Cambridge, Massachusetts.

Fernando, Tim, 1995. "Computational foundations for dynamic accounts of pre-suppositions." In Ewan Klein, Suresh Manandhar, Werner Nutt and Jorg Siek-mann (eds.), *Working Notes of the Edinburgh Conference on Computational Logic and Natural Language Processing*, Human Communications Research Centre, University of Edinburgh.

Fillmore, Charles, 1971a. "Types of lexical information." In Danny Steinberg and Leon Jacobovits (eds.), *Semantics: An Interdisciplinary Reader in Philosophy, Linguistics and Psychology*, Cambridge University Press, Cambridge.

Fillmore, Charles, 1971b. "Verbs of judging: An exercise in semantic descrip-tion." In Charles Fillmore and D. Terence Langendoen (eds.), *Studies in Lin-guistic Semantics*, Holt, Reinhardt and Winston, New York.

von Fintel, Kai, 1995. *Restrictions on Quantifier Domains*. Ph.D. thesis, Univer-sity of Massachussetts at Amherst.

von Fintel, Kai, 1998. "The presupposition of subjunctive conditionals." In Uli Sauerland and Orin Percus (eds.), *The Interpretive Tract*, vol. 25 of *MIT Working Papers in Linguistics*, pp. 29–44, MIT, Cambridge.

von Fintel, Kai, 2001. "Would you believe it? the King of France is back! (pre-suppositions and truth-value intuitions)." MIT.

van Fraassen, Bas, 1969. "Presuppositions, supervaluations and free logic." In Kirk Lambert (ed.), *The Logical Way of Doing Things*, pp. 67–92, Yale Uni-versity Press, New Haven.

van Fraassen, Bas, 1975. *Logic and Formal Semantics*. Macmillan, New York.

Frege, Gottlob, 1892. "Uber Sinn und Bedeutung." *Zeitschrift fur Philosophie und philosophische Kritik* pp. 25–50. English Translation: "On Sense and Meaning", in Brian McGuinness (ed), *Frege: collected works*, pp. 157–177, Basil Blackwell, Oxford.

Gallin, Daniel, 1975. *Intensional and Higher-Order Modal Logic*. North-Holland, Amsterdam.

Gamut, L. T. F., 1991. *Logic, Language and Meaning*, vol. 1. University of Chicago Press.

Gawron, Jean Mark, 1995. "Quantification, quantificational domains and dy-namic logic." In Shalom Lappin (ed.), *Handbook of Contemporary Semantic Theory*, pp. 247–267, Blackwell, Oxford.

Gazdar, Gerald, 1979a. *Pragmatics: Implicature, Presupposition and Logical Form*. Academic Press, New York.

Gazdar, Gerald, 1979b. "A solution to the projection problem." In Choon-Kyu Oh and David Dineen (eds.), *Syntax and Semantics 11: Presupposition*, pp. 57–89, Academic Press, New York.

Geach, Peter, 1962. *Reference and Generality*. Cornell University Press, Ithaca, New York.

Gervas, Pablo, 1995. "Compositionality and presupposition." In Ewan Klein, Suresh Manandhar, Werner Nutt and Jorg Siekmann (eds.), *Working Notes of the Edinburgh Conference on Computational Logic and Natural Language Processing*, Human Communications Research Centre, University of Edinburgh.

Geurts, Bart, 1994. *Presupposing*. Ph.D. thesis, University of Osnabrück.

Geurts, Bart, 1996. "Local satisfaction guaranteed." *Linguistics and Philosophy* 19, pp. 259–294.

Geurts, Bart, 1997. "Dynamic Dido and Commutative Aeneas." In Rob van der Sandt, Reinhard Blutner and Manfred Bierwisch (eds.), *From Underspecification to Interpretation: Papers from the ASG Workshop*, no. 29 in ILL Working Paper, pp. 163–182, Institute for Logic and Linguistics, IBM Scientific Centre, Heidelberg.

Geurts, Bart, 1999. *Presuppositions and Pronouns*, vol. 3 of *CRiSPI*. Elsevier, Amsterdam.

Geurts, Bart, 2000. "Buoyancy and strength." *Journal of Semantics* 17(4).

Geurts, Bart and Rob van der Sandt, 1999. "Domain restriction." In Peter Bosch and Rob van der Sandt (eds.), *Focus: Linguistic, Cognitive, and Computational Perspectives*, pp. 268–292, Cambridge University Press, Cambridge.

Goldberg, Jeffrey, László Kálmán and Zoltán Szabó, 1990. "Internal and external presuppositions." Ms. University of Budapest. Draft version appears in Rob van der Sandt (ed), *Reader for the Nijmegen Workshop on Presupposition, Lexical Meaning and Discourse Processes*, University of Nijmegen.

Grice, Paul, 1981. "Presupposition and Implicature." In Peter Cole (ed.), *Radical Pragmatics*, pp. 183–199, Academic Press, New York. Reprinted in Paul Grice, 1989, *Studies in the Way of Words*, Harvard University Press, Cambridge, Massachusetts, pp. 269–282. Page numbers in text refer to 1989 version.

Groenendijk, Jeroen and Martin Stokhof, 1984. *Studies in the Semantics of Questions and the Pragmatics of Answers*. Ph.D. thesis, University of Amsterdam.

Groenendijk, Jeroen and Martin Stokhof, 1990. "Two theories of Dynamic Semantics." In Jan van Eijck (ed.), *Logics in AI. European Workshop JELIA '90*, pp. 55–64, Springer, Berlin.

Groenendijk, Jeroen and Martin Stokhof, 1991a. "Dynamic Montague Grammar." In Jeroen Groenendijk, Martin Stokhof and David Beaver (eds.), *Quantification and Anaphora I*, DYANA deliverable R2.2a, Center for Cognitive Science, University of Edinburgh.

Groenendijk, Jeroen and Martin Stokhof, 1991b. "Dynamic Predicate Logic." *Linguistics and Philosophy* 14, pp. 39–100.

Groenendijk, Jeroen, Martin Stokhof and Frank Veltman, 1995. "Coreference and modality." In Shalom Lappin (ed.), *Handbook of Contemporary Semantic Theory*, Blackwell, Oxford.

Groenendijk, Jeroen, Martin Stokhof and Frank Veltman, 1997. "Coreference and Modality in Multi-speaker Discourse." In Hans Kamp and Barbara Partee (eds.), *Context Dependence in the Analysis of Linguistic Meaning*, pp. 195–216, University of Stuttgart.

Gunji, Takao, 1981. *Towards a Computational Theory of Pragmatics — Discourse, Presupposition and Implicature*. Ph.D. thesis, Ohio State University.

Hajičová, Eva, Barbara Partee and Petr Sgall, 1998. *Topic-Focus Articulation, Tripartite Structures, and Semantic Content*. Kluwer, Dordrecht.

Halliday, Michael, 1967. "Notes on Transitivity and Theme in English. Part 2." *Journal of Linguistics* 3, pp. 199–244.

Hausser, Roland, 1976. "Presuppositions in Montague Grammar." *Theoretical Linguistics* 3, pp. 245–280.

Hawkins, John, 1978. *Definiteness and Indefiniteness*. Croom Helm, London.

Heim, Irene, 1982. *On the Semantics of Definite and Indefinite Noun Phrases*. Ph.D. thesis, University of Massachusetts at Amherst.

Heim, Irene, 1983a. "File Change Semantics and the Familiarity Theory of Definites." In Rainer Bäuerle, Christoph Schwarze and Arnim von Stechow (eds.), *Meaning, Use and Interpretation of Language*, pp. 164–189, De Gruyter, Berlin.

Heim, Irene, 1983b. "On the projection problem for presuppositions." In Michael Barlow, Daniel Flickinger and Michael Westcoat (eds.), *Second Annual West Coast Conference on Formal Linguistics*, pp. 114–126, Stanford University.

Heim, Irene, 1990. "Presupposition Projection." In Rob van der Sandt (ed.), *Reader for the Nijmegen Workshop on Presupposition, Lexical Meaning, and Discourse Processes*, University of Nijmegen.

Heim, Irene, 1992. "Presupposition Projection and the Semantics of Attitude Verbs." *Journal of Semantics* 9, pp. 183–221.

Heim, Irene and Angelika Kratzer, 1998. *Semantics in Generative Grammar*. Blackwell, Oxford.

Heinämäki, Orvokki, 1972. "Before." In *Papers from the 8th Regional Meeting of the Chicago Linguistic Society*, pp. 139–151, University of Chicago.

Hendriks, Herman, 1989. "Type Change in Semantics: the Scope of Quantification and Coordination." In Ewan Klein and Johan van Benthem (eds.), *Categories, Polymorphism and Unification*, Universities of Edinburgh and Amsterdam.

Herzberger, Hans, 1973. "Dimensions of truth." *Journal of Philosophical Logic* 2, pp. 535–556.

Hintikka, Jaakko, 1962. *Knowledge and Belief*. Cornell University Press, Ithaca, New York.

Hobbs, Jerry, Mark Stickel, Douglas Appelt and Paul Martin, 1990. "Interpretation as abduction." Tech. Rep. 499, SRI International, Menlo Park, California.

Horn, Larry, 1969. "A presuppositional analysis of *only* and *even*." In *Papers from the Fifth Regional Meeting of the Chicago Linguistics Society*, pp. 98–107, University of Chicago.

Horn, Larry, 1985. "Metalinguistic Negation and Pragmatic Ambiguity." *Language* 61, pp. 121–174.

Horn, Larry, 1986. "Presupposition, theme and variations." In *Papers from the Parasession on Pragmatics and Grammatical Theory, 22nd Regional Meeting of the Chicago Linguistics Society, Part 2*, pp. 168–192, University of Chicago.

Horn, Larry, 1989. *A Natural History of Negation*. University of Chicago Press. Reissued with new introduction (2001), David Hume Series, CSLI Publications, Stanford.

Horn, Larry, 1990. "Showdown at Truth-Value Gap: Burton-Roberts on Presupposition." *Journal of Linguistics* 26, pp. 483–503.

Horn, Larry, 1994. "Pragmatics, implicature and presupposition." In R. E. Asher and J. Simpson (eds.), *The Encyclopedia of Language and Linguistics*, Pergamon Press, Oxford.

Horton, Diane, 1987. "Incorporating agents' beliefs in a model of presupposition." Tech. Rep. CSRI-201, Computer Systems Research Institute,, University of Toronto.

Horton, Diane and Graeme Hirst., 1988. "Presuppositions as beliefs." In *Proceedings of the International Conference on Computational Linguistics, COLING*, pp. 255–260.

Janssen, Theo, 1984. *Foundations and Applications of Montague Grammar*. Ph.D. thesis, University of Amsterdam.

de Jong, Franciska and Henk Verkuyl, 1985. "Generalized quantifiers: the properness of their strength." In Alice ter Meulen and Johan van Benthem (eds.), *Generalized Quantifiers: Theory and Applications*, vol. 4 of *GRASS*, pp. 21–43, Foris, Dordrecht.

Kadmon, Nirit, 1990. "Uniqueness." *Linguistics and Philosophy* 13, pp. 273–324.

Kamp, Hans, 1981. "A theory of truth and semantic representation." In Jeroen Groenendijk, Theo Janssen and Martin Stokhof (eds.), *Formal Methods in the Study of Language, Part 1*, vol. 135, pp. 277–322, Mathematical Centre Tracts, Amsterdam. Reprinted in Jeroen Groenendijk, Theo Janssen and Martin Stokhof (eds), 1984, *Truth, Interpretation, and Information; Selected Papers from the Third Amsterdam Colloquium*, Foris, Dordrecht, pp. 1–41.

Kamp, Hans and Uwe Reyle, 1993. *From Discourse to Logic.* Kluwer, Dordrecht.

Kamp, Hans and Antje Rossdeutscher, 1994. "DRS-Construction and Lexically Driven Inference." *Theoretical Linguistics* 20, pp. 165–235.

Kanazawa, Makoto, 1994. "Dynamic generalized quantifiers and monotonicity." In Makoto Kanazawa and Christopher J. Pi non (eds.), *Dynamics, Polarity, and Quantification*, CSLI Publications, Stanford.

Karttunen, Lauri, 1971a. "Counterfactual Conditionals." *Linguistic Inquiry* 2, pp. 566–569.

Karttunen, Lauri, 1971b. "Implicative Verbs." *Language* 47(2), pp. 340–358.

Karttunen, Lauri, 1971c. "Some Observations on Factivity." *Papers in Linguistics* 5, pp. 55–69.

Karttunen, Lauri, 1973. "Presuppositions of Compound Sentences." *Linguistic Inquiry* 4, pp. 167–193.

Karttunen, Lauri, 1974. "Presuppositions and Linguistic Context." *Theoretical Linguistics* 1, pp. 181–194.

Karttunen, Lauri, 1976. "Discourse referents." In James McCawley (ed.), *Syntax and Semantics 2: Notes From the Linguistic Underground*, pp. 363–385, Academic Press, New York.

Karttunen, Lauri and Stanley Peters, 1977. "Requiem for presupposition." In *BLS3, Proceedings of the Third Annual Meeting of the Berkeley Linguistic Society*, pp. 266–278, Berkeley, California.

Karttunen, Lauri and Stanley Peters, 1979. "Conventional Implicatures in Montague Grammar." In Choon-Kyu Oh and David Dineen (eds.), *Syntax and Semantics 11: Presupposition*, pp. 1–56, Academic Press, New York.

Kasper, Walter, 1992. "Presupposition, composition and simple subjunctives." *Journal of Semantics* 9, pp. 307–331.

Kay, Paul, 1992. "The inheritance of presuppositions." *Linguistics and Philosophy* 15, pp. 333–381.

Keenan, Edward, 1971. "Two kinds of presupposition in natural language." In Charles Fillmore and D. Terence Langendoen (eds.), *Studies in Linguistic Semantics*, pp. 45–54, Holt, Reinhart and Winston, New York.

Keenan, Edward, 1992. "Beyond the Frege boundary." *Linguistics and Philosophy* 15, pp. 199–221.

Kempson, Ruth, 1975. *Presupposition and the Delimitation of Semantics*. Cambridge University Press, Cambridge.

Kempson, Ruth, 1979. "Presupposition, opacity and ambiguity." In Choon-Kyu Oh and David Dineen (eds.), *Syntax and Semantics 11: Presupposition*, pp. 283–297, Academic Press, New York.

Kiparsky, Paul and Carol Kiparsky, 1970. "Fact." In Manfred Bierwisch and Karl Heidolph (eds.), *Progress in Linguistics*, pp. 143–173, Mouton, The Hague. Reprinted in János Petöfi and Dorothea Franck (eds) 1973, *Präsuppositionen in Philosophie und Linguistik — Presuppositions in Philosophy and Linguistics*, Athanäum Verlag, Frankfurt, pp 315–354.

Kleene, Stephen, 1952. *Introduction to Metamathematics*. North-Holland, Amsterdam.

Klein, Ewan, 1975. "Two sorts of factive predicate." Pragmatics Microfiche *1.1*. Frames B5–C14.

Kracht, Marcus, 1994. "Logic and control: How they determine the behaviour of presuppositions." In Jan van Eijck and Albert Visser (eds.), *Logic and Information Flow*, pp. 89–111, MIT Press, Cambridge, Massachusetts.

Krahmer, Emiel, 1993. "Partial Dynamic Predicate Logic." ITK Research Report 48, University of Tilburg.

Krahmer, Emiel, 1994. "Partiality and dynamics." In Paul Dekker and Martin Stokhof (eds.), *Proceedings of the Ninth Amsterdam Colloquium: Volume 2*, pp. 391–410, ILLC, University of Amsterdam.

Krahmer, Emiel, 1995. *Discourse and Presupposition*. Ph.D. thesis, Tilburg University.

Krahmer, Emiel, 1998. *Presupposition and Anaphora*. CSLI Publications, Stanford.

Krahmer, Emiel and Kees van Deemter, 1998. "On the interpretations of anaphoric noun phrases: Towards a full understanding of partial matches." *Journal of Semantics* 15, pp. 355–392.

Krifka, Manfred, 1992. "Presupposition and focus in dynamic interpretation." *Journal of Semantics* 10.

Kripke, Saul, 1972. *Naming and Necessity*. Blackwell, Oxford.

Kripke, Saul, ms. "Presupposition and anaphora: Remarks on the formulation of the projection problem." Princeton University.

von Kutschera, Franz, 1975. "Partial interpretations." In Edward Keenan (ed.), *Formal Semantics of Natural Language*, CUP, Cambridge.

Lagerwerf, Luuk, 1998. *Causal Connectives Have Presuppositions: Effects on Coherence and Discourse Structure.* Ph.D. thesis, University of Tilburg.

Landman, Fred, 1981. "A note on the projection problem." *Linguistic Inquiry* 12, pp. 467–471.

Landman, Fred, 1986. "Conflicting presuppositions and modal subordination." In *Papers from the 22nd Regional Meeting of the Chicago Linguistic Society*, pp. 195–207, University of Chicago.

Langendoen, D. Terence and Harris Savin, 1971. "The projection problem for presuppositions." In Charles Fillmore and D. Terence Langendoen (eds.), *Studies in Linguistic Semantics*, pp. 373–388, Holt, Reinhardt and Winston, New York. Reprinted in János Petöfi and Dorothea Franck (eds) 1973, *Präsuppositionen in Philosophie und Linguistik — Presuppositions in Philosophy and Linguistics*, Athanäum Verlag, Frankfurt.

Lappin, Shalom and Tanya Reinhart, 1988. "Presuppositions of quantifiers: a processing account." *Linguistics* 26, pp. 1021–1037.

Larsson, Staffan, Peter Ljungloef, Robin Cooper, Elizabet Engdahl and Stina Ericsson, 2000. "GoDiS — an accommodating dialogue system." In *Proceedings of ANLP/NAACL-2000 Workshop on Conversational Systems*.

Lasersohn, Peter, 1993. "Existence presuppositions and background knowledge." *Journal of Semantics* 10(2), pp. 113–122.

Levinson, Stephen, 1983. *Pragmatics*. Cambridge University Press, Cambridge.

Levinson, Stephen, 2000. *Presumptive Meanings*. MIT Press, Cambridge.

Lewis, David, 1979. "Scorekeeping in a language game." *Journal of Philosophical Logic* 8, pp. 339–359. Also in Rainer Bäuerle, Urs Egli and Arnim von Stechow (eds) 1979, *Semantics from Different Points of View*, Springer, Berlin.

Link, Godehard, 1986. "Prespie in Pragmatic Wonderland: Or the projection problem for presuppositions revisited." In Jeroen Groenendijk, Dick de Jongh and Mark Stokhof (eds.), *Foundations of Pragmatics and Lexical Semantics*, pp. 101–126, Foris, Dordrecht.

Lönning, Jan Torre, 1997. "Plurals and distributivity." In Johan van Benthem and Alice ter Meulen (eds.), *The Handbook of Logic and Language*, pp. 1009–1053, Elsevier, Amsterdam.

Lorenz, Sven, 1992. "On the role of reasoning about change in the projection of presuppositions." Report 234, IWBS, IBM Germany.

Marcu, Daniel, 1994. *A Formalisation and an Algorithm for Computing Pragmatic Inferences and Detecting Infelicities*. Ph.D. thesis, University of Toronto, Computer Systems Research Institute. Available as *Technical Report CSRI-309*, Computer Research Institute, University of Toronto.

Martin, John, 1977. "An axiomatisation of Herzberger's Two-dimensional Presuppositional Semantics." *Notre Dame Journal of Formal Logic* 18, pp. 378–382.

Martin, John, 1979. "Some misconceptions in the critique of semantic presupposition." *Theoretical Linguistics* 6, pp. 235–282.

McCawley, James, 1979. "Presupposition and discourse structure." In Choon-Kyu Oh and David Dineen (eds.), *Syntax and Semantics 11: Presupposition*, pp. 371–388, Academic Press, New York.

McCawley, James, 1981. *Everything That Linguists Have Always Wanted to Know about Logic (but Were Ashamed to Ask)*. University of Chicago Press.

McGuinness, Brian (ed.), 1984. *Gottlob Frege: Collected Works*. Basil Blackwell, Oxford.

Mercer, Robert, 1987. *A Default Logic Approach to the Derivation of Natural Language Presuppositions*. Ph.D. thesis, University of British Columbia.

Mercer, Robert, 1992. "Default Logic: Towards a common logical semantics for presupposition and entailment." *Journal of Semantics* 9, pp. 223–250.

ter Meulen, Alice, 1995. "Context and anaphoric presuppositions." Ms. Indiana University and University of Groeningen.

Moens, Marc and Mark Steedman, 1988. "Temporal ontology and temporal reference." *Computational Linguistics* 14(2), pp. 15–29.

Montague, Richard, 1974. "The Proper Treatment of Quantification in Ordinary English." In Richmond Thomason (ed.), *Formal Philosophy: Selected Papers of Richard Montague*, Yale University Press, New Haven.

Morgan, Jerry, 1969. "On the Treatment of Presupposition in Transformational Grammar." In *Papers from the Fifth Regional Meeting, Chicago Linguistic Society*, pp. 167–77, University of Chicago. Reprinted in János Petöfi and Dorothea Franck (eds) 1973, *Präsuppositionen in Philosophie und Linguistik — Presuppositions in Philosophy and Linguistics*, Athanäum Verlag, Frankfurt, pp. 373–88.

Morreau, Michael, 1995. "How to derive conveyed meanings." In Ewan Klein, Suresh Manandhar, Werner Nutt and Jorg Siekmann (eds.), *Working Notes of the Edinburgh Conference on Computational Logic and Natural Language Processing*, Human Communications Research Centre, University of Edinburgh.

Mullally, Joseph, 1945. *The Summulae Logicales of Peter of Spain*. Notre Dame Publications in Mediaeval Studies, Notre Dame, Indiana.

Muskens, Reinhard, 1989. *Meaning and Partiality*. Ph.D. thesis, University of Amsterdam.

Muskens, Reinhard, 1990. "Anaphora and the logic of change." In Jan van Eijck (ed.), *JELIA'90*.

Muskens, Reinhard A., 1995. *Meaning and Partiality*. CSLI Publications, Stanford.

Neale, Stephen, 1990. *Descriptions*. MIT Press, Cambridge, Mass.

Oh, Choon-Kyu and David Dineen (eds.), 1979. *Presupposition*, vol. 11 of *Syntax and Semantics*. Academic Press, New York.

Peters, Stanley, 1977. "A Truth-Conditional Formulation of Karttunen's Account of Presupposition." In *Texas Linguistic Forum 6*, University of Texas at Austin.

Peterson, Philip L., 1979. "On representing event reference." In Choon-Kyu Oh and David Dineen (eds.), *Syntax and Semantics 11: Presupposition*, pp. 325–355, Academic Press, New York.

Piwek, Paul and Emiel Krahmer, 2000. "Presuppositions in context: Constructing bridges." In Pierre Bonzon, Marcos Cavalcanti and Rolf Nossum (eds.), *Formal Aspects of Context*, Kluwer, Dordrecht.

Postal, Paul, 1972. "A Few Factive Facts." *Linguistic Inquiry* 3(3), pp. 396–400.

Prince, Ellen, 1978. "The function of existential sentences in discourse." In *Papers from the 14th Regional Meeting, Chicago Linguistic Society*, pp. 362–376, University of Chicago.

Prince, Ellen, 1986. "On the syntactic marking of presupposed open propositions." In Anne M. Farley, Peter T. Farley and Karl-Erik McCullough (eds.), *Papers from the Parasession on Pragmatics and Grammatical Theory, 22nd Regional Meeting of the Chicago Linguistic Society*, pp. 208–222, University of Chicago.

Ramsey, Alan, 1992. "Presuppositions and WH-Clauses." *Journal of Semantics* 9(3), pp. 251–286.

Reichenbach, Hans, 1947. *Elements of Symbolic Logic*. Dover Press.

Reinhart, Tanya, 1982. "Pragmatics and Linguistics: An Analysis of Sentence Topics." *Philosophica* 27, pp. 53–94.

Roberts, Craige, 1987. *Modal Subordination, Anaphora and Distributivity*. Ph.D. thesis, University of Massachusetts at Amherst.

Roberts, Craige, 1995. "Domain Selection in Dynamic Semantics." In Emmon Bach, Eloise Jelinek, Angelika Kratzer and Barbara Partee (eds.), *Quantification in Natural Languages*, pp. 661–700, Kluwer, Dordrecht.

Rooth, Mats, 1987. "Noun Phrase Interpretation in Montague Grammar, File Change Semantics, and Situation Semantics." In Peter Gardënfors (ed.), *Generalized Quantifiers*, Reidel, Dordrecht.

Rossdeutscher, Antje, 1994. "Fat child meets DRT. a Semantic Representation for the opening lines of Kaschnitz' 'Das dicke Kind'." *Theoretical Linguistics* 20, pp. 237–305.

Rullmann, Hotze and Sigrid Beck, 1998. "Presupposition projection and the interpretation of which-questions." In Devon Strolovitch and Aaron Lawson (eds.), *Proceedings of SALT 8*, pp. 215–232, CLC Publications, Cornell.

Russell, Bertrand, 1905. "On Denoting." *Mind* 14, pp. 479–493.

Russell, Bertrand, 1946. *The History of Western Philosophy*. Allen and Unwin, London. Page numbers in text refer to Counterpoint edition, Unwin, 1985.

Russell, Bertrand, 1957. "Mr. Strawson on Referring." *Mind* 66, pp. 385–389.

Sæbø, Kjell Johan, 1996. "Anaphoric presuppositions and zero anaphora." *Linguistics and Philosophy* 19, pp. 187–209.

Sanchez Valencia, Victor, Ton van der Wouden and Frans Zwarts, 1994. "Polarity, veridicality and temporal connectives." In Paul Dekker and Mark Stokhof (eds.), *Proceedings of the Ninth Amsterdam Colloquium*, vol. 3, pp. 587–606, ILLC, University of Amsterdam.

van der Sandt, Rob, 1982. *Kontekst en Presuppositie: Een Studie van het Projektieprobleem en de Presuppositionele Eigenschappen van de Logisch Konnektieven*. Ph.D. thesis, Nijmegen Institute of Semantics.

van der Sandt, Rob, 1988. *Context and Presupposition*. Croom Helm, London.

van der Sandt, Rob, 1989. "Anaphora and accommodation." In Renate Bartsch, Johan van Benthem and Peter van Emde Boas (eds.), *Semantics and Contextual Expression*, Foris, Dordrecht.

van der Sandt, Rob, 1991. "Denial." In *Chicago Linguistic Society II: Papers from the Parasession on Negation*, University of Chicago.

van der Sandt, Rob, 1992a. "Presupposition projection as anaphora resolution." *Journal of Semantics* 9, pp. 333–377.

van der Sandt, Rob, 1992b. "Text structure and discourse structure." Ms., University of Nijmegen.

van der Sandt, Rob, ms. "Discourse systems and echo-quotation." To appear in Linguistics and Philosophy.

van der Sandt, Rob and Bart Geurts, 1991. "Presupposition, anaphora and lexical content." In Otthein Herzog and Claus-Rainer Rollinger (eds.), *Text Understanding in LiLOG*, Springer, Berlin.

Schiebe, Traugott, 1979. "On presupposition in complex sentences." In Choon-Kyu Oh and David Dineen (eds.), *Syntax and Semantics 11: Presupposition*, pp. 127–154, Academic Press, New York.

Schöter, Andreas, 1994. "Evidential bilattice logic and lexical inference." Technical EUCCS RP-64, Centre for Cognitive Science, University of Edinburgh.

Schöter, Andreas, 1995. *The Computational Application of Bilattice Logic to Natural Reasoning*. Ph.D. thesis, University of Edinburgh.

Schubert, Lenhart K. and Francis Jeffry Pelletier, 1989. "Generically speaking, or using Discourse Representation Theory to interpret generics." In Gennaro Chierchia, Barbara Partee and Ray Turner (eds.), *Properties, Types and Meaning*, vol. II, pp. 193–268, Kluwer, Dordrecht.

Searle, John, 1969. *Speech Acts: An Essay in the Philosophy of Language*. Cambridge University Press., Cambridge.

Seuren, Pieter, 1985. *Discourse Semantics*. Blackwell, Oxford.

Seuren, Pieter, 1988a. "Lexical meaning and presupposition." In Werner Huellen and Rainer Schulze (eds.), *Understanding the Lexicon*, pp. 170–187, Niemeyer, Tübingen.

Seuren, Pieter, 1988b. "Presupposition and negation." *Journal of Semantics* 6, pp. 175–226.

Seuren, Pieter, 1990a. "Burton-Roberts on Presupposition and Negation." *Journal of Linguistics* 26, pp. 425–453.

Seuren, Pieter, 1990b. "Review article: The Limits to Debate, Noel Burton Roberts." *Linguistics* 28, pp. 503–516.

Seuren, Pieter, 1991. "Präsuppositionen." In Dieter Wunderlich and Arnim von Stechow (eds.), *Semantik: Ein Internationales Handbuch der zeitgenössichen Forschung — Semantics: An International Handbook of Contemporary Research*, pp. 287–318, Walter de Gruyter, Berlin/New York.

Sgall, Petr, 1995. "Presupposition of existence and of uniqueness, and allegation." In Hans Kamp and Barbara Partee (eds.), *Context Dependence in the Analysis of Linguistic Meaning*, pp. 395–408, University of Stuttgart.

Sgall, Petr, Eva Hajičová and Eva Benešová, 1973. *Topic, Focus and Generative Semantics*. Scriptor Verlag, Kronberg.

Soames, Scott, 1979. "A projection problem for speaker presuppositions." *Linguistic Inquiry* 10, pp. 623–666.

Soames, Scott, 1982. "How presuppositions are inherited: a solution to the projection problem." *Linguistic Inquiry* 13, pp. 483–545.

Soames, Scott, 1989. "Presupposition." In Dov Gabbay and Franz Guenther (eds.), *Handbook of Philosophical Logic*, vol. IV, pp. 553–616, Reidel, Dordrecht.

Sperber, Daniel and Deidre Wilson, 1984. *Relevance: Communication and Cognition*. Basil Blackwell, Oxford.

Stalnaker, Robert, 1972. "Pragmatics." In Donald Davidson and Gilbert Harman (eds.), *Semantics of Natural Language*, pp. 389–408, Dordrecht, Reidel. Reprinted in János Petöfi and Dorothea Franck (eds) 1973, *Präsuppositionen in Philosophie und Linguistik — Presuppositions in Philosophy and Linguistics*, Athanäum Verlag, Frankfurt. Page numbers in text refer to the 1973 version.

Stalnaker, Robert, 1973. "Presuppositions." *The Journal of Philosophical Logic* 2, pp. 447–457.

Stalnaker, Robert, 1974. "Pragmatic presuppositions." In Milton Munitz and Peter Unger (eds.), *Semantics and Philosophy*, pp. 197–214, New York University Press.

Stalnaker, Robert, 1979. "Assertion." In Peter Cole (ed.), *Syntax and Semantics*, vol. 9, Academic Press, London.

Stalnaker, Robert, 1998. "On the representation of context." *Journal of Logic, Language and Information* 7, pp. 3–19.

Strawson, Peter, 1950. "Referring." *Mind* 59, pp. 320–44.

Strawson, Peter, 1952. *Introduction to Logical Theory*. Methuen, London.

Strawson, Peter, 1964. "Identifying reference and truth values." *Theoria* 30.

Thomason, Richmond, 1972. "A semantic theory of sortal incorrectness." *Journal of Philosophical Logic* 1, pp. 209–258.

Thomason, Richmond, 1979. "Truth-value gaps, many truth values, and possible worlds." In Choon-Kyu Oh and David Dineen (eds.), *Syntax and Semantics 11: Presupposition*, pp. 357–369, Academic Press, New York.

Turner, Ken, 1992. "Defending semantic presupposition." *Journal of Pragmatics* 18, pp. 345–371.

Veltman, Frank, 1986. "Data semantics and the pragmatics of indicative conditionals." In Elizabeth Traugott, Alice ter Meulen, Judith Reilly and Charles Ferguson (eds.), *On Conditionals*, Cambridge University Press., Cambridge.

Veltman, Frank, 1996. "Defaults in update semantics." *Journal of Philosophical Logic* 25, pp. 221–261.

Vermeulen, Cees, 1992. "Sequence Semantics for Dynamic Predicate Logic." *Journal of Logic, Language and Information* 2, pp. 217–254.

Whitehead, Alfred North and Bertrand Russell, 1910. *Principia Mathematica*, vol. 1. Cambridge University Press.

Wilson, Deidre, 1975. *Presupposition and Non-truth-conditional Semantics*. Academic Press, London.

Wilson, Deidre and Dan Sperber, 1979. "Ordered entailments: An alternative to presuppositional theories." In Choon-Kyu Oh and David Dineen (eds.), *Syntax and Semantics 11: Presupposition*, pp. 299–323, Academic Press, New York.

Zeevat, Henk, 1991. *Aspects of Discourse Semantics and Unification Grammar*. Ph.D. thesis, University of Amsterdam.

Zeevat, Henk, 1992. "Presupposition and accommodation in update semantics." *Journal of Semantics* 9, pp. 379–412.

Zeevat, Henk, 1994. "A speculation about certain triggers." In Rob van der Sandt and Peter Bosch (eds.), *The Proceedings of the IBM/Journal of Semantics Conference on Focus*, vol. 3, pp. 669–676, IBM, Heidelberg.

Zuber, Ryszard, 1977. "Decomposition of factives." *Studies in Language* 1(3), pp. 407–421.

Index